CRIME IN NINETEENTH-CENTURY WALES

CRIME
IN
NINETEENTH-CENTURY
WALES

David J. V. Jones

CARDIFF
UNIVERSITY OF WALES PRESS
1992

British Library Cataloguing in Publication Data

Jones, David
   Crime in Nineteenth-century Wales
   I. Title
   364.109429081

   ISBN 0-7083-1142-3

Typeset by Alden Multimedia Ltd., Northampton
Printed in Great Britain by Biddles Ltd., Guildford

Contents

Illustrations

All illustrations are produced by kind permission of the National Library of Wales

Graphs

Tables

Preface

The definition of crime is not an easy matter. Murder and theft have always been viewed as delinquent behaviour, but there have been other activities in modern times which have been defined as criminal by new legislation or have ceased to be so. In other words, crime is an 'artificial construct' and 'a moving frontier'. During the nineteenth century there were many changes in the legal code, and in state and public attitudes towards delinquency. A few reformers then, as now, wished to race ahead of public opinion. One of these, the vicar of Nefyn, complained to the education commissioners of 1847 about the wide extent of 'offences which are not (yet) punishable by law . . . in this country'.[1] For the purposes of this monograph, however, the writer will be concentrating on those activities legally defined as criminal.

It could be argued that the title of this book is a deceit. Perhaps a better one would be 'Crime and Authority', for all students of crime know that political decisions are behind much of what they encounter. Many years ago it was suggested that the law was 'the critical instrument' of authority and control in modern Britain.[2] According to Marxist historians, Michel Foucault, and other philosophers and social scientists, industrial capitalism and the centralized state required an appropriate legal system, one which sanctioned control by the powerful few over the subject many. Although the terror of the law was reduced after the early years of the nineteenth century, the people were, it is claimed, hedged about with innumerable regulations, supervised by an army of policemen, and, when they transgressed, placed in dark corrective institutions. In this situation, popular notions of equality before the law and of the independence of the judiciary were mere 'illusions'. 'Consensus masks coercion', and those coerced were, and are, the working class.[3] In the modern 'policeman-state' it has been only the poorest members of society who have felt the full weight of authority.

What has never been fully explained, in such theories of domination, is the role of the people in the politics of crime. In recent years several prominent historians have denied that the criminal law was ever just the expression of the dominant will of an élite, and have suggested instead that it was based on values widely shared throughout British society. In an attempt to establish this fundamental point, they have gathered their research around a number of difficult questions. When and why did state law supplant other popular forms of justice? How did the various classes both view and use the criminal law? Was there some truth in the traditional notion that all free-born citizens were protected by the rule of law, and that everyone was equal before it? What was the real nature of the 'Bloody Code' of the eighteenth century? How did 'the people' respond to the important changes in law, policing and punishment in the nineteenth century? The latest generation of historians of crime, writers such as John Beattie, David Philips, Peter King, Michael Ignatieff, Clive Emsley and Vic Gatrell, are beginning to address these questions, and major research projects are underway.

The history of crime has become in the last twenty years a popular area of study. This was not always so; whilst books by modern criminologists and sociologists proliferated, there was almost nothing on the historical dimension of crime. Sir Leon Radzinowicz's *A History of English Criminal Law and its Administration*, Parts 1–5 (London, 1948–86), stood alone. Students in Wales, as an England, had to rely on a few county studies, often written by ex-policemen with access to official sources, and on popular histories such as K. Chesney's *The Victorian Underworld* (London, 1970). The classic work of this genre was by Dr J. J. Tobias, of Bramshill Police College, entitled *Crime and Industrial Society in the Nineteenth Century* (London, 1967). It was an important and controversial study, and was partly responsible for the surge of historical interest in the subject. In the 1970s and 1980s the history of crime became one of the most popular fields of research, and conference papers and books appeared in rapid succession. It is now, of course, an integral part of many GCSE and A Level History courses, not least in Wales.

In 1974 the present writer was awarded a grant to make a preliminary investigation of the sources available for a study of crime in nineteenth-century Wales. It emerged that Wales has been fortunate in the survival of records. Those of the court of Great Session, before its demise in 1830, are of much better quality than those of its English counterpart, the court of Assize. The Quarter Session records are also a treasured possession of Welsh record offices, though in a few instances, notably in Cardiganshire, large collections have long since disappeared. Petty Session material is a greater problem; there is a major gap before the 1880s, when districts were first obliged to retain the records of police courts. Only counties like Anglesey and Glamorgan have much evidence of local justice prior to that date.

The historian can, however, turn to other sources to replace and complement the above. Government papers are helpful, especially the run of judicial, police and prison statistics which began in 1805, as well as the

Home Office books and letters, and reports of select committees and royal commissions. These can be set against the local prison and police documents, which are located either at record offices or museums. The gaol books, and reports of governors and chaplains, in the Caernarfonshire, Pembrokeshire, Mid Glamorgan and Gwent record offices, for example, deserve to be better known, but others are frankly disappointing. The police occurrence books, registers of charges and diaries are particularly valuable, though sadly many of these have been lost or destroyed. Exceptions are the deposits in the record offices at Hawarden and Dolgellau, and in the Bridgend and Cwmbrân police museums.

Newspapers provide the historian with different problems; their interest in crime is unabating, and they contain information that cannot be found in official records, but the coverage is patchy. Amongst the journals used for this study were the *Caernarvon and Denbigh Herald*, *The Cambrian*, the *Cambrian News*, the *Cardiff and Merthyr Guardian*, the *Carmarthen Journal*, the *Monmouthshire Merlin*, the *North Wales Chronicle*, the *Shrewsbury Chronicle*, the *Welshman* and the *Western Mail*. The footnotes give an indication of these and the other sources used, though they are no more than a guide. It is impossible to document every case and opinion in this book.

This monograph began life as a response to demands from Welsh scholars who are studying, and being examined in, the history of crime. It will, it is hoped, be followed by a similar account of twentieth-century crime. The purpose of this book is to give a general survey of crime during the period when it emerged as one of our great modern 'problems'. I have tried to examine the roots, extent and seriousness of this problem, and to see whether modernization has meant an inevitable increase in delinquency and a change in its character. At the present time, when Welsh people are beset by rising crime rates, an arson campaign, prison riots, attacks on policemen, juvenile hooliganism, and horror stories of murder, rape, and burglary, it is interesting to have a historical perspective.

The hardest part of the exercise has been to balance the provision of information with a commentary upon it. To the surprise perhaps of some readers, I have used the criminal statistics as the basis of the work. Collecting them has been arduous and time-consuming, and using them can be dangerous. They are not a neutral nor an easy source, but they cannot be ignored. At best, they are a ricketty scaffolding from which one can gain access to a vast and intimidating building.[4] The statistics are set out, analysed, and related to the literary evidence.[5] At every point I have tried to consider the views of contemporaries and, to a lesser extent, of modern historians of crime.

In one book, covering a hundred years, problems of selection inevitably arise. Unlike some of my colleagues, I thought it right to examine not only offences against persons and property, which are the obvious threats to society, but other crimes as well. An investigation of all the cases dealt with at the criminal courts, minor as well as serious, and even the mundane breaches of licensing, vagrancy, education and other regulatory Acts, deepens our understanding of the purpose and character of nineteenth-century policing. Other things have been omitted.[6] There is little here, for example, on the reactions in Wales to the Whitechapel murders of the 1880s, or on the threat from popular disturbances. I have also taken for granted that the reader knows something of the ideological framework, and the conflicting positivist, socialist, and structuralist views of delinquency.

Crime is such a normal and common activity that it cannot be hermetically sealed. Any study of nineteenth-century crime is about power, politics and social change, at every level of the community. The writer cannot avoid themes like industrialization and modernization, the fears of revolution and the roots of stability, the balance between control and consensus, the relationships between the governors and the governed, and the special characteristics of Welsh society and culture. There are many questions raised in and by histories of crime, and it is hoped that this book will stimulate further research. It is, after all, a comparatively new subject, though one which is becoming increasingly familiar to history teachers and lecturers.

Finally, I should like to thank all those who have rendered assistance, and convinced me that such a book ought to be written. The University College at Swansea, the Social Science Research Council, and the Nuffield Foundation gave me grants at one time or another on this and related projects. I also wish to express my gratitude to Professor Ieuan Gwynedd Jones, Dr David Howell, Jeremy Glenn, Audrey Philpin, and Susan Jenkins, and to the archivists who have guided me through difficult country. I owe a special debt of gratitude to my former colleague, Alan Bainbridge, and to Mary Bodger of the Computer Centre at Swansea.

David Jones
March 1992

Abbreviations

ARO	Anglesey Record Office, Llangefni
CDH	*Caernarvon and Denbigh Herald*
CJ	*Carmarthen Journal*
CMG	*Cardiff and Merthyr Guardian*
CRO	Caernarfonshire Record Office
CLRO	Clywd Record Office, Hawarden
DRO	Dyfed Record Office, Haverfordwest
GRO	Gwent Record Office
HO	Home Office Letters and Papers
MGRO	Mid Glamorgan Record Office, Cardiff
MM	*Monmouthshire Merlin*
MRO	Merioneth Record Office, Dolgellau
NLW	National Library of Wales
NWC	*North Wales Chronicle*
PP	Parliamentary Papers
PRO	Public Record Office
SC	*Shrewsbury Chronicle*
SWPM	South Wales Police Museum, Bridgend
TC	*The Cambrian*

1

Wales and the Legal Code

Wales had a reputation throughout the nineteenth century for being the least criminal and most orderly part of the British Isles. 'The Welsh, as a class', said the chairman of the Merioneth Quarter Sessions in 1871, 'are exceedingly honest'.[1] 'The state of crime is so different...', agreed one of the first prison inspectors in 1837, 'and the habits of the lower orders so different,...' that Wales could be regarded as a special case.[2] 'There are few districts in Europe', noted the education commissioners in 1847, 'where murders, burglaries, personal violence, rapes, forgeries, or any felonies on a large scale, are so rare.' This was not a novel judgement. Arthur Aikin and other travellers in the eighteenth century were impressed by the 'untainted' nature of the Welsh peasantry and by the absence of drunkenness and disorder amongst the 'lower orders' of the towns. Their pre-marital sexual habits were the only 'blot upon the national character'. Judges of the late eighteenth century were also delighted by the small numbers for trial, and by the half-empty gaols, a tribute to the efforts of a caring and resident gentry.

During the nineteenth century, Dissenting ministers, eisteddfoddau prize-winners, and literary and political nationalists added their own colouring to this popular picture of 'a country without crime'. It became part of the larger myth of the 'pure Welsh' propounded by 'Ieuan Gwynedd' and his friends. Wales, in their eyes, was the home of the 'true Britons', spiritually re-born in the eighteenth century, and resistant to the corrupting influences of atheism and materialism. The classic exposition of the case for 'Cymru lan' (innocent Wales) or 'Gwlad y menyg gwynion' (land of the white gloves) can be found in the writings of Henry Richard, the pacifist west-Walian who gained prominence as a Congregational minister and Liberal MP. In his *Letters and Essays on Wales* (1866) he declared that in the area of delinquency, as in so many others, the Welsh showed a marked superiority to other nationalities.[3] Like the philanthropist Thomas Phillips, the Swansea minister Thomas Rees and others, Richard used court statistics to prove that the level of serious crime in Wales was exceptionally low. Nor did the praise of her inhabitants end there, for immigrant miners, navvies, tramps, holiday-makers and other outsiders were blamed for much of the criminal behaviour that was recorded. Even popular disturbances, with which the Welsh were sometimes associated, were, it was argued, largely inspired by external agitators.

One newspaper editor, ignoring the political riots which were currently disturbing his region, said in December 1830 that Wales had, since medieval times, settled down to an 'impressive tranquillity'. He recalled how enthusiastically the late, and present, monarchs had been received on their visits to the Principality. There was not, he declared, a regular soldier on domestic duty in his country.[4] Others noted at this time that Captain Swing had few followers west of Monmouthshire, and they delighted in the failure of English trade unionists to stir the men of the north and south Wales coalfields. It was, we are later told, no accident that the Chartist attack on Newport in 1839 occurred in an area where English influences were strongest. The Rebecca riots were, conceded Henry Richard and Thomas Phillips, an exception to this rule, but the dangers of a native revolt had, in their opinion, been deliberately exaggerated. On many occasions Wales was contrasted with Ireland; whilst the latter had its Fenians, and its terrifying agrarian outrages, the former country rarely troubled the central government. The typical Taffy was therefore neither a rebel nor a thief. The new professional police, and the soldiers sent into the Principality, were hardly necessary.

Alternative views of the Welsh and crime gained less publicity. Thomas Biddulph, from Amroth Castle, told the Home Secretary in July 1839 that the number of 'petty thefts and depredation' in his district of Pembrokeshire 'vastly exceeds the average in a similar amount of population in the English counties'. He received support for his views from Thomas Davies, agent of the Duke of Beaufort, and from contributors to the report on Welsh education in 1847. They insisted that in the 'underworld' of 'the least educated part of the [Welsh] community', 'petty thefts, lying, cozening, every species of chicanery, drunkenness' and latent rebellion could be found.[5] Such opinions were less common in the second half of the century, but they did not entirely disappear. During the debates over the Liberal triumphs of 1868 and 1874, and over the evils of Welsh landlordism, writers in the *Standard* and *The Times* stated that the oppressed *gwerin* were less respectable in their daily life and protests than Henry Richard and 'Adfyfyr' imagined[6]. Similarly, at the time of the great poaching raids in late-Victorian Radnorshire, and during the north Wales quarrymen's strikes of the same period, Anglicized leaders of Welsh society refused to accept the nationalists' claim that their followers were normally 'honest' and 'moral' people who lived in almost 'crimeless communities'.

Crime, order and justice

Much of the above debate turned, as always in modern times, on the

validity of the criminal statistics. From an early date there were people who
were suspicious of the empty Great and Quarter Session calendars. Landowners, magistrates and constables declared that the number of cases at
the higher courts bore no comparison to the number of offences daily
committed. In 'quiet, harmless' Pwllheli and Kidwelly, residents mocked
the single-figure returns of crime sent annually to the Home Office, and in
Caernarfon, Carmarthen, and Chepstow, where frequently 'no information was given to the police', there were reports of 'a good deal of pilfering
and much petty thieving', 'many vagabonds infest[ing]' the main streets,
and decent people being afraid to venture out after dark.[7] But perhaps the
greatest cynicism was reserved for the official statistics of crime from the
south Wales coalfield. Edmund Head, assistant poor-law commissioner,
preferred to believe the evidence of his own eyes; he compared the district
in 1839 to a penal colony, inhabited by 'bad characters', and 'runaway
criminals and vagrants', and the popular risings at Merthyr in 1831, and
at Newport eight years later, gave an urgency to his message.[8]

In the late nineteenth-century, as the number of cases heard at Assizes
and Quarter Sessions fell dramatically, a healthy scepticism developed
about the value of legal proceedings as an index of Welsh character.
Certain judges no longer accepted the white gloves at maiden Assizes with
quite the grace of days gone by. 'Gentlemen, I would willingly congratu-
late you on the non-existence of crime in your several counties IF it did not
exist;' said Lord Justice Brett to the grand juries of Cardiganshire and
Pembrokeshire in the 1880s, 'but as I believe it does exist, though, by some
means it is not brought before me, my congratulations must assume a
modified form.'[9]

This comment raised important questions about the evidence of criminal
activity and the manner in which the legal code was considered and
administered in Wales. Much law-breaking went unseen or unreported. In
the early years there were towns and villages where the forces of law and
order were hardly visible, and this continued to be the case in some country
districts until the end of the century. Vicars on the Llŷn and Gower
peninsulas complained in the troubled aftermath of the Napoleonic Wars
that smuggling, and stealing from farms, had become a way of life because
the parish constables were 'useless' and the victims 'unwilling to prosecute'.
Thomas Jenkins, in a letter to Charles Morgan Esq. in the autumn of 1830,
claimed that horse stealing had recently become very prevalent in west
Wales, but very few offenders were brought to justice. More than thirty
years later, another letter writer denounced the scale and openness of the
illegal shooting of partridges in northern Cardiganshire and asked why
respectable inhabitants lacked the courage to report the poachers.[10]

Unfortunately, detailed estimates of the extent of such criminal activities
were rare. An exception was the weekly list of robberies, first published in

the *Cardiff and Merthyr Guardian* in 1860, but even this was not complete. The police records are occasionally helpful. In Merioneth an officer in 1885 drafted a list of twenty-four serious offences committed in the quiet village of Gwyddelwern, over half of which were never entered on the charge-sheets. Two years later, in the same county, a retiring constable left his successor secret instructions about the number of respectable people whom he suspected of criminal activity, chiefly of poaching, and who had been privately cautioned by him for highway offences and for breaches of the Contagious Diseases (Animals) Act and other regulations.[11] One wishes that more contemporaries had been equally indiscreet.

Perhaps the most interesting, if partial, comments on hidden delinquency were made when self-appointed spokesmen requested a permanent police presence in their communities. 'He believed', said one contributor to the debate of 1839–40 over the need for a Glamorgan police, 'the agricultural parishes to be fully as prolific in crime as mineral districts and named two parishes in the Hundred of Ogmore which gave more trouble ...than any in the Hundred of Newcastle.'[12] 'Allow me to call the attention of the county magistrates to the defenceless condition of the district between Hirwain and Penderyn', ran one letter to a newspaper in 1859. 'Scarcely a week passes without a robbery being committed. Last week no less than three farms were visited, and a considerable quantity of poultry stolen. Sheep are frequently lost, but the thieves are never caught...A district of this nature requires different treatment from towns and civilised places. The natives have been accustomed from their infancy to a kind of nomadic life, and it is next to impossible to infuse into their nature a proper sense of the rights of property. Poaching is a favourite employment.' Only, said the writer, a constable stationed at Penderyn, and supervised by the Glamorgan county police, could change this state of affairs.[13]

It was a source of annoyance to this 'SUFFERER', and to those like him, that the victims of crimes sometimes chose to ignore the experience. 'Pilferings from gardens by needy neighbours, and twitching linen from hedges by idle or distressed wayfarers and such like depredations are known and suffered;...', wrote Edmund Hyde Hall in *A Description of Caernarvonshire* (Caernarfon, 1809–11). So, too, was the misappropriation of goods by employees, until payments in kind, allowances and perquisites were completely superceded by the money wage. 'Victorian observers would have been struck', says one modern historian, 'by their forefathers' relative indifference to crime as a "problem", and by their relative satisfaction with the apparently arbitrary and capricious mechanisms which contained it'.[14]

To understand this 'indifference', we need to step backwards in time. After the experiences of the late sixteenth and early seventeenth centuries, when people grew obsessed with the social and moral dangers of the large numbers of poor people in their communities, there was a return to a more relaxed approach to delinquency. One student of early modern Wales tells us that in the first half of the eighteenth century only a small number of serious offences were prosecuted, and most assaults, petty thefts and other crimes were borne in silence.[15] This tolerance can be romanticized and exaggerated, but, as Michel Foucault has pointed out, it made sense given the limited power of the state and people's political perceptions.[16] In 1750 only a certain amount of crime could be dealt with by the courts. To change this situation required a fundamental re-thinking of the nature and expense of government. In the interests of liberty, and especially the liberties of local communities, each section of society had its 'tolerated illegality'.

D. Parry-Jones explains how this worked in practice.[17] Each village lived by two concepts of order, the official and the popular, which occasionally conflicted. Rural communities were riddled with petty conflicts, but it was often better to live with these than the damaging finality of court proceedings. Good relationships were important in the social and economic life of the village, and even persistent trouble-makers, violent and disorderly men, and petty thieves might be tolerated. Taking these offenders before the magistrates was an admission that the preferred forms of control had failed; it was also expensive and might cause more tension than the actual crimes. Informing, at least on local people, was frowned upon, and giving evidence to the authorities brought embarrassment and even threats. Parish constables, who were caught between the two codes, were careful not to offend either the magistrates or the villagers. They issued countless admonitions in the eighteenth and early nineteenth centuries, and chose their presentments carefully, knowing what villification and violence might follow a false move. No one in a court case, least of all the victims, escaped scot free.

A reluctance to prosecute was something which continued, in some communities, well into the nineteenth century. Amongst those who benefitted from this were mischievous juveniles, violent and promiscuous males, farmers with diseased and straying animals, pilfering neighbours, and even, so it was said, a rare murderer. A glance at the Flintshire and Merioneth police diaries reveals that when constables confronted victims with second-hand reports of stolen potatoes, cabbages and milk, they were sometimes told by these people that they had no wish to initiate 'doubtful' or 'malicious' actions against close friends. Police constable William Evans of Pennal, in Merioneth, recounts in his diary how one farmer would not proceed against two neighbours, even when they confessed to stealing one of his sheep.[18] In another part of Wales there were more embarrassing reasons for inaction. When sea captains, commercial travellers and 'persons moving in respectable spheres' were robbed by prostitutes, the men were, said one Cardiff gentleman in 1860, 'as deeply interested in keeping the circumstance a profound secret as [were] the thieves themselves'.[19]

The problems which the police faced in this regard can be seen in the few occurrence books which have survived from the nineteenth century. In them we find instances of victims refusing to take the matter further when the guilty party turned out to be one of their employees, a relative, a person of importance, and a fellow member of a congregation or a club. Typical were the cases of Hugh Evans, a Merioneth farmer, who in 1885 'did not wish to prosecute his servant', the quantity of hay stolen being 'too small', and of Mr Philips of Barmouth, who a year later, 'refused to take out a search warrant, and says he would never prosecute' two respectable ladies who were in his shop when a gold ring disappeared.[20] Perhaps, as in these cases, it was in the victims' interests to keep the matter quiet. One account of the Welsh psychology, published in 1877, implied that people would do almost anything rather than cause offence, or lose face.[21]

Rather than incurring the cost and publicity of court proceedings, employers in town and country often used other sanctions. Landowners and farmers removed unreliable servants, and their families had to rely on the Poor Law which, as it emerged after 1834, was almost designed to penalize the awkward and anti-social members of rural society. Industrial masters had their own systems of fines and dismissals. The Dowlais Iron Company early in the century sacked most of its workmen 'detected in theft', knowing that other employment would be difficult without a proper discharge note. There were even employers, in both town and country, who accepted criminal losses in prosperous times, and took legal action only when an example was necessary or when they wished to remove a particularly obstructive workman. Large companies, late in the century, adopted a rather different approach and prosecuted more readily.[22]

Seeking satisfaction through the courts had never been the most popular method of obtaining redress for crimes committed. One common response was for the victim to confront the suspected criminal, and demand reparation. Where the offence was simply pilfering or minor assault, both parties were usually glad to bring the matter to a speedy conclusion, and even serious breaches of the peace might be settled without recourse to the law. No one knew this better than the first professional policemen. After eight months in the job, Captain Napier, head of the Glamorgan constabulary, complained in 1842 of 'a species of clanship...[which] renders the Welshman peculiarly averse to give evidence against a neighbour, even should he belong to a different country than himself.' He reported that 'depredators are encouraged', because the injured parties, especially in the rural districts, were prepared to accept a compromise rather than incur the expense and delay of a trial. This applied to 'quite serious crimes', as well as petty offences. Napier cited a case of a servant robbing his master of a sack full of clothes, together with a watch and money belonging to a fellow servant. The thief was closely pursued by his master and the police, but when he dropped the sack, 'he was suffered to escape, as they (the owners of the property) declared themselves perfectly satisfied by the restoration of the stolen goods'.[23]

Both inside and outside the legal system, many people looked for compensation, compromise, and apologies rather than strict punishment. In medieval times the attempt to reconcile the criminal and the victim had been an important aspect of court procedures. At every point of the legal process, compromises could be reached. To give force to these agreements, they were sometimes written down and witnessed by magistrates, solicitors, clergymen, and acknowledged community elders. Such deals, so common in medieval and early modern Wales, can also be found in the early nineteenth century, when they were encouraged by paternalist gentlemen like Lewis Evans of Abernant near Carmarthen. In some rural Petty Sessions of this period prosecutions over cutting wood, stealing milk and assault ended, more often than not, it seems, with a compromise between the parties. When a legal conviction for these property crimes ensued, it was widely regarded as a 'malicious prosecution', or one deliberately chosen to 'expose the practice' and give publicity to the penalties.[24] One is reminded of Alan Macfarlane's comment about an earlier period: 'a harsh penal code existed, but...a great deal of flexibility and compromise was permitted in its application'.[25]

As time went by, a greater proportion of complaints seem to have resulted in a full prosecution. The chief constable of Cardiganshire informed the county magistrates in 1867 that of the 547 persons summoned and apprehended in the previous six months, twenty-seven per cent had 'compromised'. His counterpart in Monmouthshire estimated that his rate was fewer than one in five. He reported that some 688 cases, many of which were assaults, were settled out of court in 1865.[26] Settlements were, as he well knew, not always possible or welcome. When the crimes were sheep stealing, burglary and arson, and the offenders were known, there was a determination, certainly on the part of the authorities, to bring them before the Assizes. Requests for a compromise, and offers of financial reparation and public apologies, were turned down. In the case of lesser offences, however, it was easier to arrange deals. Police constable Evans of Deri near Bargoed describes in his diary how, in the autumn of 1871, he witnessed an agreement between Thomas Thomas and Mr Saunders of Mardy Farm over a sheep killed by a dog, and the court registers of the 1870s and 1880s confirm that a large number of assault cases, and about one in eight of trespasses after game, were 'settled' before the verdict was announced.[27]

Another response to delinquency, adopted by people of power and property, and by the police, was to offer a pardon or caution in the first instance. Notices to that effect appeared in the press. 'I do hereby in this public manner ask my master's pardon for such misconduct', began one of them, inserted by a waggoner in 1808 when saved from gaol, 'and [I] am very thankful to him for his leniency to me'.[28] The Wynnes on their huge north Wales estate sometimes asked wood stealers and poachers to sign a confession of their guilt, which might be used in future against them. From the books of gamekeepers, bailiffs, and constables it is clear that many people appeared in court only after they had broken promises and ignored warnings. Thus Hugh Morgans, a poacher of Llandrillo, was cautioned twice by Edward Parry, gamekeeper to Henry Robertson, before being caught a third time and convicted in January 1860 by the Corwen magistrates.[29] Some watchmen and constables proved to be more generous than others. The policeman stationed at Leeswood in 1868–9 handed out cautions to a large number of farmers, carters, publicans, tramps, trespassers and drunks.[30] To the concern of his superiors, he felt that charges should be brought against only the most determined and dangerous of criminals.

There was, in addition, an unknown amount of delinquency which never came to the attention of any official. Some victims of crime ignored the legal system altogether, and sought satisfaction elsewhere. Civil society in the nineteenth century had its own dispute and grievance procedures, both the older versions, centred on battles over honour, and the newer, and less violent ones, sanctioned by the family, the work unit, the chapel and the neighbourhood. Reminiscent of earlier times, a bellman was sent round the town of Lampeter in 1810 proclaiming a fight between the victim and the accused in a stealing case. The two women fought with cudgels, and one of them managed to re-establish her honour before the constables intervened.[31] There were similar battles, waged with less ceremony, in the muddy streets of Blackwood and Rhiwabon.

Alternatively, matters were resolved by a third party. Advice and decisions were obtained from 'y dyn hysbys' (the wise man) of the village, the clergyman, and chapel elders. Many grievances in nineteenth-century Wales were left for the chapel to resolve. Conflicts between members were ended by a word from a minister, or, if things became worse, by excommunication. Friendly and trade societies performed a similar function, and so, at a more informal level, did the street. 'Although the working class brought a significant number of criminal prosecutions to the courts and sought the magistrates' arbitration in their personal disputes,' writes a historian of late nineteenth-century London, 'to a large extent their conflicts continued to be resolved, as in the eighteenth century, informally in the neighbourhood'.[32] The Welsh newspapers indicate how this was done: a man accused of stealing had his tools destroyed, a street went silent on a libeller, and a tradesman asked the father of a thief whether he would punish the child himself or follow him to the police station. At Morriston, in the spring of 1893, about seventy women stoned the house of a man who refused to work and support his daughter.[33] In Swansea's Irish Greenhill district, where so much was settled in the street, the women stopped their husbands from killing one another by sending for the Roman Catholic priest. His intervention, and that of other intermediaries, was appreciated, if not fully approved of, by the local police and magistrates.

When informal sanctions and even ostracism failed, expulsion was tried. Some of the most awkward, immoral and unscrupulous inhabitants were driven out. It was not always done forcibly, for many of the people accused of fathering illegitimate children and of neglecting their families absconded, along with a surprising number of violent and drunken individuals, thus saving friends and the police the bother of dealing with them. Others were more stubborn, like Jemmy Thomas of the Ship Inn, near Newport in Pembrokeshire. In the early 1860s he 'much annoyed' several neighbours, and had a fight with one of them. After warnings he thought it wise to sleep every night in a house on the common some distance away, but in June 1862 'a body of men' broke into his new home. After beating him and his wife, they returned to the Ship Inn and set fire to the property.[34] There were other similar incidents, mostly reported in the countryside but also in the towns.

The Welsh were condemned by Edwin Chadwick and other legal and police reformers for their willingness to take direct action. Direct retribution had been a feature of medieval life and law, and it survived, half hidden sometimes, at all levels of society. Even amongst the upper classes, who were much praised for their civilized behaviour by judges in the Great Sessions, a strand of retributive violence can be found. The gentry, rural and urban, of eighteenth-century Wales settled some of their disputes with fists, swords and guns, and this continued for a short while into the nineteenth century. Duelling, so far as it was reported, ended in the early years of Victoria's reign, and fights between magistrates, at least in open court, were rarely mentioned after that time.[35] The upper and middle classes, however, were ready to adopt other kinds of direct action when it suited them to do so. They used their employees, or hired crowds, to destroy houses, fences, and other property placed on land which they regarded as their own. In 1848 John George, colliery agent of Lord Cawdor, and David Harries, who worked for the Bishop of St Davids, set gangs of men against each other in a conflict over boundaries.[36] It was a quick and cheap method of proceeding, and one hard to reverse. The Rebecca and Tithe rioters claimed, with a degree of truth, that they had received fine lessons in direct action from their peers.

Direct action came in many forms. Arson, for instance, and the maiming of animals, were convenient ways of settling old scores, by one farmer against another, and by angry labourers and vagrants. Hugh Evans, writing after our period, relates how individuals and families in rural Wales fought one another with the knife, the torch, and savage dogs.[37] In the autumn of 1819, on the uplands to the north-west of Rhaeadr, wide-spread anger over grazing and common rights exploded in an orgy of destruction; hundreds of sheep were maimed and killed, dogs butchered and other property damaged.[38] Throughout the nineteenth century count-less people in Wales were removed from their possession of fields, enclos-ures, and gardens, only to return and enact vengeance. 'Riot and forcible entry' and 'forcible ejectment and assault' were amongst the most common entries in the registers of the Great Sessions. The very term 'Welsh eject-ment' was used as a shorthand to describe the process whereby people ignored the legal niceties and physically drove their enemies from the disputed land. An appearance in the crown courts was sometimes an admission of defeat, after years of brutal negotiation over boundary and mineral rights, contested wills and family pride.

Attempts at obtaining instant justice, or revenge, required careful planning, assistance from friends and neighbours, and an element of ritual. Warnings, via anonymous letters, were sent of the proposed attack, and when the people came with their dung forks, axes and crowbars they had blackened faces and other primitive disguises. Fences were torn down, pits filled in, lime kilns demolished, embankments removed, and cottages, barns and stables destroyed. The experience of William Rowlands of Llangwyryfon in Cardiganshire is worth recording, though it was not exceptional. One night in April 1849, as he and his wife were sleeping, the front door was broken down. They were seized, bound hand and foot, and carried outside. Then a crowd, some of whom were disguised, took off the roof, pulled down part of the wall, and smashed the furniture.[39] The precise motive for this attack is unclear, whereas those, in the same county, on the homes of estate shepherds and enclosing gentlemen are easier to under-stand. In some, often isolated, districts this type of popular justice was reported regularly until the last third of the century. People living on the hills around Deytheur, in northern Montgomeryshire, and beneath Pencarreg mountain near Lampeter, as well as the miners of Monmouth-shire villages, were accustomed to the noise of black-faced crowds moving through the night. Inhabitants who gave information about this to the police, and promised to appear as court witnesses, were amongst those who received 'the midnight visit'.

There were times when a large part, if not the whole, of a community indulged in popular policing. D. Parry-Jones, in his *Welsh Country Upbringing* (Liverpool, 1948), recalled how the village 'set in motion a crude and

primitive machinery for enforcing its own code of conduct', over relationships between husband and wife, sexual behaviour, slander and other
misdemeanours which threatened the harmony of the community. 'It
seemed at such times', continued Parry-Jones, 'to sink down to sub-
conscious regions where it made contact with an older civilisation that
knew only the tribal law'. Community punishment took several forms:
threatening letters, public ridicule in song and verse, physical abuse,
harassment, ostracism and banishment. It was 'something before which
men crouched in fear and slunk away into hiding'.[40]

The mock trial, a feature of all western societies, was perhaps the most
characteristic response. It has been associated particularly with Rebecca,
the Scotch Cattle and the Tithe rioters later in the century, but it was, in
many areas, part of the very structure of community life and politics. Social
historians tell us that the dispensation of popular justice was related to the
activities of the crowds at medieval festivals and fair days, a time when
licence prevailed and the world was briefly turned upside down. Angry
crowds in nineteenth-century Wales enacted mock court scenes, and
tried those who had offended them. The defendants were the usual ones:
adulterers, informers and exploiters. Using much of the ritual of medieval
and early modern times, the crowd visited the guilty parties, listed their
crimes, and pronounced the punishment, all in a loud and obscene
language. At a farm near Llanidloes in April 1830 a party of men with
blackened faces denounced the sins of bailiffs, and other groups did the
same to women suspected of witchcraft and of sleeping with married men.
Such people were frequently ducked in ponds. At other times their effigies
were burnt or executed; amongst those metaphorically confined to the
flames, in 1823 and 1851 respectively, were Nicholas Miles, the very
unpopular innkeeper and constable of Newtown, and Elizabeth Gibbs of
Laugharne, the suspected poisoner, who had been acquitted in a court of
law.[41]

Whereas the north of England had its riding the stang, and the south-
west its Skimmington, the most notorious form of 'rough music' in Wales
was the *ceffyl pren*. This was a custom designed to embarrass and intimidate
its victim, and was repeated before him or her on three separate occasions.
At the head of the procession was a wooden horse, or possibly a ladder, pole
and cart, and the leaders of the crowd had blackened faces and were
dressed either as animals or as women. On arrival at the appointed spot,
a spokesman loudly proclaimed the wrongdoings of the person who had
annoyed them. Sometimes the offender was placed on the horse's back, or
its equivalent, and paraded through the streets. The practice, which was
accompanied by noise, gunfire and music, gained great publicity in the late
1830s, especially in the Teifi valley, where its appearance presaged the
outbreak of the Rebecca riots. In 1837 the participants were, for the first

time, put on trial. They claimed in court that such exhibitions of popular justice brought order and discipline to society, and not the reverse.

The *ceffyl pren* remained popular at least until the mid-Victorian years, and had wide support, even from certain magistrates and 'men of very respectable connection and high standing in the parish'.[42] When it was at its height, soon after the Poor Law Amendment Act of 1834, those embarrassed by the mob included prosecutors, informers, witnesses, criminals, bailiffs, keepers and land-grabbing farmers, as well as the more common targets of adulterers, wife-beaters and deserters, but not, so far as one knows, rapists and child abusers. In later years the crowd reverted to its original function, of controlling sexual behaviour and relationships between husband and wife, and women and youths played a more prominent role in the proceedings. At Bangor-on-Dee in 1866, for example, children placed doll effigies outside the the home of a farm worker, as a warning of the public embarrassment that was about to engulf his family. Females, too, made up a large proportion of the mobs who identified wife-beaters in the Teifi valley about the same time. Were they perhaps doing unofficially what their Cardiff counterparts did every Monday in the police court? At Solva in 1856 one demonstration was even instigated by a wife who had been shamed by her husband, whilst at Llanfair Orllwyn in September 1862, when the victim was Enoch Thomas, a promiscuous 'devil', the wooden horse was actually carried by women.[43] It needed all the police resources, and the presence of soldiers, to contain these processions in west Wales. In Cardiganshire, and in Anglesey, the *ceffyl pren* was still alive in the 1880s, though the chief constable of the former county said in 1897 that 'the crime is no longer known'.[44]

The mock trial was mainly associated with country districts but it was also for a time held in the towns and industrial villages of Wales. In early-nineteenth century Merthyr crowds with poles and ladders visited wife-beaters, adulterers, brothel keepers, bailiffs and other unpopular characters.[45] At Pembroke in 1845 five workmen put their overlooker on a ladder, and were cheered around the town. When fined by the magistrates they said that John Forest was 'a bad man', and they 'did not consider this a crime' as 'they had reformed many men so'.[46] Another kind of reforming zeal, which might have emanated from a religious source, was evident fifty years later, at Blaenau Ffestiniog. After the chapel services one Sunday evening, hundreds of people paraded Cadwalladr Hughes, a prominent Salvationist, in a donkey cart. He was accused of visiting a house 'for an immoral purpose'.[47] It was one of the last demonstrations of its type in the century. After the 1860s carrying the *ceffyl pren* began to decline, as social life, notions of respectability and policing changed, and as other sanctions and legal methods of obtaining redress were adopted.

This was symbolic of broader developments, for all over Wales attachments to older concepts of order, memories of ancient codes of behaviour, and established forms of community policing were passing away. In the process something was lost and something gained. Gradually, official methods of dealing with crimes and of resolving conflicts gained wider popularity. This 'penetration of the state into the parish' occurred at different speeds amongst different social groups and in different communities. There were, inevitably, some continuities between what we have been, and will be, describing. Popular justice contained elements of formal court procedures, for the latter were well established and respected. Victims of popular justice were often 'tried' before being convicted, with people playing the part of imaginary judges and attornies. At the same time, the system of state justice adopted elements of the popular variety. Persistent troublemakers and gossipy women were sometimes 'brought forward [before the Bench] as a duty...to the public'. No formal charges were pressed, but it was hoped that the humilation and publicity would have an impact on them. The most unfortunate delinquents were those who were subjected to a range of punishments. Respectable people in late nineteenth-century Merioneth, who were accused of serious financial and sexual offences, faced a formidable combination of popular disapproval, chapel sanctions and state justice.

The courts

The Welsh have been derided, at various times in their history, for their knowledge of the law, their reliance on attornies, and their use of the courts. One historian tells us that already in 1550 Britain had the appearance of 'being a much-governed country', where the royal law was both known and of 'overwhelming importance'.[48] In the Wales of that period the church, manorial and borough courts were as popular as the criminal courts of the crown, but in the eighteenth century there was a change, 'a fall in *all* types of civil litigation...in nearly all courts, lay and ecclesiastical, the causes of which remain obscure'.[49] The church courts were used for cases of adultery, defamation of character, marital differences, conflicts over wills, and the non-payment of tithes and rates. By the early nineteenth century this ecclesiastical jurisdiction had lost much ground. In the years 1824–6, for example, only 217 causes, mainly of slander by men and women against women, were considered at the Welsh consistory courts.[50]

Of all the manorial courts, that of the leet had particularly wide powers; it met at least twice a year, and was conducted for the benefit of those holding land in the lordship. Where it survived in the late eighteenth century, this court confined itself largely to cases involving rents and repairs, the suppression of nuisances, the licensing of ale-houses and the appointment of constables. The courts leet and baron were still operating in Welsh boroughs in 1800, together with other remnants of the judicial past, like the hundred court or court of record. These staggered on, in attenuated form, at Usk, Rhuddlan and half a dozen other places, until the mid-century, only to be finally cast aside by the growth in state bureaucracy and legal centralism. Before the end of the 1830s a sharp and general contraction had taken place in all forms of seigneurial and local jurisdiction. At Llandovery and Lampeter, for instance, nothing remained.[51] The courts described in these paragraphs were increasingly viewed as irrelevant to the needs of the new urban, industrial and secular world. In 1849 the Lloyds of Bronwydd in west Wales tried and failed to revive the baronial courts on equal terms with the county courts.

Although all these courts could punish petty crime, their main interest was in civil matters. The Welsh had a reputation for being very litigious in this area, with a passion for land, contract and inheritance law. In the eighteenth century towns like Denbigh, Carmarthen and Swansea had an array of civil courts: the courts of pleas, baron, pie powder, record, hundred, view of frankpledge, admiralty and so on. Much of the business of these courts was concerned with the recovery of debts, often quite small ones. At Swansea, the court of pleas adjudicated on causes worth over 40s., and the court baron decided on those of a lesser amount. In the boom town of Merthyr Tydfil, a court of requests was established in 1809 for the benefit of small creditors, the same institution which was burnt down by the rioters in 1831. Other, more substantial, civil causes were heard at this time in the higher courts, especially the court of Great Sessions. The last, which was unique in Britain for being both a criminal and civil court, pronounced on a large number of, chiefly debt and contract, cases a year until its demise in 1830. Thereafter people increasingly used the new county courts. The judges on the five Welsh county-court circuits presided over a mountain of business. In 1887 more than 82,000 plaints were brought before them, the great majority being valued at under £20.[52] One of the main benefits of the county courts, apart from the speed of their operations, was that they allowed the courts of criminal law to concentrate on cases peculiar to them.

The criminal courts in Wales were of three kinds, the Petty, Quarter and Great Sessions, the last being replaced after 1830 by the court of Assize. They had been established for centuries and the law which they administered was known and respected. In the eighteenth century it was greatly expanded, and made more flexible, by hundreds of new statutes, most of which were in defence of property. Although there has been some dispute about the use made of the criminal courts in early modern times, in the late eighteenth century, and even more so in the first half of the nineteenth, those seeking redress turned in ever greater numbers to them. In 1805 some ninety-eight persons were indicted at the Great and Quarter Sessions; fifty years later, when the population had doubled, the number of persons appearing at the higher courts had risen to 1,325. It was a remarkable increase, and equally interesting was the fact that the enthusiasm to prosecute people for indictable, and predominately property, crimes in the crown courts affected not only the upper and middle classes, but also lesser folk, even members of the urban working class.

The reasons for this development will be discussed later, but it is worth noting here that the Great Sessions, which had a reputation of being the most flexible and economical court of its kind, was abolished in 1830. It comprised four circuits, two judges for each, and dispensed both criminal and civil justice in the English language for six days twice a year. Being an independent judicature, the Great Sessions saved people from the inconvenience of seeking judgements in the superior courts in London. With its own attorney-general, and its collection of hard-working interpreters, this court was very popular in the more isolated and Welsh-speaking parts of the Principality, but it was an affront to those seeking uniformity in legal administration.

As part of their reforming programmes, British governments after 1817 looked closely at this legal anomaly. The first enquiries into the Welsh judicature produced a hesitant response, but that of 1829 was used by Robert Peel as a basis for action.[53] Reformers argued that by bringing Wales within the English system of county Assizes and Westminster courts, the quality of judges, barristers, and juries would be improved, but there was considerable resistance to change. Those in favour of retaining the Great Sessions were David Saunders Davies, chairman of the Cardiganshire Quarter Sessions, John Jones MP, his counterpart in Carmarthenshire, a handful of grand juries, legal men with a vested interest in the matter, and people concerned, amongst other things, with the use of the Welsh language in court proceedings. 'We beg to add', said a petition of Anglesey justices, 'that we are attached to our judicature, as the only national privilege that has been left to us as Welshmen; and as one of the ancient institutions of the country, we think that the defects ought to be amended, rather than the whole demolished,...'[54] This, and many other protests, failed and after 1830 the highest justice in Wales was administered by Assize judges, mostly of English background, who travelled on the circuits every spring and autumn. 'It is hard', said one observer a few years later, 'for a judge to do justice who is ignorant of the language of the country', but the change-over did not make much difference to the number of criminal cases heard.[55]

About four times as many cases were heard at the court of Quarter Sessions as at the Assizes. The number of these courts had been reduced by the early nineteenth century; Cardiff and Newport, for instance, no longer had their own Quarter Sessions.[56] In Carmarthen, Brecon, Monmouth,

Haverfordwest and the other towns which still enjoyed the privilege in
1835, the magistrates dealt with only a few minor cases. The major burden
thus fell on the county Sessions, held four times a year, with regular
adjournments. The expansion in the work of the Quarter Sessions would
have been impossible without a parallel increase in the number of county
JPs. By 1835 the three rural counties of Anglesey, Cardiganshire and
Radnorshire had, together, just over 500 magistrates, and Monmouthshire
and Glamorgan almost 400. One in five of these was a clergyman. Table 1
gives some idea of the social origins of these county rulers at a later date;
even in 1887 four out of five magistrates in the rural counties, and the
majority of those in industrial counties, were from noble and gentry
families. Between a quarter and a half of these were good attenders at the
Quarter Sessions, and a few characters, often with a mixed landed and
legal background, dominated proceedings. In this respect, Saunders
Davies and John Jones, whom we have just mentioned, were representative
figures.

The court of Quarter Sessions, like that of the Assize, was much prized
for its jury verdicts, but there were criticisms of the body throughout the
nineteenth century. One constant source of complaint was the location of
the court. In the largest counties, magistrates, jurymen and prosecutors
argued incessantly about the best venue. In Cardiganshire, Aberaeron and
Cardigan were chosen as Quarter Session towns, in Denbighshire,
Rhuthun and Denbigh, and in Glamorgan, Cardiff and Swansea. Another
difficulty was the range of business conducted at the Quarter Sessions, for
the court was, at least until the 1880s, the very heart of local government.
It dealt with county finances, building and road services, and many other
civil matters. Although criminal proceedings in the nineteenth century
were over remarkably quickly, there were times when the magistrates
found it hard to squeeze them into their busy schedule. With some notable
exceptions, they approved of the policy, which became marked after the
1850s, of transferring more of their criminal business to the courts of Petty
Sessions. Late in the century the number of cases brought before the
Quarter Sessions and the Assizes fell considerably, and plans were made to
amalgamate the higher courts in Wales.[57]

At the local level, crown justice in 1800 was administered by magistrates
sitting singly, or together at the courts of Petty and Special Sessions. One
justice of the peace was able to conduct examinations, bind people over to
be of good behaviour, and give judgements on minor matters. With one
colleague, and sometimes without, a magistrate pronounced on poor-law,
vagrancy, licensing, highway, work and trespass offences. Much of this
activity was not recorded; one gains the impression, from the information
which has survived, that Welsh magistrates, 'sitting at home', exercised
wide powers, even handing out sentences for breaches of the peace, slight

Table 1
Social Composition of Justices of the Peace, 1885–1887

	Anglesey, Cardiganshire and Radnorshire	*Glamorgan and Monmouthshire*	*Swansea, Cardiff and Newport*
Nobles, gentry and gentlemen	228	242	25
Clergy	24	17	4
Army and navy	27	59	–
Medicine	3	17	4
Law	4	24	–
Mayors and stipendiaries	–	–	5
Finance	–	8	2
Farmers	–	–	1
Industrial employers and managers	–	51	11
Shipowners	–	2	3
Agents and exporters	–	9	3
Merchants and tradesmen	–	17	9
Engineers	–	5	2
Artists	–	–	1
No occupation given	–	–	9
Total	286	451	79

Source: PP, 1886, LIII, and 1888, LXXXII.

damage to property, and petty thefts of food and game. Their judgements were sometimes noted and confirmed later in the local court. The court of Petty Sessions served collections of parishes and townships, and met monthly or 'when necessary'. It consisted of two or more magistrates, and no jury, and was held at first in mansions and public houses. In Cardiganshire and Carmarthenshire fourteen of the Petty Sessions were still held in public houses in 1861, but with the extension of summary justice and new legislation governing its administration, so the meetings were transferred to village, town and shire halls.[58] At Haverfordwest, where local justice was laced with political discord, the court's move to the townhall in 1832 was welcomed as an end to secrecy.[59]

In the rapidly expanding towns, where fortnightly and then weekly and daily Sessions replaced monthly ones, the availability of justices was a major difficulty. 'There are but few persons here', ran a common grouse in 1835, 'at present qualified to fill Municipal Offices'.[60] Widening the social net, however, had its problems. Samuel Etheridge, a future Chartist leader at Newport, was already in the 1820s denouncing the influence of Samuel Homfray and other industrialists on the Bench. Inspite of this and upper-class resentment, from the 1830s onwards a stream of merchants, physicians, tradesmen, industrial employers and solicitors joined the esquires and gentlemen as urban magistrates, and Merthyr, Cardiff, Swansea and Pontypridd appointed stipendiaries.[61] In the largest towns the courts of Petty Sessions became known as 'police courts'. The name was significant; they were often held at police headquarters, a trend encouraged by the Summary Jurisdiction Act of 1879, and the police were prominent as prosecutors and witnesses.[62]

The extension of summary jurisdiction has been one of the most important developments of the modern legal system. The trend was already apparent in the eighteenth century, when legislation was enacted permitting more offences to be dealt with at Petty Sessions. In doing so, it increased the powers of the magistrates, and removed the prized right of trial by jury from more people, but in return it offered them quicker, cheaper and less severe justice. A meeting of Glamorgan justices in 1816 recommended the establishment of regular Petty Sessions in the county because it would strengthen the police and provide assistance for the poor.[63] In the 1820s new legislation made it easier for people to bring malicious trespass, wilful damage, larceny, common assault, and vagrancy crimes before the Petty Sessions. A select committee of the House of Commons, which investigated the increase in numbers committed to gaol, warned in 1826 of the dangers of making these courts too popular and of giving magistrates too much power to send people to prison for only 'trifling' offences.[64]

From the mid-nineteenth century onwards the shift in balance towards state justice, administered through Petty Sessions, became even more marked. The Juvenile Offenders Acts of 1847 and 1850, the Criminal Justice Act of 1855, and the Summary Jurisdiction Act of 1879 were responsible for much of this. They transferred many offences from the higher to lower courts, and thus speeded up justice and, with Treasury subsidies, reduced its price. This legislation allowed magistrates in Petty

Sessions to pass judgement on young thieves, and on adults pleading guilty to lesser property crimes. The Caernarfon Petty Sessions, welcoming the Act of 1847, said that at last all the complaints against under-fourteen year olds could be dealt with in court, whereas in the past there had been a reluctance to subject them to the ordeal and consequences of trial by jury.[65] In fact, the more wide-ranging Acts of 1855 and 1879 had a greater impact than those of 1847 and 1850; committals to Quarter Sessions and Assizes fell, and hundreds more cases of larceny were brought to the police courts.[66]

The triumph of state justice over all other forms of arbitration and retribution in the nineteenth century can be seen most obviously at this local level. Sadly the disappearance of Petty Session records makes it impossible to fully chronicle this achievement. It has been suggested that the years immediately before and after the Napoleonic Wars marked a turning-point in the popularity of these crown courts, and the figures in Tables 4 and 5 confirm the increasing use being made of them. In 1857 16,529 persons were proceeded against in the Welsh Petty Sessions. By 1899 the figure had reached 55,027, whereas only 655 persons in that year were committed or bailed to appear at the Assizes and Quarter Sessions. As we shall see in chapter 5, the police courts were by that date exceptionally busy. They were crammed not only with criminals and witnesses, but also with women seeking affiliation and separation orders, council officials recovering debts, truant officers with lists of recalcitrant children, and constables awaiting instructions on summonses and warrants. There were always places, like Bethesda, Llandudno, Tenby and Brynmawr, which demanded better judicial facilites and more active magistrates, but in general the improvement in legal services by the mid and late Victorian years was impressive.

There is little doubt that the sharp upturn in the criminal statistics, discussed in the next chapter, was a tribute to these legal and administrative developments as much as to an increase in delinquent behaviour. Of course, these developments did not just happen. Henry Austin Bruce, Aberdare industrialist and MP, who became Home Secretary in Gladstone's first ministry, was one of those who campaigned vigorously for the changes we have been describing. He believed that they would bring great improvements in the reporting and punishment of crime. Behind the triumph of state justice was a growing determination, by governments, reformers and a large number of people, to reject the ways of the past in favour of a more concerned, comprehensive, consistent and, above all, legal response to everyday crime. As Edmund Hyde Hall noted, this was not the 'last resort' mentality of the previous century; the law was now being used positively to announce and promote new standards of behaviour.[67] Since the early nineteenth century the criminal courts have occupied a central place in the life of modern communities.

Prosecution

Although the governors of Britain were partly responsible for the increasing use of the criminal courts, there was much suspicion of public prosecutions in the nineteenth century. One of the supposed merits of the British legal system in 1800 was that the decision to proceed through the courts was largely an individual responsibility. The initiative rested with the victim of a crime, and he or she had wide powers of discretion which could be exercised at every stage of the legal process. At the beginning of our period the person who wished to charge someone with a felony had to secure his or her arrest, and this usually meant convincing a magistrate of the need for a warrant, and finding a parish constable to execute it. Once this had been done, the victim collected evidence and secured witnesses for the preliminary hearing before a justice of the peace. The latter either discharged the accused or sent the person to the higher or lower courts. About a third of those examined were fortunate, and left with a warning ringing in their ears. Not all were innocent. The difficulty of finding reliable witnesses, together with the imminent expense of a full trial, persuaded many victims to withdraw their prosecutions at this time, or to come to an understanding with the person apprehended.

Of the many cases of violence against wives reported to the police, it was, said Henry Austin Bruce in 1875, 'notorious that only a small proportion of them is (fully) prosecuted;...'[68] There was often, as Captain Napier suggested in his report of 1842, an element of intimidation behind the charges withdrawn and the out-of-court settlements; householders accepted inadequate reparation for malicious damage, for fear of worse to come, domestic servants were warned about the dreadful consequences of a failed action over rape, and 'bullies', who protected thieving prostitutes, forced their victims to accept cash payments. Several determined female prosecutors, who ignored all these threats, were attacked within hours of leaving court.[69] Perhaps, as the mayor of Caernarfon claimed in 1862, one result of the new police presence was that people were less ready 'to compromise felonies as they formerly did'.[70] The other main reason for not going to the higher courts was the simple realization, which affected women more than men, that the whole business might be embarrassing, unsuccessful and probably expensive. The legal system recognized that these doubts had to be overcome. Once the preliminary hearing of a felony charge before a magistrate had taken place, and a decision to proceed

Table 2

**Prosecutors at Monmouthshire Quarter Sessions, Easter 1843–
Michaelmas 1844**

Social Group	Number
Gentlemen, yeomen, and farmers	24
Employers, agents and managers	20
Retailers	40
Skilled manual workers	16
Unskilled manual workers	37
Constables	21
Females	9
Total	167

Source: GRO, QSR 0161-68. Quarter Session Recognizances, 1843–44.

agreed, recognizances were made out binding everyone to appear at the
coming Sessions or Assizes.

An analysis of the Monmouthshire Quarter Session records in the first
half of the century confirms the important role played throughout by
private rather than public figures; at least two out of three prosecutors in
court were the victims of the crime, and some of the others were the agents,
friends and relations of the wronged party (Tables 2 and 3). All the work
of prosecution, such as getting clerks to draw up indictments and even
presenting the case in open court, had to be done by these individuals, or,
in a minority of instances, by their attorneys. Parish constables, and the first
professional policemen, usually prosecuted only when they had been
injured by the defendants, and when the crime was larceny from the
person, rioting and other street offences. It took some time, as the inspectors of constabulary admitted, before people surrendered control of their
complaints to policemen and their solicitors. Only, it seems, very late in the
century did the police become the main initiators of criminal cases at the
higher courts, and then not in every county.[71]

The situation at the Petty Sessions was somewhat different. Much of the
business at these courts, from the earliest days, had been concerned with
regulations. Prosecutions were brought, on behalf of the community,
against individuals who failed to obey the laws governing poor relief,
ale-houses, weights and measures, customs and excise and the highways.
Even in these local courts, however, most of the prosecutions were brought

Table 3

Victims of indictable crime in the Abergavenny, Bedwellty, Chepstow and Trevethin divisions of Monmouthshire 1818–1842

Social group	Number
Gentlemen, yeomen and farmers	40
Employers, agents, and managers	38
Retailers	57
Skilled manual workers	38
Unskilled manual workers	78
Constables	12
Females	30
Total	293

Source: GRO, Calendar of Quarter Session Depositions, 1818–42.

by individuals. They were encouraged in this, especially after the Jervis's Acts, by the growing use of summonses rather than warrants in Petty Session cases. A summons could be obtained from a police court for about 2s. One London historian claims that perhaps a quarter or a fifth of assault and property cases at the police courts were conducted by members of the working class.[72] The Petty Session records of Glamorgan for the 1860s and 1870s indicate that as many as a third of prosecutors were from this social group, though over the next twenty years more companies, officials, magistrates' clerks and policemen were responsible for the charges. In Monmouthshire the Ebbw Vale, Rhymney and Tredegar iron companies took hundreds to court in the late nineteenth century, whilst in some divisions of Caernarfonshire and Merioneth at this time police prosecutions accounted for between a half and three quarters of the total. At the Barmouth court, police constables D. Rowlands and Enoch Roberts, and Serjeant Charles Ashton, were extremely busy.[73]

The change from private to police prosecution was gradual and represented an important transfer of power and discretion. In the second quarter of the nineteenth century the first professional police were obliged to accept some of the norms and controls of the communities in which they were placed. Like their predecessors, the parish constables, they took only a selection of known offenders to court. The first 'bobbies' turned a blind eye to many crimes, and handed out countless cautions and pardons to troublesome youngsters, drunken farmers, fraudulent and obstructive tradesmen, audacious vagrants and hawkers, and even a few petty thieves. The last were sometimes instructed to hand back the goods stolen. PC James James of Merthyr in 1860, who took no action over a fifth of the offences known to him, had a soft spot for beer-sellers, drunken and riotous men and female coal-stealers.[74] Criticism of these policemen was voiced in the local newspapers, but when victims and the public refused to help solitary constables, and when it was difficult to get hold of a magistrate or to keep people in custody, inactivity and compromise were understandable.

Gradually the new police were encouraged to take a more positive role not just in the reporting and detection of crime, but also in prosecuting offenders. In 1877 the Pembrokeshire chief constable reprimanded those in his force who 'regularly report all correct' and do 'not bring up more cases than they can possibly avoid'.[75] His counterpart in Caernarfonshire asked inspector Jones of Bangor in December 1859 why the reports of thefts made by the public to his officers had not been taken further.[76] Questions of a similar nature appeared in the press and police committees, and sharp-eyed observers compared the scale and character of police prosecutions in one Welsh district with another. Why, it was asked, were so few vagrants taken before the courts in certain Montgomeryshire and Pembrokeshire parishes, and why did the police in the Bridgend and Tywyn divisions enter 'not proceeded with' alongside the names of scores of people found in a drunken state? Ultimately chief constables had to answer all such queries, for it was their task to impose uniformity and it was they who decided to initiate, or withdraw, many of these prosecutions.

The police, and their legal representatives, took on more cases as the years passed. The development was carefully monitored, not least in Caernarfonshire where, in the 1890s, the costs of William George of Criccieth, and the three other police solicitors, were minutely scrutinized. Critics of the growing police influence over the criminal administration talked of vindictive prosecutions, unsupported evidence, and forced confessions.[77] The reduction in acquittals and discharges in the late nineteenth century was an indication that the police became more careful, and proficient, at presenting cases, but suspicions remained. A report by the judicature commissioners in 1874 stated that 'the police are in a great many cases important witnesses, and when a prosecutor is also a witness, there is a risk of his becoming biased in his testimony', and it concluded with a recommendation that public prosecutors be appointed.[78] This was something which had been considered before, in the 1830s and 1850s, because of the low quality of prosecutions. In 1879 the post of Director of Public Prosecutions was established by Parliament, but he was given no more than a minor advisory role.

One reason why successive British governments resisted the temptation to extend the centralized system of crown prosecution from Ireland to the mainland was the cost of legal cases. If crime was a problem, so, too, was the expense of dealing with it. At the beginning of the century, prosecutors at Assizes and Quarter Sessions had to pay £10–20 per case in fees, charges and allowances, and about a tenth of that at Petty Sessions.[79] People thought long and hard before committing themselves to a prosecution. Even in 1883, S. H. Jones-Parry felt that the 'empty gaols and blank calendars' of his homeland could partly be explained by the 'fear of loss of time and money in prosecuting, and the dread of being placed at the mercy of lawyers'.[80] As most cases of theft had to be tried by a jury before the 1840s, the costs involved were frequently well in excess of the amount stolen. Complaints about the excessive costs, which contributed to the Rebecca troubles, encouraged the government to regulate fees and increase the financial assistance given to prosecutors and witnesses. After 1752 a series of Acts, notably Peel's Criminal Justice Act of 1826, offered state aid to private, and especially poor, prosecutors, first in felony and then in certain misdemeanour cases, but not everything was covered. Magistrates sometimes compounded the problem by refusing to allow costs for a successful prosecution where the victim had inadequately secured his or her property.

It has been assumed that this help with expenses, which increased substantially in the second quarter of the century and became comprehensive by the fourth, made a significant difference to the number of court cases. Yet one can exaggerate its impact. Men and women doggedly pursued an offender even when it was financially disastrous to do so. 'I am not aware of its [inadequate remuneration] having prevented the prosecution of offenders or deterred witnesses from attending', said Robert Oliver Jones, chairman of the Glamorgan Quarter Sessions in 1872. 'Generally persons who have been robbed or injured give the offenders in custody, or inform the police in the first moment of anger or suffering, and then the cases have to go on. The question of expense is, in Quarter Sessions cases at all events, not thought of in the first instance.'[81] An analysis of the Anglesey court records in the 1860s bears this out; outraged owners wanted to prosecute youths for stealing the smallest objects, and only the charity of magistrates brought the legal proceedings to a close.[82]

Robert Oliver Jones was also dismissive of the financial burden of legal representation. Attornies, solicitors and barristers were increasingly used in the courts from the turn of the century, first by the prosecutors and then by the defendants. At the Great Sessions, Assizes and Quarter Sessions, where typically about a dozen lawyers were in attendance, they began to dominate proceedings. By the 1860s cases of embezzlement and fraud were adjourned whilst defendants secured professional help. The Welsh had a reputation for producing, and using, many attornies. One judge in Carmarthenshire in 1837, condemned them, and the practice of having numerous witnesses on both sides of a case.[83] Indeed, one of the charges against the Great Sessions was that 'a large assembly' of attornies, of indifferent quality, lengthened proceedings, made deals amongst themselves and milked the complainants.[84] There is evidence that in the criminal, and especially the civil, business of the higher courts, legal fortunes were made and prosecutors and defendants brought to ruin. Robert Oliver Jones had little sympathy for them. 'Persons of the better class who have got into trouble will obtain the assistance of Attorneys of reputation', he stated in 1872, 'and the lower class of prisoners who are defended are almost invariably persons of bad character, and... deserve no more protection than they now get.'[85] At the time when he was speaking, at least two-thirds of the poorest people who appeared in the courts, as prosecutors and defendants, were not represented.

What has surprised historians is the fact that hundreds, if not thousands, of ordinary people used the crown courts. Whatever their views of the expense and class-biased nature of the legal system, these people sought assistance from it. This was not without precedent, for in the eighteenth century at least a third of prosecutors were small tradesmen, artisans and labourers.[86] In property cases it was common to find the poor, and not-so-poor, on opposite sides of the court. The Monmouthshire Quarter Session records of the years 1818–42, admittedly from an exceptional county, show that well over a quarter of the prosecutors in that county were working class, and many of these were miners and labourers (Tables 2 and 3).[87] In Glamorgan, two decades later, it was a similar story, whilst of the 100 prosecution recognizances which have survived in the Anglesey Quarter Session records for 1838–54, five were of gentlemen and esquires, fifteen of farmers, twenty-four of retailers, twenty of labourers or husbandmen, sixteen of other members of the working class, seven of policemen and thirteen of others. Thomas Roberts, husbandman of Llanfigael, who pursued William Williams for larceny, was thus a more representative figure at the court than Thomas Peers Williams Esq. of Llandegfan.[88] The Petty Session evidence is more difficult to find, but, as we noted earlier, it seems that about a third of the prosecutors at the Glamorgan Petty Sessions in the mid-Victorian years were working class; they included poor labourers, seamen and prostitutes as well as the labour aristocrats, all seeking retribution for assault, larceny, unpaid wages, attacks by vicious dogs and other sufferings.[89] In court they sat alongside the many shop-keepers, dealers, publicans and other retailers who were, proportionately, the most litigious people in nineteenth-century Britain.

One historian, who is determined to offer a non-Marxist perspective, states that 'the whole of the criminal system, especially the prosecution system, was designed primarily to protect the people, overwhelmingly non-élite, who suffered from crime'.[90] It is a large claim, but the evidence

FIVE GUINEAS
REWARD.

WHEREAS

Some Person or Persons did on the Night of Saturday or early on Sunday Morning last, Steal a number of GEESE and other FOWLS, from the Yard of Mr. EDWARD ELLIS, of Celyn.

Whoever will give Information of the Offender or Offenders, so that he or they may be brought to Conviction, shall receive TWO GUINEAS from JOHN MAUGHAN, Esq. Secretary to the Whitford Association for the Prosecution of Felons, and a further Reward of THREE GUINEAS from Mr. EDWARD ELLIS.

December 22nd, 1828.

JAMES DAVIES, PRINTER, CROSS-STREET, HOLYWELL.

A reward offered by the Whitford Association, 1828

of Tables 2 and 3 gives superficial support to it. Three out of five prosecutors, and victims, were retailers or manual workers. These people were affected more than most by the property crimes and violence of the nineteenth century. Jewish businessmen in south Wales, men like Coleman Follick and Louis Barnett, pawnbrokers, were especially vulnerable, as were inn and lodging-house keepers.[91] An analysis of the first 100 robberies reported to the police in the Holywell division during 1890–1 indicates why the middle and lower middle class were so prominent as prosecutors. Nineteen per cent of victims were hotel proprietors and innkeepers, another 19 per cent were shopkeepers and dealers, 16 per cent were male workmen, 15 per cent were farmers, 12 per cent were females, 9 per cent were companies, masters and agents, 7 per cent were gentlemen and clergymen, and 3 per cent were others.[92] The wealthiest inhabitants of country and town were rarely prosecuted in the higher courts by people of a lower social status, but the former used the criminal law rather less than was once thought. According to Table 2, gentlemen, large employers and their representatives comprised a quarter of the total seeking help at the Monmouthshire Quarter Sessions. Although this was a considerable proportion, there was, at the beginning of our period, some anxiety that the most prominent members of society were reluctant to prosecute.

The emergence of the Associations for the Prosecution of Felons reflected a growing determination to change this state of affairs. These were established in the last thirty years of the eighteenth century and in the first sixty years of the nineteenth. The Eifionydd, Bangor, St Asaph, Whitford, Rhiwabon, Corwen, Llanfyllin, Talgarth, Swansea and Abergavenny associations were just a selection of the better known institutions. A few notables joined these bodies, though members were usually middle-ranking propertied people and the obligatory clergyman.[93] They entered into an agreement to report offences, and prosecute the perpetrators. By offering rewards they attracted information from informers and a few semi-professional thief-takers. Solicitors were employed to prosecute offenders, and each association obtained about a dozen or more convictions a year. Some of the Welsh associations were apparently quite effective, but with the installation of professional police in all counties and large boroughs after 1856 they ceased to be very active.

Part of their work was, in fact, taken over by the Game Associations, and especially by the Fishing Clubs and Boards which were set up in the mid-Victorian years to execute the new legislation on seasons and licences. These also retained solicitors, and gave bonuses to their keepers, bailiffs and watchmen for every prosecution.[94] In the 1860s these conservators were responsible for bringing many fishermen and game poachers before the courts. The Wye Preservation Society, set up in 1862, employed thirty-seven watchers who secured twenty-five convictions for illegal salmon fishing in its first full year.[95] One of the complaints of Welsh Liberals, often made in the last two decades, was that the police and magistrates, when apprehending and prosecuting offenders, gave undue weight to the wishes of these landowning clubs. At a meeting of the Carmarthenshire Standing Joint Committee in 1890, when a violent poaching affray near Llanelli was discussed, Gwilym Evans asked why the police 'took up' all manner of 'small [poaching] prosecutions', but never one against aggressive gamekeepers.[96]

The establishment of corporation and county watch committees in the 1830s and 1850s respectively, and of standing joint police committees in 1889, were important developments in the history of prosecution. In these meetings people expressed views on police policy and sought to influence its direction. Some of the early urban watch committees kept tight control over policing. John Bird and his Cardiff colleagues 'instructed' their superintendant on a wide variety of matters. After the County and Borough Police Act of 1856 chief constables exercised more independence. Not all the requests from private individuals, traders and employers were attended to, and not all the demands of the police committees were acted upon. The Flintshire committee rarely challenged the decisions of its chief constables.

Police chiefs were occasionally reprimanded for a casual approach to prostitution and disorderly conduct, and for ignoring victimless crimes like drunkenness and breaches of the licensing laws. In the last years of the century they came under increasing pressure from the moral reformers on the police committees. These demanded action against Sunday traders, licensees, gamblers, drunkards, swearers, vagrants, gypsies and prostitutes. In the 1890s Richard Roberts in Anglesey, Thomas Gee in north-east Wales, and minister William Thomas in the south-west, hounded chief constables and helped to transform the character of recorded crime.[97] In Caernarfonshire, a successful campaign, jointly run by Lord Penrhyn and D. P. Williams in 1893, resulted in the county police taking proceedings against all persons who swore and used obscene language in public places.[98]

These police committees were the target of pressure groups. One of the stated purposes of the Cardiff Association for Improving and Enforcing the Laws for the Protection of Women, the Arfon and Conwy Vale Temperance Association and the female Ffestiniog branch of the National Vigilance Association was to provide evidence of wrong-doing and persuade the police to follow up their complaints. Like the society for the reformation of manners in the early eighteenth century, and the anti-vice societies a hundred years later, these new associations raised money for prosecutions. They were opposed, in the watch committees, by representatives of the Cardiff Licensed Victuallers Association and other conservative institutions. As we shall see in chapter 5, prosecution policy was also influenced by press campaigns and by the work of voluntary agencies like the NSPCC and the RSPCA. At the annual meeting of the Anglesey and Caernarfonshire branch of the latter charity in February 1893, inspector Yates reported that during the previous year they had brought seventy-five cases before the courts, mostly of cruelty to horses.[99]

Apart from the police, the most common prosecutors at the end of the century were other representatives of local and central government. Commissioners and inspectors of health, education, excise, and poor relief, collectors of rates, revenue, and other duties, and all manner of major and minor officers, constantly used the lower courts. Public prosecutions were not new, as we have seen, but the scale and range of official actions in the courts increased significantly during the second half of the nineteenth century. At least a third of the cases before most police-court magistrates in the 1890s were of this kind. It is an indication of how modern government hi-jacked the criminal-justice system, much as it did the business of education and the administration of social welfare.

The changing pattern of prosecution sharpened the debate about the nature and purpose of the legal system. One of the main defences of the system in 1800 was that it reflected individual needs, and acted as a bulwark against the might of a centralizing state and powerful vested interests. Private prosecutions, even if burdensome and costly, gave the illusion that everyone had a part to play in the legal process, that somehow the law transcended political, class and sectional interests. No doubt this was one reason why the law was highly regarded by the public as well as by the rulers of society. In 1899 it was more difficult, in some ways, to decide for whose benefit the law was being administered. Private prosecutions, chiefly for assaults and property crime, were still fairly common, but most were of a public kind, and almost all were financed by the Treasury. Apologists of the criminal-justice system at the end of the century maintained that it was being run by the state and its professionals, efficiently and non-politically, in the interests of the whole nation, or at least of those who believed in order and civilization. The state, which had once been regarded as the greatest threat to liberty, 'gradually became the implicit source of rights, for it could fairly claim that rights were conditional on the order which it alone had the resources to protect'.[100]

Not everybody liked the new developments. As the business of dealing with crime passed out of the people's hands, questions of influence, control, and liberty, became ever more important. In September 1875 the *Haverfordwest and Milford Haven Telegraph* wondered 'how much the liberties of the public' were now lodged 'in the hands of policemen'.[101] Although they claimed to be the best guarantors of order and justice, the police, the court officials and the lawyers were moving beyond the reach of ordinary people. 'Who controls the police?' was the most interesting question raised in the Welsh standing joint committees of the late nineteenth century.[102] Whoever controlled policing and prosecution had a major influence on the purpose and execution of the criminal law. It became easier for governments, and the interfering 'meddlers', whom Edmund Hyde Hall so disliked, to use the legal system in a positive and selective fashion. The criminal law, which in the eighteenth century had been 'an expensive discipline of last resort', now began to occupy a prominent and not always welcome place in people's lives. The Cardiff youths of 1900 who appeared in the police court on charges of drunkenness, swearing in public and kicking a football in the street, experienced both the freedoms and the controls of the modern age.[103] For good or ill, after the late nineteenth century the story of the Welsh and crime would never be quite the same again.

2

A General Survey: the Criminal Statistics

Despite the problems outlined in the last chapter, a general survey of crime in the nineteenth century must begin with the published national statistics. The year 1810 marked the first appearance in the Parliamentary Papers of the county figures, back-dated to 1805, of people committed for trial at the Great and Quarter Sessions in Wales. Thirty years later, after pleading from Samuel Redgrave at the Home Office, more details were added of the sex, age and literacy of these offenders and of the nature of their crimes. The major change, however, followed upon the international statistical congress of 1853 and the passing of the County and Borough Police Act three years later. From that moment onwards, many new annual tables of information on crime, criminals, police and prisons, were published. The two most interesting, and used, of these returns were of indictable offences reported to the police and of offences determined summarily. They provided, and have continued to provide, the basis of our yearly reports on the criminal state of the nation.

There was a lively discussion amongst contemporaries about the value of these figures, especially when they were first collected, and again after 1893, when a major overhaul of the judicial statistics took place. In Britain the leading figure in the debate was Rawson W. Rawson, who developed the fascinating ideas of European social scientists like Lamberte-Adolphe Quetelet and André-Michel Guerry about the regularity and significance of the annual crime rates. Although Rawson had no doubts about the importance of the new statistical information, he had some sympathy for the chief constable who declared that 'the amount of crime in a county is a matter of book-keeping'.[1] At the local level it took a while for occurrence and charge books to be supplied to each of the police stations, and for standard forms to be issued to all the forces and courts. In 1860 the inspector of constabulary for north Wales said that the criminal statistics were 'much more correct' than in previous years.[2] Gradually the Home Office insisted on greater uniformity, though its own Departmental Committee of 1892–5 claimed that there were still serious deficiencies in the collection and tabulation of the figures.[3] Some modern academics have registered their doubts about this evidence by ignoring it in favour of 'the sure-footed terrain of human feelings', but most historians of crime continue to use the government information.[4] There is a widely held belief

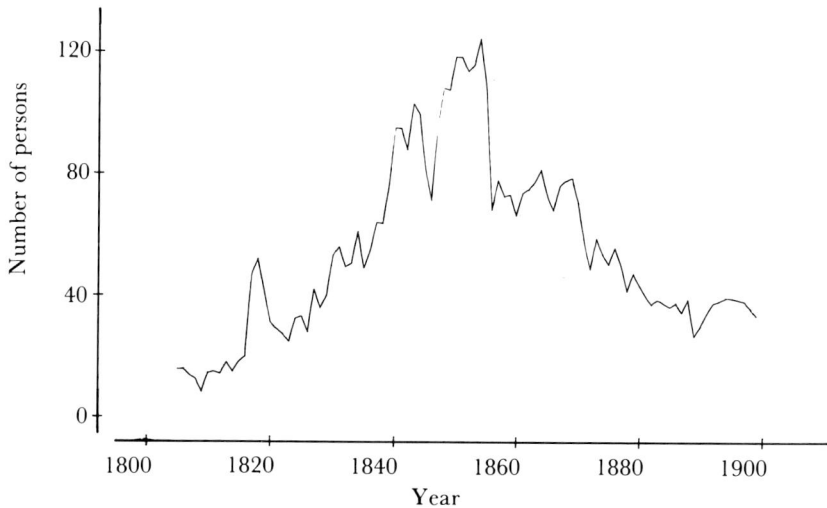

Basic rate: per 100,000 of population

Graph 1. Persons committed for trial, or bailed, 1805–1899.

that, apart from their other disclosures, statistics give vital clues to long-term changes in social behaviour.[5]

The crime rate

Graphs 1, 2 and 3 are based on the information given in the published tables. The figures of criminals proceeded against at the higher and lower courts differ greatly, and have to be considered separately. The changes in the statistics of reported and prosecuted indictable crime in Wales mirror those in England and several other western European countries, though not precisely so.[6] After a long decline in the annual totals of Welsh indictments for much of the eighteenth century, there was a rise in the last two decades, which continued until the early 1850s, by which time the English statistics were already falling. The spectacular nature of the increase on Graphs 1 and 4, in both male and female indictments, can only be compared, in modern times, to the 'explosion of crime' since the Second World War, and both have been linked to the problems of change and modernization. In the 1840s Friedrich Engels, Archibald Alison, the Reverend John Griffith and others looked to the future with 'the most melancholy forebodings'.

The sharpest upturns in the statistics occurred in the early part of the Napoleonic Wars, during the first years of the peace, in the run-up to the Reform crisis of 1830–2, and at the time of the economic depressions of the late 1830s and late 1840s. Judge Bosanquet, speaking to the Cardiganshire

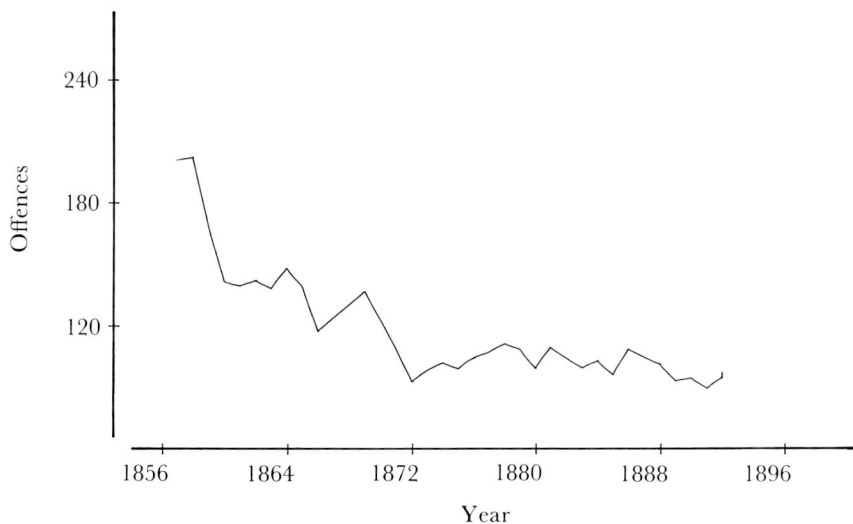

Basic rate: per 100,000 of population

Graph 2. Indictable offences known to the police, 1857–1892.

Basic rate: per 100,000 of population

Graph 3. Persons proceeded against for offences determined summarily, 1857–1899.

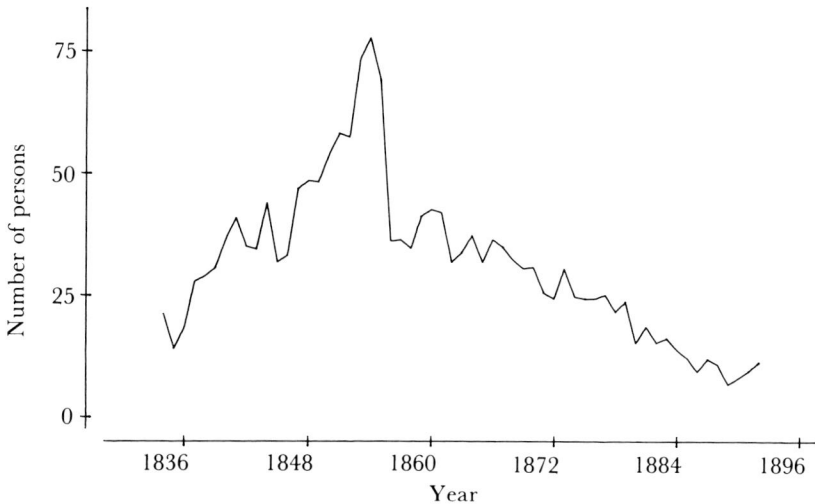

Basic rate: per 100,000 of population

Graph 4. Females committed for trial, or bailed, 1834–1892.

Assizes in 1833, said that these figures of people committed to the higher courts actually reflected the 'rising level' of crime, but he felt that the the the scale of the problem was less serious inside the Principality than outside. In 1851, a total of 1,376 people were committed for trial or bailed to appear at the Assizes and Quarter Sessions, some one in 845 of the population, more than seven times the proportion of the year 1805. This was better than the equivalent English rate of one in 655 in 1851, but not by as much as Henry Richard, Bosanquet and others suggested.

After the high reaches of the early 1850s there was a sharp fall in the rate of indictable crime to a lower plateau in the 1860s, and then another drop in the early 1870s before the fairly consistent and gradual decline of the last three decades. In 1875 Henry Austin Bruce, retired Home Secretary, addressed the National Association for the Promotion of Social Science on these crime figures. His mature reflections on their importance was conveyed by this metaphor: 'We have gained the summit-level. A broad table-land has still to be crossed, "not without dust and heat"; but soon the further ridge will be gained, and with assured step and with increased speed we shall descend the rugged slope, and gaze with wistful eyes into the impenetrable depths beneath us.'[7] As he pointed out, and as we shall see later, the fall in the annual totals of recorded indictable crime was not uniform across all communities, nor all offences, but the trend was unmistakable. By the last decade, when there was a major change in the compilation of the statistics, the anxiety of the early Victorians had been replaced by a mood of confidence. In 1899 the rate of people tried in Wales for indictable crimes was only slightly better than that in England, but at one person in 2,994 it was much better than that of fifty years before. 'With regarded to crime', concluded the chief constable in his statement to the Denbighshire Standing Joint Committee in April 1895, 'I am happy to say that the country is in a most satisfactory state'.[8]

Judgements of this kind tended, perhaps understandably, to ignore the evidence of offences which were not dealt with at the higher courts. The 'problem' of crime has usually been defined in terms of the most serious threat to persons and property. Significantly, national information on cases heard at the Petty Sessions was collected fifty years after that from the courts of Assize and Quarter Sessions. Prior to 1857 the historian has to rely for a picture of petty crime on local records. Of the people bound over and convicted by magistrates sitting alone, we know almost nothing. The impression, from the scraps of surviving evidence, is that more cases were heard at every level in the late eighteenth and early nineteenth centuries. In thinly populated Merioneth, justices such as Richard Watkin Price and Richard Hughes Lloyd were obliged 'on their own behalf' to deal with a large number of poachers, trespassers, vagrants and stealers of wood and vegetables during the war years.[9] The records of Flintshire also reveal a substantial increase in 'out-of-court' convictions in the years 1815–18 and 1820–25.[10]

Although most Petty Session records before the 1850s have long since disappeared, we can tell from the prison registers and the occasional parliamentary paper that these lower courts were increasingly busy. The number of people admitted to Haverfordwest gaol, for instance, rose in the post-war years, and then again, more sharply in the early 1820s, early 1830s and early 1840s. In the twelve months after October 1816 there were seventy-eight on its prison register; by 1826–7 the number had trebled, and in 1833–4 and 1843–4 it was 409 and 406 respectively, excluding debtors. At Rhuthun county gaol and house of correction, eighty-two people were admitted in 1827, ninety-four in 1830, 129 in 1832, and 150 in 1834.[11] In Wrexham and Dolgellau it was a similar story, and the kind of people filling the cells were vagrants, idle, disorderly and riotous persons, thieves and poachers, individuals guilty of assault and malicious damage, and those who had disobeyed bastardy orders, other poor-law regulations and work contracts.[12]

Tables 4 and 5 are records of prisoners committed and convicted under summary process between 1814 and 1854. They have been ignored by most historians of crime. Although some returns are missing from the Welsh gaols at the beginning of this period, they are a useful guide. They indicate sharp increases in convictions at the Petty Sessions prior to 1823, and in 1839, 1842, 1844 and 1848. A further breakdown of the figures in Table 5

Table 4
Number of persons committed each year to Welsh gaols under summary process, 1814–1829

Year	No. of gaol returns	Wales	Anglesey, Cardiganshire & Radnorshire	Glamorgan & Monmouthshire
			Number committed in:	
1814	17	136	40	9
1815	17	162	36	21
1816	17	211	50	16
1817	18	305	75	30
1818	20	458	81	26
1819	21	428	77	51
1820	21	516	68	104
1821	22	566	88	123
1822	24	668	91	203
1823	24	815	105	245
1824	24	740	98	197
1825	24	690	82	164
1826	26	714	110	181
1827	26	802	77	211
1828	26	929	103	257
1829	26	867	78	249

Source: PP, 1831, XV. These figures were compiled 'in so far as the same can be made out'.

shows that the number of people, especially of a young age, imprisoned in Wales for offences such as vagrancy and trespass trebled and quadrupled in the early Victorian years. Sadly, the totals of Welsh people who were fined, instead of gaoled, for misdemeanours in this period cannot be recovered, though odd references suggest that these, too, were increasing.

Even more difficult to discover is the number of people charged with crimes, which was always larger than the number who were eventually taken to court. The only detail on this is to be found in those counties which

Table 5
Persons imprisoned, having been summarily convicted, 1836–1854

Year	Wales	Anglesey, Cardiganshire & Radnorshire	Glamorgan & Monmouthshire	For assault (Wales)
1836	859	95	353	245
1837	823	88	293	213
1838	858	81	392	176
1839	1005	150	411	212
1840	994	87	460	179
1841	1072	80	526	210
1842	1319	91	652	325
1843	1488	180	656	280
1844	1944	198	763	306
1845	1976	210	758	296
1846	1358	221	539	274
1847	1487	188	645	262
1848	2249	302	875	348
1849	2080	218	929	348
1850	2009	172	911	476
1851	2237	153	1062	530
1852	2094	136	1141	477
1853	2168	131	1302	404
1854	2139	93	1343	447

Source: PP, 1837, XXXII-1857, VII.

had the first professional constabularies. The Glamorgan chief constable reported in April 1851 that as many as 2,916 people had been summoned or arrested in the previous year, about one in fifty-six of the population policed by his force, almost fifty per cent more than the rate of seven years previously. In his Merthyr district the rate and the increase were even higher. As a comparison, it has been estimated, from various sources, that the rate of people charged in the south-western counties of Wales during the second quarter of the nineteenth century reached a peak in 1843–5, when approximately one in 100 of the population was summoned and apprehended.[13]

In the second half of the century there was a change in the pattern of recorded crime. A sharp divergence occurred between the statistics of offences determined summarily and those of indictable crime. As the latter fell, so the number of people dealt with at the lower courts continued to rise (Graph 3). The steepest and longest increase took place between the late 1850s, when the statistics began, and the mid-1870s. During that period, courts had to stay open for longer during the week, and at Pontypridd and Swansea stipendiary magistrates were appointed in the summer of 1872 to streamline business. After the mid-1870s the rate of Petty Session cases fluctuated, reaching a peak in 1899. In that year, assuming no one attended more than once, one in thirty-six of the Welsh population appeared at the Petty Sessions, more than twice as many as in 1857, and just above the England figure. If Wales had become a less criminal nation by the end of the century, as some claimed, this was statistically true of only the most serious types of offences. In parts of Wales the number of cases dealt with at the lower courts was especially high. Of the 55,027 offences determined summarily in 1899, seventy-three per cent were in Glamorgan and Monmouthshire, where just over half the population of the country resided.

Regional variations

Before attempting an explanation of these statistics of both serious and petty crime it is worth looking in more detail at the regional differences, and at the categories of offences. Anglesey, Cardiganshire and Radnorshire have been chosen as representative of the rural counties, and Glamorgan and Monmouthshire of the most industrialized.[14] With a few notable exceptions, contemporaries were convinced that there was less crime in rural Wales than outside, and the statistics in Table 4 and Graph 5 give some support for this view. Whereas one in 1,140 of the population of the three rural counties was committed for trial or imprisoned under summary process in 1821, in the industrial ones the rate was one per 831. Thirty years later the respective figures, based on Table 5 and Graph 5, were one per 586 in Anglesey, Cardiganshire and Radnorshire and one per 215 in Glamorgan and Monmouthshire.

The differential can also be seen within counties. In April 1851 the Glamorgan police force, which did not cover the boroughs of Cardiff, Swansea and Neath, gave the following proportions of people apprehended and summoned in the four districts of Merthyr, Newbridge, Bridgend and Swansea over the previous twelve months. The difficulties of the sources

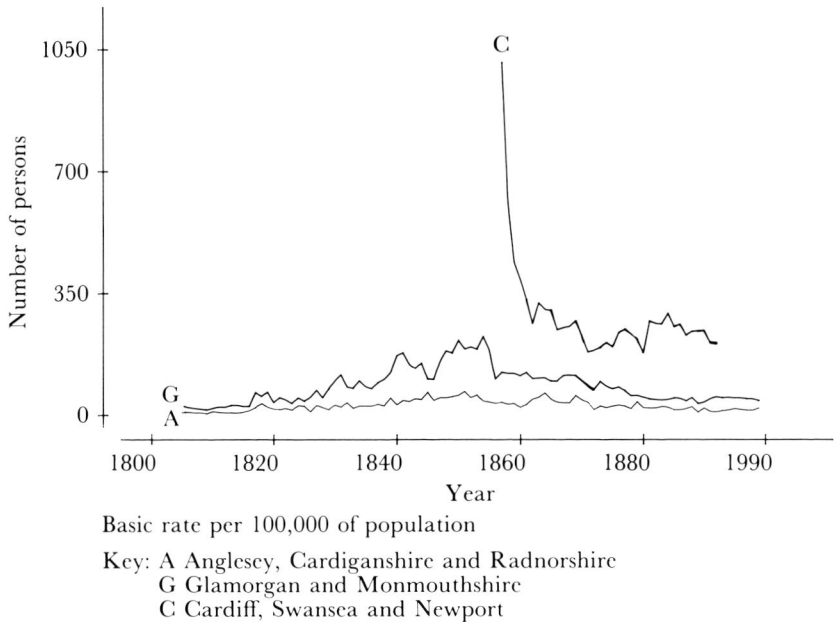

Basic rate per 100,000 of population

Key: A Anglesey, Cardiganshire and Radnorshire
　　 G Glamorgan and Monmouthshire
　　 C Cardiff, Swansea and Newport

Graph 5. Persons committed for trial, or bailed, in rural and industrial counties, and indictable offences reported in urban communities, 1805–1899.

make accuracy impossible, but the differences between the heavily industrialized Merthyr area and the semi-rural hinterland of Swansea are well delineated:[15]

Police Division	Population	Acreage	Persons apprehended and summoned	Crime rate
Merthyr	67,819	77,931	1,651	1 per 41
Bridgend	23,422	109,511	422	1 per 56
Newbridge	32,391	126,209	407	1 per 80
Swansea	39,680	144,589	436	1 per 91

As a comparison, the Caernarfonshire chief constable presented a similar table for 1895, which showed that, even allowing for the variable levels of policing, the rate of recorded offences in the agricultural division of Pwllheli was much lower than that of the other urban and semi-urban areas:[16]

Police Division	Constables	Population	Acreage	Indictable Offences	Summary Offences
Caernarfon	22	37,541	78,436	68	619

Bangor	17	25,324	57,108	74	324
Conwy	18	22,168	89,270	66	643
Pwllheli	16	30,854	147,619	26	171

How to account for the favourable situation in the rural communities was a question of much interest to contemporaries. For some the key factor was the density of population. The half-empty gaols of rural counties at the end of the eighteenth century proved that 'those violent passions which engendered crimes are invariably most prevalent in populous districts'; a scattered agricultural people could not become 'addicted to crime'. Travellers in the Welsh countryside found an explanation for this 'lack of crime' in the character of the peasantry and the quality of the social relationships. Poor farmers and labourers were described as 'of a steady, plodding stamp', 'contented' and lacking the energy and initiative required for delinquency and rebellion. Although the income of servants was low, it was regular and sometimes received in kind. During hard times, these people had a reputation for bearing privations with a fortitude unmatched in Britain, and in a manner very different from that of their urban cousins.[17] 'Drunkenness is rare in this neighbourhood;', said the Reverend John Price of Bleddfa in Radnorshire in 1846, 'the poorer classes are really honest, quiet, and industrious'.[18] 'The agricultural labourers are in general', concluded a fellow clergyman in 1842, 'a much more moral class than the operatives in the town'.[19]

The reasons for this difference were, it was said, to be found in the close relationships, co-operative mentality, and religious feelings of the rural community, and in the effective agencies of authority and control. Benjamin Malkin, writing in 1807, believed that the quiescence of the peasantry stemmed from not having 'the means of comparison and choice'.[20] Deference, even 'feudal dependence', was apparently strong in rural Wales. Judges and chairmen of Quarter Sessions compared the resident landowners of Wales favourably with their Irish and English counterparts. 'All my friends among the neighbouring landlords try to do their duty towards their dependants, with whom they are in complete sympathy,' said C. R. Williams of Dolmelynllyn, 'and this may account for the contentment and absence of crime which is proverbial in Merioneth'. In Lleufer Thomas's opinion, the close relationships that still existed in the 1890s between master and servant, and the voluntary or enforced attendance at church and chapel, produced 'in all the ... parts of rural Wales, an almost total absence of all serious crime ...'[21]

Such statements have to be set against the 'tolerated illegality' in the countryside, and the low level of policing throughout the nineteenth century. As we have seen, some observers felt that the 'problem' of crime in farming districts was as bad as that in industrial ones, and John Glyde, a Suffolk statistician, claimed that it was worse. The increase in the Welsh crime rate was initially, like the population explosion, fairly uniform across the nation, as Tables 4, 5 and Graph 5 indicate. If we extract from these incomplete and selective statistics the annual totals for Anglesey, Cardiganshire and Radnorshire, and relate them to population growth, it appears that the rate of known indictable and summary crime rose by some 500 per cent between the end of the war and 1848. The main increases were prior to 1818, possibly in the early 1830s, when most of the information is missing, in 1839 and especially between 1842 and 1848.

The statistics in Table 5 are particularly interesting. They show that, contrary to received wisdom, the number of people imprisoned for lesser crimes rose faster in the group of rural counties between 1836 and 1848 than in the industrial. In west Wales these statistics increased by almost 300 per cent during the late 1830s and early 1840s, at a time when its population growth had slowed to a trickle. This provides a fascinating background to the Rebecca story, and to the debate over Welsh morality and habits contained in the education report of 1847. However it is interpreted, Table 5 confirms that rural people were not 'innocent of crime', and we can be certain that many of the migrants to Merthyr Tydfil took their delinquent behaviour and rebellious instincts with them.

From Table 5 and Graph 5, we can see that rates of reported indictable crime and imprisonments in Anglesey, Cardiganshire and Radnorshire rose to an early peak in the mid-century and then declined. There was a temporary halt to this decline in the 1860s, and an increase in offences determined summarily, causing the chairman of the Anglesey Quarter Sessions to mutter about the misplaced 'pride...upon the absence of crime' in his county, but there was, in general, a growing satisfaction with developments in rural Wales. A generation after Rebecca rode across west Wales, the images of the countryside were of 'peace', 'innocence' and 'tranquillity'. Rural Wales was again, and especially, 'the land of white gloves'. 'As a rule,' commented the Welsh Land Commission of 1896, 'a farming neighbourhood is a model of peace and quietness...As a rule,...the country districts are comparatively free from all serious crimes,...'[22] Crime, agrarian outrage and trade-unionism in the late nineteenth century were identified as something which afflicted outsiders. In Anglesey the criminal scapegoats were the Irish labourers of Holyhead, and the travelling beggars. The chief constable of Radnorshire declared in 1885 that if tramps were kept out his county 'we shall be almost free of crime'.

Industrial Wales, by contrast, was associated with high levels of crime. Visitors to the Principality during the Napoleonic Wars wrote of the 'tainted' nature of those working amongst the dirt and noise of the mines and factories. It was often said that places like Merthyr Tydfil attracted the 'worst elements', and changed the 'natural simplicity' of the peasantry into 'the drunken depravity' of the industrial work-force. According to one report, the 'black domain' of the south Wales coalfield 'contains a larger proportion of escaped criminals and dissolute people of both sexes than almost any other populace'. The Reverend Richard Davies, magistrate at Brynmawr, believed that the state of this industrial population in 1847 was worse than the statistics implied, but he was content to use them 'as our guide and index'.[23] Historians can do no more; as we saw earlier, the rate of recorded crime was already higher in Glamorgan and Monmouthshire in 1821 than in the three selected rural counties, and thirty years later the gap had widened. The increase in recorded crime in south-east Wales until the mid-century was extraordinary and almost continuous. The figures in Tables 4 and 5, and Graph 5, indicate that in Glamorgan and Monmouthshire the rise was halted only briefly in the mid-1820s and mid-1840s.

It was widely recognized that the most heavily industrialized regions made a major contribution to the last Welsh peak of indictable crime in the late 1840s and early 1850s. Sir John Campbell, chief justice, speaking in 1855, commented on the dichotomy between the recently improved situation in south-west Wales and the long list of court cases in the south-east. He pointed out that, whilst commitments to gaol had fallen by a half in Cardiganshire and Carmarthenshire since the days of Rebecca, in Glamorgan they had doubled. He refused to believe that the industrial population was less prosperous, educated and policed than its rural counterpart. On the contrary, like several observers, he wondered whether there was an unwelcome connection between delinquency and industrialization, modernization and affluence. 'It will be a sad reflection to find that an increase of crime is a consequence of increased prosperity', he mused, 'and that crime must follow in the train of wealth'.[24]

Ironically, he was speaking at the very moment when the number of persons committed to the higher courts in Glamorgan and Monmouthshire was about to fall sharply, helped no doubt by the Criminal Justice Act of 1855 and the growing use made of summary jurisdiction. In the parliamentary reports of 1846 and 1847, which examined the state of the mining population and its education, claims were made of a recent improvement in social behaviour and peaceable habits. 'It is right to acknowledge', was one comment on the miners of Monmouthshire and Breconshire, 'the existence among the population of many, and it is believed, an increasing number of persons, correct and estimable in their mode of life,...'[25]

The picture was not completely rosy. Graph 6 shows that the rate of Petty-Session cases in Glamorgan and Monmouthshire rose fairly consistently until the end of the century, as did the number of people apprehended and summoned by the Glamorgan police, but a half of these proceedings were a tribute to the authorities' determination to enforce the Licensing Act of 1872 and the legislation controlling education and the highways.

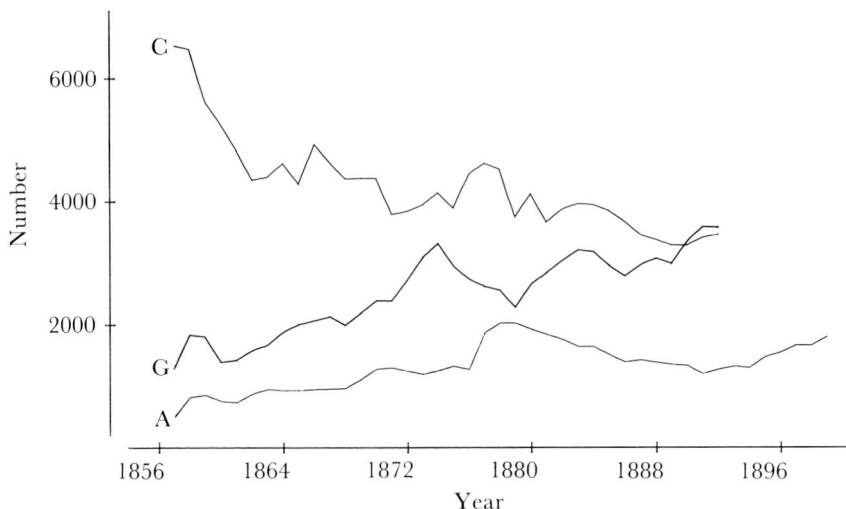

Basic rate per 100,000 of population

Key: A Anglesey, Cardiganshire and Radnorshire
     G Glamorgan and Monmouthshire
     C Cardiff, Swansea and Newport

Graph 6. Offences determined summarily in rural and industrial counties, and in urban communities, 1857–1899.

Moreover, as Graph 5 indicates, the rate of serious crimes reported to the police in Glamorgan and Monmouthshire in the second half of the century moved comfortably in the right direction. Although they had moments of concern, and occasional alarm, the chief constables of industrial Wales shared in the 1880s and 1890s some of the optimism of their rural colleagues.

The amount of crime in individual Welsh towns during the nineteenth century is more difficult to estimate, chiefly because of the disappearance of virtually all the records for the early decades. In the parliamentary reports of the 1830s people complained of the threat to property, the level of disorderly behaviour, and the inadequacy of the police in places like Newtown and Newport (Monmouthshire), but figures of delinquency were rarely given. People simply assumed that the rate of crime was higher in the town than in the country. The first available statistics support this. In 1841 it was estimated that there was one court case for every fifty-four of Swansea's population, compared to one per fifty in Merthyr and one per sixty-seven in Neath. Unfortunately, the totals of reported crime are missing.[26] When we have details of these, twenty years later, one indictable offence was reported to the police of Cardiff, Swansea and Newport for every 302 of their combined populations, and one person was proceeded against at the Petty Sessions for every twenty-one. In Brecon, Carmarthen and Haverfordwest the respective figures for their combined populations were one per 1,170 and one per fifty-three, worse than that of their counties but only by a half.

Exactly why the urban crime rate, of all but the smallest country towns, was so high, even by the standards of the mid-twentieth century, was never satisfactorily explained.[27] The simplest explanation, which cannot be verified, is that people were more prepared to report offences in Cardiff than in the small towns and villages. As we shall see later in this chapter, people also believed that city dwellers actually committed more crimes. There were complaints, in the parliamentary reports, of the materialism of these inhabitants, of their rising expectations and of their determination, in the difficult times, to maintain a basic living standard. Speeches and sermons of the period highlighted the lack of religion and other social restraints, and there were references to both the anonymity and crowded existence of city dwellers. 'A vision of hell', was one minister's impression of Cardiff on a Saturday night, and his words expressed his dislike of non-Welsh immigrants and of the behaviour of the disillusioned and desperate poor. There was also the paradox of the endless opportunities for crime in large conurbations, and the greater likelihood of coming across a policeman. By the end of the century there were twice as many constables per head of population in Cardiff, Swansea and Newport as in our three rural counties.

Although the evidence is fragmentary, and changes in boundaries add to the difficulties, there seems little doubt that the rate of indictable and summary prosecutions in these towns rose with that of the counties during the first half of the century. The information in Table 6 is of limited value, but it shows the importance of the year 1848. The figures of prisoners committed in Swansea, Carmarthen and Aberystwyth, for example, during that year of revolutions were the highest of the early Victorian period. Other statistics of urban crime suggest that the 'triumph over crime and disorder' was evident at an earlier date than is often supposed. The peak in recorded offences in several English cities was reached early, in the 1830s or early 1840s. The confidence of urban propagandists like Thomas Plint, the positive remarks of visiting journalists, and Queen Victoria's favourable comments on an urban tour in 1851 seem to have been well founded.

Sadly, we are unable to plot the peak of recorded crime in Cardiff, Swansea and Newport, but it is interesting that in Graphs 5 and 6, the totals of reported indictable crimes, and of offences determined summarily, are both falling sharply from their beginning in the 1850s. This was a unique combination, and, in the light of the unprecedented expansion of these three towns, an extraordinary one. The assumption that continuous

Table 6
Prisoners committed, either for time or trial, in six Welsh boroughs, 1836–1853, with the number of police

Year	Prisoners committed in Beaumaris, Welshpool, Aberystwyth, Carmarthen, Monmouth and Swansea	Police
1836	120 (no returns from B., A. and C.)	14 (cost £370)
1837	199 (no return from C.)	18
1838	188	20
1839	186	23
1840	229	22
1841	205	22
1842	203	23
1843	241	31
1844	303	30
1845	207	33
1846	145	35
1847	234	34
1848	400	36
1849	255	36
1850	340	36
1851	285	43
1852	280	42
1853	233 (no return from Beaumaris)	41 (cost £2,143)

Source: PP, 1854, LIII.

urban growth would forever be accompanied by moral decline, lawlessless and violence had proved to be a fallacy.[28] In the case of serious crimes reported to the police there is a dramatic drop from the mid-century to a much lower level. By 1871 this rate had reached about its lowest point in the three Welsh towns, and there were certain years subsequently, such as 1876, 1881 and 1884, when the graph moved temporarily in the opposite direction. Each of these reverses was a source of annoyance to the chief constables and town elders, and provided a little ammunition for those who argued that the ultimate threat in the nineteenth century was not from Charles Dickens's Coketown, but from the ever-expanding city.

These regional variations in the national story of crime add to our understanding of the mid- and late-Victorian debates over the morality of Wales against England, Welshmen against immigrants, and rural communities against industrial and urban ones. In their exposition of the moral and social superiority of their countrymen, Henry Richard and linguistic, religious and political nationalists chose to concentrate on 'Wales Proper', ignoring those districts, ports, and large towns which had 'long ceased to be distinctively Welsh'.[29] Statistically it made sense to do so. In 1891 one indictable crime was reported for every 1,061 persons in Glamorgan and Monmouthshire living outside the three main towns, and one in twenty-eight of this population appeared before the lower courts. In Anglesey, Cardiganshire and Radnorshire the respective figures were one per 4,484 and one per eighty-three. The situation in Cardiff, Swansea and Newport is more difficult to determine, but in the same year it seems that one indictable crime was reported for every 478 of their combined population and one offence was dealt with at the Petty Sessions for every twenty-nine. Compared with these variations, the differences between Wales and England were comparatively minor; in 1891, the former still had proportionately fewer serious crimes reported to the police and fewer committals to the Assizes and Quarter Sessions, but slightly more offences were dealt with summarily. The last was rarely mentioned. The *Caernarvon and Denbigh Herald*, campaigning in 1889 for a reduction in the number of higher courts, expressed the general delight that the inhabitants of Wales displayed a greater respect for life and property than people elsewhere in Britain.[30]

Categories of crime

To fully understand the confidence behind such a statement, we need to glance at the changing incidence of the major crimes. Contemporaries divided crime into three broad categories: offences against the person, offences against property, and those which breached various regulations. Questions have been asked about the value of using such broad categories, and whether the third class should be included at all in studies of crime, but they are a convenient way of starting our analysis.[31] The most common crimes in the first two categories were assault and theft, and the prevalence of these was taken as a measure of the moral standing of a community. In Merthyr Tydfil, widely regarded as the most depraved of industrial towns in the first half of the nineteenth century, almost a third of the 1,050 people convicted outside the Assizes and Quarter Sessions (185 cases) in the calendar year of 1850 were charged with assaults and a fifth with stealing, whilst another two-fifths were evenly divided between those convicted of being drunk, causing wilful damage, deserting the family, and not paying maintenance, poor-rates and wages[32]. During the next half century, in Merthyr, and in Wales as a whole, these proportions changed markedly. In 1861 the national breakdown of all recorded offences against the person, against property and against regulations was in the ratio of 22:23:55, and thirty years later 13:14:73.

The proportions in the first two categories were lowest in the most rural of counties, and highest in the major towns. The differences, however, were remarkably slight. In 1861 a fifth of the recorded crimes in Anglesey, Cardiganshire and Radnorshire were against the person, whilst in Glamorgan and Monmouthshire and their major towns it was a quarter. Thirty years later the proportion of violent crimes had fallen to a tenth in the rural counties, thirteen per cent in the industrial, and fifteen per cent in Cardiff, Swansea and Newport. Crimes against property, from burglary to malicious damage, accounted for a quarter of the total in Anglesey, Cardiganshire and Radnorshire in 1861, thirty-one per cent of the total in Glamorgan and Monmouthshire and twenty-three per cent in the large towns. In 1891 the proportions of property crimes in the three areas had dropped to eleven, fourteen and fifteen per cent.

What emerges from these statistical snapshots is the similarities across the different communities, not the opposite as is often assumed. The theft/violence ratio, sometimes taken as an index of modernization, was fairly even in all the districts, though we should remember that many assaults never became court cases. The popular notion of the 'more primitive' rural communities being areas of predominantly inter-personal conflict, and the 'modern' urban districts of property crime, has to be revised. Howard Zehr's conclusions on this do not seem applicable to Wales, nor do his general comments on the extent and 'modernization of criminal behaviour'. He tells us that both assaults and stealing became more common in the nineteenth century, the rising theft rates being 'an acceptance of modern society's values'.[33] In Wales the rate of criminal violence was in decline in all regions well before the end of that century, and so, in contrast to France and Germany, was the rate of property offences. Clearly, Welshmen as well as 'Englishmen [have] obstinately refused to behave in the way in which many modern academics would like them to have done'.[34]

The third and largest category, of victimless crimes, has been the one most neglected by historians. This class included drunkenness and breaches of the education, highway, public health, poor-law, vagrancy and other national and local Acts. Drunken and disorderly conduct accounted for sixteen per cent of recorded crime in Wales in 1861, and for twenty-nine per cent in 1891, the proportions being higher in the rural than in the urban districts. All these prosecutions reflected 'an increasing concern to uphold moral, social and sanitary standards through the expansion of state regulation'.[35] In the police occurrence books and the Petty Session registers of these years, such offences fill page after page. Thus of 723 crimes recorded in the Tywyn, Barmouth and Corwen occurrence books for 1884–99, twenty-six per cent were of drunkenness and other offences against the licensing laws, twenty-six per cent were crimes against the Vagrancy Acts, thirteen per cent were larcenies, seven per cent were assaults, and most of the rest were suspected breaches of the poor-law, highway, and pedlars Acts.[36] Both the rise in the rate of these prosecutions in the second half of the nineteenth century and the decline early in twentieth, were regarded by experienced observers as a sign of progress. People were being, and becoming, civilized.

The seriousness of such crimes, many of them committed by the poorest members of society, was largely in the eye of the beholder. For some reformers, the people who appeared in the local police courts for these misdeamours were no less criminal than other offenders, but Henry Austin Bruce, speaking in 1875, offered a different opinion:

> It is undoubtedly true that some of the offences dealt with summarily must be numbered among crimes, as, for instance, larcenies proceeded against under the Juvenile Offenders' and Criminal Justice Acts, as well as the more serious cases of assault...but the increase (of summary convictions) mainly exhibits itself in offences, which it would be an abuse of language to characterise as crimes, and which must be provided against and dealt with in a very different manner.[37]

The graphs show how the rate of offences in this and the other two categories changed over the period. They will be looked at in more detail in the next three chapters. Offences against property such as theft formed an important part of the rising crime rate during the first half of the century, but after the climax of the early 1850s the graph of property offences fell away, only to recover somewhat in the early 1880s, helped by the effects of the Summary Jurisdiction Act of 1879 (Graphs 13 and 15). The rate of crimes of assault and other forms of violence against the person occasionally mirrored that of property crimes, as in the years 1835, 1841 and 1846, but over much of the century there was no correlation between them. The rise in the statistics of criminal violence fluctuated wildly, but lasted for three-quarters of the century, with outstanding heights being reached in 1843, 1859 and 1874 (Table 5, and Graphs 8 and 9 on page 67). During the last, and highest plateau, newspapers in Wales, as in England, were full of the evils of violent burglars, street muggers, and dangerous convicts out on licence. As we shall see in the next chapter, people living in the largest towns of mid-Victorian Wales experienced a rate of assaults which has rarely been equalled in modern times. Only after the mid-1870s was there a consistent fall in the reported acts of violence, a trend which contemporaries welcomed as the dawn of a new era.

In fact, a look at the graphs confirms that the last twenty years of the century witnessed a decline in the known incidence of all those crimes, including vagrancy and game-law offences, which had caused some anxiety only a decade before. The exceptions to the rule were the statistics of white-collar crimes, and of burglary and house-breaking, all of which were fairly low anyway. What made this decline even more impressive was the amount of new legislation then being added to the statute books and the extra policemen available to report crime. Even the rate of offences determined summarily began to slow down in the 1880s and 1890s (Graph 3). Although more people were prosecuted for cruelty to animals, and for certain highway and revenue misdemeanours at this time, in general the mid-Victorian boom in police-court cases was not sustained. The best example of this were the prosecutions for drunkenness and disorderly conduct, which increased in astonishing fashion prior to the Licensing Act of 1872 and for a few years afterwards. Then followed a decline, which was temporarily reversed at the turn of the century, but continued later.

Welshmen in the 1890s were gently mocked for the statistics of drink and other victimless crimes, though it could be argued that these were a tribute to the higher standards of behaviour being set in the Principality. What mattered, however, for Henry Richard, Henry Austin Bruce and the editor of the *Caernarvon and Denbigh Herald*, was not these lesser offences, but the low and declining incidence of attacks on people and property. The 'moral statement' of reported indictable crime was, it was widely believed, the best indication of the criminal health of a community. The Welsh in 1900 seemed more civilized and law-abiding than their grandparents and great-grandparents had been.

Explaining the statistics

It is important in this, as in any discussion of crime rates, to establish that contemporaries, no less than modern criminologists, had conflicting views of the extent of delinquency in society. A minority of observers argued that it remained fairly constant across the years; criminal statistics fluctuated simply because society repeatedly changed its mind over the nature and amount of delinquent behaviour which it would tolerate. 'We now know', agrees one historian of crime, 'that what was increasing in the first half of the nineteenth century was not crime but the prosecution rate, a very different matter'.[38] It is possible that the reduction in prosecution expenses might have played its part in this, but there were other, and perhaps more important, influences at work.

As we saw in the last chapter, responses to crime in 1800 were changing, and this was true of some members of the public as well as of the rulers of society. Exactly why this happened is not clear. In the sixteenth century, so we are told, the phenomenon of a rising population made people more aware of the problem of crime and disorder, as well as of the moral dangers of sexual impropriety and idleness. There are parallels here with Wales of the late eighteenth and early nineteenth centuries. In the countryside the pressure of population on land was greatest in the war years, and immediately afterwards, as the violent resistance to enclosures and the removal of squatters illustrates, whilst in the towns the presence of ever-increasing numbers of people, especially of the poor and young kind, must have been only too obvious. The middle class in places such as Cardiff, Merthyr, Wrexham and Llanidloes lived, for a while at least, alarmingly close to the 'dangerous poor'. They demanded police changes and prosecuted many of the offenders. At the Montgomeryshire town, the Reverend E. Pugh described in 1839 how the respectable inhabitants were being driven 'to extreme measures' by the constant 'insubordination, defiance of all authority, dishonesty, and nightly depredations, fighting [and] drunkenness,...' Even the homes of employers in Llanidloes were not safe from these ruffians.[39]

People from the 1780s onwards were encouraged to change their standards, and approach to delinquency, by an interesting collection of individuals and pressure groups. Edmund Hyde Hall spoke of their 'restless spirit of meddling', and accused them of wanting 'absurd and tyrannical Laws' to 'hedge about the poor' and trap them in 'vast and rectangular buildings'.[40] In west Wales, these 'meddlers' included David Williams of Bronmeurig in Cardiganshire, with his disturbing memories of the French Revolution, Dr Bowen, the surgeon of Carmarthen, applauding another association for the prosecution of felons, and Miss Thomas, the 'civilizer' of Redberth Lodge in Pembrokeshire, the very personification of the society for the reformation of manners. They sought, amongst other things, to create 'an honest, sober and independent labourer' by making him dependent on money wages, rationalizing the poor rates, and reducing the scale of gleaning, begging, poaching and all manner of 'primitive and violent' pastimes. Along with sympathetic magistrates and clergymen, they urged people to treat crime as a serious problem, and deliberately associated it with anxieties about outsiders and sedition. Henry Leach, chairman of the Pembrokeshire Quarter Sessions, told an audience in April 1848 that 'the greater number of' serious crimes was carried out by 'trampers: men who come to prey upon the fruits of your industry, and not to live upon their own – who preach about politics and not about labour,...'[41]

The men and women who appeared in the Welsh courts and prisons in the early nineteenth century provide clues to the pyschology of their prosecutors. There were thieves, robbers and burglars, indicted chiefly by members of the middle and lower classes, but there was also an exceptional number of poachers and 'idle and disorderly' individuals who refused to act responsibly towards their children, wives, employers and society generally. Of the 317 'out-of-court' convictions recorded in the Flintshire records for 1815–30, many of which resulted in fines, forty per cent were for taking game or fish, and many other males and females were brought before the magistrates in these years on bastardy, affiliation, and vagrancy charges. Some unfortunates even spent months in gaol on 'suspicion of felony' or whilst sureties were being obtained for their future good behaviour.

Prison inspectors in the 1830s said that many of the offences for which adults and especially juveniles were being sent to gaol 'were formerly disregarded, or not considered of so serious a character as to demand imprisonment'.[42] The Vagrancy Act, the Malicious Trespass Act and the Offences against the Person Act of the 1820s were a conscious effort by the legislators, with considerable backing from local magistrates, to widen the range of punishable activity and deal with it promptly in Petty Sessions. In 1848, when the highest figures of summary convictions are recorded in Table 5, forty per cent of those imprisoned had fallen foul of the Vagrancy Act, fifteen per cent had committed an assault, ten per cent had offended against the poor-law, and six per cent had been found guilty of a malicious trespass.

This was more than 'the last resort' policing of the eighteenth century. It was, in the opinion of Benjamin Disraeli and some of Henry Leach's opponents on the Pembrokeshire Bench, a determination to invent a crisis where none existed. Simple criminal acts were invested with a new meaning and symbolism. They were viewed as part of a wider malaise, which had its roots in the traumatic economic, social and political changes of the period. 'The people of this place [Nefyn] are in the most wretched condition that I have seen, for insubordination, disorder and ignorance –', said the Reverend William Jones, 'disorder in the most comprehensive sense of the word'. 'It is impossible', agreed Dr Phillips of Pontypool in the same report of 1847, 'to think of the social and political conduct of the people without alarm'.[43] As Disraeli pointed out, each set of rising statistics was a statement of fear, and a further sanction for the legal, prison and police reforms of the 'damnable Whigs'.

Taking up this theme, William Meyrick, the conservative solicitor, stated in 1841 that such 'panic' measures made his town of Merthyr Tydfil seem much worse than it actually was. At a meeting held to discuss the need for a stipendiary magistrate and improved policing, he infuriated Josiah John Guest by declaring that the town had always been 'remarkably free of crime, and particularly aggravated crime – so much so that he did not believe that there was a place to be found in the world so free from crimes as Merthyr,...'[44] He was not alone in this judgement; there was, in both rural and urban Wales, a small minority who questioned the significance of the crime statistics. In 1842, one of the worst years in the history of crime, the judge at the Glamorgan Assize said that the changes in the number of offences 'arises not so much from an increase in the quantity of crime as from an increase of detection through the agency of a more vigorous system of police'.[45] At a somewhat later date, Henry Austin Bruce made a similar point about the cases at the lower courts; in his opinion 'the greater part' of the increase in proceedings owed more 'to the more vigorous enforcement of the law and to the higher requirements of modern civilisation, than to the actual increase in the number of offences.'[46]

Such a mechanical interpretation of the crime rate had much to commend it so long as the statistics kept rising, but when they began to fall it became harder to sustain. It has been suggested, however, that the decline in the number of indictments in the second half of the nineteenth century, like that in the late seventeenth and early eighteenth centuries, could be attributed to a reduction of social pressures, chiefly of population on resources, and to the growth of political stability. The comparison is not a direct one, for the rise in population continued after 1850 and was prodigious in south-east Wales and the largest towns. Yet there was economic improvement at the same time, and this, together with the changing social geography of urban life, helped to bring a kind of accommodation between the classes. In Cardiff and Merthyr, a wide range of social missions modified the class indifference and hostility of the past. It is just possible that this lessening of the fear of social and political revolution in the years after 1848, and the emergence of other social issues, contributed to 'a decline in the reporting and prosecution of the lesser and smaller offences', but there is little evidence of it.[47] Contemporaries were convinced, and so are most historians, that the falling statistics of crimes against the person and property in the late nineteenth century were a reflection of a genuine reduction in criminal behaviour.

In the most popular interpretations of the crime rates, at least of the more serious offences, statistics were always regarded as neutral phenomena, 'the true account of delinquency'. Increases in the reporting and prosecuting of crime were blamed on a decline in moral standards and not the reverse. Most people seemed agreed, for example, that 'crime has much increased' everywhere in the years before Victoria came to the throne. Years like 1817–9, 1830–4, and 1839–44 were widely recognized as being periods of economic and social tension, when perhaps the ties of deference and obedience were loosened, and restraints cast aside. A study of the newspaper reports of these years gives the impression that there *were* more thefts and burglaries at these times. Those who lived through the post-war famine in rural Wales described how, in spite of the sharp rise in poor-relief payments, people lived from hand to mouth, always on the look-out for extra and illegal sources of income. In 1817 all the records are unanimous that there were more food, sheep, clothes, and wood thefts, and that the growth of game preservation was matched by an increase in poaching. This was when, suggested witnesses before the Welsh Land Commission, 'Taffy' earned his reputation for being a thief. Similarly, in 1842–4 and 1848 there were many claims, in legal and other documents, that criminal behaviour in both country and town was on the increase, and people took greater care of their property and person.

The pessimism of these years was well conveyed by the Reverend John Griffith of Aberdare, in his Glamorgan Assize sermon of 1850. In his judgement, the criminal statistics denoted a real change for the worse in human behaviour:

> There is no sign of the times so painful, as that crimes and offences are greatly on the increase. The most thoughtless startle at the march of guilt, when they see prisons too narrow for their multiplied inhabitants. Never, surely, was there a nation in the state this is now. It is justly regarded as one of the strangest and most ominous in the world. Never has there been a condition so anomalous...the nation itself is pre-eminent for its public virtue, its pure religion, its strict justice, and its impartial laws...Civilization has, probably. never been carried higher, yet, possibly, seldom seen lower...[48]

Ironically Griffith was speaking at the very moment when other people found signs of a change for the better. In Merthyr, Llanelli, Swansea and a number of other towns, there were references to the 'better habits' and order that had already been noted in the countryside. The reporter of the *Morning Chronicle*, who travelled to the Welsh iron capital in 1850, was impressed by the change that had come over the town since the days of the Chartists.[49] Within a few years, there was a consensus, in most parts of Wales, that criminal behaviour was on the decline, and that 'the country was never in a more quiet, peaceable and prosperous condition than at present,...' In January 1860 Thomas Hughes of Ystrad, the chairman of the Denbighshire Quarter Sessions, confirmed that 'crime was very low in the county, as low as he ever remembered it;...'[50] What is difficult to decide is whether such views were independent of, or influenced by, the official rate of indictable crime. Whichever was correct, Thomas Hughes was certain of one thing; the police force had not decreased its efforts.

After the mid-1870s there was universal agreement that the criminal statistics reflected a genuine reduction in the amount of delinquency in society, a fact confirmed by the most sophisticated historical analysis. 'Something extraordinary happened then...' writes our most perceptive historian of crime.[51] In a period of quite exceptional population and urban growth, of which Cardiff and Swansea were outstanding examples, the decline of theft and violence was, we are told, 'an achievement' unique in modern times. 'There never was,' wrote L. O. Pike in 1876, 'in any nation of which we have a history, a time in which life and property were so secure as they are at present...'[52] In support of this opinion, Henry Austin Bruce and other optimists drew attention to the police tables of known criminals and suspected persons at large in the country. In 1860 there were 8,537 of these in Wales; by 1876 the number had dropped to 4,199. For the remainder of the century, as each annual total of reported indictable crime affirmed the decline, the addresses in court assumed a very different character from those of 1850. Chairman J. Scott Bankes of the Flintshire Quarter Sessions declared in the summer of 1885 that no one could deny that there had been a real 'diminution of crime of all kinds'.[53] His self-appointed task, and that of others like him, was to explain the delinquency that remained and to eliminate it.

Crime, the economy and social change

Understanding delinquency had become a fashionable activity by the late nineteenth century. This had not always been so. In the previous century crime was often dismissed as the waywardness of a few souls who freely chose the path of wickedness. 'Everyone must keep hold of his evil nature', said William Jones, the Independent minister, in 1802. Only exceptional individuals, like Robert Owen, the Newtown socialist, and William Antony, the Carmarthen Chartist, claimed that people were somehow forced to commit illegal acts by modern society, with its competition, *laissez-faire* mentality, and obsession with property. More popular, and increasingly so in the mid-century, was the idea that crime was to be found amongst certain types of people. They were variously described as having a physique, mentality and life-style different from the rest of the population. For some they were 'a mobile criminal fraternity', and for others 'the hereditary criminal class'. In the 1860s, when vagrants, released convicts and prostitutes alarmed the rural and urban authorities in Wales, the threat from such a class seemed real enough.

For the rest of the century, analyses of criminals became rather more scientific. Studies of groups of prisoners suggested that they were predominately from the wretched and embittered ranks of 'fringe labour', often with deprived family backgrounds, and sharing some of the depressive and addictive traits of the mentally ill. It was estimated that a tenth of inmates were 'mentally weak', like Hyam Jacobs, the fraudulent Cardiff jeweller, who tried to pawn his face, and a few were seriously disturbed. About half a dozen prisoners were sent from Wales to Broadmoor each year, and almost a hundred criminal lunatics were received into the gaols or deposited in county and borough asylums.[54] The deputy superintendant of the Glamorgan Asylum believed that his inmates had much in common with alcoholics and 'habitual criminals', and were influenced in the same way by economic circumstances.[55]

However, it was not in the nature or the interests of those who dealt with criminals to make too much of this information. Explanations of delinquent behaviour from Welsh magistrates, lawyers, chaplains and policemen were rather superficial in character and moral in tone. The social reports compiled by these experts during the first two-thirds of the century hardly advanced people's understanding of delinquency. They were more a commentary on change and the evils of modern society than an objective survey of the people in their care. E. G. Williams, the Swansea prison chaplain, who interviewed large numbers of prisoners, reported that 264 of them had become criminals in 1861 because of 'drink', 278 through 'bad company', and ninety-two from 'other causes'.[56] Robert Oliver Jones, the Glamorgan stipendiary who dealt with more cases than anyone else in our period, was even more disappointing in his analysis. He concluded in 1871 that 'three-fourths of the mischief and crime which exists in this country arose from the habit of drunkenness'.[57] It was a common view, with a long history. In the education report of 1847 it was said that when 'clergymen and magistrates, who used to frequent them', ceased to do so, the public houses and especially the beershops became the 'source of all crime'.[58] Even Henry Austin Bruce, a future Home Secretary, used similar language in the 1850s, though he also attempted to relate crime to other factors, like population growth and the state of trade.[59]

In their enquiries into delinquency, contemporaries spent less time on the economic context than historians have done. In a country where at least a third of the population was in a state of primary or secondary poverty it was thought unlikely that unemployment, low wages and price fluctuations had a major impact on social behaviour. The Royal Commission on the County Constabulary of 1839 affirmed: 'in scarcely any cases is [crime] attributable to the pressure of unavoidable want or destitution; ...it arises from the temptation of obtaining property with a less degree of labour than by regular industry'.[60] Henry Nicholl MP, saw no evidence of 'any pressure of want or difficulty' on the many offenders from the large towns and manufacturing districts of south Wales.[61] Even the fact that so many of the inmates of the Glamorgan and Monmouthshire gaols were unmarried labourers, unburdened by large families, was used against them. In the opinion of Bruce in 1875, it was only people who were both poor and pauperized who disgraced the working class. Pauperism, which he believed was on the wane, was a lack of will and energy, leading to dependence on charity, the degredation of begging and ultimately petty crime.

These opinions were not shared by the people in the dock; men, women and children in court protested that destitution alone had obliged them to commit a crime. 'It was nothing but want that induced me to steal', 'I can't get work', and 'I had no choice' were excuses repeated time after time, even when people had nothing to gain by them. As we shall see in later chapters, the poverty of vagrants and servants, and of female and juvenile thieves, was so common that magistrates grew accustomed to it, and historians are apt to ignore it. Only the exceptional case catches the eye. 'Year in and year out', concludes one modern writer, 'it is chronic as much as episodic deprivation which...is encoded in the doleful catalogue of boots, shoes, loaves of bread, sides of bacon, lumps of lead, etc. which confronts any student of court records up to the 1930s at least'.[62] The background of so many of these offenders was described as 'very poor', 'indifferent' and 'neglected'. 'Poverty', exclaimed a correspondent of *The Welshman* at the time of Rebecca, 'has been the parent of crime in all ages...'[63]

For all their denials, the police became more anxious when food prices rose and work became harder to find. In a report of 1878 on reformatory and industrial schools in Wales, the inspector had no doubt that 'part of the increase' in recorded juvenile crime was due to the depressed state of trade. 'There has been less demand for labour, and of the number of boys out of work it would be strange if some did not get into trouble'.[64] Alarm bells also sounded when the very poor were given a stark choice between survival and a criminal act. In 1838 a petition was sent to John Jones, MP for Carmarthenshire, complaining about the 'alarming increase in crime', desertion and infanticide since the passing of the Poor Law Amendment Act.[65] Thirty years later, when vagrants were refused all poor relief in some of the north Wales counties, the judge, who sentenced them to penal servitude for their malicious response, acknowledged that they 'were in some sort of way driven to this [arson].'[66]

If there were a relationship between the economy and social behaviour, the persistent one, for most contemporaries, was that between high wages, drunkenness and crime. 'I believe,' said a judge at a Welsh Assize in 1860, 'wealth has as much to do with crime as poverty.'[67] As the real income of all workers, and especially of those in industrial districts, began to rise in the second quarter of the century, there was a feeling that they needed better education, higher standards of morality and more policing to benefit from the extra income. 'Educate the people first,' demanded Rowland Jones, the Cardiff prison chaplain in October 1875, 'then, if the commerce of the country will allow it, pay them high wages'.[68] Until that time 'the workman is as little to be trusted with money as the Red Indian with drink'.[69] Parliamentary reports of the mid-century, and an angry Monmouthshire chief constable in 1880, claimed that sustained industrial booms invariably meant more beershops, drunkenness, violence and other crimes.[70] It was, insisted Henry Austin Bruce, the combination of industrial affluence and ignorance which explained why such regions of Wales took rather longer than the others to join the falling crime statistics.

The evidence of Graph 7, when set against the others in this volume, shows the limitations which must be placed on all these conflicting views.[71] There is no consistent correlation between the reports and trials of indictable crime, and the economic indicators of prices, money wages and real wages. In the years immediately after the Napoleonic Wars, a fall in living standards *was* accompanied by a rise in recorded crime, and from 1868 the reverse was true. 'The main cause of the increase of crime in the agricultural districts' in the former period, concluded a select committee report in 1826, 'appears clearly to be the low rate of wages, and the want of sufficient employment for the labourer.'[72] Yet there were many other years, more so perhaps in Wales than in England, when economic difficulties for the working class were accompanied by lower than expected criminal statistics, and when real wages and crime rates rose together. In 1850, when Revd John Griffith was complaining about unprecented levels of delinquent behaviour, the wages of agricultural labourers, industrial workers and artisans were increasing, prices were low, and more people than ever were migrating from the countryside to improve their economic propects. As for non-indictable offences, the rate of people dealt with at Petty Sessions was even less affected by economic forces.

The best correlation, across the century, was between the recorded incidence of theft and changes in the economy. This was true in all communities after the 1780s, as unemployment and poverty affected workers in the villages as well as the towns. Larcenies were usually most common, as in the late 1860s, when real wages fell sharply, and least common, as in the early 1870s, when they did the reverse.[73] Even at the time of the last significant upturn in the rate of stealing, in 1879–82, immediately after the important Summary Jurisdiction Act, the economic context in the most affected counties was the drop in the living standards of the industrial workers. It seems that such workers were more inclined to poach and take food, coal, and other items during 'episodic deprivation', though strikes, including those at Rhiwabon in 1848, across the south Wales coalfield early in 1875, and of north Wales quarrymen a decade later, were accompanied by a fall in drink-related offences.

The statistics of family crimes, like failing to maintain children, wives and relatives, and of offences against the game and vagrancy laws, moved less in tune to the rhythm of economic change, but in industrial south Wales law-breaking of this kind was often greater during hard times. Crimes of violence, by contrast, were more numerous when money wages increased, and the same can be said of drunken and disorderly behaviour,

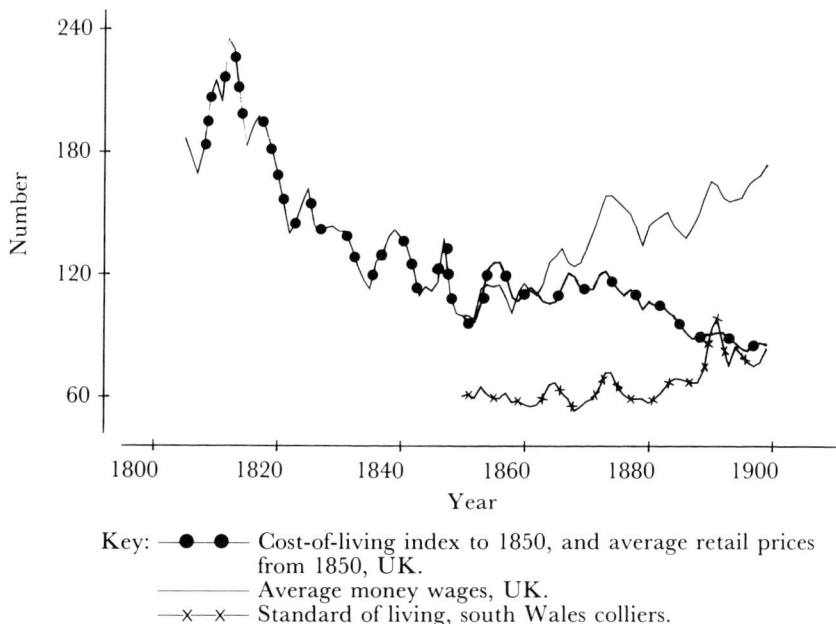

Key: —●—●— Cost-of-living index to 1850, and average retail prices from 1850, UK.
————— Average money wages, UK.
—x—x— Standard of living, south Wales colliers.

Source: see section on Sources and Data at the end of this book

Graph 7. Standard of living: United Kingdom and Wales, 1805–1899.

at least for much of the 1860s, 1870s and 1880s. Such figures helped to convince Rowland Jones, chaplain of Cardiff gaol, and his friends, that, outside the rural areas, crime had become by the last quarter of the century more a manifestation of affluence than indigence. There were even those who wondered in these years whether the commercial prosperity of Swansea and Cardiff had adversely affected middle-class as well as working-class morality. Our graph of the white-collar crimes of embezzlement and fraud suggests that they were committed, or reported, most when business was at a low ebb (Graph 17).

Prosperity, like poverty, had different effects on criminal behaviour in different situations. The boom in trade that accompanied the expansion of the railways drew, we are told, a 'mature' reaction from the people of Carmarthen and west Wales.[74] It brought 'a decrease in crime and even petty offences', something which was contrasted with the deleterious impact of sudden prosperity in the Glamorgan mining districts. Even in the latter, however, the effects were mixed. Mr Williams, the Congregational minister of Hirwain, claimed in 1846 that high wages brought an increase in comfort and respectability for some, and more dissipation, drunkenness and crime in others.[75] A detailed study of Merthyr, only a few miles to the east, has confirmed the dangers of attributing too much to changes in living

Table 7
**Seasonality of reported indictable crime, for ten years between 1857
and 1892**

Place	Oct.–Dec.	Jan.–March	April–June	July–Sept.	Total
Anglesey, Cardiganshire & Radnorshire	168	173	188	182	711
Glamorgan & Monmouthshire (excluding 3 major towns)	1873	1763	1547	1744	6927
Cardiff, Swansea & Newport	1417	1203	1078	1053	4751
Wales	4901	4426	4083	4250	17660

Source: PP, 1857–8, LVII – 1893–4, CIII. Years chosen – 1857, 1860, 1864, 1868, 1872, 1876, 1880, 1884, 1888, 1892.

standards. The apprehensions for larceny in that police district between 1842 and 1866 did not vary as much as the economic indicators. The number of recorded thefts rose considerably in the bad economic winters of 1847–8, and 1856–7, but in other difficult periods not so much, a phenomenon which, English historians believe, became increasingly the norm. The same Merthyr records also indicate that whilst arrests for violence and drunkenness usually increased in the months of high wages, there were more exceptions to the rule than Glamorgan prison chaplains ever admitted.[76]

Information on the seasonality of these crimes gives another dimension to the discussion. As Table 7 shows, reports of indictable crimes, which were overwhelmingly against property, were most common in the quarter October–December. In the largest towns the police were busiest in the six months from October to March, whilst in the rural counties the reverse was true. From an analysis of 13,313 offences committed at Merthyr in the years 1847, 1850–1, and 1855–8, it seems that larcenies were most common in the winter season, and both assaults and drunkenness in high summer, the typical pattern of modern urban crime. From another large sample, it seems that January was the most popular month for crime in the Tywyn, Barmouth and Corwen police districts during 1884–99, but July, August and September ran it a close second. August, in fact, provided the highest monthly figures for larcenies as well as assaults and drunkenness. As expected, most game offences in these Merioneth areas occurred between September and February, and vagrancy crimes were common in the spring and autumn.[77] How to explain these seasonal patterns is a difficult matter; economic circumstances were only a part of the answer.

For those in authority, the economic context of criminal behaviour was always less important than its social and moral roots. In fact, the most substantial speeches and writings on Welsh crime used delinquency as an index, and indictment, of the more alarming developments in society. Almost without exception, they mentioned the pressure of population and the depressing features of the new urban and industrial environment. Much was written about the physical conditions of life, the changes in the home and family, and the presence or otherwise of religion and education. 'Happy are the Welsh', said judge Alfred Wills in March 1890, 'that they mainly dwell in small and scattered communities,...'[78] 'Wales is innocent [of crime],' agreed Henry Austin Bruce, '...because it has the good fortune to enjoy all the [right] conditions...a sparse population, no towns of vast size, no great accumulation of valuable and unprotected property; and it rejoices in the absence of that [fatal] combined pressure of poverty and temptation...'

There was a general conviction that densely populated districts contributed to criminal behaviour in multifarious ways: through biological, cultural and environmental influences, and by offering exceptional opportunities and anonymity for criminals. 'Evil communication corrupts good manners; and evil associations are inevitable in these resorts of the miserable, the vicious, the drunkard, and the criminal', stated one writer. 'Foul air depresses; depression craves for stimulants, and stimulants beget drunkenness and its long train of curses. Crime is promoted by security from detection and punishment, and the difficulties of detection and the facilities for escape are multiplied in these Alsatias which are found in all our larger towns.'[79] As this writer implied, the largest towns of Wales, from Carmarthen and Merthyr at the beginning of the century, to Swansea and Cardiff some years later, were synonymous with delinquency, or rather their slums and crowded quarters were. In precisely those places where the cholera flourished, the 'foundations of morality are sapped'. With Merthyr's 'China' in mind, William Kay, medical officer of health, reported in 1854 that 'the worst conditioned districts furnish the largest number of offenders'.[80] It was a satisfying thesis, which we shall examine in some detail in chapter 6, but it begged several questions about middle-class anxieties, prosecution policy and the actions and locations of the urban police.

Urban living had, it must be remembered, its defenders as well as its critics. For Josiah John Guest, as for Thomas Plint and Edwin Chadwick, the great economic and social changes of the nineteenth century offered the pleasing prospect of a higher state of civilization, and a more orderly and disciplined way of life. Yet, if the ultimate goal was laudable, the immediate problems of rapid urbanization and industrialization were only too apparent. Henry Thomas, the tetchy chairman of the Glamorgan Quarter Sessions, argued passionately in the mid-century that the new towns, and especially the new works, in his county were the source of the decline in moral standards. Rapid immigration, the intermixture of nationalities, social neglect, economic fluctuations and conflict, and the temptations of unprotected property were just some of the conditions of industrial life of which he disapproved. He placed the responsibility for the crime statistics of mining towns like Merthyr on the shoulders of those 'ruthless masters' who had undermined 'the religious and moral feeling amongst the lower classes'.[81] 'When, said Sir William Grove in 1872, one moved from an agricultural to an industrial and manufacturing district in south Wales, one 'must expect a greater number of crimes and misdemeanours as a consequence of the more severe conflict of opposing interests'.[82]

In the most populated parts of Wales the state of the family was regarded as of the greatest importance in determining who turned to crime. There were complaints that rapid urbanization and industrialization had disrupted the natural pattern of family life. It was alleged that the husband's role had been undermined, women had been driven out to work and 'demoralized', and neglect and early work experience had encouraged independence, indiscipline and violent behaviour in the young, female as well as male. 'Whilst children of both sexes are allowed to drink, smoke, swear and talk obscene language, before 12 years of age', said the Catholic pastor at Merthyr Tydfil in 1842, 'they cannot be expected to come up to the morality even of Canadian savages.'[83]

Parental neglect was not confined to any period or place. In 1839, the chairman of the Caernarfonshire Quarter Sessions blamed the rise in petty crime in his county on the lack of family interest in the upbringing of children.[84] Fifty-three years later, after a spate of garden robberies, the same comments were made in Merioneth, with a request to bring back the use of the birch rod. Even so, it was in the large towns and mining areas of Wales that crime was most commonly linked to family problems. Reports on the young male and female criminals in these districts revealed that as many as a third of them had been abandoned, orphaned or raised by one parent. Albert Spacey, nine and a half years of age from Nantyglo, with a widowed mother on poor relief, Moses Jones, fourteen years of age from Newport, with a drunken father, and orphaned John Cromwell, of the same age and town, were typical of the young and 'entirely neglected' thieves sent to the reformatories in the mid-century.[85] Some, as we shall see in chapter 6, had been brought up to a life of crime, whilst others had been forced on the streets when family support ceased. What united them all, according to Robert Oliver Jones, was the absence of moral guidance.

Virtually all the commentators of the mid-nineteenth century were agreed that education and religion, in the home and outside, were needed to change these patterns of anti-social behaviour. The ignorance of the first generation of industrial workers was, said one reformer, 'such as cannot be described.' One of the purposes of the public meeting at Merthyr in March 1847, to 'establish a good, cheap and unsectarian education' for the children of the working classes, was 'to stop crime'. It was part of a wider movement to increase the number and quality of educational establishments in Wales, and within a generation Welsh towns had an impressive range of poor, charity, ragged, industrial, British and National schools. J. H. Whalley, an old paternalist, argued in the Montgomeryshire Quarter Sessions of 1862 that by educating the poor they were just producing cleverer criminals, but his point was quickly ignored. Henry Austin Bruce, a supporter of the Education Act of 1870 and a pioneer of schooling for young delinquents, was a more representative figure. He maintained in 1875 that education had convinced many working people of the futility of crime. This was his explanation for the increasing proportion of criminals who came from the lowest and most ignorant depths of society.

Revd John Griffith of Aberdare warned of the dangers of being too complacent about this situation. He had none of the secular optimism of his distinguished friend, and insisted that only religion and passionate moral teaching could change the habits of the lumpen proletariat:

> . . . the people, be assured, require something more to keep them steady than eating and sleeping wages; and if wisdom and forethought give it them not, knavery and discontent will. If millions are not taught – taught systematically and taught religiously, millions will surely teach in their own rude, harsh way...there are growing millions in this empire, without not only God in the world, but without reason, or intelligence...It is true, the more respectable and industrious of the working classes will send their children to school...But the struggle is not with them; the battle is not on that field. To rouse the depraved, to reform the vicious, to sober the drunken, and to awaken the mere animal...much more must be done than merely raising schools and providing masters.[86]

Although the Anglican Giffith chose to ignore it, Wales already had a formidable reputation as a religious nation. Time and again judges referred to this, and to the wise paternalism behind religious education, as the strongest reasons for the comparatively low number of indictable court cases in the Principality. The historian might question whether people were becoming more religious after 1850, but those who dealt with criminals every week were convinced that the missionary zeal of the

revived Church of England and the pervasive chapel culture had a beneficial effect on social behaviour. 'There is at present a far better observ-
ance of the Sabbath than I have ever witnessed here;...' said one Neath
petitioner in 1860, 'The habits of the people [recently] have assumed a
more prudent character; their homes are more comfortable than they were;
there is less poverty and less crime.'[87]

A 'bright and encouraging light'

It is fascinating, at this distance in time, to see how quickly the debate on
the problem of crime turned into another on the move 'towards legality'.
When the decline in the committals to Assizes and Quarter Sessions
became apparent, people felt the need to explain, not just the British trend,
but also Wales's special place in it. One judge, in south-west Wales in 1860,
set the framework for the discussions:

> What has produced the change [from the high crime figures]? We must take
> into account the general improvement of the country, both here and in
> England. All classes of society are more intelligent, more moral, more
> religious than they were at the beginning of the present century...The social
> debaucheries and dissipation which were then common are now abandoned
> and denounced. The political agitation and revolutionary sentiments which
> then drowned the good sense of the people, have perished...The probability
> that crime might escape punishment and the temptations which then existed
> to do wrong, have been removed by a vigilant police and the overwhelming
> disgrace of conviction for crime. We in this part of Wales have participated
> in these improvements, but this does not explain the peculiar – almost total
> immunity from crime which we enjoy.[88]

As we shall see in chapter 7, it was generally assumed that the improvements in policing, and the increase in the conviction rate, acted as a
deterrent force against those contemplating crime in the second half of the
nineteenth century. About the effects of changes in punishment, especially
the reforms within the prison system, people were more equivocal. Dr
Bowen, the Carmarthen surgeon, and Edwin Chadwick, both of whom
compared crime to a disease, wondered if it might be possible, with the
right treatment, to eradicate it altogether, but by the end of the century
there was a growing feeling that punishments of every kind had a very
limited impact on the crime rate. The Gladstone committee on prisons in
1895 adopted a pragmatic approach to the treatment of criminals. Rather
than waste time and money on more reformatory experiments and further
medical and anthropological research into the causes of, and remedies for,
delinquency, it concluded that 'much can be done by the recognition of the
plain fact that the great majority of prisoners are ordinary men and women

amenable, more or less, to all those influences which affect persons outside'.[89]

This was the attitude of most Welsh observers. They claimed that the fall in the crime statistics was part of a wider improvement in social behaviour which was itself the product of a 'fortunate combination' of factors, some of which were accidental and some planned. Economic change was regarded as a vital element in the transformation. One writer in 1877 declared that the Welsh, having become prudent and socially ambitious, were not prepared to throw away the gains of economic progress.[90] 'With the advance in wages the prisons have been locked up...' was a typical remark in rural Wales late in the century. Down to 1870, said the Welsh land commission, the improvement in the countryside 'chiefly consisted in the labourer's wages being advanced', but thereafter there was also an 'enlargement of his opportunities'. The latter included elementary education for his children and the possibility of social mobility, as well as better housing and new forms of 'profitable recreation'. The results were self-evident; although there was still some poaching, trespassing for mushrooms and blackberries, juvenile pranks and a little drunkenness, the families of farm labourers were described in the 1890s as 'morally improved', 'quiet, respectable and honest'.[91]

In industrial Wales, economic and social improvement began at an early date, and became most apparent after the difficult years of the late 1860s. Although, as we have seen, there was some debate over the immediate effects of higher real incomes in terms of drunkenness and violence, Charles Wilkins and others had no doubt that a favourable long-term change was taking place in the 'moral climate' of industrial Wales. They attributed the decline in 'riot, disorder and depravity' to more effective policing, better living standards, and especially to social propoganda and sensible paternalism. On the south Wales coalfield, from the end of the 1840s onwards, the press was full of accounts of night classes, lectures, penny readings, eisteddfoddau, concerts, excursions, and sports. Works schools, mechanics institutes and libraries were established in large numbers in the mid-Victorian years, and support was given to the efforts of the Early Closing Association, the Temperance Recreation Society, the YMCA, the Juvenile Rifle Corps, and various Boys Clubs. No one could evaluate the precise impact of such good works, but it was deemed to be most favourable on those who least needed it, 'the better class of working people'. Henry Austin Bruce and his ironmaster friends claimed that their well paid, 'steady and independent' employees caused the authorities no headaches; 'the culprits that appeared in the police court came from a very different class'.[92]

Rather more pertinent, in the light of this statement, was the experience of the 'poor and dependent', especially those living in the largest towns during the second half of the century. Thomas Hughes, chairman of the Denbighshire Quarter Sessions in the mid-Victorian years, argued that these, too, had benefited a little from the general improvement in the standard of living, but the greatest influences on them had been planned. These were of two main kinds; firstly, 'judicial coercion', the slow but remorseless effect of more regulations, stricter policing and certain punishment, and secondly, the 'counter-acting agencies' of better education, housing and recreational facilities. The police, thought Hughes, 'probably prevented a good deal of crime', but he, like modern historians, was impressed by the 'civilizing' effects of educational and environmental reform.[93] One public-health officer, appalled by the housing and sanitary arrangements of Merthyr Tydfil in 1853, argued that 'the domestic comfort and decency of the poor (who are the vast majority)' was 'the foundation' upon which improvements in social behaviour had to be built.[94] The chief constable of Swansea agreed; he recommended careful town planning to complement the 'promising' effects of compulsory education and other regulations. He claimed in the 1880s that the removal of the slums near the docks had reduced crime in his town almost overnight.[95] In one way or another, such people were determined to subject the 'residuum' to the values, controls and influence of the rest of society.

The chairmen of the Welsh Quarter Sessions, who were delighted by the short lists before them in the 1880s and 1890s, believed that the battle against crime had been fought in the Principality with a special determination and skill. Wales had been fortunate in its teachers and ministers of religion, its reforming middle class, and its own Sunday Closing Act of 1881.[96] The work of religious educationists and temperance pioneers had implanted 'self-respect', and 'ideas of reverence and decorum that are apt to remain with them [the working class] forever'. Such 'moral tuition' helped the working class to cope 'better than before' with both prosperity and depression, and substantially reduced the scale of female and juvenile delinquency. The social history of the twentieth-century has shown the limitations of such influences, but the conviction and the optimism of the late nineteenth century were infectious. Sir William Harcourt, Home Secretary, told Gladstone that the dimunition of crime was 'a bright and encouraging light on our social horizon'.[97] There were, inevitably, a few warning voices, reminding people of the large number of misdemeanours that passed unnoticed in back streets and country lanes, and expressing alarm at the short-term upswings in the rate of serious crime in the largest seaports. But Henry Austin Bruce, an earlier Home Secretary, likened this to the backward wash of an outgoing tide. Nothing was allowed to mar the celebrations, or the conviction that persons and property had never been safer.

3
Crimes of Violence

The amount of violence in society has always been a delicate matter. The general assumption is that by the end of the eighteenth century, Britain had become a more peaceful place, when compared with Stuart, Tudor and certainly medieval times.[1] The world of the private army, the duel, the blood feud and other physical retribution for imagined or actual injuries had largely gone. There were duels between gentlemen in Brecon, Laugharne, and Narberth in 1817–19, and even more reports of bloody fights between magistrates about the same time, but with these exceptions the ruling classes were praised for setting 'a good example'. At a lower social level, too, there were signs that conflicts amongst the middle and working classes in the nineteenth century were being resolved in a more civilized fashion, and the fear of sudden death from an angry opponent or ruthless criminal seems to have been gradually reduced. 'Who now sleeps with pistols beneath his pillow or hangs a blunderbus within reach of his bolster?' asked Dr W. C. Taylor in 1839.[2] Wales, more than any other country in the British Isles, had a reputation for being safe from serious violence. 'Only once in a century has a murder been committed in the county', said judge Fry at Dolgellau in 1881, 'and only twice since the days of semi-barbarism, and these offences occasioned a thrill of horror not only through the county, but throughout the Principality'.[3]

The first official reports in the 1830s from the villages and country towns give the impression of a quiet society, whose peace was only rarely disturbed by drunken celebrations, the disorder of fairs and elections, and the occasional riot and rick burning. Montgomeryshire is a good example. Its rural population was described as being 'very quiet and orderly' and accustomed to dealing with inter-personal disputes 'in their own way'. Several times a year, or more if they were farmers, they cast aside their restraint. 'The people come from the hills, where they live on buttermilk;' said an angry resident of Llanfyllin, 'and when they taste the strong ale [on market and fair days], to which they are much addicted, they are apt suddenly to fall a fighting in a very barbarous manner'. Otherwise, the Montgomeryshire villages, and market towns, were represented as 'sleepy'. 'The police is quite adequate to preserve the peace;' insisted a relaxed inhabitant of Montgomery 1835, 'we have more noise from dogs, than from anything else; ...The borough magistrates hold petty sessions, as

occasion requires; but there is little business for them.'[4] Not far away, in the
rapidly expanding manufacturing towns of Llanidloes and Newtown, the
view was rather different, and so were the demands for better policing.
Here it was possible to see violent behaviour as a threat not just to the
victims but to the new world of industry, municipal pride and middle-class
respectability.

The fear, which accompanied the first stages of industrialization and
rapid urbanization in Wales, was that a changing and disturbed society
might return to the uncivilized standards of the Celtic past. In the eighteenth century, when Welsh society was said to have been 'frequently cruel,
aggressive, brutal, bawdy and drunken', and public disorder was anticipated in Carmarthen, Wrexham and other towns, we are told that at least
half the cases at the higher courts were offences against the person.[5] This
proportion was, however, falling in the last decades, and remained low for
a short while in the nineteenth century. In the first court and gaol registers
of nineteenth-century Anglesey, Merioneth and Pembrokeshire only about
a tenth of the convicted persons had committed assaults and breaches of
the peace, and the same was true of the 317 'out-of-court' convictions in
Flintshire which have survivied for the years 1815–30. Whether these
figures were due, as one historian believes, to a decline in violent behaviour
in society at the turn of the century, or whether many assaults were kept
out of the courts, is not clear.[6]

The records indicate that after the late 1820s there was a change.
Prosecutions for criminal violence increased, stimulated perhaps by the
Offences against the Person Act of 1828, the political tension of the period,
and new police appointments. The scale of the increase after 1834 can be
gauged from Graphs 8 and 9, and Table 5. By 1851 the rate of people
committed for trial for offences against the person, and imprisoned after
Petty Session convictions for assault, had risen by almost two-thirds, and
there were certain years, like 1842–4, 1848, and 1850–2 which stand out.
In 1851 one in 1,773 of the population of Wales was so prosecuted and
convicted, and, in addition, there were many more persons fined for
criminal violence. Graph 9, which is based on much better information,
indicates that the high rate of such crimes continued for a quarter of a
century after 1851. It was a pattern repeated in other areas of Britain.

Those historians who have concentrated on the records of the higher
courts and the legislation in defence of property, have not fully appreciated
the interest which the people of the mid-century showed in criminal
violence especially if it were directed against respectable citizens, unprotected females and 'innocent newcomers'. Such matters were debated in
Parliament, and there, and in wider circles, concern was expressed that the
modern city was too prone to violence in its personal, sexual, class, and race
relations. In the census year of 1871, just before the final peak of violent

Basic rate: per 100,000 of population

Graph 8. Persons committed for trial, or bailed, for offences against the person, 1834–1857.

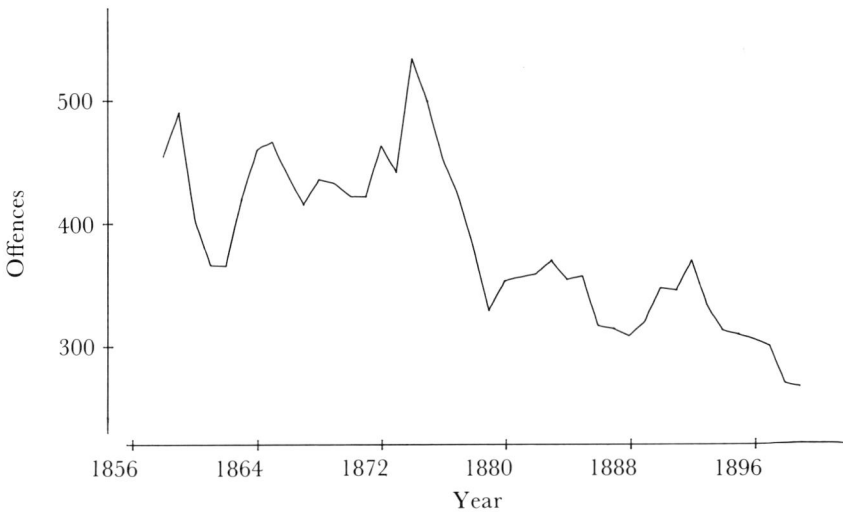

Basic rate: per 100,000 of population

Graph 9. Violence: indictable offences against the person known to the police, and persons prosecuted for assault offences determined summarily, 1858–1899.

offences, the rate of assaults in Wales matched that in England. The crimes against the person recorded in that year on Graph 9 affected one in 237 of the inhabitants of the Principality. This was, by any modern standards, an exceptional rate, especially for working-class adults.

Thereafter, Wales experienced a transformation, a remarkable fall in almost all types of violence, until the reversal in quite recent times. By 1899 the above rate had improved to one per 375. Although this was perhaps not a true reflection of changes in private behaviour, in public at least it was said that 'any man of average stature and strength may wander about on foot and alone, at any hour of the day or night...and never have so much as the thought of danger thrust upon him,...'[7] To give it a wider perspective, in 1899 the situation was good, but in 1931 it was, statistically, much better. When writing of Victorian improvement it is easy to forget that it was always a fairly violent society.

Contemporaries, and historians, have asked two main questions of these statistics: what influenced the rate of offences against the person, and was it similar across different communities? The best historian of eighteenth-century crime has suggested that the declining rate of indictments at the end of that century reflected shifts in attitude; people increasingly disapproved of violence, and conducted themselves better. Women and children, animals and convicted offenders all benefited from this.[8] Similarly, most historians of the nineteenth century have assumed that long-term movements in the statistics, of a rise and then a fall in reported violence, were caused by significant changes in private and public behaviour. Howard Zehr, for example, claims that in the first half of the century, the social dislocation of exceptional population, urban and industrial growth was accompanied by greater disorder, but he believes that once society 'adjusted' to such growth, by 1870, the rate of violent incidents, particularly of a serious kind, began to slow down.[9]

Some contemporaries claimed that social behaviour in the period between 1820 and 1880, especially in the industrial areas, was closely related to the unprecedented increases in real wages, and to the price and consumption of alcohol. According to one close observer of the criminal mind, 'families who were in ordinary times comparatively respectable' were reduced to 'idleness, drunkenness and crime' by prosperity.[10] Violent incidents were often reported in large numbers after a rise in money wages, and this was true of serious and sexual attacks as well as of the minor ones. There were similarities between the prosecutions for drunkenness and violence for much of the century, and one notices that the per capita increase in the intake of alcohol tailed off, with the assault statistics, in the later 1870s. Even so, there were years such as 1842 and 1848 when these correlations break down, and alternative views about the connections between hardship, frustration and anger have to be considered. Attacks within the family were possibly more likely at these times.

It has been argued that the highest peaks in the statistics of criminal violence matched political and social crises, when angry individuals sought to change their circumstances, and when the authorities displayed a greater desire to prosecute disorder of any kind. Individual aggression has been viewed as a substitute for, or complement to, collective protest. There were years in the 1830s and 1840s when this makes sense, but the peaks in the rate of violence after 1848 were not at times of great political anxiety and popular anger. The high figures of the mid-Victorian years cannot be explained in this way, though the subsequent decline in recorded incidents might have a connection with the growing optimism of the period. It is possible that the confidence of the authorities revealed itself in 'a growing disinclination to take proceedings for trivial assaults' in the 1890s, though one should not make too much of this.[11]

The rate of offences against the person was different across the rural, industrial and urban communities. The evidence is incomplete for the first half of the century, but there can be little doubt that the fewest pros-ecutions over violent crimes were brought in rural Wales during that period. The gap was narrowest in 1837; this was the year when the rate was highest in Anglesey, Cardiganshire and Radnorshire, and lowest in Glamorgan and Monmouthshire. Over the next twenty years, according to the information in Table 5 and Graph 8, the rate in the rural counties never returned to the level of 1837. Fuller information on all known offences against the person was given in 1858, and in that year the rate in Anglesey, Cardiganshire and Radnorshire was one per 580 of the popu-lation. As can be seen in Graph 10, it rose a little after that time, reached a peak in 1877, when it was one per 405, and then declined to a low point of one per 810 in 1891. Forty years later it was twice as good again.

Although other studies have suggested that the countryside in the nine-teenth century was as violent as the city, full of tensions and with a high tolerance of fighting and assaults, the Welsh picture seems somewhat different.[12] There was more, possibly much more, violence in the villages than the legal records indicate, as we saw in chapter 1, but the sources are unanimous that this was not, normally, a dangerous or brutal society. This was the picture drawn by the travellers at the beginning of the century, by the Welsh education commissioners of the mid-century and by the compilers of the huge reports on land and labourers at the end. There were great tracts of mid-Wales, for instance, where murder, manslaughter and serious injury were 'almost unknown'. This peaceful order was largely the product of self-control, for parish constables and policemen were few in the rural parishes; in 1899 Anglesey, Cardiganshire and Radnorshire, with a combined population of almost 135,000, had only eighty-eight of them.

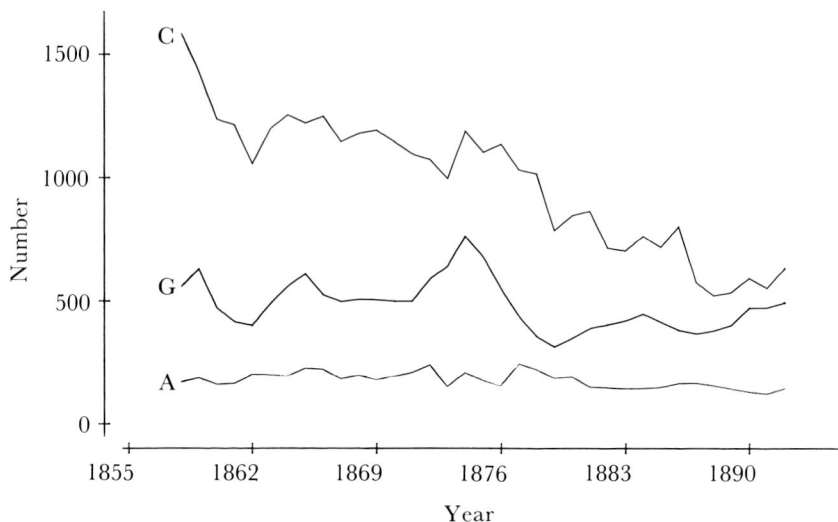

Graph 10. Offences of violence in rural and industrial counties, and in urban communities, 1858–1892.

According to the Nonconformist view of Welsh history, religious and educational influences had transformed this rural society from the 'barbarism' of the early modern era. The rural poor were portrayed in the late nineteenth century as a people who had established their own high standards of behaviour, and who appeared polite, lacking in envy, and frequently tired. 'Slow to anger' was the appropriate phrase.

Of the situation in industrial and urban Wales the evidence is more conflicting. The same statistics, which we have just examined for the three rural counties, indicate that life in Glamorgan and Monmouthshire was less safe than in any other part of the Principality. In the mid-1830s the rate of known violence in these industrial counties was comparable with that outside, but then it rose very quickly to the mid-century. In 1854 the rate of people tried for offences against the person and imprisoned for assaults in Glamorgan and Monmouthshire was seven times worse than in the rural counties. More accurate and detailed information on cases summarily disposed of and committals in Merthyr, Swansea and Neath in the years 1839–41, reveals that just under a third were for assaults, and more than one in 200 of their population was annually prosecuted for them.

In the Merthyr police district during the years 1842–59 between a third and a half of all charges were of assaults and drunken and disorderly conduct, and Henry Austin Bruce, a local magistrate, insisted that over half the male fights were settled out of court.[13] This was not quite the peaceful picture drawn by David Philips in his study of the Black Country at this time, though admittedly much of the violence in the Welsh industrial districts was of a rather petty kind. It amounted, in the eyes of a clergyman living near Brynmawr in 1846, to weekends of public-house disorder, foul language by females and juveniles, and 'strife, jealousy, bickerings, assaults and quarrelling...'[14] Even at the end of the century, when the rate of recorded violence had fallen substantially, there were areas of the south Wales coalfield where assaults, disorderly conduct, drunkenness and attacks on the police represented a large share of cases at the Petty Sessions. In the Tredegar court register of 1892 the figure was a half.[15]

As we have seen, Henry Richard and other Nonconformist observers found much to criticize about life in the largest of all the Welsh towns. In the mid-century their high streets, slum districts and docklands were described as the most likely places to witness manslaughter, muggings, attacks by and on women, public-house fights and general disorder. In 1858, when one in 113 of the people of the Merthyr district were apprehended and summoned for common assault and violence against policemen, the information on Graph 10 gives a combined rate of one violent crime per every sixty-three of the population of Cardiff, Swansea and Newport. People must have lived in real fear of being attacked; this was a level of violence almost inconceivable to the people of the early twentieth century. In 1931, when the populations of Cardiff and Swansea had increased by more than five times since 1858, the number of prosecutions for common assault had fallen by 300 per cent.

The 1850s probably witnessed the high point of urban violence in the second half of the nineteenth century. Whereas the rate of offences against the person for Glamorgan and Monmouthshire, excepting the three towns, reached its peak on the graph in 1874, with one crime per 131 of the population, in the three seaports the reduction began early and continued with few interruptions. By 1891 the combined rate for the two industrial counties had fallen to 1:212, and for the towns it was almost as good, at 1:181. As in England, France and Germany, it seems, from the police and court statistics, that it was in some way the 'novelty', not the fact, of urbanization which produced the highest rates of personal conflict.

This is something which was also emerges from the literary evidence. Dr Taylor, Joseph Fletcher, and the other defenders of city life and the factory system, believed that it would take a little time for the old patterns of work and play, the ingrained tolerance of violence and the self-regulation of rural communities to pass away, and for new forms of control, education and policing to make their mark. For such urban propogandists, the initial surge in the criminal statistics represented a growing determination to resolve conflict more formally and legally, and was a tribute to the efforts of the police, who reported and prosecuted many of the cases of violence. The police, on the instructions of their watch committees, ensured that behaviour, which had been tolerated, or hidden, in rural and semi-rural parishes, was outlawed in the town centres and inner residential districts.

Positive changes in the life of the larger urban and industrial districts were noted at an early date. Even at the time of the education report of 1847, a few of the witnesses on the north and south Wales coalfields spoke of recent improvements in the social atmosphere of their towns. 'Good order generally prevails', said John Harley of Pontypool, 'excepting only drunkenness and its consequent evils. The district is free from crimes of violence, and political agitators have not latterly produced much effect.'[16] In the 1850s visitors to the industrial heartlands were impressed by the discipline of the work and life-style and by the absence of riot and disorder. 'During a stay of several weeks in the town I never saw nor heard of altercations and fighting', said the reporter of the *Morning Chronicle* of Merthyr in the spring of 1850.[17]

From the statistics it appears that the optimism of this journalist was perhaps a little premature, but by the end of the mid-Victorian years the improvement in private and public behaviour was often remarked upon. The last quarter of the nineteenth century witnessed a sharp fall in the recorded incidence of almost all types of violent crime. It was a decline that began somewhat later than that in England, but it was nevertheless a remarkable achievement, and it continued into the twentieth century. When compared with contemporary Ireland, Wales was much more law-abiding, and especially 'innocent of great crimes'. The Welsh, unlike their Celtic friends, had a reputation throughout this period for being 'strangers to the knife and the gun', rarely given to serious outbursts of criminal anger. When such violence, especially of a public nature, occurred within the Principality, outsiders were often blamed for the trouble.

The number of serious indictable offences against the person was low throughout the nineteenth century, and continued to be so well into the next century (Table 8). There were on average only twenty cases of homicide per year at the Assizes and Quarter Sessions between 1834 and 1899, with the charge of manslaughter, or killing without prior intent, being almost five times as common as that of murder. Of the 227 persons tried for murder in this period, 117 appeared before the Glamorgan and Monmouthshire courts, and only sixteen before those of Anglesey, Cardiganshire and Radnorshire. Radnorshire, together with Merioneth, was about the safest county in Britain. When a horrific murder was committed at Penrhyndeudraeth in 1812, 'the year of blood', the *Chester Chronicle*

Table 8
Annual average of serious offences against the person, 1858–1899

Homicides (murder & manslaughter) reported to the police	22
Shooting, wounding & inflicting bodily harm reported to police	97
Sexual assaults reported to police	69
Attempts at suicide reported to police	22
Aggravated assaults on women and children proceeded against at Petty Sessions	178
Attacks on the police proceeded against at Petty Sessions	643

Source: PR, 1859(1), XXVI–1901, LXXXIX.

expressed feigned surprise that at last the 'detestable crime has extended to Wales – a country in which simplicity of manners, and the proverbial mutuality of national affection, one would have thought, would be sufficient guarantees for its internal tranquillity.'[18]

In earlier centuries, when such deaths occurred, the family of the victim sometimes agreed a private settlement with the family of the killer, and there were surprising claims in our period that a few homicides were hidden from the authorities, or kept out of the courts, by the incompetence and connivance of constables and by the silence and lies of witnesses. In the Report of the Royal Commission on the Constabulary of 1839, Thomas Yates, a Welshpool solicitor, expressed annoyance at the manner in which rural communities in Wales reacted to murder and manslaughter.[19] A few years later, when the body of a young female servant was found in a pond near Cynwyl Elfed in Carmarthenshire, the local newspaper had no doubt that the murderer was being protected by his family and friends. The point was also made about crimes just short of murder. An anonymous correspondent of 1858, describing a vicious attack on a Carmarthenshire woman in a lonely rural cottage, said that 'when it became known that a murderous assault had been committed, the poor woman herself and all the neighbours tried to put obstacles in the path of justice.'[20]

The Belgian Lamberte-Adolphe Quetelet, and other statisticians who looked at homicide in the nineteenth century, were struck by the differences between it and all other forms of crime; the number of cases remained similar from year to year, the manner of death hardly changed with the passing generations, and the murderers had little in common with other offenders. About a half of the Welsh cases were family affairs, typically a husband killing his wife, or a mother doing the same to her new-born child. In the first, and much more common instance, women were strangled, and set upon with knives, pokers, hammers and bars. John Griffith of the Haverfordwest area, who poisoned his second wife in 1811, was an exception, and proved it by confessing that he had done the same to his first spouse. Some of these husbands were undoubtedly suffering from mental illness; amongst them was an elderly Dolgellau printer, successful and prominent in his local chapel, who killed his wife in 1881, and then cut his own throat. In many instances, as in the murder of Elizabeth Harry near Monmouth in 1817, and of Mary Griffith in Anglesey thirteen years later, the brutal assault closed a long chapter of family quarrels.[21] Sexual jealousy was the spark that often ignited these smouldering personal conflicts. A Cilrhedyn horse-dealer and a Llanfair Caereinion farm labourer killed their wives in the mid-century on suspicion that they were seeing other men.[22] When these husbands were executed in public it needed all the efforts of the constables and javelin men to keep the angry spectators at a distance.[23]

Even in murders outside the family, it was frequently the case that the parties concerned knew each other intimately. Here, too, matters of sex and pregnancy turned a difficult relationship into an unbearable one. The following cases illustrate the male's blundering responses to common nineteenth-century problems. Thomas Rees of Llangadog, a part-time Presbyterian minister, and his girl-friend Elizabeth Jones, who was forbidden an early marriage by her parents, were faced in the spring of 1817 by an unwanted pregnancy. The poison which Rees administered to Elizabeth killed the mother as well as the unborn child, and the preacher was convicted and executed before a crowd estimated at 10,000 people. Twelve years later, in another *cause célèbre*, the pregnant Hannah Thomas was deserted by her Carmarthenshire lover. When she tried to persuade him to marry her as promised, he killed her with fourteen hatchet blows to the head. Meanwhile, in Breconshire, Gwenllian Morgan suffered a very similar fate; having bravely insisted on naming David Edwards as the father of her unborn child, he cut her throat. Edwards, the son of a poor mason, almost escaped from the condemned cell, by chipping away at its walls.[24] Women, for their part, committed few murders of adults, but when they did poison and stab their husbands and lovers it was the source of much public interest. This was true, for example, of Hannah Roberts, an eighteen year old of Holywell, who gave arsenic to her husband in 1842, at the request of her lover, John Parry, and of Pembrokeshire's Lydia Williams, who was given a life's sentence in 1863 for doing the same.[25]

The other murders were of friends, drinking companions, fellow workmen and servants, and the outcome of armed robberies, poaching raids and violent strikes. Foreign seamen were killed at Cardiff, Swansea and Newport, whilst in quieter market towns people died at work and in public-house brawls. In 1886, when William Samuels, a Welshpool trades- man, murdered an assistant, the police had to rescue the former from the baying crowd. In a few instances, as when Thomas Price and John Evans of Cardiganshire beat Thomas Evans to a pulp in 1822, the crime was the last stage of 'an old quarrel'. Other murders were more spontaneous, even possibly accidental, affairs. James Richards, who had been involved in the Merthyr rising of 1831, and Thomas Thomas, who was a follower of Rebecca, were convicted of murdering people whilst robbing them, and the giant Thomas Edwards – 'a resident in Wales, [but] not a Welshman' – killed young Mary Jones in 1812 when she caught him rifling her master's home at Penrhyndeudraeth. After the last incident, 'it was truely grateful to behold the zeal and activity of every individual, in rendering their utmost assistance for the attainment of justice'.[26]

A number of gamekeepers expired at the hands of poachers.[27] On one occasion, at Gurnos, a large mob cheered outside the New Swan Inn where a coroner's jury was considering the death of Mr R. D. Gough's under- keeper. There was also a degree of community support for the killing in 1840 of Shadrach Lewis, the ex-soldier, woodward and informer of Clydau in Pembrokeshire, and, ten years later, of John Thomas, the blackleg of Cwmbach, Aberdare.[28] Of course, it would be wrong to make too much of this; community feeling was often against the murderer, as was shown during the riot at Swansea in April 1866. Robert Coe of Mountain Ash was executed for the murder of his friend; as he was about to be hanged, four women with knives attacked him, and in the mêlée 120 were injured. This affair contributed to the ending of public executions in Britain two years later.[29]

Infanticide was seen, in the nineteenth century, as being different from the above murders, and this was reflected in the under-reporting of the crime, and in the punishment of the guilty parties. It had been regarded as a very serious offence in Jacobean times, but we are told that the interest in, and incidence of, such deaths declined in the eighteenth century. The real extent of the crime will never be known. Lionel Rose informs us that many children's deaths were not recorded, and inquests on the rest were few.[30] It was difficult to prove murderous intent in an age when death was so common. Infant mortality in Wales increased between 1839 and 1900, notably in the last two decades. Hundreds died every year soon after birth, and there was an unknown number of still-births. In the eighteenth century a witness was required to prove the circumstance of such deaths, and in Victorian times these had to be registered with the authorities. Not all were. Thus Sarah Bostock, a Denbighshire servant, delivered herself of a dead child in 1860, and then buried it secretly in the garden.[31] The discovery of this and other little bodies, and the intervention of employers and neighbours, led to a very small number of women appearing in court on the charge of concealing a birth.

A related crime was unlawfully abandoning children under two years of age. This 'child dropping', as it was called, was most common during hard times, and when the state reduced the help for unmarried mothers. After the implementation of the Poor Law Amendment Act of 1834, hundreds of babies were dumped outside workhouses, chapels and houses, and some expired. At public meetings in rural Wales, opposing the new bastardy and relief clauses of this Act, speakers insisted that the measures had contributed directly towards the unprecedented neglect, cruelty and death of children.[32] Each year, however, only a handful of the worst examples of concealing births and 'child dropping' came before the courts. Punishment amounted to a short period of imprisonment, for up to twelve months, or a fine and a lecture. The recipients of such sentences were often single females, mostly servants, and a much smaller number of deserted or vagrant married women.

Infanticide was not yet defined as a separate crime, and it is difficult to establish the extent of the offence. The number of court cases was always very small, and they usually involved single women who had killed newly-born babies. Murders of children over one year of age were extremely rare. William Jones of Nevern in Pembrokeshire, who knocked the life out his six-year-old daughter and was transported for life in 1848, was a strange and unpopular character, and both Hannah Prothero and Mary Hughes, who were found guilty of a similar crime, suffered from mental illness. The former committed suicide, and the latter, who hanged her offspring in 1847, was declared insane.[33] These were the obvious cases of child murder; others were more difficult to establish. Coroner's juries, confronted by small dead bodies, struggled with the evidence before them, uncertain whether the infant had expired from natural causes, neglect, or malice. Even when their verdict invited a court case, Assize juries, both grand and petty, rarely treated the offence with the seriousness given to other murders, especially if the child were illegitimate. Many prosecutions for infanticide were quashed by the grand jury and the charge was frequently reduced to concealing a birth. Acquittals were common. Only about forty per cent of the accused were tried and found guilty under the terms of the original indictment.

'I did not intend to kill him' was the successful defence of many farm and domestic servants charged with suffocating babies in coffers, drawers and blankets, but when Margaret Hughes and her daughter of Llannon in Carmarthenshire were acquitted in 1843 of killing new-born twins by dropping them down a pit, the judge had to bite his tongue. Punishment for those convicted of infanticide varied considerably. One girl was hanged at Presteigne in 1805 for the murder of her infant, and Mary Jones, a 24-year-old Caernarfonshire dairy maid, was sentenced in 1850 to be transported for the crime. The 22-year-old pauper Mary Prout, of Pembrokeshire, also got twenty years penal servitude in 1864, but these were extreme and even possibly vindictive sentences.[34] During periods of acknowledged hardship for single mothers, the authorities tended to be much more charitable. Such was the case after the Poor Law Amendment Act of 1834 when newspaper evidence and the returns of coroners suggested that about a third of all killings were of babies.[35]

Some idea of the nature of serious violence, both towards children and adults, in the second half of the century can be gained from Table 8, but the real extent of the problem cannot be determined. Each year, on average, half a dozen failed attempts at murder were reported to the police, and just under a hundred shootings, stabbings and brutal assaults, often by young male adults. In the mid-century there were complaints by judges in south Wales that such attacks were on the increase, especially in those districts where there was a 'mixed and mobile population', and this feeling merged, in the 1860s, with the national outcry over the brutality of street robbers. In Glamorgan, it was a particular source of frustration to Robert Oliver Jones that the Garotters' Act of 1863, and the harsher penalties subsequently imposed on offenders, had, it appeared, only a limited effect. Punishment for felonious, malicious and unlawful wounding at this time was typically from nine months to two years incarceration.[36]

The rate of these serious assaults in Wales did not coincide exactly with the rate of all criminal violence shown on Graph 9. The former reached peaks in 1864 and 1869, then fell after the mid-1870s, only to rise again from the low point in 1880. By 1896 the rate of serious violence had returned almost to the height of 1869, underpinning, and perhaps even reflecting, the anxiety about personal safety and 'the hooligan' during the last decade. It was widely, and rightly assumed, that a large number of the worst incidents happened in the industrial towns and seaports. As soon as detailed comparisons could be made, in 1858, Cardiff had one of the worst records for such crimes in England and Wales, and 'wounding' thereafter remained a prominent entry in its annual lists of indictable offences. When sixteen-year-old William Reynolds was charged, in August 1898, with hitting James Pike over the head with a poker, detective inspector Scott told the Cardiff magistrates that they had several young 'Hooligan gangs' in the town.[37] The chief offenders in cases of serious violence in the Welsh metropolis were in fact seamen, often Italian and Greek, and labourers and prostitutes, who, it was said, followed the example of all foreigners by keeping a knife on their person. Typical of the 'malicious stabbings' in

Cardiff was that by Richard Russell, a 22-year-old mariner, who in 1862 drew a knife on Thomas Miller, coal heaver, in a quarrel over clothes, and, when he had served his gaol sentence, did the same to Charles Walter, fellow seaman, in a brothel.

In industrial Wales serious injury, and manslaughter, were half-expected on pay nights, weekends, and holidays, during industrial strife, and in clashes between different nationalities. Bagillt in Flintshire, and Rhosymedre in Denbighshire were renowned for their street violence in the early nineteenth century, whilst in the pubs and lodging-houses of Merthyr and Aberdare, colliers, labourers and boatmen were responsible for deaths and permanent injury. People fought with their fists, and with stones and knives hidden on their person, and the language at such times was full of racial, religous and sexual taunts. Many of the worst fights occurred as the men left the comfort and control of the public house. Then the Irish in particular seemed to relish the challenge of 'a good fight', knowing that because their 'blood was in a heated condition' they were likely to evade the extreme legal consequences of their action. When two labourers kicked a fellow Irishman to death outside the Black Bull in mid-nineteenth century Merthyr, they claimed that 'they were too drunk to remember anything about it' and got eighteen months hard labour.[38] On occasions it took all the resources of the Merthyr police and the Catholic Church to control the Irish rows, especially if Orange and Green families were on opposite sides.

It would be wrong to see the behaviour of these industrial workers as being completely different from that of their country cousins. Although rural Wales had a largely justified reputation for being a peaceful society, there were more brutal conflicts than the police and court records indicated. At least until the late nineteenth century, trouble was anticipated on market-days, fair-days, and the few annual holidays. Heads were broken on journeys home from Builth and Dryslwyn, and people disfigured for life. When men had drink inside them, family feuds and quarrels over sweethearts degenerated into bloody confrontations. Several young farmers and labourers perished, for example, in the many brawls outside public houses in Llandeilo and Newcastle Emlyn during the century.[39] And always in the countryside, the 'civil war' between poachers, bailiffs and gamekeepers continued, with guns and hatchets freely used.

Punishment for manslaughter and serious injury was comparatively light, with a six- or twelve-months gaol sentence being common, but there were exceptions. In April 1817 Thomas Langslow, a prize-fighter and frequenter of fairs and wakes in the border country, was executed for cutting and maiming John Green in an affray near Knighton.[40] The authorities decided to deal harshly with him as an example to others; they were convinced that tolerance of such violence was no longer acceptable, and that firm action was needed by parish constables and fellow magistrates.

The gap between the actual incidence of violence and the number of court proceedings was especially apparent in the case of sexual assaults.[41] The published Welsh figures, which were sometimes paraded as the best evidence of the nation's superior morality, have to be regarded with scepticism. In the years 1834–57 an annual average of only fifteen cases of sexual offences were heard in the higher courts. Thereafter, when more detailed evidence was provided, an average of sixty-nine cases a year were reported to the police, with rape being seven times as common as sodomy and bestiality (Table 8). The graph of these sexual attacks has no clear pattern, although, like the other statistics of serious violence, there was a rise in the rate during the 1880s and 1890s, partly caused by the terms of, and publicity accompanying, the Criminal Law Amendment Act of 1885. Even when allowance is made for the differences in population density, an exceptional number of these sexual attacks took place in Glamorgan and Monmouthshire. The most dangerous places for women in the nineteenth century were, it seems, the roads over the hills between the south Wales industrial valleys. It was easy, in the misty nights, to lose one's way, and the person who rendered assistance often demanded an unpleasant reward. Henry Perkin, a 34-year-old collier who was imprisoned for life in 1860, committed half a dozen rapes and attempted rapes on the mountains about Blaina.[42]

The police occurrence books of Merioneth show that there were considerably more examples of indecent behaviour towards women, failed attempts to ravish, and actual rape, by men from all classes of society, than one might have expected from the records of Assize and Quarter Sessions. In this and other rural counties the victims of rape were often female servants, trapped in out-buildings and caught in lonely places, sometimes by small gangs of young labourers. Some of the women were abused by their employers; others were attacked on their way to and from chapel, usually by men whose advances they had previously ignored or resisted. In the towns sexual assault was more associated in the minds of reformers with overcrowded homes, though the records reveal that the work-place, the roads on the edge of town, and dark alleys in the docklands were just as dangerous. Besides rape, there were innumerable instances in the newspapers of 'gross and disgusting behaviour' towards women, and the masters of domestic servants at Swansea, Neath and other towns in the mid-century claimed that it was unsafe to send them on errands after dark. Rather than condemn their attackers, newspaper editors issued warnings that women would be wise to stay in their proper, domestic, place.

In the first decades of the century, when a prosecution for rape reached the Great and Quarter Sessions, the victims received little support. There

was an unspoken feeling in many sections of society that such matters were
best kept out of court, and a suspicion that prosecutions for sexual assault
were only a conspiracy to destroy someone's character. A handful of
women in rape cases were subsequently indicted for this secondary crime.[43]
Grand juries were sometimes instructed to ignore bills for rape in cases
where no resistance had been offered and when no immediate complaint
had been made. It was hardly surprising, in all the circumstances, that
victims occasionally found the ordeal too much, and gave up the prosecution. The popular male presumption, which women had to overcome,
was that somehow the latter had encouraged their attackers, even, it
appears, in the case of an eleven-year-old Cardiganshire girl who was
sexually assaulted by fifty-year-old Daniel Davies in 1831.[44] Judges were
always looking for signs of 'enticement', 'prevarication' and 'ulterior
motives' in rape cases. Juries reduced many of the charges to common
assault, and between a third and a half of the defendants were acquitted.[45]

Transportation was the punishment in the early years of the century for
a very bad case of 'aggravated' rape, though Richard Radnor was
executed in September 1829 at Monmouth for a horrific sexual attack on
a thirteen-year-old.[46] When transportation ended, long periods of penal
servitude were given to those who assaulted the very young, but a typical
sentence for other types of rape was twelve or eighteen months in gaol.
Attitudes did change, if slowly. There were rather more expressions of
anger in court as the years passed, more outbursts from the crowds which
attended rape trials, and more critical comments from the newspapers
about the sentences. In Wales, too, there was support for the Criminal Law
Amendment Act of 1885 which raised the age of consent to sixteen years.
This Act led, as we have seen, to a sudden increase in the number of cases
of sexual assault being brought before the Welsh courts, but even at the end
of the century the tolerance shown to the male defendants was as evident
as concern for female distress.[47]

By contrast, 'unnatural crimes' always produced a severe retribution, of
transportation or very long periods of imprisonment. Bestiality has been
called a 'common rural offence' in nineteenth-century Wales, but very few
people were actually charged with the crime. Incest was in a similar
category; in some ways it was the most secret yet revealing of all the
offences against the person. Two of the most notorious cases came to light
in 1848 and 1866, when the Assizes dealt with offences committed by a
28-year-old Aberdare brother on his sister, and by a Llanwonno widower
on his sixteen-year-old daughter. The widower, John Kerby, a 44-year-old
collier with three children, received a sentence of penal servitude for life.
In this example, and some of the others, a daughter had replaced, in the
mind of the offender, a sick or dead wife. Behind the shock horror of the
reports of incest, there were hints that some people in both rural and

industrial society half-condoned the practice by their silence. In the Denbighshire village of Llanerchrugog, for instance, it was said in 1847 that people accepted with apparent equanimity a father and daughter living together as man and wife, and other unspecified 'bestialities'.[48]

On a number of occasions sexual misdemeanours led very directly to another crime, that of attempted suicide. The official suicide statistics, used in a recent book on the subject, indicate that suicide was not a popular act in Wales. The author claims that people in the friendly and supportive industrial communities rarely tried to kill themselves, and she informs us that towards the end of our period Swansea and Cardiff had two of the lowest suicide rates in Britain. Self-inflicted deaths, and failed attempts at such, were indeed rare, but rather more common than Dr Anderson indicates.[49] In difficult years such as 1817, 1830 and 1848, when a considerable number of cases were chronicled, there were suggestions in the press that people were threatening to take their lives only to get charitable assistance, and, to stop this, they should be threatened with the treadmill.[50] A few were gaoled, for one or two weeks.

By the 1890s a yearly average of forty-three attempted suicides was being reported to the Home Office by the Welsh police forces, a figure well above the previous returns (Table 8). The offenders were from all classes, the clergyman and the farmer being as representative as the aged pauper, the young pregnant girl and the 'down-and-out'. Some were sad and tragic cases, having survived potions of arsenic, gun blasts in the face and hours in deep water. In one or two instances, it was difficult for the authorities, and even harder for the historian, to decide whether the young female servants who had taken toxic medicines were seeking an abortion, a common practice, or wishing to end it all. Gradually, as the years passed, the dock, prison and police authorities took what measures they could to prevent suicides, and greater sympathy was extended to those who had been through the experience. In court they were ordered to keep the peace for six months, encouraged to sign the teetotal pledge, issued with a friendly warning, and then placed in the hands of relatives and religious and private welfare agencies. A few of the depressed individuals declared that they would make another suicide attempt as soon as possible, and in recognition of the futility of the legal exercise, Parliament later removed this offence from the statute book.

As society grew in tolerance towards suicide attempts, successful and unsuccessful, the reverse was true of violence carried out against other people. During the century new legislation increased the penalties for certain types of assault, and the courts, the police and the press even began to take violence within the home, and between working-class males in public, more seriously. Most of the prosecutions at this time were over common rather than aggravated assault, and there were many more of these than in the eighteenth and early twentieth centuries.[51] Of the 7,781 offences against the person recorded in the peak year of 1874 on Graph 9, eighty-six per cent were of this type, and almost all the cases were heard in the local police courts, especially those of Glamorgan and Monmouthshire. Three years before, at the time of the census, more than half of the Welsh cases of common assault were committed in these two industrial counties, against one in 242 of their inhabitants. Cardiff, Swansea and Newport, which were removed from these totals, had even higher rates. In contrast, only one in 491 of the population of Anglesey, Cardiganshire and Radnorshire in 1871 was charged with common assault. Although this rural figure continued to rise until 1877, at every point in the nineteenth century a person was less likely to be attacked in a village than in a town (Graph 10).

The magistrates who dealt with the vast collection of people charged with common assault were soon able to identify distinct groups and types, on either side of the courtroom. Eight out of ten offenders were male, but about a fifth of these committed violence against females. The latter were attacked in public houses, at work, in the streets and behind closed doors, and they received little protection and sympathy. Domestic servants were especially vulnerable, as the court cases show. Thus when John Augustus Jones of Wellington Terrace, Caernarfon, was given a sentence of one-month's hard labour in 1860, it emerged that he had continually abused his servant Mary Williams.[52] In 1853, as parliamentary interest in the subject began to grow, the most battered groups of women and children gained additional protection. An Act provided a maximum prison term of six months or a fine of up to £20 for those convicted of 'aggravated assault' (resulting in actual bodily harm) on all females, and on males under fourteen years of age. Each year an average of 178 people, mostly from Monmouthshire and Glamorgan, were proceeded against under this legislation (Table 8).

It is clear from these cases that the greatest danger to women lay within the home. A large number of wives, both legal and common-law, were attacked by men. Although family violence had become less acceptable by the end of the eighteenth century, we are told that even in the first half of the nineteenth, especially in 'low neighbourhoods', 'wife beating was taken for granted'.[53] In the worst cases, as we saw in chapter 1, they were given some protection by the practice of carrying the *ceffyl pren*, but when this disappeared females had to rely increasingly on the police and the courts. The wife of Thomas Lloyd of Lampeter was one who sought their help. Her husband was brought before the Petty Sessions for cutting her with a hatchet, and was put away for six months. Like some of the other irresponsible husbands, Lloyd had strong views on how his partner should behave, and wanted things done 'properly'. Magistrates were often of a like mind.

At the Llanbadarn Petty Sessions in 1864 they dismissed a charge of assault against James Evans the blacksmith, and advised him to make his alcoholic wife an allowance and get rid of her.[54] Wives knew when to expect trouble, and the press, in its sardonic coverage of Monday morning's court proceedings, often used the heading 'Marriage Bliss'. Regular weekend performers were Henry Lloyd of Carmarthen and Thomas Stephens of Cardiff. In 1886, not for the first time, the latter knocked his wife unconscious whilst he was in a drunken state.[55]

By this date, according to Nancy Tomes, in her survey of London crime, such attacks on working-class women had fallen from their mid-century height. The Welsh evidence, at least of aggravated assaults on females, supports this view. After a peak in 1864, and especially after a lower one in 1874, the rate of prosecutions fell gradually to the low of 1899. Almost certainly the downward trend, which was in line with that of many other violent offences, cannot be related to a declining interest in wife-beating, or to a growing reluctance on the part of women to report their husbands. Women were more open about this than we think; in Cardiff, Swansea and Newport wives embarrassed police-court officials by seeking help and summonses, and by parading their bruises and those on their children.

They had a mixed reception. A few chief constables demanded firm, even repeated, evidence of physical injuries before allowing their men to become entangled in a family dispute. If, when wife-beating was reported to the police, the man was 'found...quiet' when the officer arrived, and if he could be taken up on a charge of drunkenness instead, usually no action ensued over the initial complaint. Even when violent husbands were brought to court, magistrates were inclined to dismiss them with a warning about future conduct. Thus when Jane Grindley took Samuel before Anglesey justices in 1822, Samuel was bound over to keep the peace. Later small fines were inflicted, and teetotal pledges signed, but imprisonment of up to six months, and separation orders, were given with reluctance.

Of violence against children we know very little. Child-welfare legislation was passed to give better protection to factory, street and schoolchildren, but comparatively few people were prosecuted. In some instances, when children were assaulted whilst living away from home in domestic and farm service, magistrates supported their masters' disciplinarian line. On rare occasions apprentice boys struck work as a protest against brutal and vindictive employers. In the centres of heavy industry, fellow workers and the wider community had strong feelings about the worst cases of abuse. 'If...a child or young person was ill-used or ill-treated in any of the works by the masters or overmen', said John Roberts, the Pontypool superintendant of police in 1841, 'the men would come out until the matter was arranged.' At Merthyr in 1833 a man who whipped a tram boy was beaten to death, and, thirteen years later, when a stepmother was accused in the same town of cruelty to a child, a mob threatened to lynch her.[56] Second partners of quarrelling husbands and wives, and foster parents, carried out many of the reported assaults in the home. In a society which accepted the physical chastisement of children, it was only exceptional cases which were taken to court. One or two of the children who were brave enough to complain of their treatment reappear in the records, battered but not completely submissive.

The rulers of Victorian Britain were torn between 'the sacrilege' of interfering with family life and legal patriarchy, and the fear that violent homes were a source of delinquency and crime.[57] As we shall see in chapter 5, Parliament, at least until the Prevention of Cruelty Acts of 1889 and 1894, left the initiative in the matter of child abuse and cruelty to voluntary agencies, especially to the NSPCC, whose case-load in Wales grew substantially towards the end of the century. The inspectors received considerable assistance from those who, a century before, might have organized a *ceffyl pren*. In 1899, 253 people, two-thirds from Glamorgan and Caernarfonshire, were charged with cruelty to children at the Assizes, Quarter Sessions and courts of summary jurisdiction. We shall never, of course, know the full details of changes in parental attitudes towards their offspring. Some historians think that during the most difficult years of the industrial revolution, things probably became worse for the most vulnerable members of society, and improved with the better conditions and 'evangelical conscience' of subsequent decades, but it would take much research to support such a thesis.

Fights within the home were a problem for the extended family, neighbours and the police. At Rhuthun in November 1894, the mother-in-law of Thomas Davies intervened on the side of his wife, and Davies smashed a broom upon her head.[58] Those living in close proximity were also attacked for expressing embarrassment over family rows. In the villages and towns of the early nineteenth century, arbitration and the threat of community action were sometimes used to curb such disorder, and chapel disapproval of open family conflict was strong. Parish constables were anxious not to become involved in this business, but the new professional police had less excuse. They grew to hate this area of their work, for requests from agitated neighbours and relatives for assistance rebounded on the authorities. Policemen were injured in family conflicts, and complainants proved to be unreliable witnesses. At Newport in Monmouthshire police constable Davies made the mistake in 1880 of trying to stop a fight in Cwrtybella Street between Michael Callaghan and his wife. Immediately all the Callaghan clan descended upon him, and he was punched and kicked mercilessly.[59]

The legal records and the newspaper reports illustrate that neighbours could both dampen down and ignite violence. Men, and an unusually large number of women, fought each other over matters to do with children, personal and family honour, and property. In the countryside there were painful battles over the ownership of land, the position of boundaries and grazing rights. William Lewis and his three sons of the parish of Haroldston West in Pembrokeshire fought Peter Jones and his three sons in 1854 over the correct line between their two farms, and were only prevented from killing each other by outsiders.[60] Much of this anger was contained, for farmers had to get on with one another, and there were informal village sanctions against, and third-party attempts to prevent, too much physical conflict. Every now and then, however, the wrong sheep in a field or another deliberate act of trespass proved too much and the police became involved. Rachel Rees of Wiston, Pembrokeshire, received a knife in the back over the disputed ownership of a field, and on Christmas Eve 1888 Ellis Griffith of Llandanwg, near Harlech, struck Salmon Jones repeatedly about the head in a frenzy over stray ewes.[61]

In the towns and industrial villages tensions between neighbours arose over the the behaviour of juveniles, noise in the street, the disposal of ashes, the beating of carpets, and even more mundane matters. By no means all these clashes were resolved in the courts, but one gains the impression over time that summonses and cross-summonses became a more popular way of dealing with assaults. 'The attraction of the police court, particularly for the lower classes, has been extraordinary,...' wrote one English contemporary in 1868.[62] In a typical case, at the Llandudno police court in May 1895, Grace Hughes, accompanied by her two children, told a long story of how she had been assaulted by neighbour Elizabeth Jones. The children had quarrelled in the backyard, and the mothers had interfered.[63] Missiles were then hurled, and other people joined in the row. Exasperated policemen and magistrates tried and failed, in this and many similar cases, to get the parties to reach an amicable compromise, and then bound them over to keep the peace for six or twelve months.

Rather more serious for the authorities were the attacks on officials. These were numerous, and well reported. Very early in the century several justices of the peace were the target of popular anger, but generally it was lesser mortals who suffered. They included in their number excise, poor-law, and sheriff's officers, watchmen and keepers, and parish and police constables. These had the difficult tasks of executing court orders, obtaining money and property, defending privilege, and apprehending suspected criminals. Amongst the most vulnerable officials were those isolated and undefended men who had to enforce unpopular dues. Collectors at the toll-gates constantly appeared in court, complaining that travellers had abused and physically injured them. The Rebecca riots were, to that extent, only the worst episode of a long-running saga. Others who had reason to fear the public's wrath were the collectors of the various municipal and market tolls, as well as customs and excise officers, and those trying to obtain poor rates, church rates, tithes and taxes. At Llansteffan, for example, in April 1807 labourers beat and kicked William Thompson, an excise officer, as he was about to secure 292 gallons of foreign brandy, rum and gin.[64] In many of these affrays women, who were most often at home, proved as determined as the men. In 1810 the wife of Samuel Jones of Wrexham was committed for three months for assaulting a parish officer and resisting the execution of a distress warrant for the non-payment of poor rates.[65]

Of all those attacked, bailiffs, keepers and policemen were perhaps the most common targets. The first of these had a reputation for being arrogant and extortionate, but they had a thankless task, for they were the front line of authority. They had to deal with people who had refused, or were unable, to pay fines, rents and other dues. Such was their treatment that in Llandudno, and other places, it was 'a matter of impossibility to get men...to do their duty as bailiffs, because of the rough treatment they were subjected to,...'[66] The non-payment of house and farm rents was the source of the greatest conflict. In Swansea's Greenhill and Cardiff's Butetown, penniless tenants and their goods vanished overnight, whilst the most desperate barricaded themselves behind locked doors or waited expectantly with savage dogs.

In the countryside, violent opposition to bailiffs was most intense during difficult times, like the 1790s, the post-war slump, the years of Rebecca, and the late-1860s, when indebtedness increased and so did fears of repossession. The work of recovering property was thwarted, crowds of relatives and friends launched counter-attacks on bailiffs, and impounded cattle, horses and sheep were rescued. In all of this conflict, much depended on the attitude of officials and the support given to them by the constabulary. At Llansawel in 1837 a force of twenty-six bailiffs lost a battle with a crowd over levied goods, but when a large number of families were ejected from their Caernarfonshire cottages in 1862 policemen with drawn swords ensured compliance. At Maesteg, constable John Davies spent a good deal of time in the late 1860s respectfully 'keeping the peace while common bailiffs were executing a warrant of distress', and he was rarely challenged.[67] One newspaper, commenting on the changing situation in 1854, hoped that the days 'of [mobs] bullying and threatening violence' were at last 'past and gone'.[68]

The attacks on keepers were of a different character from those on bailiffs, and more serious. Most of them occurred during poaching raids, though there were ugly incidents in the streets and public houses, and at the homes of the unfortunate victims. The responsibility for this 'rural war' was shared equally between those on either side of the property divide. The

£100 REWARD

WHEREAS on the night of FRIDAY, the 27th of NOVEMBER instant, JOSEPH BUTLER, Keeper to the Right Honourable The Earl of Lisburne, was Shot dead by WILLIAM RICHARDS, of Cefncoch, in the Parish of Llangwryddon, in the County of Cardigan: the above Reward will be paid for the apprehension of the said William Richards.

The said William Richards is about 28 years of age, 5ft. 9in. or 10in. high, slight figure, long thin legs, with stooping gait, light hair slightly curled, thin sandy whiskers, long thin face, lower teeth overlapping upper teeth, long nose rather Roman, full grey eyes, speaks very little English; is supposed to be dressed in a dark home-made coarse coat, corduroy breeches and leggings, striped check shirt, and lace-up boots, clumsy feet, and has been operated upon for a bruise in the testicle.

All information to be addressed to the Superintendent of Police at Aberystwith.

Crosswood, 30th November, 1868.

J. COX, PRINTER AND STATIONER, PIER STREET, ABERYSTWITH.

The shooting of a keeper, 1868

late eighteenth and early nineteenth centuries witnessed a remarkable growth in the preservation of winged game, and in the employment of men to watch woods and covers. Later, when more interest was shown by landowners in the trade in rabbits and fish, even more watchmen were needed. As these people were armed with guns and clubs, and as night poaching in particular invited harsh punishment, their clashes with gangs were frightening affairs. Amongst the affrays which ended with death and serious injuries to keepers were those at Picton Castle in February 1842, near Cardiff in March 1848, and at Clarach in January 1867.

Worried governments launched enquiries into the extent of the bloodshed. In Wales, where fish preservation was as important as that of game, some of the worst attacks were on water-bailiffs and other watchmen employed by the conservators. The climax of one confrontation was the 'second Rebecca riots' along the salmon rivers of mid-Wales in the later decades of the century.[69] About Rhaeadr and Newbridge a number of water-bailiffs were caught and severely beaten by bands of disguised poachers. The newspapers expressed outrage at the events, but there was another side to the story. Some of these bailiffs were tough ex-criminals, and gamekeepers, too, often started the violence. One appeared at the Mold police court in 1895 on a charge of assaulting a tenant farmer who was taking rabbits on his own land.

For obvious reasons, the authorities were anxious to remove constables from this area of perpetual conflict. When the police supported keepers and bailiffs, they were in turn subjected to popular hostility. The full extent of violence towards the parish and police constables is a matter of current historical debate. A search of the Great Session records at the turn of the century suggests that parish, and special, constables were often attacked by men and women, both when they came to the aid of bailiffs and when they were arresting and escorting prisoners. In the immediate post-war years, part-time constables Richard Williams of Rhuthun and Nicholas Miles of Newtown were singled out for brutal attention.[70] It seems that the first paid policemen in these Welsh towns had a very difficult time in executing certain municipal regulations. At Carmarthen there was a series of angry protests culminating in the Christmas Eve riots of 1828 when James Evans, the head constable, and his lock-up house were attacked.

Assaults on peace officers were a direct threat to county and national government, and partly for this reason they were listed separately in the records. The number of cases tried at the Assizes and Quarter Sessions was small, usually below twenty, but in the second half of the century an annual average of 643 assaults on the police were dealt with at Welsh Petty Sessions (Table 8). At least a quarter of the offenders came before the Cardiff, Newport and Swansea magistrates. Some of the assaults, as the diaries of constables James James of Merthyr and James Row of Pontypridd illustrate, were rather innocuous affairs, no more than the stubborn refusal of drunken or militant workmen to be arrested.[71] When related to population, the statistics of attacks on the police published after 1858 reveal an almost continuous decline. Can these figures be related, as some writers have suggested, to changes in working-class attitudes towards the new agents of the state? It is possible, though violent behaviour is not the only, or even perhaps the best, indicator of popular views.[72]

In the early days, there was a number of unpleasant incidents, as the professional police established their authority and objectives in the villages of Wales, and when they entered Merthyr's 'China' and other 'rough' urban districts for the first time. There were a few serious anti-police riots in the mid-century, notably the Newcastle Emlyn disturbances over several days in March 1845, when only 'the interposition of the better affected portion of the townspeople' saved the constables 'from a violent death'.[73] Much of the hostility shown towards the police sprang from their role in enforcing unpopular legislation, like the Poor Law Amendment Act of 1834. There was anger, too, when the men in blue appeared to act on behalf of landowners, especially over the game laws, and of industrialists, during wage disputes, as we shall see. But perhaps the greatest cause of trouble, and the spark that ignited the riots at Newcastle Emlyn, was the police support for the licensing laws and local Acts regulating behaviour in public places. Most of the violence against the police occurred at the weekend, when public houses and drinking clubs disgorged their inmates. At Glanconwy, for example, one late evening in 1895, labourer Enoch Hughes hit a policeman and, when he was arrested, his friends raced from the public house to the station and launched a second attack.[74] Once they reached their late twenties, most of these people gave up the fight, but for Grace Roberts of Llanrwst, John Garraghty of Bangor, and one or two others, it became a way of life.[75] Punishment was a prison sentence of three to six months, about twice as long as that for a common assault on someone else.

Many of the assaults which we have been describing were drink-related, and it makes sense, therefore, to look at the problem of drink here rather than with other victimless offences in chapter 5. The extent of drunkenness and disorderly conduct in Wales has always aroused controversy. The Methodist revival, and the work of others wishing to reform manners, had increased the awareness of the problem. The public house was regarded by many reformers of the early nineteenth century as the key institution of disorder, and towns like Swansea and Merthyr Tydfil had by-laws to bring it under greater control. However, the available statistics of the early nineteenth century do not suggest that, prior to the late 1820s, many people were actually punished for ale-house offences and drunkenness. The Beer Act of 1830 added to the difficulties of improvers, and its repeal, and

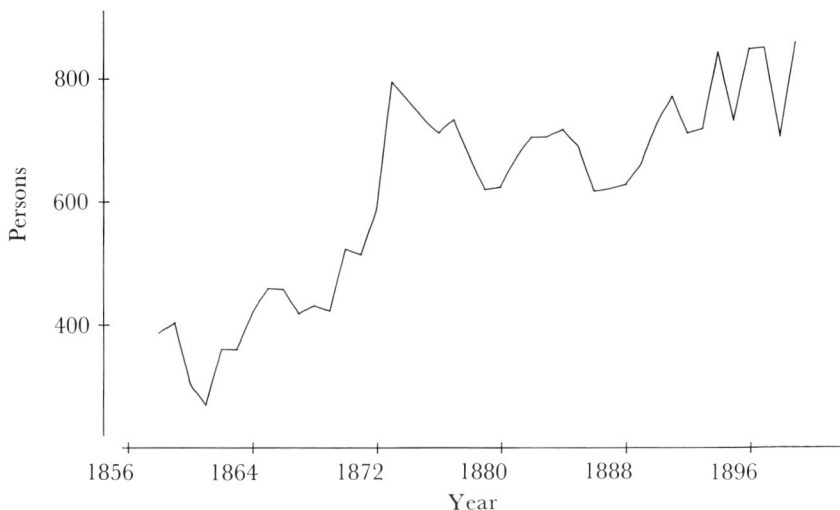

Basic rate: per 100,000 of population

Graph 11. Persons proceeded against for drunkenness, and for being drunk and disorderly, 1858–1899.

demands for more stringent licensing laws, became the subject of mass petitioning. The temperance and teetotal movements had considerable support in Nonconformist Wales. The arrival of the professional police forces was equally important; at last the drink reformers and the authorities had the means to check drunken behaviour. Unfortunately, the recording of this crime, and the prosecution of offenders, varied greatly from area to area, and from period to period. In some districts the police ignored much drunkenness, especially if respectable citizens were involved and when the inebriated caused no disturbance.[76] When David Smith, the Cardiff solicitor, was fined 5*s*. for being drunk and incapable, the mayor on the Bench said that it was an unusual and sad occurrence.[77]

Graph 11 must therefore be viewed with caution. It is a compilation of all cases of drunkenness, and drunken and disorderly conduct in Wales returned to the Home Office. More than four-fifths of people in these cases were convicted, a similar proportion were males, and punishment was usually a small fine. By the 1890s the number of persons before the courts had risen to such a height that it accounted for about a third of all cases at Petty Sessions. The rate of such proceedings, about one per 116 of the population in 1899, has rarely been been equalled since. In 1931 it was only half as bad. Magistrates of the late nineteenth century spoke about 'unprecedented signs of debauchery', and even the defenders of Wales wondered privately if this had become the 'besetting sin' amongst her 'lower classes'.[78] But the statistics reflected the impact of legislation, and the decisions of police committees and chief constables as much as any moral decline. The Caernarfonshire and Denbighshire police committees, under pressure from outside bodies, asked their police chiefs to consider charging every drunk 'found rambling' in the streets. In the land of Thomas Gee, it was no longer possible to ignore the noisy crowd reeling out of 'a wedding house' or celebrating Christmas Day. Indeed, the police caused many of the worst disorders by blundering arrests, first of the drunkard, and then of his rescuers. At Llansteffan, where constable John Morgan in 1891 pursued a rigorous campaign against heavy-drinking farmers and labourers, the counsel in one case said that this policeman had to understand that 'the Welsh were an exciteable race', and that all the village was against him.[79]

It was often claimed, especially at the time of the mid-century debate on education, that a Welsh man and especially a Welsh woman rarely drank to excess. The statistics do not support this; the rate of cases of drunkenness within the Principality was not that different from the one outside. What does emerge from the Welsh figures, however, is the disparity between the rural, industrial and urban situations, something which Benjamin Malkin had noted on his tours. In the 1850s the rate of drunkenness, and drunken and disorderly conduct, in Anglesey, Cardiganshire and Radnorshire was exceptionally low, fewer than one in 500 people being proceeded against in the Petty Sessions. By comparison, the rate for Glamorgan and Monmouthshire in the mid-century was nearer one in 300 and for Cardiff, Swansea and Newport worse than one in 100. What is interesting, and not well chronicled by contemporaries, was the subsequent rise in the rate of prosecutions in the three rural counties, of almost 400 per cent, to a peak in the 1877–9. Thereafter the rate fell, until a small rise at the very end of the century. In 1899 the inhabitants of Anglesey, Cardiganshire and Radnorshire were twice as good, in terms of court appearances, as those of Glamorgan and Monmouthshire.

The Petty Session registers confirm that rural as well as urban authorities had their 'Black List' of regular drunkards, and, in spite of the bands of hope and late-Victorian chapel frowns, there was even a little drunkenness amongst the sweethearts and wives of farm labourers. After the hiring fairs, Christmas Eve, and Whit Tuesday, magistrates in the countryside were always busy. In 1846 the Principal of the College at Trefecca, hardly an unbiased witness, claimed that it was rare to 'meet with farm servants returning from any considerable distance with their master's waggon or cart [without being] intoxicated, while it is quite lamentable to witness the number of drunken farmers returning from market on Saturdays.'[80] Respectable inhabitants of Builth, Brecon and Cardigan complained at the same time that young farm workers, in receipt of better earnings, crowded into their towns at weekends, and prevented all sleep with their drunken antics. By the late 1870s, on the eve of the Welsh Sunday Closing Act, there was some anxiety about this state of affairs, but the later descriptions of restrained behaviour by the rural population were, to some extent, borne out by the above statistics. Market days in the 1880s and 1890s had certainly lost much of their old excitement.

In the towns, drunken and disorderly behaviour was visible, annoying and occasionally alarming. The court returns from Cardiff, Swansea and Newport, within Graph 11, reveal that the rate of proceedings was highest in the late 1850s, though it rose again to a secondary peak in the early and mid-1870s. The Merthyr statistics, which run from the 1840s to the 1860s, are comparable. In 1858, the worst year, 532 people in this police district were convicted of drunkenness and twenty-three discharged. It is not too hard to imagine the live pictures behind these urban figures. One visitor to Bangor in 1841, who arrived about 8 a.m. on a Sunday, was astonished by the sight of drunken men and women brawling in the city, and twelve hours later he witnessed a repeat performance.[81] At Barmouth, and several other places, it was this conduct which brought residents together in the 1830s to demand better policing and lock-ups. What worried middle-class residents was the extension of drunken brawls, from the poorest districts into the main streets, and out into their suburbs. At Bangor, Tywyn and other towns along the Welsh coast, where people feared that such behaviour would drive holiday-makers away, the police spent their evenings moving drunken and disorderly seamen, prostitutes, vagrants and navvies out of sight. Drunken married women, one of the smallest categories, caused particular embarrassment; they were reminded, when their husbands were not, of the shame which they brought on their sex and family.[82] If they were chapel members, the elders took a similar line.

Contemporaries were convinced that this was a crime which became more prominent when the price of drink and food fell, and people had money to spare. Seamen arriving at Newport, Cardiff and Swansea sometimes spent the first weeks of their leave in and out of police custody, and it was widely reported in the mid-century that drunkenness was 'most of the trouble' with highly paid industrial workers. At Bagillt and Flint there were stories of the *noson lawen* degenerating into a continuous weekend drinking session. 'Drunkenness is the crying sin of our working class', said Revd Thomas Davies of the industrial parish of Trevethin in 1846, 'and by the facility which beer-houses afford of inducing people to drink, multitudes are led astray'.[83] Temperance groups, chapels and schools did their best, and the Wine and Beerhouse and Sunday Closing Acts of 1869 and 1881 were much praised, but the rate of drunkenness in Glamorgan and Monmouthshire rose relentlessly throughout the second half of the century.

The correlation between this rate and the movement of real wages on the south Wales coalfield was remarkably close, but it is worth noting that there, as elsewhere, the 'habitual drunkards' in the gaol registers were usually not the better-off workmen, but poor 'down-and-outs'. David Jenkins of Pontypridd, 'Peggy Clarach' at Aberystwyth, John 'Angel' Jones of Tywyn, and Daniel Jones in Carmarthen, all spent a lifetime cadging money for alcohol, fighting the police, and staggering from one cell to the next. Although fining was the recommended form of punishment, most of them could not afford to pay, and some courts anyway preferred the deterrent of a gaol sentence of seven or fourteen days.[84] The effect was minimal. John Stone, a wandering Bangor tailor, spent months in prison, but was still charged thirty-nine times between 1875 and 1895, confirming a chaplain's comment that such people were the most 'irrecoverable' of offenders. Ann Awbrey, the permanently 'drunk and disorderly prostitute' of Carmarthen, and Jane Griffiths, Elizabeth (Neathy) Jones and Mary Ann Williams, her counterparts at Caernarfon, Swansea and Newport, had over 176 convictions between them. Drunks, both male and female, were the archetypal criminals of late-nineteenth-century Wales, and the Inebriates Act of 1898 was designed to deal with the worst of them.

The extent of disorder, of an everyday variety, in nineteenth-century Wales is not easy to determine. In the 1830s and 1840s, when economic and social change was accompanied by political ferment and the mass immigration of starving Irish families, it was perhaps not too surprising that the leaders of urban society should complain about the numbers of people who were idle, disorderly and riotous, though the records do suggest that they had reason for their concern. As in the 1980s and 1990s, however, it seems that disorder was endemic in just a few districts within the biggest towns and seaports, and then only for a while. Merthyr's 'China' district was described as 'dangerous to enter' until 1843, when it was permanently settled by policemen who achieved their victory by hard physical conflicts with John Jones (Shoni Scuborfawr), the prize fighter and others. In this, and other large towns, however, the level of disorder seems to have dropped in the second half of the century, especially after the 1870s, whilst in the market towns life was comparatively peaceful, except at weekends.

In industrial Wales much depended on the size and character of the setting. In some of the smaller Flintshire and Glamorgan mining communities, it was said in the 1840s and 1850s that 'the people though ignorant are of very peaceable habits as a mass'. 'As a body they [the lead miners of Talargoch] may be described as sober, well conducted and quietly disposed men,' said the vicar of Meliden in 1856; 'seldom of late years has a fight taken place at the Meliden Monthly Fair – a thing of frequent occurrence at one time.'[85] The men of the quarrying communities to the west had a similar reputation. 'The Queen may be proud to rule over such a body of men', said one English traveller in 1869.[86] Elsewhere, in the large mining towns, there was, after the many complaints of 'riotous conduct' in the mid-century, also some evidence of improvement, but even in the 1870s and 1880s there was much street fighting, casual and organized, which James Row of Pontypridd, Fred Dagg of Aberdare and other policemen just about managed to control. 'A large crowd obstructing the highway. Dispersed them, and sent fighters home' was a typical entry in their journals between Friday and Tuesday nights. The Bedwellty and Tredegar court registers leave no doubt that profane language, disorderly behaviour, and assaults on the police were a fact of life on the south Wales coalfield in the 1890s, as they had been fifty years before.

On the state of the countryside, opinions were a little divided; whilst its population seemed essentially 'law-abiding', and, according to Lleufur Thomas, ever more 'temperate in their habits', there were reports of farm servants 'looking for life' on midnight jaunts, shouting at crossroads, and celebrating 'with excessive enthusiasm' the harvest season. Letter-books from Flintshire and Merioneth in the 1860s and 1870s reveal that village constables, no less than than urban, had to deal with disorderly and noisy inhabitants, and the vandalism of 'parties of young men'. On occasions the conflict owed something to the introduction of policemen where, for a long time, there had been none. Henry Simpson of the Flintshire Constabulary was told to leave one village in May 1868 because they disliked his 'interference' with their usual practice of playing and drinking on the highway.[87] At the end of the century, there were a few country places, like Llansantffraid in Montgomeryshire, which remained notorious for drunken hooliganism.

Apart from the close connection between the pub, drunkenness and disorder, contemporaries associated disturbances with the insolent young, sexually promiscuous females, outsiders of almost every kind, and the 'lower orders' at play. In Caernarfon and Pwllheli in the 1840s respectable inhabitants condemned virtually all those young people who were 'beyond the different religious circles'. Boys and girls were accused of spending 'all their free time' in drinking, gambling, fighting and throwing stones at the police, middle-class residents and church-goers. The Cardiff police were directed in the 1860s and 1870s to watch for 'the nuisance caused' by teenagers 'annoying residents'.[88] In the countryside, young farm servants were also condemned for chasing girls, and abusing middle-aged females and elderly cottagers. The newspapers in the second quarter of the nine-teenth century describe the range of their activities. There were weekend battles between the youths of neighbouring villages in the Teifi valley, whilst at Carno and Berriew in Montgomeryshire late-night revellers taunted the staid residents; and no fair day of that era was complete without a bruising encounter between 'the country lads' and the showmen, or with the special constables sworn in for the day.

Prostitutes, vagrants and other outsiders were often singled out as the most disorderly members of society. 'Ladies of the pave', especially Julia Carroll of Merthyr, 'the heroine of a hundred brawls' and Sarah Banner ('the great Western') of Carmarthen, had truly formidable reputations as fighters, and they often appeared in court charged with attacking each other. Beggars and vagrants were less inclined to cause trouble, though there were spectacular exceptions. It was, in fact, only too easy to blame outsiders for outbreaks of violence. As we have already seen, many of the breaches of the peace in places like Pembroke Dock and Swansea were attributed to seamen. The Irish were synonymous with trouble at Holyhead and Llanelli, whilst police sergeant Gill, and constables Jones and Nott, had their hands full with the imported dock-workers at Barry. Radnorshire's chief constables also found that railway navvies, vagrants and damn-builders were convenient scapegoats for conflicts in their county. Further north it was a similar story. The building of the Chester to Holyhead railway, and the one from Ffestiniog to Porthmadog, was accompanied by 'riots and affrays' along the way. It was, said a number of observers, only the close contact with railwaymen, quarrymen, fishermen, lead miners, and colliers which excited 'bad feeling' and 'disorder' amongst the normally peaceful farm workers.[89]

In many of these descriptions of disorder, it is difficult to decide whether the evidence reflected a decline in moral standards or changes in tolerance and policing. One can see this, for example, in relation to those customs and recreations of rural Wales which had an element of violence in them. Wild riding at weddings brought injuries and death, and the crowds demanding ale and gifts on Old and New Year's Day, watching Whit-Monday cock-fighting and badger-baiting, and playing football on Shrove Tuesday, sometimes turned very unpleasant indeed. At Cardigan, on 31 December 1859, the 'rabble', from within and without the town, finished the evening by throwing mud at houses, breaking windows and kicking in doors.[90] Those who suffered at these times, or who wished, like Revd Llewellin Llewellin of Lampeter, to reform the 'lower orders', left magistrates in no doubt that the villages and market towns of rural Wales were not yet havens of peace.

From the 1830s onwards the attempts to change the 'out-worn habits and customs' became more organized. At Llandysul the vicar, Revd Enoch James, won in 1837 his final victory in the sixteen-year-old battle against kicking football on Old Calan, and elsewhere prosecutions against cock-fighting, bull-running, and similar enjoyments were brought, and then withheld, on 'a promise not to do so in the parish again.'[91] By the early 1850s there were reports from all over the Principality that holidays were

now a time for Sunday School and Rechabite processions, and the contribution of the police to this was much applauded. Twenty years later the
old customs, like wild riding, are mentioned much less frequently. One
senses, from the speed with which the old ways disappeared, that there was
considerable support for these changes, but the effort to stop crowds, with
their torches, burning tar-barrels, guns and fireworks, celebrating Christmas
Eve and Guy Fawkes night was a more difficult business. The Dolgellau
police were trying and failing to outlaw the second of these riotous nights
as late as the 1880s.

There has been some debate about the manner in which village sports
and customs were carried over into industrial life. Popular recreations like
cock-fighting, chasing animals, foot racing, wrestling and prize fighting
seem to have initially flourished in the new towns. The first generation of
north Wales colliers were condemned for spending 'their leisure hours, and
the Sabbath in particular, in the public houses, in noise and riot; assembling together along the road-sides, or sauntering in the adjacent fields;
they had dog-fights, bull-baitings, and fights and broils amongst themselves.' These, and the work stoppages for fairs and festivals, were the
occasion for heavy drinking and crowd troubles. On the days of the Cefn
fair, above Merthyr, in the 1830s and 1840s, workmen 'perambulated the
streets, reeling, vomiting, and quarrelling,...'[92] Yet, if contemporaries are
to be believed, within a short time there was a 'revolution in [these] habits'.
'The brutal and brutalizing pastimes of our ancestors are now gone', said
one newspaper in 1857, adding three years later the rider that only the
'most ignorant and dissipated of the lower class of working men' clung to
the old ways. According to the description of the old Twynywaun fair near
Dowlais in the diary of constable Evans for 1872, improvement was slow.[93]

It was a short but important step from the disorder which we have just
described to the disturbances associated with communal discipline, social
and industrial tension and popular politics. Whenever a crowd gathered,
it was always possible that a peaceful procession or celebration could be
turned into an attack on their enemies. Welsh people in the eighteenth
century rioted over bread prices, militia laws, poor relief, the latest
commons enclosure and much more. They did so according to fairly strict
and well-understood rules, and in Wales, as elsewhere, there was considerable tolerance of this form of community politics. The turning-point in
attitudes was the 1790s when the unprecedented rioting was confused with
sedition, and when men of property organized themselves into defence
corps. For some time thereafter collective action was regarded by the
central government as criminal, dangerous and a threat to the established
order.

We have, in chapter 1, noted the manner in which the crowd imposed
its own brand of morality in respect of adultery, promiscuity, family

violence and the like. Occasionally the same crowd humiliated informers, bailiffs, policemen and any outsiders who had become obnoxious to them. Minorities were a likely target in any community, and nineteenth-century Wales witnessed several vicious attacks on those of the Roman Catholic and Jewish faiths, and on the English, the Irish, and other immigrants. People were man-handled and windows smashed during the agitation over the Roman Catholic Emancipation Act of 1829 and the 'papal aggression' in 1850–1. The rather ambiguous reaction of the authorities to such disturbances shows the wide support for this kind of community pressure.

Some of this violence occurred in a semi-rural setting, as when English railway workers at Bancyfelin and Ferryside in 1851 drove Irish navvies from their homes, but much of it was a feature of the industrial villages and towns.[94] Amongst the worst incidents were attacks on English and Irish workers near Mold, at Swansea, and along the heads of the valleys, all in the 1820s. In the most ferocious clashes, in the vicinity of the Bute and Tredegar ironworks in March 1826, the 'foreigners' agreed to return only with military protection.[95] In the mid-century there was even more violence, including the clashes with Cornish copper and lead miners at Amlwch and near Aberystwyth, the attacks on Lancashire men in Flint-shire, and other troubles at Pyle, Llantrisant, Dowlais and Nantyglo.[96] The use of Scottish and English blacklegs during the Tumble strike of 1893 provided perhaps the best example of crowd violence; in spite of Mabon's strictures, and the arrival of Llanelli policemen and the Inniskillen dragoons, a combination of processions, hymn-singing and naked aggression proved successful.[97]

Between 1879 and 1882 there was also a number of large anti-Irish demonstrations at Ebbw Vale and Tredegar, and twenty years later people remarked on the smouldering discontent over 'the Blacks' at Cardiff. During some of this violence, houses, shops, churches and synagogues were gutted, and a few men stabbed. Punishment for such crimes was selective; examples were made of ringleaders but many of the arrested, notably the youngest, were just bound over. As the police chiefs readily admitted, most of the clashes were short-lived, and not as serious as parallel conflicts in certain other countries, but it was an indication of tensions, especially over employment and wages.

'Athough a law-abiding people generally, the Welsh, when fully aroused by a sense of wrong, are very apt to take the law into their own hands', declared D.C. Davies in 1883, 'and, regardless of consequences to themselves, like their old turbulent and independent forefathers, try to eradicate the wrong by main force.'[98] He was seeking to explain the riots and rebellions that had occurred in the Principality since the days of Edward I. In our period the rural counties witnessed, in the Napoleonic War years, and just afterwards, both food and enclosure riots which needed soldiers to bring them under control. In addition there were the angry outbursts of squatters then, and indeed at various times throughout the century. The records of the courts reveal that the battle over common and waste land, and over grazing and turbary rights, was more protracted than has been acknowledged. Conflict took place between a variety of opposing groups, with the big men being as vindictive as the small. 'I am sorry to say, that in the enjoyment of these rights [grazing rights on common] there is,' said Thomas Frankland Lewis, MP for Radnorshire in 1844, 'the utmost possible violence exercised on the part of the strong against the weak,...' Across the uplands where his county met Cardiganshire, and in the hilly country of north Montgomeryshire, cottages were torn down, squatters removed, fences broken and animals killed in two Victorian generations of bitter, and largely hidden, warring. Better known were the evictions by landowners after the elections of 1868 and 1874, and the farmers' controlled response. Of organized direct action by farm servants and labourers there was remarkably little. 'Captain Swing' had a few poor followers in Flintshire, Montgomeryshire, Monmouthshire, Glamorgan, Carmarthenshire and Pembrokeshire, but the very nature of the rural economy and society in Wales made such open protests unlikely.[99]

Much of the village's anger at rapid economic, social and political change eventually found expression, in west Wales, in the Rebecca riots. Between 1839 and 1844 there were over 500 attacks on turnpike gates and, more worryingly, on other types of property and on persons.[100] The troubles convinced Queen Victoria's ministers of the need to implant professional police and soldiers in this, supposedly peaceful, part of her realm. The Caernarfonshire riots of 1859–67, when miles of walls were torn down, the 'second Rebecca' poaching raids across mid-Wales, which lasted even longer, and the extensive tithe riots of 1886–95, all indicated that perhaps Sir James Graham had been right. One is struck, however, in the last of these rural troubles, by the ritual and discipline. Beginning in north-east Wales the tithe riots quickly spread to mid and south-west Wales; crowds, who were summoned by horns in the manner of the Rebeccaites, tried with bludgeons, pitchforks and threats, to intimidate their enemies and reinforce solidarity amongst the farming community. When they failed, heads were broken, and auctioneers, bailiffs and policemen reviled. Discussion in the local councils and the Welsh press over the Tithe riots revolved around the question of whether too much, and insensitive, policing had been the catalyst which had turned a 'quiet people' into a furious mob.[101]

For a while in the early nineteenth century, the violence of industrial relations and popular politics was almost a fact of life. Peaceful trade-unionism took a long time to establish a permanent hold. In its place the workmen often resorted to forms of direct action, like destroying tools and pit props, and intimidating blacklegs, agents, and employers. In Mont-

The police and the Tithe riots, c. 1890

gomeryshire, during a five-week strike, weavers in 1830 smashed the windows of their masters in an attempt to equalize wages, and twenty-six years later the masons of Pembroke Dock turned in similar fashion upon unemployed workers seeking their jobs.[102] In some of these conflicts, the participants tried to legitimize their protests by wearing the costumes, and carrying the effigies and placards, of the *ceffyl pren*. The Talargoch lead miners, about whom we heard earlier, were encouraged to remain on strike in 1856 by a party of 'some twenty or thirty persons, some of whom were dressed in women's clothes, and carried firearms,...' Those caught by the police, at least in the lesser industrial disputes, could expect to spend two months in gaol.

Violence on a large scale was a matter of much greater concern, both to the magistrates and to the Home Office. In 1816 virtually the whole of the south Wales coalfield was brought to a halt by marching gangs, which intimidated workmen, threatened shopkeepers, and brushed aside armed special constables. Soldiers, in large numbers, eventually secured the peace, and this time the men's leaders were caught and sentenced. Despite the Prince Regent's pleasure at the outcome, one type of violence was replaced by another; during the next forty years on the eastern half of the coalfield the Scotch Cattle came and went. These miners, in their cattle skins, black faces and women's clothes, were the most obvious manifestation of direct action in industrial relations, but there were others.[103] Captain Napier had to deal with them all in Glamorgan, and yet by the mid-1840s his reports suggest that the attitude and behaviour of the miners were changing for the better.

In the mid-Victorian years industrial affairs were conducted in a more civilized fashion. The Anglesey miners strike of 1860, that of sailors at Holyhead in 1872, and the protests on the south Wales coalfield in 1853, 57–8 and 67–8, were notable for a 'degree of restraint and of discipline'.[104] The leaders of the men's unions counselled peaceful agitation, and won much support for their stance. Of course, illegal activity, either covert protest or open violence, still continued in the mining areas. Tensions during the late 1860s led to clashes with the police, sabotage, and worse. The deaths and injuries at Mold in 1869 and in the Rhiwabon area in the spring of 1882 were a reminder of the dangers of industrial conflict, and the century ended with violence from south Wales dockers and hauliers, and North Wales quarrymen.[105]

The number of court cases of people charged with rioting was never very large. Only twenty people per year, on average, stood trial at the higher courts between 1834 and 1899 on charges of riot, sedition, breach of the peace and pound-breach. The figures reached a peak in the years 1839–44, when the average was seventy-six, but after 1855, and even more so after the early 1860s, the graph falls very sharply indeed. In the second quarter of the century, when these cases were comparatively numerous, a rising proportion of the proceedings was the outcome of political demonstrations. During the most serious of these, Home Secretaries became rather cynical about the popular myth that the Welsh were a peaceful race, with a deep sense of loyalty to the crown.

The first memorable experience of Welsh street politics was in 1831, when the Reform crisis produced rioting in at least a dozen towns, as well as the Merthyr rising, a determined attempt to by-pass the polite politics of the Westminster élite.[106] This was followed eight years later by an even more alarming affair, the Newport insurrection, the high-point of physical-force Chartism, and the most bloody battle on mainland Britain in the nineteenth century.[107] There was much interest in the effects which this defeat had on the 'rebellious Welsh'. In a short period of time, it was claimed that people had become more 'careful and provident', and changed their hopes and priorities.[108] The contribution of the continuous military and police presence towards this re-adjustment is hard to quantify; contemporaries were inclined to give more credit to the new efforts in the field of popular education, and to the beneficial influences of economic change and social reform. There was nothing subsequently, despite the beginnings of a general strike in 1842, the Fenian outrages in south Wales, and attacks on Anglesey police stations in 1887, to match the scale and seditious motives of the Chartist rising, but the political scene remained lively. The conflict between Liberals and Tories in 1868 resulted in ugly demonstrations, especially in Gwent, where £4,000 of damage was done.[109] Nor did it end there, for inhabitants of north and mid Wales had to face more election riots during the next twenty-seven years. So, for that matter, did many other districts in Britain; as Donald Richter reminds us, even the late Victorians were more riotous than we imagine, and the police liked to have troops standing by.[110]

It is not easy, therefore, to make a final, definitive, statement about the level of violence in nineteenth-century Wales. The amount of homicide and grievous bodily harm was, when compared with the rest of the British Isles, low. It was probably lower than it had been in early modern times. Family feuding, clashes over honour, status and property, electoral politics, highway robberies, and burglaries now resulted in few deaths, and when people were attacked they often received only minor injuries. There were certainly more petty assaults recorded in our period than in the eighteenth and for much of the twentieth centuries. The statistics of Graphs 8 and 9, and Table 5, show that during the second and third quarters of the nineteenth century, prosecutions for assaults were high, except perhaps in the countryside. The pattern, which is mirrored elsewhere in western Europe, could have been the result of more violent behaviour, or of changes in attitude, prosecution and policing.[111] Many people, including

Henry Thomas, chairman of the Glamorgan Quarter Sessions, believed that the former was true, and argued that mid-Victorian life was exceptionally violent, drunken and disorderly.

Whether this amounted to a serious threat to the social and political structure was a different matter. Much of the casual violence, though not all of it, was ignored by governments, but popular disturbances, on the other hand, always evoked a response. The risings of 1831 and 1839, and the Rebecca troubles of 1839–44 made a deep impression on the political leaders of Britain, especially so because of the reputation which Wales enjoyed. Great efforts were made to explain, and end, such dangerous protests. 'It was the remarkable political success of the second half of the century', writes John Saville, 'that violence from below became localised; in political terms it was marginalised.'[112] After the mid-century there was a change in the threat posed by public violence. Rioting continued, especially at times of local and general elections, but it was more predictable and, for various reasons, less of a danger to the state. Other forms of disorder were also curbed, not least by the presence of more policemen who gave the task a high priority. It was harder, in both village and town, to continue some of the customs and practices of the old communal culture, and funerals, weddings, fairs, markets and other occasions for gatherings became more respectable, even dull. By the 1880s and 1890s the transformation was evident to all. In his last report of the century the Cardiganshire chief constable expressed his delight that 'the carrying of effigies', and other types of 'unseemly conduct' were 'a thing of the past'. Although he wished to give his policemen the credit, these changes in public behaviour were the outcome of many developments.[113]

The parallel changes in private behaviour in the last decades were more difficult to uncover and explain. The decline in recorded assaults seems to have been a little slower than that in England. It began after the 1830s or 1850s in some places, and generally after the late 1870s. By 1891 only one in 968 of the inhabitants of Anglesey, Cardiganshire and Radnorshire were charged with common assault, and one in 244 in Cardiff, Swansea and Newport. Family violence and most other types of offences against the person also appeared to be declining, though the statistics of serious violence and sexual assaults, which were associated with the areas and the practice of heavy drinking, rose in the 1880s and 1890s. The rate of serious offences against the person did, however, descend in the early twentieth century, confirming the general feeling that life, like property, had never been safer. This rejection of violence was, so contemporaries tell us, especially marked amongst women and slowest amongst the poorest, least educated and most mobile members of society. The behaviour of the powerless seemed, not for the first or last time, to be the least rational.

Historians, as well as criminologists, are divided over whether these trends in the criminal statistics have any value in themselves or whether they simply reflect the political and social interest in violence. As we have seen, people in the early modern period had a greater tolerance of brutality and could do less about it. In the late eighteenth and early nineteenth centuries attitudes changed somewhat, perhaps encouraged by the great social changes, evangelicalism, and fears of revolution. 'There was', argues one historian, 'some shifting of the line dividing acceptable from unacceptable conduct and a strengthening of feelings of shame, guilt, and repugnance about acts that had once raised no eyebrows.'[114] The sensitivity of people like the vicar of Nefyn to 'profane language and swearing', threatening behaviour, and the slightest sign of disorder was extraordinary by any standards. Yet, as the danger of upheaval receded after the mid-century, and as the urban middle class moved out to their suburbs and the regular police patrols began, it has been suggested that the interest of authority in violent behaviour might have declined.[115] It was, after all, much more of an immediate threat to working-class men and women than to anyone else; very few of the victims of assaults in Table 3 were of the upper and middle class.

One wonders, however, whether the watch committees and police constables really did relax their efforts. Instead, it appears from their records that as one small victory was achieved they moved on to another. At Flint in 1895 the mayor took up the problem of 'a lot of young fellows who made a practice of standing round street corners, and making insulting remarks to the people. It must be done away with.'[116] Even if middle-class people lost some interest in private and public violence, there is evidence that poor men and women kept the police courts busy with their complaints. A desire to have a peaceful life was something which crossed class lines. Barry's Trades Council in 1898 welcomed firm action in their town against the kind of language and behaviour which had annoyed the mayor of Flint, and the police were occasionally thanked by working-class residents for curbing disorder.[117]

The overwheming impression, therefore, is that private and public behaviour was actually improving at the end of the century. It was, on reflection, much as Francis Place and Edwin Chadwick had predicted. They had been hopeful that the very process of modernization, with its emphasis on individualism, efficiency and order, and the need for education and controls, would gradually civilize the population. After the mid-century, there were more and more references to 'better manners' and the 'orderly and sober' attitudes of working people. Although perceptions of violence vary greatly according to age, sex, class and place, there was a general concurrence in Alfred Marshall's comment: 'all ranks of society are rising; on the whole they are better and more cultivated than their forefathers were...'[118] In the early decades of the twentieth century, the rate of offences against the person fell sharply, as did that of drunkenness.

The improvement was attributed to economic confidence, religious and educational initiatives, new ways of spending leisure, and better policing. By the 1880s many people were living in communities where controls and culture worked, externally and internally, in favour of a more peaceful resolution of tension and conflict and a greater sensitivity towards the appalling effects of violence and cruelty. 'Reason', said H.H. Vivian in 1876, in a statement which was of wider significance than he intended, 'has asserted her sway'.[119] Of course, there remained areas of concern; at the end of the century there were complaints about the extent of drunkenness, street violence and sexual assaults in the Welsh mining towns and seaports, and the industrial disturbances of the 1890s were a harbinger of much worse to come. Until all this was controlled, chief constables doubted whether the police could ever give sufficient time to their other task of preventing and solving property crimes.

4
Crimes against Property

Crimes against property comprised, for at least half of the nineteenth century, the largest group of offences dealt with in the courts. At least seventy-five per cent of cases at the Assize and Quarter Sessions, and up to twenty-five per cent at the Petty Sessions, were of this type. This was not, when set in a wider ideological and social context, too surprising. One historian of the early modern period has written of a 'transition from a general concern over order to a more limited one concentrating on the defence of property'.[1] The eighteenth century was a commercial age, when new forms of wealth were being developed and when, especially in Wales, people were becoming more concerned about the ownership of mountain, common and waste land, and about rights over the seashore, rivers, woods, footpaths, and industrial resources. Laws in defence of property filled the statute books, many of them having been passed in fairly recent times. Amongst the most famous legislation of the eighteenth century was the Black Act of 1723, which created a number of capital offences, the Acts introduced to protect banking and commercial arrangements, and the laws which outlawed certain gleaning, hunting and fishing practices. For the legislators at least, the threats to property seemed more real than the problem of violence.

The support for strict laws in defence of property was wider than at first appeared. If, as Adam Smith, William Blackstone and others insisted, the major function of eighteenth-century law was to safeguard the ruling élite and its property, it was also true that many of the lower middle class and working class shared the anxiety about losing what they had so carefully earned.[2] Although, as we saw in chapter 1, petty thefts were not always prosecuted in village communities, and, although some of the new legislation was disliked and resisted, it would be wrong to exaggerate the tolerance of property offences.[3] If they understood the forces which gave rise to this type of crime, when they were its victim ordinary people used the courts. There was, as the cases of slander and even suicide indicate, considerable shame attached to accusations of stealing.[4] By the end of the century, about the worst thing that could still be said about Taffy was that he was a thief.

How much of a thief Taffy really was cannot easily be ascertained. Much depended on where Taffy lived, and what moment in time is chosen.

In the villages of the eighteenth century one has the impression that there was a large amount of borrowing, poaching, mouching, gleaning, and sharing of goods, which was on the very margins of legality. It was simple to remove items, and, if there were a complaint, to return them. A great deal was tolerated, depending to an extent on the character of the person concerned and his or her relationship with the victim. The wealthier members of society often permitted workmen to have their perks and the poor to collect cheap fuel, whilst cottagers, too, accepted that the hungry had to survive. Only occasionally was legal action taken, perhaps against a persistent offender, an outsider, an awkward employee and a vindictive neighbour, and then efforts were made to save them from being tried for a capital offence. Other controls and sanctions were preferred to restrain and punish thieves. For most of the early and mid eighteenth century the number of indictments for property crime was small.[5]

Late in that century more complaints about offences against property were laid before the magistrates, and the prosecutors included large numbers of artisans and labourers as well as people of the middle and upper classes (Table 2). Exactly why this increase happened is not clear, though the most thorough treatment of the subject suggests that it reflected both an actual increase in property crimes and a growing intolerance of them.[6] By the turn of the century the great majority of cases at the higher courts were of this type, and the rate of these prosecutions continued to rise, especially in the post-war years, the early 1840s, the late 1840s and early 1850s. The police and judicial statistics of the most numerous property crimes, namely stealing, larceny, pickpocketing and other offences 'committed without violence', reached a peak in the mid-century and fell to a low point in the 1870s, only to rise again sharply in the early 1880s, before a last long decline (Graphs 14 and 15).

The other graphs, of robbery, burglary and break-ins, of arson and malicious offences against property, of embezzlement and fraud, and of breaches of the game laws, follow slightly different lines. The statistics for all these crimes are unsatisfactory for the first half of the century, but Graph 12 confirms the literary evidence that such offences were becoming more common. In the second half of the century, the rate of malicious damage to property and offences against the game laws remained on a high plateau from the late 1860s to the early 1880s, before falling, like most property crime rates, in the last fifteen years of the century (Graphs 18 and 19). Burglary, break-ins, robberies and white-collar crimes are the exceptions to this general rule. Graphs 12, 13 and 17 reveal their similarities with, and the differences from, other rates of property crime. The rates of burglary and embezzlement were comparatively high at the end of the century. This was important, because both types of crime had, and still have, a considerable impact on public opinion, but the number of court

Basic rate: per 100,000 of population

Graph 12. Persons committed for trial, or bailed, for offences against property, committed with violence, 1834–1857.

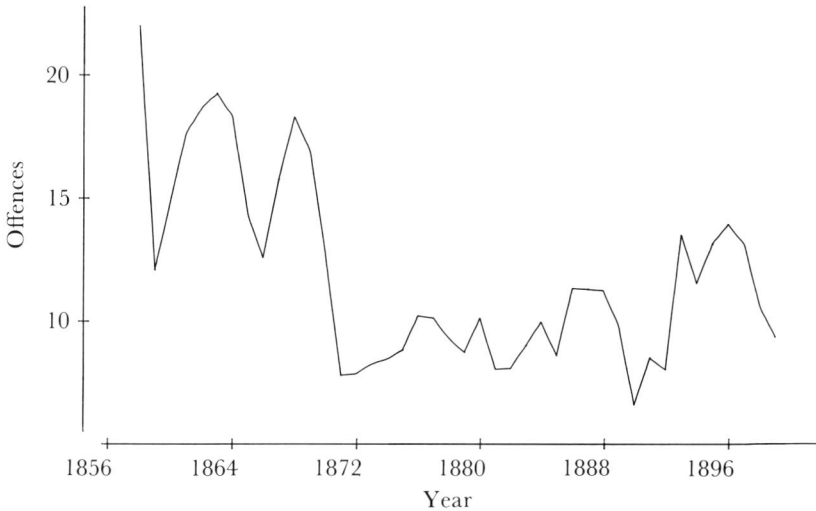

Basic rate: per 100,000 of population

Graph 13. Indictable offences against property, committed with violence, and known to the police, 1858–1899.

Basic rate: per 100,000 of population

Graph 14. Persons committed for trial, or bailed, for offences against property, committed without violence, 1834–1857.

Basic rate: per 100,000 of population

Graph 15. Reported indictable offences against property, committed without violence, and offences of stealing, embezzlement and receiving stolen goods determined summarily, 1858–1899.

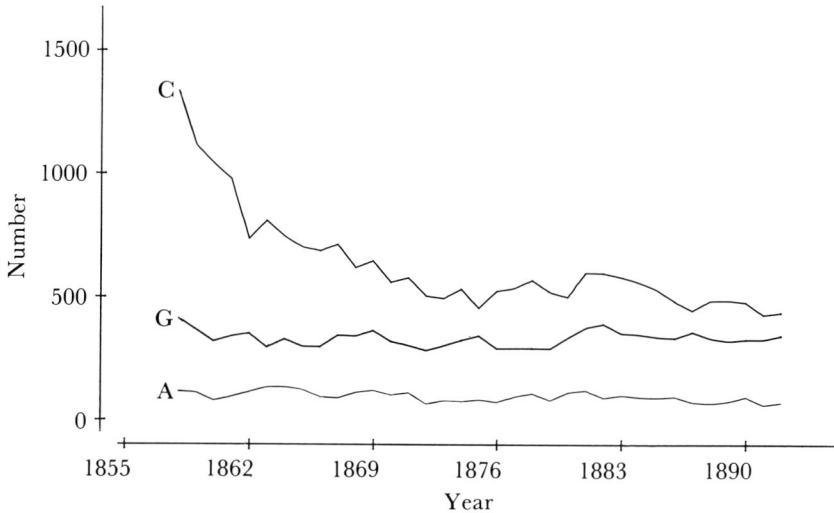

Basic rate: per 100,000 of population

Key: A Anglesey, Cardiganshire and Radnorshire
G Glamorgan and Monmouthshire
C Cardiff, Swansea and Newport

Graph 16. Offences of stealing in rural and industrial counties, and in urban communities, 1858–1892.

cases hardly justified the interest shown in them in 1900. The overwhelming impression, to be gleaned from the returns, is that people's property at the end of the century had never been safer. Taffy was becoming less of a thief. When compared with that of England for 1891, the Welsh rate of property crimes was significantly better.

The scale and character of Taffy's thieving varied from one community to another. If we take the figures of reported indictable offences against property committed with and without violence, and combine them with cases of stealing, embezzlement, receiving and game-law offences dealt with at the lower courts, there was in 1861 one of these crimes for every 318 of the Welsh population. This was, in sharp contrast to the offences discussed in the last chapter, similar to the rate of property crime in the years after the First World War, though burglaries and break-ins were then more common and larcenies less. The rate in the three rural counties of Anglesey, Cardiganshire and Radnorshire in 1861 was one in 621, in Glamorgan and Monmouthshire one in 255, and in Cardiff, Swansea and Newport, which were excluded from the county totals, one in ninety-nine. This was close to the figures for common assault mentioned in the last chapter. So it seems, at least superficially, that not only life but property also was safest in the countryside. Thirty years later the three rates in the

Crime in nineteenth-century Wales

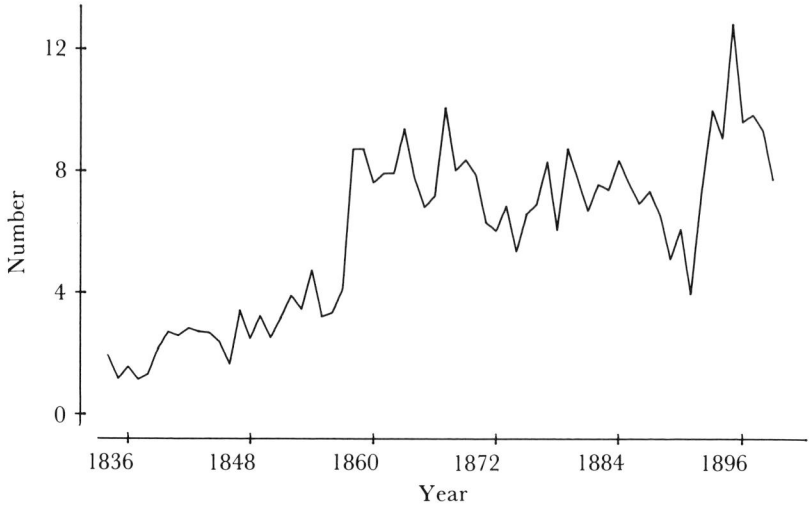

Basic rate: per 100,000 of population

Graph 17. Embezzlement and fraud: persons proceeded against at Assizes and Quarter Sessions, 1834–1857, and indictable cases reported, 1858–1899.

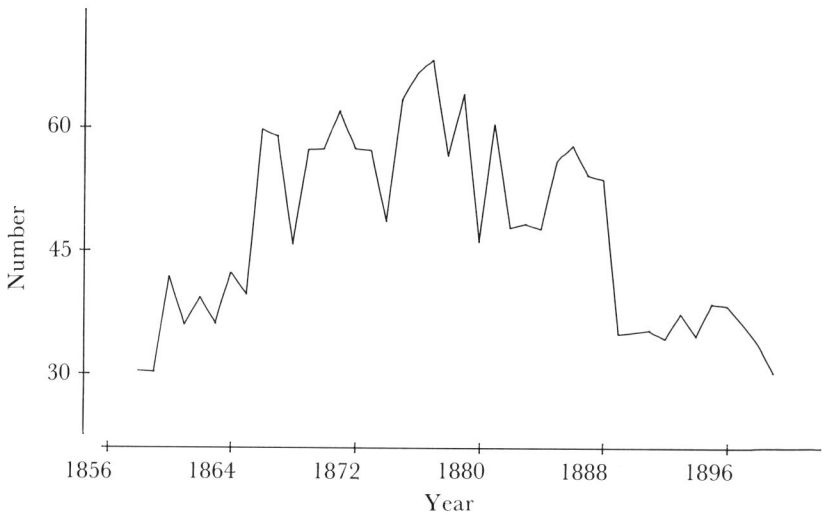

Basic rate: per 100,000 of population

Graph 18. Offences against the Game Laws, determined summarily, 1858–1899.

Basic rate: per 100,000 of population

Graph 19. Indictable offences of malicious destruction of property known to the police, and offences of malicious damage determined summarily, 1858–1899

rural, industrial and urban areas had improved to one in 968, 258, and 219.

These differences came as no surprise to contemporaries. They were convinced that the restraints on thieving in the countryside were stronger and the opportunities more limited. The controls were of a moral and physical kind, and internal as well as external. As Benjamin Malkin and other visitors noted early in the century, the rural poor had low expectations, and bore privations with remarkable stoicism. John Beattie tells us that only real necessity produced peaks in the level of recorded property crime in the eighteenth century. Thieving was not well regarded in the village, though whether, as D. Parry-Jones states, it was 'the most despicable crime' is open to doubt.[7] It was certainly a risky activity; the chances of being identified as the criminal were considerable, and the consequences hard to predict. Robbery, burglary and stealing were difficult in a community where people knew each other well. This was one reason given for 'almost a total absence of all serious crimes among agricultural labourers,...the offences that are most commonly met with are petty pilfering and trespassing in search of game and fish...'[8] The wives of these labourers, who spent less time outside the home as the century wore on, had few chances to steal anything. Between a third and a half of apprehended rural criminals were, in fact, either servants who had the opportunity and the secrecy to purloin goods, or tramps who passed through the villages at speed.

Apart from what was standing and moving in the fields, and kept openly about barns and dwelling houses, not many goods were immediately accessible in the countryside. Almost half of the 317 out-of-court convictions in Flintshire between 1815 and 1830 were for poaching and taking milk and wood.[9] According to the Merioneth police occurrence books of the 1880s, a quarter of rural property crime was poaching, 14 per cent was the stealing of clothes, often from lines and hedges, 12.5 per cent was malicious damage, including arson, 11 per cent was the stealing of animals and fowls, and the rest was fairly even divided between breaking and entering, embezzlement and obtaining goods by false pretences, thefts of cash, removal of jewellery and clocks, the taking of tools and knives, the illegal collection of fuel, and the consumption of food and drink.[10] Most of the goods stolen in the countryside were kept by the thieves, but there was a small illegal trade with hawkers and dealers. Although the proportion of food thefts in Merioneth was lower than in other analyses of eighteenth- and nineteenth-century rural crime, we should not make too much of this. As we shall see, there were offences in the countryside, like the milking of cows and the taking of vegetables and underwood, which were greatly under-represented in these police books.

In the industrial districts and towns of Wales the situation was rather different. One of the complaints about these places in the early nineteenth century was that they lacked controls and offered temptations. Without the influence of the squire, the church and even perhaps the close community, the people were said to have grown daring, independent, and acquisitive. There were claims that the simplicity and integrity of the 'lower orders' had been subverted by the affluence, freedom and modern values of city life. This applied, as we shall see in chapter 6, to women and juveniles as well as to adult males; all seem to have committed many more crimes in the town than in the village. The town had two physical benefits for these thieves; there was much accessible and valuable property which was poorly protected, and the environment offered some anonymity for offenders and places to dispose of their booty. The disadvantages, which helped to keep the urban crime rate above the rural, was the extensive police presence and a greater willingness to prosecute.

The character of recorded property crime in Merthyr and Cardiff in the third quarter of the century, illustrates some of these points.[11] A quarter of the goods stolen was clothing, another fifth were coal, wood and metals, fifteen per cent were watches, silver and other valuables, ten per cent were food and drink, and five per cent was cash. An analysis of the juvenile cases produces a similar result, but gives a higher proportion of thefts of food, drink, coal, metals, tobacco, cigars and snuff. Many of these goods were taken from shops, stalls, workshops, sheds, and doorways, as well as from houses, drinking places and hotels. Burglary, break-ins and robbery were usually more common in the towns than the villages, and so was removing cash, watches and handkerchieves from the person. Of the above total of property crime in Merthyr and Cardiff, fifteen per cent of cases were of stealing from the person, an offence which was rare in the villages, and which was gradually disappearing from the towns.

The pattern of modern property crime which has caused anxiety in the late twentieth century can already be seen in embryonic form in the largest towns of Wales before the end of our period. In 1888, and 1895, for instance, there were ninety-eight burglaries, break-ins and violent robberies reported to the police in Cardiff. This, in a town of some 129,000, was almost a quarter of the Welsh total. Members of the watch committee discussed measures 'to suppress...this nightmare', and the police force was increased by ninety-nine men in the last decade. It was a natural response, but in the long term, as Graph 16 shows, Cardiff, Swansea and Newport, as well as the rural counties, and, to a lesser extent, the industrial counties, experienced a general decline in property crime during the last quarter of the century. In addition, there were reductions about the same time in the rate of female and juvenile thieving. One of the country's leading statisticians, examining this evidence, argued that everyone should give thanks for an 'exceptional immunity from crime'.[12]

The statistics of property crimes, which will be used in the rest of this chapter, must, however, be regarded with suspicion. It is worth reminding ourselves that information about property offences in the nineteenth century came mainly from the victims. There is evidence in the police occurrence books that some people were too keen to report thefts, whilst others were the reverse. 'Felonies and other offences from time to time reported', said the Caernarfonshire chief constable in 1861, 'have turned out on subsequent enquiry to have originated through mistakes or through wilful perversion of the truth'.[13] In rural counties scores of angry vagrants were accused of property crimes which never took place; farm animals had simply strayed, and householders later recalled that they had mislaid or sold the 'stolen goods'. In a few instances, when animals were killed and property set on fire, the damage was self-inflicted. On the other hand, many crimes were not reported, or at least never reached the courts of Assize, Quarter and Petty Sessions. Landowners and industrialists relied on insurance policies to recover some losses, and, like lesser fry, kept quiet about petty misdemeanours, saving face and money. Everyone knew that the detection rate for certain crimes hardly justified the bother of reporting them.

Three groups of crimes make the point about the problems of relying on the official statistics: wrecking, currency offences, and embezzlement and fraud. The first of these flourished in the eighteenth century, in spite of its being a capital offence. It was a crime easy to commit, and difficult to prevent. The establishment of coastguards along the Welsh coast early in the nineteenth century made a difference, but less perhaps than was suggested. Richard Scott, commander of the Porthcawl coastal station, said in 1839 that when ships were wrecked in the area, local families refused to give up the old, illegal, claim to a portion of their contents.[14] In Denbighshire in 1824 there was a similar feeling that stealing from wrecks was 'no great moral offence'. The Carmarthenshire Proclamation Society, appalled by the situation in the post-war years, distributed a sermon by the rector of Bishopston church, Swansea, on the evils of plundering from wrecks, and promised rewards to informers. On the Cefn Sidan sands, by the mouth of the river Gwendraeth, a notorious danger spot for shipping, stewards of Lord Cawdor, magistrates, clergymen and special constables fought the crowds with swords. Even when the authorities rescued the goods lying on the beach, they were sometimes stolen from the warehouses a few days later.

The formation of county police forces, and the appointment of many excise, customs and coastguard officers, increased the risks for looters, but the attraction of sudden wealth was overwhelming, and people entertained the fanciful notion that at the very least they could obtain a reward for the return of the goods. When the *Royal Charter*, with 400 passengers and 79,000 ounces of gold, was washed onto the rocks near Moelfre in Anglesey, fortunes were made overnight. One of the problems, of course, was disposing of such valuables. People who tried to sell ship's stores in Carmarthen, Haverfordwest and Llanelli markets were pounced upon and dealt with at the Petty Sessions.[15] By the end of the century wreck-plundering was in decline, in both south and north Wales. Public attitudes towards the offence underwent a gradual change. At no time, however, was the number of wreckers reported and arrested very large.

The same was true of those who made money from counterfeiting coins and forging banknotes. Each year no more than a score of people came before the higher courts for offences against the currency, the rate declining after the 1850s. Besides pedlars, hawkers and other mobile 'smashers', those convicted included tradesmen, craftsmen and housewives. The full-time criminals worked in pairs and gangs, calling at fairs and markets wherever possible. In the last years of the war, and especially in the post-war depression, hundreds of people seem to have been involved in the business. Although the evidence is missing, it is possible that some of these travellers were part of large criminal networks of coiners, such as have been found in the seventeenth and eighteenth centuries. Caernarfon and Cardigan posted up warnings about the danger which these people posed 'to trade'. At Caernarfon in 1810, one of the worst years, the constables managed to arrest husband-and-wife teams who had packs of counterfeit notes and were about to make a killing at the fairs.[16] Of the women who were apprehended, most were taken simply for passing illegal notes and coins, though Sarah Chandler and Margaret Watkins, who were transported from Radnorshire and Monmouthshire in 1817, were skilled forgers.[17]

The ability to make fine replicas of banknotes was highly prized. In the winter of 1817–18, after superb reproductions had been found across south Wales, the equipment which had produced some of them was discovered in a house at St Clears. William Baines, one of the operators of this machinery, offered to share his secrets with the Bank of England in exchange for a pardon from the death penalty.[18] A death sentence, sometimes commuted to transportation, was not uncommon at this time for the worst offences; poor John Greenwood had the gruesome honour in May 1812 of being the last person to be publicly hanged in Merioneth. Within fifty years, the punishment had been reduced to a few years imprisonment, or less. At the same time, the uttering of false currency was made more difficult because of the new police forces and the first detectives. In Merthyr, during 1840, constables James Millward and Thomas Thomas confiscated a mould which had been responsible for the 'great glut of base coin at present current in this vicinity', and when a gang in the winter of 1850 flooded towns in south Wales with forged £5 notes, prompt police action and a reward of £50 resulted in the arrest of the ringleaders.

It was many years before the same policemen devoted much of their time to white-collar crimes like embezzlement and fraud.[19] They have always been amongst the most under-reported of offences. Action in the courts against abuses in the commercial world was infrequent and difficult. Graph 17 is therefore of limited value, but it does indicate that the cases known to the police reached a peak late, in the mid-1890s. At the end of the century, as the interest in middle-class offenders grew amongst social scientists, there was an uncomfortable feeling that perhaps this class was as criminal as the working class.[20] In the days before special police squads and private investigators, it was hard to obtain information on embezzlement and fraud. Companies often preferred private cautions and dismissals to public action, and only changed their mind when the swindling became too great and embarrassing. Thus when Robert Jones Evans, a clerk of Llanwnda in Caernarfonshire, appeared in court in 1893, his sentence of eighteen months hard labour was for a succession of frauds and thefts. Ten years before, the clerk of the Nantlle Vale Building Society, anticipating a similar downfall, departed for Canada, with several thousand pounds.[21] The Post Office was a keener prosecutor, demanding punishment which would serve as an example to all their employees. One of their clerks, convicted in 1862 at Cardiff, of embezzling 10*s*. 6*d*. and twelve stamps, received a sentence of four years penal servitude.[22]

The number of legal proceedings was small. In 1899 sixty-one people were committed for trial accused of embezzlement and fraud, and fifteen for forgery, whilst an additional thirteen cases of embezzlement were dealt with at the lower courts. In the last group of cases, only a few pounds were taken, but some of the other crimes involved thousands. Typically, there was one court case for every two offences reported to the police, and the annual rate of convictions, as for most property crimes, varied between sixty and seventy-five per cent. Punishment of twelve months imprisonment was quite common, though the Cardiff solicitor who received this in 1882 for forging three cheques to the value of £16. 6*s*. 10*d*. was apparently surprised by his fate. A number of his profession were charged with white-collar crimes, as were accountants, and especially clerks and agents. Representatives of insurance companies and mail order firms, and ticket collectors of all kinds, were accused of withholding some of the money which passed through their hands. When they eventually appeared in court the public and the press took an exceptional interest in them.

Fraud took many forms. Members of the middle class gained money dishonestly by false wills, deeds and orders, whilst the working class concealed and removed household articles in an attempt to defraud creditors. So far as one can tell, obtaining goods and money by false pretences had always been an attractive proposition, but it was one, said the chairman of the Monmouthshire Quarter Sessions in 1880, which was becoming increasingly popular.[23] It was committed by a wide section of society. Agents cheated clients, businessmen stayed at hotels without paying the bill, and married men defrauded enlisting officers. Farmers also obtained advances by pretending that they had a sale coming, and beggars played confidence tricks on gullible housewives. William Williams took money from people across south Wales by pretending that he had been cruelly treated by the French during the Napoleonic Wars, and other charlatans preached chapel sermons and then disappeared with the collections.[24]

If one were known to the victim it was harder to escape detection. Men and women bought clothes and boots on credit, giving the name of a relative or employer as surety. Margaret Griffiths, a 24-year-old from St Mellons, was transported in 1814 for calling at shops in Cardiff, taking food, clothing, and other goods, and promising that her husband would pay later.[25] Unscrupulous servants, at the beginning of the hiring year, told credulous tradesmen that their masters had agreed to pay for a set of clothes and boots. In 1885 Merioneth magistrates publicly reprimanded a shopkeeper who had given a 16-year-old girl items of clothing on the strength of a pencilled note, supposedly from her employer.[26] Perhaps to ward off such embarrassment, other victims refused to reveal similar

Table 9

The main offences against property dealt with at Assizes, Quarter Sessions and Petty Sessions in 1861

Burglary and break-ins	79
Robbery	18
Embezzlement	12
Receiving stolen goods	31
Fraud	45
Forgery and offences against the currency	12
Cattle, horse and sheep stealing	17
Offences against the Game Acts	462
Larceny, to the value of £5, in dwelling houses	11
Larceny, from the person	89
Larceny, by servants	33
Larceny, simple	391
Larceny, by offenders under 16 years (Criminal Justice Act)	259
Larceny, under the value of 5s., on pleading guilty	1162
Larceny, or larceny from the person, attempts to commit	355
Stealing fruit and vegetables	158
Stealing fencing and wood	42
Stealing trees and shrubs	36
Arson	8
Malicious destruction, wilful damage and trespass	934
Total	**4154**

Source: PP, 1862, LVI.

examples of duplicity to police and magistrates. Fraud, together with embezzlement and stealing from one's employer, was one of the under-reported crimes; a court case was sometimes a carefully considered exercise in public relations.

This examination of white-collar crimes, as well as of coining and wrecking, has illustrated the difficulties of estimating and characterizing property crime in the nineteenth century. There was a vast amount of illegal activity, much of which was hidden from contemporaries, and thus from historians. The public perception of property crime then, as now, was largely influenced by the court cases about which they read each week. Table 9, a compilation of proceedings at the Assizes, Quarter and Petty Sessions in 1861, is an analysis of the Welsh prosecutions. It is no more than a snapshot. Certain of the crimes, such as highway robbery and coining, belong to an earlier age, whilst others were a sign of things to come. The main value of the table, for the reader, is that it provides a reference point for the detailed discussion of property crime in the rest of this chapter.

Of the all those listed in the table, offences against property committed with violence have always received the most attention.[27] This category included burglaries, break-ins of domestic and commercial property, highway and street robberies, sacrilege, and piracy. The number of these offences was small; despite the publicity and anxiety about them, no more than 274 cases were reported to the police in a year, and of these a high proportion were committed in Glamorgan and Monmouthshire, with Cardiff pre-eminent. It was widely believed that the rate of these crimes rose with real wages, but a comparison between Graphs 12 and 13, and 7, reveals that such a simple explanation is inadequate. The rate was at its height between 1850 and 1868, with a disturbing, though lower, peak in the 1890s. Despite the efforts to catch the perpetrators, and the improvement in the detection rate later in the century, only about a half of the reported cases became a matter for the courts. Punishment for offences with violence was always severe; until the 1830s, for example, highway robbery and burglary carried the death sentence.

Highway robbery was, so far as we know, most prevalent in the early years of the century, when there were few policemen to patrol the lonely country roads and the turnpikes, and when people carrying rents and wages had little protection.[28] In these years scares about the activities of highwaymen and footpads were common. In the spring of 1810, in the vicinity of Wrexham, John Jones, a blacksmith of Hope, attacked John Wynne, the foreman of a local lime-works, and relieved him of the men's wages. In the struggle Wynne died, and six months later Jones was hanged on Flint Marsh. Although it was not so in this case, many of the highway robberies at this time were the work of two or more people, with mud or masks covering their faces. Two men, so disguised, seized a tenant farmer of Carno parish, in March 1812, as he was on his way to hand over the half-yearly rent, and left with his £20.[29] Other gangs, sometimes members of criminal confederations or 'swell mobs', took even more money from auctioneers, merchants, and collectors of rents and poor-rates, as they were returning home late at night. Nor were the drivers of passenger and mail coaches completely safe; figures appeared in the dark and demanded a financial return for allowing them a safe passage.[30]

Highway robbery was rarely reported in the second half of the century, but street robbery continued to annoy the authorities. Within towns it seems that the streets were most dangerous in the evenings, especially at weekends. Violent robberies from surprised predestrians were given as one of the reasons why Monmouth and Chepstow appointed night-watchmen and welcomed gas lighting. From time to time, as English historians have shown, society became rather paranoid about this crime. In the 1860s and 1890s, partly one suspects because of national publicity over garotting, the police of Cardiff, Swansea and Newport took extra precautions against street robbers. In the ensuing court cases, a number of 'habitual criminals' were convicted of the offence, but, contrary to received wisdom, so were other types of people.

This mixture of professional and part-time criminals was true of all kinds of robbery on the open road. There were a number of Dick Turpin characters, and skilful exponents of the art like Benjamin Richards and Ann Evans, the 'Emperor' and 'Empress' of Merthyr's 'China', but there were also many less romantic offenders. Amongst those convicted were travelling tradesmen from north Wales, farm labourers living near Welshpool, unemployed railway workers in Monmouthshire, and Cardiff youngsters looking for easy pickings. Almost without exception, all these highway and street robbers received sentences of death or transportation, and, when these ceased, long periods of penal servitude.

So did the burglars, and those repeatedly arrested for breaking and entering. Society, or rather the press, judged the efficiency of the policing authorities on their ability to prevent and detect this particular crime. Its nature varied somewhat, depending on the place and size of the property under threat. In the countryside, especially in the first half of the century, isolated mansions and large houses were visited by disguised and armed men, and women, too, who took cash, silverware, jewellery, and watches to the value of several hundred pounds. During one burglary, in the parish of Llansadwrn, Ann Lloyd and three other local women dined on a victualler's salmon and bread, and disappeared with candlesticks, pans and tallow. In some of the worst cases, reminiscent of earlier times, the offenders battered down the doors of the rich, held the residents at knife or gun-point and demanded details of where valuables were hidden.[31]

Armed gangs also intimidated female cottagers and elderly farming couples, but many, and increasingly most, of the burglaries of these homes were carried out stealthily by passing tramps and dishonest neighbours.[32] These moved in when the owners of the property were out working, or at divine service. In November 1829 they raided the house of Micah Thomas, Baptist minister, near Abergavenny, when he was in the middle of his sermon.[33] When everyone was at home in the evening, then churches and chapels were broken into, and so, at the turn of the century, were village railway stations, post offices and creameries.

In the towns there were more opportunities for burglaries and break-ins, but also greater risks. The newspapers indicate that most towns experienced 'a rash' of these offences at one time or another in the first decades of the century, with counting houses a main target. It was customary at this time to blame the raids on gangs of outsiders. These were, it was assumed, part of 'extensive confederations which then existed for the purpose of carrying on a regularly organized system of robbery', but in the post-war depression they were joined temporarily by groups of unemployed colliers and other out-of-work labourers.[34] In these years, before the arrival of professional policemen, the wealthier inhabitants co-ordinated the work of protecting property and prosecuting these criminals. Associations appointed watchmen, and rewards were offered for information on burglars. One of those taken was John Hardy, who robbed the house and stable of his master, near Llandovery. He was executed in 1817.[35] When people like Hardy were arrested, they were accused of long lists of crimes. In January 1830 coach loads of Merthyr Tydfil's inhabitants came to the police office to identify goods found in the possession of Henry Phillips, Gwenllian Phillips, and Elizabeth ('Betsy Paul') Morgan. Twenty-five years later, William Phillips, William Johnson, and Charles Green were charged with burglaries in towns right across south-west Wales, but then, to the obvious delight of the press, failed to break out of Haverfordwest gaol.[36]

In time street-lighting, night-watchmen and police forces made life more difficult for these criminals, and altered the character of their work. House break-ins became more like snatch-and-grab raids, with clothes and boots the prime targets. Raids on shops were often quick affairs as well, with windows broken and goods hurriedly pocketted. Entering deep into locked shops and warehouses, where shutters and bars had been installed, required higher skills, but the rewards were good. In 1857 £1,000 worth of jewellery was taken from Rayners at Swansea, under the noses of the police, whilst in a more typical affair some years later at a shop in Holt, near Wrexham, £45 was removed from the till, and the thieves then helped themselves to a meal of sweets and chocolates from the shelves.[37] At the end of the century there were also a few spectacularly successful raids in Cardiff, which might have increased the attraction of the crime, and pointed the way to twentieth-century developments.

Security was improved before the end of our period, but magistrates and chief constables continued to express concern at the vulnerability of commercial premises, especially in the winter months when so many of these offences occurred. Police success in preventing and detecting these crimes depended greatly on being in the right place at the right time. They had some achievements. On a number of occasions they surprised mischievous children, gangs of youths, destitute women, and men who had been, or were currently, working at the very place being ransacked. Most of the people who were apprehended for burglaries and break-ins were, in fact, unemployed adult males, from the district and outside, a smaller number of boys and girls, and a handful of professionals like Frederick Reidell, the German who patrolled the Llandudno area before his death in 1901. The last group included people who became folk heroes, men such as Thomas

Phillips from St Dogmaels, and John Jones, who was given fourteen years' penal servitude in Merioneth in 1880 after breaking into three more jewellers' shops. The main difference from their predecessors of fifty or a hundred years before was their rejection of violence. This was, said a Monmouthshire judge in 1880, his only consolation when he was presented with rising statistics of serious property crime.

There was a distinction, by no means absolute, between the most notorious burglars and the people responsible for the offences committed against property without violence. There were about twenty times more recorded instances of stealing than of robbery, burglaries and break-ins. The rate can be seen in Graphs 14 and 15, and the fluctuations in the rate were discussed in chapter 2. Of those cases of stealing which came before the courts, only one in six were dealt with at the Assizes and Quarter Sessions. Decisions over where to prosecute were taken in relation to the nature and value of the goods stolen, and the age and plea of the offenders. The stealing of farm animals, larceny in a dwelling house, and more serious cases of larceny from the person and by servants, as well as of receiving and obtaining money by false pretences, were a matter for the Assizes and Quarter Sessions, whilst, from the mid-century onwards, adults pleading guilty to larceny and juvenile thieves usually attended the Petty Sessions.[38] Although the estimated worth of the stolen goods was a legal fiction, the average theft in these court cases was certainly no more than £2 in value. This set it apart from the property offences which we have already considered.

For the purpose of this book, all the many types of larceny can be discussed under a few main headings; those which took place at one's home and the homes of others, those committed at work and by the families of workers, those executed in the streets, pubs and shops, and the stealing of animals, fish and birds in the countryside. Theft within the home was carried out by family members, lodgers, neighbours, vagrants and other visitors. The number of court cases involving family and friends was small. As soon as they were identified as the probable criminal, the victim was inclined to become 'an unwilling witness'. This was the term used of William Parry, when the police told him in 1885 that his thief was almost certainly Rowland Edwards, a neighbouring Merioneth farmer.[39] A word of warning was often sufficient for guilty friends to return the goods taken 'by mistake'. In contrast, lodgers, tramps and hawkers were readily accused of theft by householders, even of offences which had never taken place.

Money was a powerful attraction for all domestic thieves, though watches, umbrellas and other valuables were also popular. In 1862 a collier at Merthyr received twelve months hard labour for taking the life-savings (£80) of his landlady, and two years later a forty-year-old female of the

same town was sentenced to two months for removing a settee from the
house which she was renting. Landlords frequently appeared in court to
prosecute lodgers who had left with more than their belongings. Thus
George Maker of Newport brought proceedings in 1880 against Mary
Frost, when he discovered, after her departure, that she had sold one of his
sheets and pawned another. She received a sentence of twenty-three days
hard labour.[40]

Clothes and food were taken more than anything else from within and
outside the home. Each year there were hundreds of cases, in country and
town, of items being removed from back-kitchens, clothes lines and hedges,
and of poultry, vegetables and fruit disappearing during the night.[41] This
annoyed the working class, as much as anyone else. Cottage gardens and
orchards were a magnet in the summer months, and once losses became too
much, the well-to-do employed watchmen, kept guard dogs, and asked the
police to search every vagrant in the vicinity. By the 1880s tramps could
expect two months' hard labour for such offences, and local residents, with
no previous convictions, two weeks. Seventy years earlier things had been
different; William Williams was whipped through Llanelli in 1810 for
taking apples from a garden, and Evan Hughes, in Merioneth, was shot
dead in 1817 by an angry householder.[42] As the many convictions under
the Act for the better protection of property in fields and orchards show,
the crimes of this last year fully tested the patience of gentlemen and
farmers.[43]

Amongst the people charged with larcenies from houses were servants,
especially female ones. Recorded cases of substantial theft by butlers,
coachmen and other servants of the aristocracy were comparatively rare
and always treated seriously. Thomas Gunn, gardener, and John Jones,
coachman, at Vaynor Park were fortunate to escape execution in 1812 for
having removed, over a long period of time, some two hundred bottles of
wine. Jones was doubly lucky, because three months later he escaped from
Montgomery gaol.[44] Stealing from the homes, and hotels, of the middle
class was more common, so the records tell us. The temptation for the
poorest female domestics, and the lowly boots boys, to purloin their
masters' property was strong, and became even stronger, it seems, just
prior to leaving their employment. A visit to a pawnshop was almost the
signing-off note. An extreme case was that of a charwoman who appeared
at the Quarter Sessions in Cardiff in 1882 on a charge of stealing ten plates,
when she already had five previous convictions for taking sheets, a
pinafore, a cushion, a frock, a coat and a cigar case from other employers.
One can compare her sentence of seven years penal servitude with the
fourteen days hard labour given to another charwoman, Ann Pugh of
Dolgellau, a 'good character' who, eight years before, stole a cash box from
her master, a grocer. Shop assistants were in rather similar situation to

domestic servants, though they were not often brought to account. Perhaps their bosses, like those of insurance, finance and railway companies, allowed for a certain amount of misappropriation.[45]

In the country, where payments in kind were given to farm labourers with their wages, no one was too surprised that small amounts of hay, oats, cabbages and eggs were dishonestly added to the list. During harvesting and threshing small losses were expected. If farmers discovered that male and female employees had been persistently deceiving them, rather than support a prosecution they often preferred to caution or dismiss the unreliable servants. So when the police approached John Silvester Esq. about the loss of rabbits on his north Wales estate in January 1884, he told them that Hugh Morris, his employee, had been sacked and he wanted 'no further action'. There was a suspicion in a number of the court cases of petty thefts by farm servants and labourers that employers were acting out of spite, and juries took account of this. In 1840, when a Carmarthenshire jury acquitted William Thomas, who was charged with stealing a small amount of hay from Edward Adams of Middleton Hall, the sheriff exploded in anger and the courtroom broke into laughter. Some workers, not wanting to face this ordeal, took matters into their own hands; William Williams of Holyhead, a mason's labourer on Lord Stanley's estate, fled to south Wales in 1895 knowing that he was about to suffer the legal consequences of chasing after his master's rabbits.[46]

Although farm servants and labourers were not prosecuted as often as the urban and industrial poor, it would nevertheless be wrong to claim, as some observers did, that their families were free of crime. A close look at all the sources reveals that many women and children took milk, vegetables, wood and other gleanings to keep the domestic economy going through the winter months. The collection of underwood was, together with the milking of cows, probably the most common crime of the countryside.[47] In the winter of 1817–18, when estate agents brought poor families to court for cutting and carrying away wood, the most sympathetic reporters said that they could 'half understand' the prevalence of the crime, and attempts were made to rescue those taken into custody.[48] 'Old offenders' who picked up sticks for the fire could expect up to a month in gaol, but those who ran a small business in stolen trees and branches were dealt with more harshly. Fines of £15, or six months imprisonment, were the norm. Thomas Evans of Llannon in Carmarthenshire cut and sold great quantities of young ash and oak trees during 1817 for making coal baskets, and over the Christmas season every year there was a profitable trade in stolen holly and ivy.[49]

Such was the scale of these activities that people were interested in the motives of those who decided to apprehend and prosecute a selection of these criminals. When Elizabeth Lloyd 'in advanced pregancy' was sentenced to one week's imprisonment at the Llandeilo Quarter Sessions in 1830, on a charge of milking cows, many in the court felt that the prosecution must have been malicious. Frequently, as when 'wretchedly poor' Mary Eynon, with a child in her arms, was charged with stealing turnips, prosecutors asked for a caution only, the main purpose of the case being to deter those who had evaded arrest. During the potato famine of the mid-century, these crimes reached epidemic proportions. Acres of cabbages, turnips and mangels disappeared in Carmarthenshire alone. Responsibility for this was shared between unscrupulous middle-men, who received and then re-sold the vegetables, poor families, and gangs of women working quietly at night. Nor was this the end of such illegality; dozens of women in the same county were annually charged with taking straw, leaves, nuts, reeds, sand and peat. It was a reminder to the 'lower orders', said the Tory *Carmarthen Journal*, that they had 'no rights' in such property.[50]

At the industrial workplace, and the dockside, vast quantities of clothing, metals, wood, tools and other materials went missing. The stealing of flannel was 'all too prevalent' amongst the workers of Newtown and Llanidloes, as was the disappearance of copper and iron in the foundries of Amlwch and Merthyr. In west Wales, William Chambers, Richard Nevill, James Child and their friends in the coal and copper industries prosecuted scores of employees and their families.[51] In court the watchmen of the works admitted that hundreds more had slipped their net. Similarly, the dock police at Swansea and Cardiff acknowledged that it was impossible to guard all the ships and wagons in their care. They identified three classes of dock criminals. A number of them, including ships' pilots, hauliers and canal boatmen, were always 'on the make'. So were gangs of unemployed youths on the waterfront, who supplied the marine dealers and pawnbrokers. Finally, there were the workers themselves who were caught at the dock gates with brass, copper, and rope under their coats. One excuse for this practice was that 'it has always been done', and, after all, their employers had 'plenty to spare'. The same attitude can be found amongst some of the railway, post office and local-government employees, though comparatively few of these appeared in court.

In the industrial villages and towns coal stealing was an ever-present fact of life. 'Women and children of all ages, sent out expressly by their parents, are seen at all hours following the tram-waggons', said the rector of Machen in 1847. Printed notices were circulated on the south Wales coalfield in 1836 reminding people that the offence was a felony, but forty years later the *Aberdare Times* still referred to it as one of the most common 'of our social crimes'.[52] It was at its height during the winter months. The largest employers, like the Guests of Dowlais and the members of the

Newport Coal Society, appointed watchmen and paid policemen to limit the damage. When cautions, exhortations and dismissals failed, as in the late 1840s and early 1850s, they turned to the courts for assistance. It was a policy pursued with some vigour by the Powell Dyffryn and Ebbw Vale coal and iron companies a generation later.

One of the defences of workmen was that they had a right to free coal, but once again it was the wives and children who were usually arrested. It was said that children in Dowlais were trained to commit this crime; in 1852 one eleven-year-old boy was sentenced to six months' imprisonment, two previous convictions having been proved against him. This was exceptionally harsh; punishment for coal stealing, both before and after the Criminal Justice Act of 1855, was lighter than that for many property offences. In February 1880 the Tredegar magistrates, faced with two men and seven women in the dock, issued a warning that in future those with a previous conviction for coal stealing would be sent to gaol. A few months later, when more women were brought to the same court, the prisoners' invective was directed, as it often was, at the 'blackleg' witnesses for the prosecution.[53] Single and widowed mothers told these magistrates of their poverty and of the temptations of coal lying about the tracks, but there were also repeated stories of women running a black-market trade in fuel around the houses.[54]

The streets were, of course, an important arena of crime. Armed robbery, stealing from open stalls, and pickpocketing were problems in all the largest towns of early nineteenth-century Wales. The court records of larceny from the person give us some clues to the popularity of this particular crime. In 1834 twenty-four people were committed to the Assize and Quarter Sessions, charged with this offence; in 1858 the number was seventy, with another 224 dealt with at the Petty Sessions. Twenty-four years later the respective court figures were thirty-six and 122. There was little doubt, in this instance, that the last figures represented a genuine reduction in criminal behaviour, and that a permanent police presence had contributed to it. Much of our best information on larceny from the person comes, significantly, from the earlier period. At that time a typical sentence for a first offence was six months hard labour, and for a second, transportation.

Those found guilty included fleet-footed youths, members of 'swell mobs', prostitutes and their 'bullies'.[55] They operated at auctions, markets, fairs, and races, in the noisy confusion of public houses, shops and brothels, and at the largest railway stations. Handkerchieves, watches and above all, cash, to an average value of £2 or £3, were removed with professional ease. In the first half of the century the newspapers were full of accounts of gangs of travellers who attended the Wrexham, Llangollen and Aberaeron fairs, and cheated those present either by fixed games of chance or by removing their wallets and purses. On one occasion, angrily reported in the south Wales press, the bailiff of Lewis W. Dillwyn of Penllergaer lost £61 at the Neath fair.[56] Special constables, and later the professional policemen, did their best to keep watch wherever hundreds and thousands of people were gathered, and a few magistrates and head constables took a legal risk and ordered suspected pickpockets to be held in the lock-ups until after the crowds had gone. In the 1870s it was reported that people could at last attend fairs and steeplechases without fearing for their property.

In the larger towns, gangs of youngsters, chiefly male, preyed on women shopping at the weekends, and adult females took advantage of men with money to burn. Some of the children were very young indeed, and there were claims that these operated under the direction of men like Llewellyn Price of Cardiff, a notorious character of the 1880s.[57] The court cases, especially against disorderly prostitutes, confirm that members of both the middle and working classes carried large sums of cash about their persons. Drovers, bailiffs, tradesmen and sailors were likely targets for pickpockets. Ellen Coghlan and Minnie Maguire of Cardiff, Sarah Davies of Merthyr, and their counterparts in Holyhead, admitted that, with the help of their 'bullies', they made more money from this kind of stealing than from sex. Like so many other thieves, they found drinking places to be the perfect environment for their crime. As was acknowledged under cross-examination, their victims frequently had only the vaguest recollection of what had been done to them after they had become inebriated.

Shops, markets, and lodging-houses were other places where stealing was rife. Clothing, food, and footware, in that order, were the things most commonly taken. Every week the Welsh police received reports of the loss of hundreds of trousers, dresses, shirts and coats, and of vast quantities of bread, potatoes, butter, meat, poultry, cheese, eggs and fish. At Cardiff the poorest families had a particular liking for eating stolen beef fat and herrings with their stolen bread. Angry stallholders in the markets and arcades of late-nineteenth century towns demanded greater police protection, only to be told that their open displays of goods for sale invited trouble. Mr Stephens, who owned a shop in Bute Street, Cardiff, was formally reprimanded in 1860 for hanging clothes over the pavement.[58] The implication of the magistrates' warning was that they would not support any more prosecutions against those who were 'so tempted'. Ironically, there was a small number of stallholders and dealers, notably sellers of poultry and game, who turned criminal to supply their trade, and then grumbled about the morals of customers.

There is very little evidence of gangs controlling the trade of shop-lifting. Many labourers in their twenties, and a few tramps, were apprehended for the crime, but it was always, and correctly, associated with women and youngsters. They were to be found, for instance, in the several hundred children under sixteen years of age who were proceeded against each year in the lower courts for larceny. Four-fifths of these cases were in Glamorgan and Monmouthshire, and especially in Cardiff, Newport and Swansea. Swansea had, said its chief constable in the 1880s, scores of very young children who lived rough and survived by pinching food from the shops and stalls of the town centre. Much of it was consumed within minutes of the crime. When the goods stolen were not of immediate use, they were pawned or passed to receivers. Henry Thomas, chairman of the Glamorgan Quarter Sessions in 1852, was convinced that receivers actually employed young boys to steal.[59]

Women, both single and married, were discriminating in their illegal shopping. In the large towns, they travelled at weekends from the poorer districts to the high streets, and, with the occasional help of their children, chose the food for the Saturday and Sunday meals, and snatched the boots and shirts which their families needed. In contrast to male shop-lifters, only a small minority of these women pawned goods, or took clothes to receivers. In fact, offenders were identified because they were wearing the very clothes which they had stolen only hours before. A few of them looked, and were 'very respectable', like Elizabeth Ward of Welshpool, whose husband tried to replace the stolen dresses, and Emily Williams of Wrexham, who was led screaming from the dock in 1860, but most were described in court as 'bedraggled' single and married women in their twenties, with very limited means of support.[60] They received perhaps a two-month gaol sentence, not as much as their younger sisters who stole from the person, but similar to the punishment of the female thieves of the countryside.

In rural communities the equivalent of this urban self-help was the taking of milk, vegetables, eggs, fuel, poultry, farm animals, game birds and fish. The amount of such crime can never be known. Deirdre Beddoe tells us that the 'incidence of animal thefts was in fact far higher in Wales, than in the rest of mainland Britain',[61] but it is extremely difficult to prove this proposition. Defenders of the Welsh, who gave evidence before the education and land commissions, claimed that the low number of recorded property offences in the villages bore witness to the honesty of the native population.[62] There were, on the other hand, landowners and farmers like George Rice Trevor of Dynefwr who denied that the cases reported to the police and prosecuted in court matched the extensive losses which they suffered. So far as they could judge, these thefts were the work of three groups of people: local residents who committed an occasional offence, a few villagers whose trade benefited from sustained illegal activity, and outsiders, like tramps and hawkers, who were often blamed for rural crime.

The stealing of farm animals was the responsibility of the first two groups. At the start of the nineteenth century this offence carried the death

penalty. Between 1800 and 1818 eighty-nine people were capitally convicted of stealing sheep, horses and cattle on the south-west Wales Great
Sessions circuit, but only a handful were actually executed.[63] Mary Lewis
of Llangelynin parish, Merioneth, a practised thief, was transported for life
in 1801, whilst Elizabeth Richards of Pembrokeshire, another sheep
stealer, escaped both death and transportation in 1810 because of her
pregnancy. Henry Hall, who was executed eight years later in Montgomeryshire for horse stealing, was one of the last to pay the ultimate
price.[64] The removal of the death sentence seems to have made little
difference to the popularity of these crimes. The number of persons committed for stealing farm animals after 1834, when transportation and long
periods of imprisonment were the normal punishments, was fewer than
fifty per year and falling for much of the time, a statistical fact which drew
cynical remarks from those who suffered the most. Sheep stealing was
undoubtedly very common, especially on the open moors. Lambs were
caught and eaten by hungry labouring families, especially during the
winter months, and even more, one suspects, were added to other farmers'
flocks, or quickly slaughtered by unscrupulous butchers.

'Sheep-stealing is becoming a wholesale business' ran one report of the
1820s.[65] During the late 1840s and early 1850s, when several hundred were
lost in Pembrokeshire and Carmarthenshire parishes, it was said that gangs
of sheep stealers were at work.[66] Some individuals were heavily involved in
the crime, both as thieves and receivers. In 1882, for example, Morris John
Jones of Maentwrog, a 33-year-old farmer and butcher, was sentenced to
twelve months hard labour for taking as many as eighty-seven sheep.[67] The
stealing of cattle and horses was a more difficult exercise, but one which
offered farmers, dealers, drovers and butchers a good return. In 1829 so
many disappeared in the south that watchmen were engaged night and
day on estates, and farmers travelled many miles for news that someone
had sold a £6 animal for half the price. Some of the stolen beasts were
walked across north and south Wales to the coalfields in the east. One
would like to know more about this trade in stolen animals, for it
strengthened the belief of chief constables that rural crime was more an
expression of capitalist endeavour than of hunger or protest.

The same point was often made when discussing poaching. The taking
of rabbits, game and fish has been excluded from the figures of stealing
given so far in this chapter. This reflects the way in which contemporaries
regarded, and catalogued, the crime. Parliament passed a series of Acts in
the eighteenth and nineteenth centuries, determining the property in birds
and game, and the rules by which they could be killed and sold. In our
period the most famous legislation included the Game Act of 1831, the
Night Poaching Acts of 1828 and 1844, the Game Licences Act of 1860, the
Poaching Prevention Act of 1862, the Salmon Fishing Act of 1861, and the

GAME.

To Poachers and others who buy or sell Game.

An Association having been formed for the preservation of the Game, Persons are employed to lay informations against unqualified Persons who are in the habit of destroying Game, and also against any Person whatever who shall sell or buy the same.

Any communications will be thankfully received by Mr. JESTON HOMFRAY, Solicitor, Cardiff, who is authorized by the Association to assist and prosecute any informations.

Cardiff, 5th January, 1821.

B. LLOYD, PRINTER, HIGH-STREET, CARDIFF.

A warning to poachers, 1821

Ground Game Act of 1880. In addition, there were several important local Acts early in the century for protecting the rivers in Welsh counties. Helping to execute all this legislation were game associations, fishery boards, a small army of keepers, watchers and bailiffs, and the police.

The outcome was, according to one modern writer, something akin to civil war in the countryside, especially where the village population claimed to be acting in defence of custom and the peasant economy.[68] Comments at the time of an inquest on a poacher shot dead at Glan Conwy in 1860 illustrate his point. 'Poachers without exception are a class the most disreputable on the face of the earth...They are too lazy to work, too mean to honestly earn their bread...' said the coroner. The *Caernarvon and Denbigh Herald* replied thus: 'the laws that would... make private property out of public vermin, destroy in the minds of the uneducated ...the sanctity of legislation;...'[69] One of the most bitter conflicts over rights and regulations involved the Tywi Board of Conservators and the coracle men, from the mid-1840s onwards. Another was the long-running dispute in west Wales over the Salmon Fisheries Acts of 1861–5, which affected the livelihood of more than a thousand fishing families, and a third made Thomas Mostyn reluctant to return to his north Wales home. In a letter of 1859 he described how gangs of poachers 'not only shoot the game' at Gloddaeth, 'but they make great havoc in knocking down walls and breaking the fences and gates...', and on one occasion they even entered the mansion itself.[70]

The preservation of birds, game and fish grew at a slower pace in the Principality than in, for example, East Anglia, but it gathered momentum in the second quarter of the nineteenth century. Most landowners were interested in the pleasure of the shoot, but some, like the De Rutzens of Slebech and the Lisburnes of Crosswood experimented with the farming of rabbits and fish for the food market, and others later decided to let their shooting and fishing to English businessmen. All these attempts to build up the stock in rivers, scrub and woods proved irresistible, not just to country dwellers but also to sporting miners and unemployed workmen living on the edge of towns. Hugh Roberts, Elias Williams, amd William Robinson, labourers of the Conwy area, collected dozens of convictions for the crime in the last years of the century, together with a few for drunkenness and disorderly conduct.[71] The lead-miners of west Wales were said to have been addicted to poaching, especially when they were on short-time work. These people poached in ones and twos, or, when the prospects were good and the defences formidable, in gangs. In 1835 there were reports that gangs about Abergele and along the Teifi had operated for years without detection.[72] Every night, until their capture in 1857, Jonah John, William Owen and William Watkins set almost a hundred snares on a warren at Laugharne, and sent their catch to the local markets.[73] Night poaching required considerable skill, courage and organization, but much of this criminal activity was very casual, with a rabbit picked up on the way from work, and a fish grabbed out of season.

In Wales the radicals of the mid-Victorian era complained of the privilege, protection and policing associated with the Game and Fishing Acts. Minister Henry Harries Davies of Beaumaris deliberately sought arrest to illustrate the iniquity of the game laws, and public meetings were held to protest against aspects of the legislation. These voices had an impact on the way in which the laws were administered, but the apprehension and prosecution of poachers never ceased to cause trouble. The great majority of offenders were reported, and denounced in court, by people generally viewed as spies of the landed classes, and judgement was made not by a jury but by one or two of the landowners' friends, sitting on the Bench at Petty Sessions. On occasions the treatment of Welsh poachers, tenant farmers and buyers of game was raised in Parliament.

Punishment varied, from transportation and penal servitude for the worst cases, to fines of a few shillings for a trespass, and £2–5 (with gaol for non-payment) for setting snares, sporting on a Sunday and taking salmon out of season. Tenant farmers and their friends also risked £5 fines for shooting without a licence, keeping a dog to destroy game, and being in possession of game on their own land. In court the poachers, like the wreckers and coal stealers, were inclined to see themselves as special criminals. They showed remarkable composure and not a little humour. John Williams, the Narberth mole-catcher, told the Petty Sessions in 1853 that he forgave the magistrates and the witnesses, and then began his customary coughing fit to save himself from the treadmill. Seven years later, old David Jenkins, at the Bridgend court, explained how his partial blindness allowed him to see flies on the water, but caused him to miss Captain Treharne's notice on the river Ogmore.[74]

During the first half of the nineteenth century comparatively few poachers appeared in the higher courts. This gives a rather false impression, for some 126 'out-of-court' convictions filed in the Flintshire records for 1815–30 were of this type. Many were from the years 1817, 1822–3, 1825–6 and 1829–30. In Merioneth, too, many farmers and labourers were prosecuted in the homes of the gentry in the post-war years, with fines common, some as high as £20, half of that amount going to the informers. Returns from the Great, Quarter and Petty Sessions, though incomplete, show that there was a substantial increase in the number of cases brought to open court during the second quarter of the century. In the year ending Michaelmas 1844, 436 people were convicted of Game Law offences in the courts of Wales, several times the figure of twenty years before, and certain years, like 1836, 1843 and 1851, were prominent in these statistics.[75] According to Graph 18, the number of such persons proceeded against at

Petty Sessions rose to a peak of about a thousand in the mid-1870s, and declined sharply a few years after the passing of the Ground Game Act. 'We very seldom have a game case or fight about poaching' was the exaggerated boast of a good number of Welsh magistrates at the end of the century. Lord Kenyon, speaking in 1894, claimed that landowners had lost some of their enthusiasm for pursuing the offenders.

The number of cases brought for offences against the fishing Acts were only about a third of the proceedings under the game laws, and, apart from exceptional figures immediately following the Act of 1878, the annual rate began a long decline after the 1860s. This was not because of inactivity on the part of the authorities; the mid-Victorian years witnessed major efforts to impose long closed periods, new rules for line and net fishing, and stricter regulations for coracles and other small boats. On the rivers Dyfi, Wye, Teifi, and Tywi, resistance to conservation was particularly strong, and the water-guards, even with bonuses for convictions, faced an uphill struggle. The reappearance of Rebecca, first in west, and then in mid Wales, to give legitimacy to mass poaching expeditions was a sign of the popular feeling.[76] Police constable Hughes in Merioneth describes in his diary how, on 10 January 1878, he came upon a large gang of fish poachers, with blackened faces and hoods over their heads. 'I advised them to go home, as they were out for an unlawful purpose', he wrote in his journal. He was told to turn back, or he 'would be killed on the spot'. A spear was stuck in his chest, and he was pelted with stones all the way home.[77] In later years, as people became used to the changes in fishing laws, there were claims that more Welshmen were treading the 'path of legality', something confirmed by the Land Commission of the 1890s. Yet the widespread use of explosives in the Gwendraeth, Dee and other rivers in that decade, and the revival of open poaching by hundreds of people in Radnorshire soon afterwards, did cause concern.

In special circumstances, the poaching gangs went beyond their usual remit. There were occasions when they added ritual, and supporters, to their nightly proceedings, and, when their work was done, took their spears and lights to the property of conservators, burning ricks, smashing weirs, and firing guns at houses. Sir James Drummond, a leading figure on the Tywi and the Cothi, lost dogs and haystacks, and received threatening letters. The coracle men, always 'a turbulent race', attacked the property of landowners and the nets of rival fishermen. Weirs were a popular target; angry crowds removed those at Beddgelert in 1805, Northop in 1816, Blackpool (Slebech) in 1830, Llechryd in 1843, and many other places.[78] In a way these weirs could be compared with the fences of commons enclosure, and the destruction of both reminds us that when customs and rights were set aside, the powerless had only one, immediately satisfying, response. Thomas Llewellyn, whose family was involved in the dismantling of the Blackpool weir, justified the act by telling his interviewer that only a few years before the fishing in the river had been free and open.

This malicious destruction was of a different type from the property crimes described so far in this chapter, and it was often regarded more seriously. From their beginning, the returns of Quarter Session and Assize cases had a separate category for malicious offences, and into it were placed cases of arson, machine-breaking, damage to trees, fences, walls and gates, and the maiming and killing of animals. The last were perhaps the most disturbing; dogs, donkeys, and horses, as well as pigs, sheep and oxen, were poisoned and mutilated in private and public battles over common and grazing rights, boundary disputes and other matters. In typical examples, David Davies and Margaret Davies were gaoled in 1851 for cutting and wounding sheep belonging to John Owen, a farmer of Llanfihangel Genau'r Glyn, who had once taken them to court, and employees in the same county, having lost their jobs, cut the teats and hamstrings of cows owned by their old masters. Hostility to landowners, industrialists and policemen was also expressed in this way, though the innocent victims in these instances tended to be valuable horses. In a strange north Walian episode in 1870 one extended family was alarmed when the the tongues of their horses were cut, and horrified when one of the humans later received the same treatment.[79]

Despite the offer of rewards, it was not too surprising that, for all except a dozen years, fewer than twenty of the worst cases of malicious destruction were taken before the higher courts. Most of the minor offences, which were often connected with trespass, were left to the magistrates in Petty Sessions. After the enabling Act of 1827, they imprisoned just under a hundred people on average per year until the 1850s, and fined others. High peaks in the numbers gaoled came in 1842–4 and 1848–9. In the second half of the century, when we at last get comprehensive annual totals of the proceedings at the higher and lower courts, it is apparent that a few more people each year were prosecuted for wilful damage and trespass than for poaching game and fish, though considerably more of the defendants in the former cases came from the industrial counties and large towns. The figures on Graph 19 prompt the thought that violence against both property and the person in Wales was probably at its height in the mid-1870s, and/or the authorities took it most seriously at this time.

Much of this destruction of property was hardly worth the name, like breaking the top bar of a gate whilst in the act of trespass and removing part of a wall in a fight over rights of way and ownership of a close. Yet there were times when this crime deservedly made the headlines: the post-war years for example, and the early 1840s.[80] During these two difficult periods, there was an exceptional number of cases of cutting trees, poisoning and maiming animals, breaking gates, fences and walls, ruining corn fields, and pulling down houses in the countryside, and smashing tools, destroying pit props and machinery, and burning wagons in the industrial districts. Some of this is well known to students of Welsh history, but there were many cases which passed virtually unnoticed at the Petty Sessions. In April 1850, for instance, Cardigan shipwrights 'maliciously injured' the tools of men working at reduced wages, and John Williams, who left a holding near Aberystwyth, was fined for damaging trees in his own garden. The latter prosecution was, so we are told, a warning to people not to be so vengeful at the end of a tenancy.[81]

Many of the people who committed this kind of crime had few other ways of expressing their feelings and grievances. A good example were the workhouse inmates, temporary and permanant, who tore their clothes, destroyed bedding and broke the windows of union property. This damage is not included in Graph 19. Each year in the second half of the century an average of thirty-nine people were prosecuted under the Poor Law Acts for the crime, and in 1868–70 the number trebled. It has been shown elsewhere that Bangor, Hawarden, and Haverfordwest were amongst the unions most affected. At Narberth, and several other places, attempts were even made to set fire to workhouse buildings. When these attacks are added to the number of people charged with other forms of disorderly conduct in the workhouse, to be discussed in the next chapter, it appears that there were moments in the mid-century when this institution of discipline became a place of 'incipient rebellion'.[82]

Arson was the most feared of all these malicious property crimes, and it was frequently accompanied by the sending of threatening letters. In the early years, before the comprehensive security of fire insurance and fire engines, some of the victims successfully recovered their losses from their Hundreds. One such was John Gough, who lost £200 worth of farm buildings near Newtown in 1810, about the same time as a clothing factory was disappearing in smoke not many miles away.[83] Gough, and his friends whose hay ricks were fired in 1815–17, 1830–1, and 1843–4, knew that it was extremely difficult to catch the offenders, in spite of large rewards and harsh sentences. Until the 1830s incendiarism carried the death penalty, and even when this was removed, sentences of transportation and long periods of penal servitude were the standard punishment. Eleanor Williams, who was convicted, despite her protestations, of firing a Carmarthenshire farmhouse and stables, was conveyed to Van Diemen's land with her son in 1841.

During the years of the Rebecca riots and in the 1860s the number of recorded arson cases was well above the annual Welsh average, and there were districts, such as Llandeilo and Llandovery in the late 1850s and early 1860s, where it was deemed necessary to have anti-fire committees and patrols.[84] Yet none of this truly compared with the number of fires in the

FIVE POUNDS REWARD.

WHEREAS, either on Sunday Night, or early on Monday Morning, the 14th instant, the "MOSS HOUSE," the property of Lord A. E. Hill Trevor, M.P., Brynkinalt, was maliciously Set on Fire and totally destroyed.

Whoever will give such Information as may lead to the apprehension or conviction of the Offender or Offenders, shall receive the above Reward of Five Pounds, on application to the Treasurer of the Chirk Association for the Prosecution of Felons.

☞ Information to be given to J. PURCELL, Police Officer, Chirk.

W. H. LEVER,
SECRETARY.

Chirk, 19th March, 1864.

Arson in Denbighshire, 1864

worst affected English counties. It is possible that some acts of Welsh incendiarism were not reported, especially, one suspects, those which were part of hill-country feuding. On the other hand, several people, often female, appeared in the courts for only threatening to commit arson. The motivation of the arsonists varied greatly. A small number of fires were started deliberately for the insurance money, whilst those discovered in south-west Wales during 1843, and in mid and north Wales in 1863, were an expression of collective anger and protest. During the 1860s eighty-two people were brought before the Assizes in north Wales, mainly in the eastern counties, for setting ricks and sheds ablaze. The vagrants, and unemployed labourers, who comprised two-thirds of these defendants, claimed that the farmers and poor-law authorities had denied them food and shelter. The judges, who gave them long prison sentences, agreed that they had been badly treated.

Most of the arson attacks in nineteenth-century Wales were private acts of malice, a revenge for a real or supposed slight. Thus Thomas Davies of Cynwyl Caio in August 1854 set fire to the home of David Davies, for having pulled down a building which he had erected on a disputed sheepwalk, and Elizabeth Harry of Llandough did the same to her own dwelling house a few years earlier in a dispute over rent. Many of the fires, including a spectacular blaze in Radnorshire on 19 May 1838, took place at the very moment when a tenant was required to leave the property.[85] When farm and domestic servants, who seem to have committed fewer of these crimes, were found guilty, it was either a reaction to a dismissal or a plea for help. There was also a handful of offenders suffering from pyromania. Henry Burke, a tramping painter of Rhyl, was one, and so was Howell Jones, a 23-year-old Glamorgan labourer who carried out a personal war against employers and landlords who crossed him.

In addition, there were the equivalent of the modern vandals. Vandalism has always been present in both rural and, so the records tell us, especially modern urban society. Newspapers throughout the nineteenth century convey the exasperation felt about those anonymous people, presumed to be of a young age, who had nothing better to do than disfigure trees, smash windows, wrench door-knockers, break street lamps and signs, and light fires in churches, schools and empty houses. At Usk in the early spring of 1842 the gates, doors and windows of 'several of the most respectable families of the town' were systematically destroyed over several nights. A few years earlier, similar events had encouraged the authorities at Caernarfon and Haverfordwest to discuss better policing and lighting for their towns.[86] The *Carmarthen Journal* said in 1847 that such apparently pointless property crime was in its way more sinister than the other forms.[87] Subsequent decades were marked by more window smashing, damaging of hydrants and placing stones on railway lines. Poor David Jones, a ten-year-old who was convicted of the last offence in 1869, was treated to fifteen strokes of the birch and one month in Carmarthen gaol. How much effect such punishment had we cannot say, but in in the late nineteenth century the number of people charged with vandalism was falling.

This decline was in line with the recorded incidence of poaching, and most of the other offences against property, a trend which was to be reversed fairly quickly in the early twentieth century. As Graph 16 reveals, the rates were different across rural, industrial and urban Wales, but the overall trend was in the right direction. The confidence of the early 1870s was undermined a little by the recovery of the theft statistics ten years later, and by that of the burglaries, break-ins and robberies in the 1890s, but Henry Austin Bruce, amongst others, refused to be over-influenced by the latest events and bad publicity over a small number of unsolved serious offences. When they reflected on the situation of a century or more before, late-Victorian people were convinced that both they and their property were safer, a view shared by most historians. One thing cannot be disputed; the fall in the rate of property crimes was not the result of a declining interest in the subject.

Contemporaries were intrigued by the extent of offences against property and by the dangers which they posed to authority, the economy, and civilized behaviour. Chief constables in the second half of the century were obliged to make an annual return to the Home Office of the value of the goods stolen in indictable offences. From these it can be seen that a handful of embezzlements, forgeries and frauds were worth several hundred pounds, and some burglaries, break-ins and robberies from the person were estimated at over £50. At Llandudno in the autumn of 1893 one hotel robbery netted £91, another £40, and a theft from a bathing machine some £85. However, the re-sale value of stolen goods was often much less than these figures, and between a quarter and a half of the stolen property was recovered.

Most thefts, of every kind, were very ordinary affairs. When added together it is clear that the average value of serious property offences reported to the police was below £10. In Caernarfonshire during 1892, for example, when embezzlement cost £190 in just one quarter, the total worth of goods stolen was £449, about £7 for each crime.[88] Unfortunately we do not have similar evidence for larcenies dealt with at the Petty Sessions, but when the legislation provided for it, in 1863, almost a thousand adults, willing to plead guilty, were proceeded against for larcenies of less than 5s. in value. A sample of the first 100 thefts reported in the Holywell police division in 1890–93 gives an average value of just over £2 each, the greatest losses being sustained by gentlemen, hotel proprietors and farmers.[89] Judged on these terms, the real cost of property crime to society was, and has remained, 'relatively trivial'.[90] Nor was it quite the frenzied battle which Engels portrayed between the rich and the 'have-nots'. Property crimes do have a stronger inter-class dimension than violent behaviour, and this is particularly true of the female offences in both town and country, but an estimated third of the victims were working class (Table 3).

This raises the question of how property crimes were regarded by society. People, in authority and outside, undoubtedly viewed some offences, and offenders, differently from others. Magistrates themselves could be annoyed when the most trifling cases were brought to court, and made donations to help some of the poorest defendants who had broken the law 'to keep body alive'. Even ill and starving tramps received a smattering of sympathy, though if police found cash on their person the reverse was true. For their part, ordinary people reacted to property crimes in a varied way, condemning some offenders, and excusing others. It has been suggested that the response was influenced by whether the act was carried out by a professional or a casual criminal, but the attitudes were more complex than that. When the working class were themselves the victims of theft, it is especially interesting to compare their reactions. Some resolutely refused to supply information to the police, but in most cases it seems that artisans and labourers were prepared to take offenders to court. One can understand the anger of a charwoman, a laundress and a carpenter of the Holywell area, who lost between them almost £45 in the 1890s, but others in the same district demanded action over 3*d*., 6*d*. and 9*d*.

The nature of the crime made an obvious difference to the response to it. Some offences, such as arson, maiming and machine-breaking, coal and wood stealing, and gleaning on old common and forest land, had a degree of support from those sections of the population who rarely suffered from them. Many people also refused to recognize wrecking, smuggling, and certain breaches of the game and fishing laws as 'moral offences'. Towards the end of the century we are told that, in an increasingly respectable world, even these ceased to be regarded as 'social crimes', but in Wales the political and social conflict of the Tom Ellis era perpetuated the discussion over the propriety of obeying 'gentry laws'.

In an effort to make sense of the multiplicity of these views, one historian has drawn up non-official categories of property crime. He makes a clear distinction between actions such as poaching which were illegal but legitimized by public opinion, and which might contain a strong element of protest, and actions such as fowl stealing which were both illegal and not legitimized by public opinion. Another historian has suggested keeping the category of 'protest' offences, and separating the rest into 'acquisitive' and 'survival' crimes. It is a promising beginning, but the main problem, which is only too apparent in this chapter, is contained in his question: 'where do we draw the line?'[91]

Before we can take the matter further, more research is needed on the organization of property crimes, and on the precise nature of the crimes and the criminals. Some of this will never be recovered. Commercial crime, for instance, did not receive the attention it deserved in the nineteenth century, and so we cannot imagine the scale and planning of the operations. Organization, at least of a primitive kind, was important in most property crimes. Unless the goods were immediately consumed, worn or spent, criminals, like any other seller, needed a distribution network and a market. On many occasions the thieves who fell into police hands had been too anxious to pass on their booty; the sensible offender waited for time to elapse and sold it some distance from his or her home. Counterfeit coin, and stolen valuables, metals, animals, fish and game were sometimes taken, or sent, many miles across country.

At the end of the chain was a small number of fairly respectable merchants, victuallers and petty manufacturers, and a larger group of shady characters in the 'lowest haunts' of the main towns. When William Evans, a Holywell gentleman, lost 19 lb. of lead pipe in June 1890, it found its way, via William Davies, the rag collector, to Michael Cuddy, marine storehouse dealer, and then to the police. Receivers were generally safe from the police; each year on average only forty-two people were prosecuted for accepting stolen goods. In their anxiety over these hidden 'guardians of crime', contemporaries were inclined to exaggerate the size and threat of the criminal underworld. Captain Napier's descriptions in 1841 of an integrated criminal and distribution network across south Wales turns out to be only a collection of rather nebulous 'swell mobs' and notorious 'pot-houses'.[92] The receivers, whom the police numbered at 323 in 1860, and 119 thirty-two years later, were by occupation pawnbrokers, ironmongers, metal dealers, marine storemen, rabbit, fish and game dealers, rag-and-bone men, and the keepers of brothels, beerhouses and lodging-houses.[93] It was, in Wales at least, part-time work on behalf of a part-time industry.

The professional criminals, gangs and receivers of our period cannot be compared to their equivalents in the late twentieth century. Permanent criminal organizations did exist, with their roots in the darkest corners of the largest towns, but they were rare. Few gangs and few 'habitual criminals' lived for very long by crime alone. Two people who were said to have achieved this state were Sarah Davies, the Merthyr prostitute of the 1840s, and David Callaghan, the poacher of Holyhead, right at the end of the century. It was a hard existence, with irregular income and an implacable enemy. The newspapers gave undue importance to the professionals, and to the differences between them and other offenders, in the story of nineteenth-century property crime. Although someone like John Jones (Coch Bach y Bala), with his break-ins and compulsive thieving across north Wales, made the headlines, it is worth recalling that the typical property crime found in the records was the taking of clothes, food and fuel by ordinary folk. Most people, especially in the countryside, who appeared in court on charges of taking or destroying goods were given 'good' or 'unknown' characters. As we have seen, there was, on occasions, an element of capitalist enterprise and communal protest in their actions, but most of it was done to supply an individual and immediate need. One is left with the impression in the late nineteenth century that these people, and particularly the females amongst them, were becoming less willing and less able to behave in this fashion, and perhaps felt less pressure to do so. This in turn encouraged the state to extend its controls into other areas of social life.

5
Other Offences

The difficulty of defining, and estimating the amount of, crime has been illustrated by the removal in very modern times of certain breaches of traffic laws from the annual criminal returns. A century ago there were similar problems, which occupied the collective mind of the Departmental Committee on Criminal Statistics. In its report of 1895 the Committee noted that the courts of summary jurisdiction were widely used to decide matters which appeared to be more civil than criminal. 'Having a chimney on fire, failing to secure a child's attendance at school, disobedience to a borough bylaw or to road regulations under the Highway Acts, are treated by English law as criminal offences and punished on conviction by fine, which is enforced by criminal imprisonment.'[1] After some discussion about the nature of these offences, and the haphazard manner in which returns were made of their numbers to the Home Office, the Committee concluded that in future those which, like Sunday trading, led to a 'technical conviction' should be included with other offences determined summarily and those which which were dealt with by an order, like arrears of maintenance payments, should be entered in a new table of quasi-criminal proceedings.

It is customary for historians of crime in the last two centuries to ignore offences other than those against the person and property.[2] As we have seen, Henry Austin Bruce also took them less seriously, but no one, least of all the ex-Home-Secretary, doubted their importance. Ministers of the crown were very interested in them, for regulative legislation was at the heart of the revolution in government during the nineteenth century, and breaches of laws controlling licensing, vagrancy and the like were often associated with the crimes described in the last two chapters. In fact, these 'technical offences' took up a large amount of the time of magistrates and the police. Three out of every ten out-of-court convictions in Flintshire between 1815 and 1830 were of this type. In 1836 breaches of the same laws was responsible for a third of the imprisonments in Table 5, and a half in 1849. These people were proceeded against for swearing, deserting their families, evading a demand for rent, selling food and drink without proper weights or a licence, taking an unlawful toll, driving recklessly, paying wages in goods, bull-baiting, and being 'of the description of gypsies' and 'incorrigible rogues'.

Graph 3 reveals the staggering increase in the number of cases determined summarily in the second half of the century. The increase was
especially marked before the mid-1870s, and this affected the industrial
and rural counties more than Cardiff, Swansea and Newport. How to
explain this is a difficult matter; it is possible, as was suggested at the time,
that the higher rate of crimes against the person and property in the large
towns gave the authorities less time for other types of policing. In Anglesey,
Cardiganshire and Radnorshire, where many publicans, hawkers, pedlars,
and beggars came before the courts, the rate of cases determined summarily declined sharply and consistently after the late 1870s, but in Glamorgan and Monmouthshire the rate was higher in 1899 than at any time
in the century. Licensees, parents of rebellious schoolchildren, dog-owners,
drivers, street traders, reluctant rate-payers and owners of disorderly
houses were prominent targets in these industrial counties. By 1899 a total
of 55,027 people were proceeded against at the lower courts in Wales,
which, if each appeared only once in the year, represented one in thirty-six
of the population. Four out of every five of these defendants were charged
with offences other than those against the person and against property, and
one of the main victimless crimes, namely drunkenness, we have already
considered in chapter 3.

For the American Arthur Cleveland Hall, writing in 1902, the number
of these proceedings was a sure sign of the march of civilization and the
ordering of urban society, and he argued that the changing rate simply
reflected the influence of new legislation and more policing.[3] Amongst the
important statutes to which he was alluding were the Public Health Act of
1848, the Adulteration of Food and Drugs Act of 1860, the Habitual
Criminals Act of 1869, the Prevention of Crimes Act of 1871, the Licensing
Act of 1872, the Employers and Workmen's Act of 1875, the Elementary
Education Acts of 1870–91, and the Criminal Law Amendment Act of
1885. Most of these extended the regulatory powers of the state and the
police, and reduced the freedom of the citizen, including that of suspected
and convicted criminals.

The number of people in the nineteenth and twentieth centuries who
have been charged with offences other than those against persons and
property has sharpened the debate about the purpose and nature of the
legal code. Early social reformers like James Kay-Shuttleworth and Joseph
Fletcher proposed that the law and the police, together with education,
should be used to civilize and modernize the population. They were not the
first to think in this way, for an attempt had been made in the late sixteenth
and early seventeenth centuries 'to redefine and mark out anew the
boundaries of permitted behaviour', but not, it must be said, in quite such
a comprehensive way.[4] Although liberal in some senses, the nineteenth-
century reformers supported legislation which invaded the inner sanctum

of family life and ordered the daily existence of ordinary people. In their eyes, the public-health, social and political crises of the 1830s and 1840s illustrated the necessity for such interference, and the better circumstances and resources of later years made it possible. With the perceived physical threat to the state, to property and to the person on the decline after the mid-century, it was, said Robert Oliver Jones, time 'to set new standards'. Yet greater intervention, which all Victorian governments supported in practice if not in theory, was not always a popular idea. It marked a break with old forms of politics and community regulation, and with old notions of freedom and individual – chiefly male – responsibility.[5] In Parliament and in court, amongst householders, husbands, parents, and traders, the tone of the opposition was contained in the sentence: 'it is my business'.

Amongst the most unpopular legislation was that which hit the pockets of the Welsh population. Information on the resistance to the various revenue laws in the early years of the nineteenth century is thin, for most people were fined rather than imprisoned. We know that excise officers took large numbers of people to court. In the eight months, from August 1806 to March 1807, for example, over 350 people were convicted of crimes associated with illegal brewing, many of them from east Pembrokeshire and west Carmarthenshire.[6] In this area the work of excise officers like Mr Rowlands of Narberth, and the fines of £5 to £100, brought furious responses from those who made and sold alcohol without a licence. Even the grand juries of south-west Wales, in their petitions of 1831–2, support-ed the right of small farmers to make their own malt and beer, rather than having to resort to public houses.

Near the coast there was a chance of obtaining alcohol from smugglers. Smuggling had been big business in eighteenth-century Wales, when duties on tea, coal and other basic goods transported by sea were high. Despite tough legislation against evading and attacking customs officers, the government was faced with formidable gangs, an effective distribution network, collusion between the criminals and the local population, and a number of dishonest magistrates and customs men. Large quantities of brandy and gin, together with tobacco and other goods, continued to be imported illegally, at least until the establishment of the coastguards in the 1830s. In Llanon (Cardiganshire), Haverfordwest and Gower during the Napoleonic Wars, officers discovered hundreds of untaxed casks, and were attacked by crowds as they tried to confiscate them.[7] Lord Cawdor, who physically fought the smugglers, did as much as anyone in these years to stop 'this illegal trade'.

By the mid-century, the customs and excise services had been reor-ganized, and it became more difficult, and less profitable, to escape paying duties. Smuggling, and trying in other ways to evade taxes on imported goods, was apparently on the decline. In their report for 1858 the commissioners for customs said that 'no contraband transactions have occurred during the year of sufficient extent or pecularity to call for notice'. For the rest of the century much of their time was devoted to the everyday crime of 'not fully declaring' goods, by seamen entering the major Welsh ports.[8] Ordinary sailors could expect to pay full or treble duty on small amounts of hidden tobacco and alcohol, but the fine for 'systematic' evasion, and blind-eyed captains, was £100. In July 1850 the Cardiff magistrates agreed to support a petition to the Customs Board to reduce the statutory penalty of £100 which they had just imposed on the master of the *Eldon*.[9]

Non-payment of other revenue demands brought increasing numbers to court. In 1858 only 113 cases of offences against the revenue laws came before the Petty Sessions, but forty years later the figure had risen tenfold. Amongst those caught by the Inland Revenue were gentlemen and professional people without the appropriate licences for their firearms and private transport.[10] Hundreds more were summoned for refusing to pay tolls at the turnpike gates and market halls. Caernarfonshire carters, Llangwm oysterwomen and Newport orange-sellers, for instance, fought a constant battle with council officers and patrolling constables on market and fair days. Church rates were another point of contention, especially when money was needed to finance the Anglican revival of the mid-century. Sometimes, as when over 600 church-rate defaulters crowded into the Aberystwyth court in 1847, non-payment was part of an organized protest.[11] How many people appeared for not paying their rent was a different matter, and much harder to quantify. As we saw in chapter 3, these tenants often removed themselves and their goods just before the bailiffs arrived.

Hundreds of people every year, including many Cardiganshire and Pembrokeshire hill farmers, attended court because they had not paid their highway and poor rates. The rising figure in south-west Wales during the late 1830s and early 1840s was an index of the growing poverty and anger that became the Rebecca riots. Richard Rees, cabinet-maker of Llanelli, who could not pay the highway rate, entered a plea of bankruptcy, but, as with so many of his friends, it 'was not allowed'. At Merthyr, where the evidence is unusually good, at least 526 people were summoned for the non-payment of poor rates in the years 1855–8.[12] When the arrears were very small, 'the monies were [often] paid before the cases were called on'. Later in the century, when towns like Merthyr and Swansea provided better services for its householders, some of the latter resented the increased charges of local government, especially the new water and sanitary rates. Mr Tweeney, newsagent at Grove Place, Swansea, was just one of many who protested. Non-payment resulted in court orders for the requisite amount, together with costs, followed by fines, distraints, and, ultimately, imprisonment.[13] The magistrates acknowledged that they disliked sending men such as Mr Tweeney to gaol, but, like the police, they had to enforce the law.

Amongst the most used legislation of the nineteenth century were local Acts and by-laws. In 1899 just over 5,000 people were prosecuted under borough and county by-laws, for ignoring building and market regulations, and other controls. The number was a tribute to the emergence of an ordered urban society, the appointment of well-paid inspectors, surveyors and collectors, and the readiness of householders to inform on their neighbours. Under old paving and improvement Acts, people had always been summoned for dropping filth near their front doors, allowing water to overflow, and not pruning hedges, but the Victorians went further. To the delight of Dr Bird who said of Swansea people in 1845 that they 'build where and how they please', town dwellers increasingly needed planning permission to alter buildings and change the drains. It took individuals some time to realize how quickly and quietly freedom passes away. 'I will not do it', George Robinson, blockmaker, told the Swansea magistrates in 1860 when instructed to pull down his new home, 'nor will I give the Local Board or the Surveyor liberty to do so.' 'We don't need your liberty', replied Mr Harvey on behalf of the Board.[14]

At work, too, people found it hard to escape the law. The police, the armed forces, the merchant marine, the workers on the railways and those in the Post Office had their own regulations, whilst lodging-house keepers, beer and wine merchants, pawnbrokers, dealers in petroleum and explosives, hawkers and other sellers in the nineteenth century were required to have annual licences and inspection. People were summoned for failing to register lodging-houses, using gunpowder at improper times, and demanding excessive charges and fares. Much police time was given to this work. Each year in the later nineteenth century the Welsh police granted, and checked, thousands of pedlars' licences.[15] Hawking without a certificate, a common offence, resulted in a 10*s.* fine or fourteen days imprisonment in the 1880s. Nor did it end there, for these sellers were reported for obstructing the footpaths, setting up stalls outside market halls, and holding illegal auctions.

During these years the state also placed new responsibilities on parents, as we shall see later, and on the owners of dogs. First hundreds, and then thousands, of dog-owners appeared in court annually. In 1899, for instance, 2,442 people were proceeded against over offences relating to dogs. They were charged, amongst other things, with having a dangerous animal, not keeping the dog under proper control and allowing a dog to kill sheep. The police found the work arduous; they had to collect and dispose of strays, and report breaches of the new Dog Licensing Act. In 1878 the Inland Revenue requested greater police co-operation over the latter, and promised detecting officers a small reward from the money recovered.[16] In Pembrokeshire the police initiated proceedings against 148 people in 1881 for having a dog without a licence, and gained a conviction in 132 cases. For a first offence, an owner paid a fine of between 2s. 6d. and 10s. In the most heavily policed districts of this period, where so much was enforced by a 10s. fine, even keeping chimneys and pavements clean, one can detect some annoyance that virtually every facet of human behaviour was coming under scrutiny.

Complaints about these proceedings under summary jurisdiction were indeed rather more common than reformers admitted. They were of four main kinds. One grievance was that there was simply too much new legislation, which was not fully understood and which sometimes conflicted with traditional ways of doing things. In the remoter districts of rural Wales, there were still people at the end of the nineteenth century who would or could not pay their highway rate, but offered instead to work on the roads for a few days a year, as their grandfathers had done. In refusing this statute labour, the magistrates said that 'we are not to keep a custom if it is contrary to the law'.[17] Some of the new standards of public hygiene also marked a break with familiar practices. Food merchants resented both the changes and the scientific support upon which inspectors and magistrates increasingly relied. In court, traders questioned the worth, convenience, and costs of the regulations, but, after an initial period of grace, they were shown the error of their ways. When A.J. Sheppard, for the Local Government Board, took butcher Phillips before the Tredegar Petty Sessions in March 1880, for having five carcasses of mutton 'unfit for food', the magistrates gave him the mitigated penalty of £5 rather than £20, 'as it is the first case of the kind brought before us'. No doubt it helped that one of them, Dr Coates, personally knew Phillips 'to be a respectable man', but the other butchers of Tredegar and Pontypool who soon followed him into court were not so fortunate.[18]

A second, related, complaint was over the manner in which the courts were being used. Official prosecutors such as collectors, inspectors and policemen, often seemed inflexible and unwilling to accept apologies and compromises. The weekly parade in the Petty Sessions of those who had not paid their rates and duties was increasingly regarded as a necessary public exercise, and less sympathy, and fewer concessions, were held out to the poorest of these offenders with the passage of time.[19] Indeed, there were moments during the court cases when everyone realized, in a blinding flash, just how much ultimate power now resided in the hands of local-government committees, with their strict rules and officials. At St Asaph Petty Sessions in February 1860 several people, charged with breaches of the Nuisance Act, pleaded with magistrates to intercede on their behalf with the appropriate committee. The Bench replied that the nuisance committee was under the democratic control of ratepayers, and the function of the court was simply to enforce, by orders, fines and distresses, the will of that body.[20] There were occasions when the boards and committees over-reached themselves, and magistrates declared that some of the statutory fines which they demanded were excessive, but there was not too much that could be done by way of protest.

A third complaint was over the representative nature of those pressing hardest for social improvement through legal and police action. In a number of Welsh districts, for example, support for the ban on Sunday trading, drinking and recreation was matched by less publicized statements in favour of relaxation and choice. In Cardiff, despite the rise in prosecutions in the late 1850s and early 1860s, and again in 1870 and 1882–3, at least 125 shops were open on a Sunday, many in the Butetown area.[21] Shopkeepers who appeared in court there, and in the Monmouthshire mining towns, sometimes refused on principle, both to abide by Sunday closing and to pay the fines, citing as their excuse the requirements of the labouring population. In the capital, where there were even attempts to stop pigeon races on a Sunday in the 1880s, a pamphlet was printed called *Black Glamorgan*, setting out an alternative case for popular recreation on the Lord's Day. The same kind of dialogue accompanied the moves towards compulsory vaccination and education. As the number of court cases show, especially in places like Newport, Cardiff and Swansea, a determined minority of people remained unconvinced that all aspects of state welfare and moral reform were in their best interests. Magistrates, who were increasingly doctors, lawyers, and ministers, as well as gentlemen, disagreed.

One such conflict, which excited much interest, was fought out in Neath during 1858–60. At the centre of the controversy was police superintendant John Lynn, a teetotaller who launched a personal crusade against 'low' lodging-houses, drunkenness, gambling on licensed premises, insanitary habits, swearing, playing pitch and toss and football in the streets, and desecrating the Sabbath. Such was his unpopularity with poorer sections of the population that posters were printed calling upon people to escort him out of the town, to the sound of tin kettles. Perhaps his greatest mistake was to have alienated, by 'his zeal' and 'impartiality', a section of middle-class opinion. Admiral Wardle, an important local figure, felt that Lynn had improved the habits of the people, but had gone overboard in his enthusiasm. A meeting of the town council decided on his removal, after mistakes had been spotted in his accounting. Lynn later joined the Cardiff police, and continued to be a focus of controversy.[22]

The final complaint, which was often heard in the cases discussed in this chapter, was that the authorities dealt more harshly with the the poor than with people of a higher social status. This, it was claimed, was true at every stage of the legal process. Amongst the hundreds of people summoned and apprehended under preventive legislation, it was difficult to find one from the higher orders. The poorest members of society were often arrested just on suspicion under the police and vagrancy Acts, and later released or acquitted in court. The diary of police constable William Evans of Pennal, Merioneth, reveals that the public had some sympathy with such unfortunates, and the latter made their own feeble protests. Ephraim Barret, 'a most repulsive-looking fellow', tore his clothes to pieces after being arrested by the Newtown police in 1862. 'I don't see why a man should be brought upon suspicion', he declared in court, and was then given seven days imprisonment for his behaviour.[23] There were claims, too, that the Victorian reforming legislation, over matters as different as animal rights, work contracts, drink and pollution, was largely class specific. The activities of the middle, and especially the upper, classes in these areas of life were never followed with quite the same interest as those of the working class.

In defending the owners, and the customers, of disorderly and bawdy houses in Cardiff in 1860, solicitor Bowen contended that 'the whole affair was a crusade against the poor man, while the rich were allowed to go free'.[24] The same charge was made in relation to the Weights and Measures Act. Sir John Mansel said at the Quarter Sessions in 1846 that Act was, much to the disadvantage of the poor man, a 'nullity' in Carmarthenshire, but fellow magistrate, John Lloyd Davies, resisted the appointment of the rural police as inspectors under the Act because they would become 'domestic spies' and would not be tolerated in the county.[25] In later decades, as local government became more democratic, a larger number of tradesmen, contractors, professional men and other people of wealth and privilege were prosecuted, but certain inequalities always remained.[26] In many, but by no means all, of the cases dealt with at Petty Sessions, where there was no recourse to trial by jury, there seemed to be a built-in bias in favour of residents against outsiders, masters against employees, sellers against buyers, welfare officers against recipients, and men against women.

It is impossible in one chapter to discuss all the offences other than those against persons and property. The main ones can be seen in Table 10. Within Wales certain categories of these 'moral' or 'technical' crimes attracted special attention: those affecting the family and the home, those concerned with health, food and drink, those against Acts controlling work, industrial relations, poor relief and vagrancy, and those in the area of roads and transport. Graph 20 covers the first group. It is a combination of court appearances for ignoring bastardy orders, and for deserting and neglecting to support the family. Not surprisingly, these offences were influenced by changes in the standard of living. The economic implications of maintaining illegitimate children were well known in Wales; in fact, its

Table 10
The main victimless crimes dealt with at Petty Sessions in 1881

Adulteration of Food, etc. Act	104
Contagious Diseases (Animals) Act	132
Cruelty to animals	446
Customs Acts	125
Disobeying bastardy orders	514
Elementary Education Acts, offences against	3724
Employers and Workmen's Act, 1875	695
Excise Acts (including Hawkers' and Pedlars' Acts)	725
Highway Act	1752
Licensing Act, 1872, drunkenness, and drunk and disorderly	10522
Licensing Act, 1872, other offences	1680
Local Acts, and borough by-laws, offences against	1665
Public Health Acts	88
Poor Law Acts, deserting, or neglecting to support family	715
Poor Law Acts, disorderly, and damaging conduct, in workhouse	138
Railway Acts	234
Turnpike Acts	274
Vagrancy Act, disorderly prostitutes	445
Vagrancy Act, begging	1080
Vagrancy Act, having no visible means of subsistence, etc.	364
Vaccination Acts, offences against	74
Weights and Measures Acts, offences against	518

Source: PP, 1882, LXXV.

rural population had a reputation, largely undeserved, for having an exceptionally large number of bastards. When these were born, the first reaction of the mothers, at least in the countryside of the early nineteenth century, was to make private deals with the fathers. If this failed, then these women were forced to seek help from the parish.

The parish sometimes found a foster home for the bastard child, but it

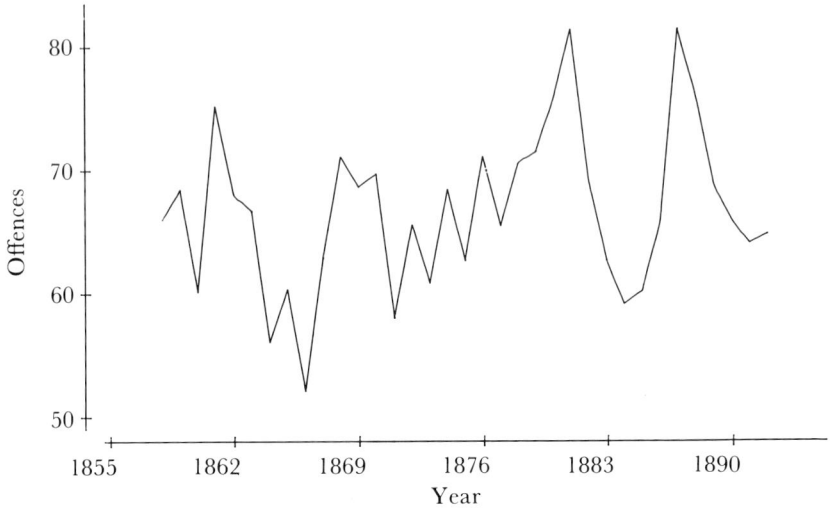

Basic rate: per 100,000 of population

Graph 20. Offences determined summarily of disobeying bastardy orders, and of deserting or neglecting to support the family, 1858–1892.

was important to establish the responsibilities of the fathers and mothers in this matter. When problems arose, one or other, and sometimes both, of the parents were taken to court. Before the Poor Law Amendment Act of 1834 scores of Welsh women were, every year, given three months hard labour or heavy fines for crimes associated with bastardy, such as refusing to swear to the identity of the father, but this hardly compared with the number of men who were prosecuted. For example, Sarah Nash, Susan Griffiths and Ann Rees were committed to Haverfordwest gaol in the twelve months after October 1831 for disobeying an order of bastardy, and they were joined by twenty-four males on similar charges. A number of the latter, like James Thomas, the nineteen-year-old shipwright of Burton, were discharged early 'having satisfied the parish'.[27]

Local and national governments took an interest in these matters mainly because of the expense. A large share of poor-law expenditure went on unmarried mothers, unsupported children and aged parents, and the workhouses were full of them. Until the Act of 1834 the courts generally relied on the evidence of the mother as to the identity of the father of her bastard child, and maintenance orders were made out, with penalties and gaol for those men who fell behind with payments. The Act made life easier for these fathers, and male imprisonments were reduced to a trickle. At the same time, reports of female desertion of children and infanticide increased sharply. In fact, the agitation against the new bastardy clauses in Wales persuaded the government, ten years later, of the need to modify them.[28] The result can be seen in the following figures. In 1836 only twenty-two of the men convicted at Petty Sessions on bastardy charges were imprisoned; in 1845 the number leapt to forty-eight, and doubled again by 1851.

Of course, those with wealth and legal counsel who were accused of fathering 'base children' always had an advantage, but Charles Brigstocke, a Carmarthen vestryman, was wrong when he said that 'no rich man is ever forced to pay'.[29] Like some of the property crimes mentioned in the previous chapter, the issue of bastardy brought a small number of respectable people into the dock. Men of commerce, ministers, farmers, as well as working men, had the embarrassment of seeing their names in the local press. When, as often happened, they later ignored the paternity orders and maintenance payments, the mothers had to seek union help again and another court action ensued. At this point, Rowland Evans and Rowland Rowlands, butchers of the Aberdyfi–Tywyn area in the 1870s, always 'paid on demand'.[30] A cheaper, if illegal, alternative for the exasperated mothers, and one adopted by Rebecca and angry neighbours throughout the century, was to leave these illegitimate children outside the homes of their fathers.

The legal statistics of proceedings at the lower courts for disobeying bastardy orders, and for neglecting or deserting the family, moved in different directions. Typically, in the second half of the century, about four or five hundred people were in court annually on bastardy charges, many of them being inhabitants of Carmarthenshire, but the numbers fell markedly in the 1880s and 1890s. The reverse was true for the second offence; in 1875 there were some 547 cases of neglect and desertion, but by 1888 this had risen to 906, when well over half the cases were from Glamorgan. In a representative case, William Davies, an unemployed copperman, deserted his family, saying that he no longer had the means to feed them. He was given one month's hard labour for such arrogant behaviour, and his wife and children entered the Swansea workhouse.[31]

Some of the prosecutions for desertion were made on the initiative of distressed females, but this was an issue which also concerned the authorities. Early in the century they committed a few men to the county gaol at Dolgellau, their only crime being 'threatening to leave his family'. At Corwen in the 1860s and 1870s Robert LLoyd, who did more than threaten, was pursued relentlessly; he received five short gaol sentences for beating his wife and neglecting to support his family.[32] One suspects that, unlike the poor-law union, his dependants were rather glad to see the back of him. Family duties were becoming harder to impose, as the years passed, because of the greater mobility of people in the period and because of the freedom enjoyed in city life. It proved easier for men than for women to escape their responsibilities, and, if caught, the males often did rather better than the runaway mothers. There are many instances of husbands, working class and otherwise, leaving home to find work, never to return, and of men and women who were unwilling to look after elderly and sick relatives. The former misdemeanour, if turned into a conviction, meant a fortnight or a month's hard labour in gaol, whilst the latter could result in a court order to contribute towards workhouse and asylum costs. The improvements in police communications made life a little harder for such deserters. Thus David Roberts, a Barmouth joiner, was arrested in Merthyr in 1884, when information on him was telegraphed around the forces, and he was sent back to face his family. Some of his friends, in a similar situation, joined the emigration ships.

There was a thin line between desertion, neglect and cruelty, especially over children. Each year, as we saw in chapter 3, babies were abandoned outside workhouses, houses and chapels, often after an attempt at affiliation had failed, and older children, too, were left 'on the parish' by families passing through the district. In a number of cases, after husbands and wives separated, their offspring struggled on by themselves. The consequences can be imagined; in the winter of 1891–2, two of John Davies's children died in the Strand, Swansea, and a third was found starving. Others were neglected, or abused, within the home. Mary Thomas of Llangefni, for instance, was fined £2 in 1895 for not providing adequate food and clothing for her stepchild, whilst nine years before Benjamin Evans of Cardiff was charged with causing the death, by starvation, of his baby daughter. The family were in lodgings, they had no furniture and his wife was ill. He told the court that he had done his best. Rather more wilful perhaps was Evan Jones of Llandudno who received two months hard labour for persistently ill-treating and neglecting his sick daughter, and much better known were the parents of Sarah Jacob, 'the fasting girl' of Lletherneuadd near Pencader, who were given twelve and six months gaol in 1870 for her manslaughter. During the 1890s the NSPCC, which prosecuted Jones, played a significant role in the sharp rise in child cruelty cases. In this area at least, the state left the initiative, and any opprobrium for unwarranted interference in the home, to voluntary movements.

Changes in family relationships during this period were signposted by legislation such as the Custody of Children and the Married Women's Property Acts of 1872 and 1882, but it was the new Education Acts which brought the law most commonly into the home. The Acts of 1870–91 re-organized the administration of elementary education, improved facilities for it, and then made it compulsory and free. In the last two decades of the century 4–5,000 people a year were proceeded against under the Acts, chiefly for not sending their children to school. The typical punishment was a 5s. fine, though in north Wales, in the very worst of cases, magistrates ordered that the children should join other young rebels on the *Clio* training school-ship, permanently anchored at Bangor after 1877. In most cases, the erring families were reported by school-attendance officers rather than by the police, for the latter disliked the task of rounding up truants.

Contrary to some impressions, the legal battle over the new education policy was fought more fiercely in the urban and industrial districts than in the countryside. In 1892, for example, when 5,619 prosecutions were launched under the Elementary Education Acts, three-quarters were in Glamorgan and Monmouthshire, and almost one in five were in Swansea, Newport and Cardiff. A large body of Ebbw Vale parents in that year was fined 5s. each for the irregular attendance of their children, but the greatest number of court cases was always at Swansea. On 23 January 1884 no less than twenty parents appeared at its police court for failing to send their children to school. Orders for attendance were made out, and on this occasion the defendants had to pay only the costs of the case. They knew, without being told, that non-compliance would result in their children being taken to Bonymaen truant industrial school.[33] Between 1882, when the establishment was founded, and 1888, 458 boys entered the school and, despite its ferocious discipline, about a third of these were re-admitted.[34] Many of the parents of these children inhabited the poorer districts of the town, though most of these did not, so far as we know, have criminal records. The chief excuse for the non-attendance of their offspring was illness, and failing to realize that thirteen-year-olds did not have an automatic right to leave school, but one can detect in their language a resentment that they had to conform to other people's standards.

The same feeling was expressed in other areas of life. There was, for instance, open and covert resistance to the legislation passed to improve health and combat disease. In the early years of the century paving commissioners prosecuted hundreds of people for throwing putrid material, and relieving themselves, in the streets. The cholera epidemics prompted health enquiries, and stimulated local as well as national action to improve medical care, sanitation, water supplies and housing conditions. On 9 November 1866, for example, the superintendant of police for the Monmouth borough, acting on instructions received from the sanitary committee, summoned a number of individuals over nuisances arising from foul and offensive privies, the keeping of pigs, and premises having no water supply. The important Public Health Act of 1875, one of a series, gave sanitary authorities the right to initiate summary proceedings against 'unfit' housing and overcrowded conditions. James Row, the Pontypridd policeman, caught Hannah Gowery early one morning, as she slept with her three children, and thirteen unauthorized lodgers.

Each year in the second half of the century two or three hundred people were prosecuted for breaches of public-health legislation, and hundreds more were charged with related nuisances under local by-laws and highways Acts. Keepers of common lodging-houses, like Mrs Ivorey in Swansea, complained that the police never left them alone. A few of them refused to pay the fines imposed on them because of the overcrowded and unhealthy state of their accommodation, and suffered imprisonment instead. One of their gripes, expressed at a public-health meeting at Merthyr in 1856, was that employers and wealthy landlords escaped the legal consequences of their inaction over such matters. There was much truth in this, though there were rare occasions when industrial companies were convicted of polluting both rivers and the atmosphere.[35]

Controlling disease also required care over the supply and distribution of food. Prior to the comprehensive Contagious Diseases (Animals) Act of 1869, amended six years later, orders were issued from time to time over the reporting, movement and sale of affected beasts. During the Cattle Plague of the mid-1860s several hundred farmers were charged with disobeying such orders. The policeman of Overton in Flintshire, who was the temporary plague officer for the district, disliked the work; from his notes, it is obvious that he had to balance the wishes of the farming community, the demands of the Quarter Sessions, the instructions of the local plague committee and the orders of his superiors.[36] In later years the number of farmers who came before the magistrates was much reduced, though police constable William Evans of Pennal, Merioneth, and other colleagues were busy in 1885–6 with an outbreak of sheep scab. One learns, from their diaries, that many cases of foot-and-mouth, swine fever, sheep scab and other diseases were not reported, and that many frightened and irresponsible farmers escaped with a caution.

For their part, tradesmen like Thomas Hughes, the Overton butcher, were frequently accused of dealing in unwholesome meat and fish, as well as of adulterating food and drink, and selling it underweight. From the number of their appearances in court, a few of the market traders of Wrexham and Swansea must have made a decent living out of selling cut-price, if inferior, food to the poor. David Thomas, butcher of Llanedi, was fined several times in 1860, on the information of inspector Bennett, for bringing unwholesome meat to Swansea market.[37] Twenty years later, when food and drugs experts were much used in prosecutions, traders complained of the level of scrutiny. In 1880, 120 people came before the courts under the Adulteration of Food Act, and sanitary inspectors in Monmouthshire seized hundreds of putrifying carcasses. At Pontypool and Tredegar the butchers joined forces, and told the magistrates that, by any criteria, the regulations were too strict.[38]

Many complaints against merchants and shopkeepers found their way to court. They were accused of making money illegally both by adulterating milk, butter, mustard, tea, coffee, gin, whisky and coffee, and by selling flour, bread and coal underweight. The use of false weights was a common offence. In the summer of 1830 'a gang of gipsy vagrants' informed on a 'great many' Anglesey traders, who were fined for 'trifling breaches' of the law.[39] The police, who replaced the parish constables as inspectors of weights and measures, cautioned hundreds of people for using defective and unjust measures. In 1860, when as many as 561 traders appeared in court to answer these charges, the patience of magistrates gave way. At Rhuthun the mayor fined a miller £5, with costs, for his 'shameful' conduct, and reminded him that 'in olden times this offence was punishable in a very severe manner'. 'It is melancholy to think', agreed the mayor of Caernarfon in the same year, 'of the number of poor persons who may be defrauded by acts like this' (a faulty coal weighing balance). *The Cambrian* newspaper, describing similar prosecutions of shopkeepers and grocers at Neath and Bridgend, suggested in 1860 that consumers should establish their own protection society.[40] Later in the century, when the numbers prosecuted were fewer, plain-clothes officers made a worthy, if vain, attempt to stamp out these and other shady commercial practices. In 1893 the Anglesey Police Committee was told that 343 surprise visits had been made to trade premises, and five summonses taken out.[41]

The regulation of drinking-houses, like that of places where food was sold and eaten, was taken more seriously as the century progressed.[42] This was not a new policy; in the late sixteenth and early seventeenth centuries the control of alehouses had been a prime target of the village officers, though it was the people of low social status who were usually prosecuted. This selectivity was also apparent at the beginning of the nineteenth century, as craftsmen, labourers and women were charged with keeping disorderly houses, selling ale without licence, and permitting tippling on a Sunday. Public houses were annually licensed at Brewster Sessions of magistrates, who were accused of being manipulated by the trade. In 1830 the Beer Act freed beerhouses of such controls, and immediately its repeal became one of the primary objectives of the puritan lobby. The keenest authorities, including those at Merthyr, used the new police to enforce their own licensing regulations, and welcomed an Act of 1849 which banned the sale of drink on Sunday mornings. Within a couple of years, over a hundred proprietors of public, and especially beer, houses were being prosecuted annually in the iron capital, and amongst those regularly punished were the landlords of the Colliers Arms and the Black Bull in 'China'. As the police diary of James James in the early 1860s shows, many other guilty Merthyr publicans escaped without a summons.

According to the police authorities, the restrictive Wine and Beerhouse Act of 1869 proved 'highly satisfactory', and three years later, Henry

Austin Bruce's famous Licensing Act set a national standard which remained until quite recent times. Its main clauses governed the sale of alcohol, the licensing of premises and the restriction of opening hours. The implementation of the Act became another matter of controversy, for nonconformist radicals on the police committees insisted that, when breaches of the law occurred, the seller of alcohol was treated more generously than the drinker. On the other hand, there were fears, expressed at the Denbighshire Standing Joint Committee in 1895, that it was only too easy for the police to 'set up' cases against keepers of public, beer and cider houses.[43] In some towns, such as Newport, as many as one in five of these people appeared in court annually, and, increasingly, decisions were taken not to renew their licences. The reponse was an angry one; petitions from the 'persecuted and ever oppressed licensed publican' rained thick and fast upon the watch committees.

As we saw in chapter 3, the rise in the statistics of drunkenness owed something to the prodigious efforts of moral and religious reformers, and to the personal commitment of chief constables. The same was true of the proceedings over breaches of the licensing regulations. Licensees were charged, amongst other things, with allowing drinking after hours and during divine services, permitting drunkenness and gambling on the premises, and refusing police access. At Carmarthen in the 1830s an attempt was made to suppress skittles, card-playing, dominoes, games of chance and musical entertainment in public houses. It failed, but not before it had inflamed feelings between the customers and the police. At Cardiff thirty years later, John Willet, secretary of the Society for the Prevention of Vice and Immorality, led another campaign. He personally checked that beersellers had proper signs over their doors and that closing times were duly observed. For his efforts, he was abused and threatened, and so was the reforming police constable David Jones of Dolgellau, who launched daring midnight raids in 1870 on drinking premises.

The diaries of constables James Row of Pontypridd and David Williams of Briton Ferry reveal that in the 1870s they spent much of their time in monitoring these licensing regulations. As a result of their efforts many non-publicans, often women, were accused of selling alcohol illegally from their homes and at lodging houses. On 10 October 1879, David Williams and another policeman dressed in navvies' clothes and drank with others at the homes of the Stoneham and Norris familes in Felindre, near Swansea, and then told them to expect a £2 fine for illegally selling beer.[44] In Irish Cardiff, where the battle was relentless, shebeens were constantly closed down, only to re-open months later. By 1880 the annual number of all such licensing prosecutions in the Principality had risen to almost 1,500. This still did not satisfy the drink reformers, and, after a vigorous publicity campaign, the Welsh Sunday Closing Act passed through Parliament a year later. It was a unique piece of Welsh legislation, and regarded by some as a first step towards Home Rule!

The Act divided the police forces and the press, as much as it divided the Welsh nation.[45] Even in the heart of Dissenting Wales breaches of the Act were recorded, and heavy fines imposed. At the Hope and Anchor in Holyhead, Ellen Jones received a £5 fine for serving beer at an open window to a crowd of men. On that occasion the look-outs were caught napping.[46] Newspaper correspondents did spot-checks on the number of people flouting the new law, and others sent anonymous information to the police. In the largest towns the police needed little help. In dockland and Irish Cardiff Sundays continued much as before. Dr Lambert assures us that the Act of 1881 led to an 'increase in Sunday drunkenness' in Glamorgan and Cardiff, but not in the rural areas.[47] In the city hundreds of people were convicted of selling beer contrary to the Act. One response, in Cardiff, as in all the largest industrial towns and seaports, was the establishment of working-class drinking clubs, which were outside the terms of the Sunday Closing legislation. It was several years before the Cardiff watch committee, following Bristol's example, closed this loophole. In Wrexham and Brymbo there were similar battles of will, but in north Wales, at least amongst Thomas Gee and his friends, much of the anger was directed at the middle-class drinkers who travelled to Betws-y-coed and Llangollen on a Sunday, booked into hotels and imbibed in comfort.

The campaign for tighter controls over drinking was matched by another against disorderly and bawdy houses (brothels). There were many examples of this, from Holyhead southwards, and the demands for action came from angry local residents as well as from moral reformers. Two of the best known chapters in this story opened at Cardiff in 1859–60 and at Newport in the winter of 1879–80. In Cardiff John Willett and John Davies laid information against Thomas Daley, Susan Strange and more than thirty other people for keeping bawdy houses. The police moved cautiously, but with an element of surprise; after documenting reports of disorder in Whitmore Lane and Bute and Christina streets, they rushed the premises and found sailors and prostitutes in bed. The chairman of the Quarter Sessions said that 'he knew very well that the law could not make people virtuous, but it could be instrumental in preserving public decency and public order...'[48] Most of the brothel keepers in the dock were found guilty, and bound over. It was not the end of the story, for in 1865 an order was made to clear all drunk and disorderly prostitutes from the streets of Cardiff, and ten years later the inhabitants of Roath persuaded the watch committee, and a reluctant superintendant, to 'suppress houses of ill-fame' in Constellation Street. Meanwhile, a few miles to the east, at Newport, another confrontation was about to take place, after more complaints from residents that their life had been ruined by carousing prostitutes and sailors. In the winter of 1879–80 Ursula Clements, Mary Ann Williams, and Harriet Haggerty, who owned nine of the bawdy houses, chiefly in Canal Parade, were prosecuted. Williams received twelve months imprisonment, but Haggarty and the chief witness disappeared before the trial came on.[49] The Criminal Law Amendment Act of 1885 made prosecutions against brothel keepers somewhat easier, but even after that date the numbers charged remained small.

Whether at leisure, or at work, people of the nineteenth century soon discovered that the state was interested in them. Work, and the lack of it, was something which had always been of concern to governments. Although there was a gradual removal of legal controls over apprenticeships and pay at the beginning of the century, Parliament found it impossible to ignore the conditions of work in the new industrial towns. The misery and tensions caused by these conditions, and unremitting pressure from reformers, persuaded the politicians of the mid-century that here, too, regulation was needed. Factory and Mines Acts were passed to control female and child labour and to reduce the chance of accidents, but inspection was poor and punishment never adequate.[50] The number of prosecutions under these Acts was remarkably small in Wales, usually well under 100 per year. Amongst the most common proceedings were those against miners who smoked underground and forgot to close air doors. Few cases were brought against employers; as a report of 1842 indicated, magistrates who were themselves industrialists, were hardly the best recipients of complaints against their colleagues.[51] This in part explained the half-hearted implementation of the Truck Acts of 1831 and 1842, which sought to outlaw the payment of wages in goods, a common practice in Wales at the time. It needed courage and money to confront the company bosses; one conviction, secured after much endeavour by the Aberdare Anti-Truck Association in the early 1850s, cost £80.[52]

By comparison the courts were used frequently in other areas of industrial relations. In strategic occupations, such as the armed forces and the merchant navy, those who broke the signed articles of employment were rigorously pursued. Between 1834 and 1854 about a hundred military men per year were imprisoned, usually for twelve months or less, for desertion and other offences. In the case of British seamen the very common practice of jumping ship was punished by two to three months hard labour, whilst foreign sailors who did the same were forcibly returned to their vessels. Those who hid them whilst on shore were also convicted. There were always, of course, many sailors who, tired of life at sea and angry about conditions, refused to obey their captains. This was true both before and after the Merchant Shipping Act of 1854. Magistrates prefered to adjourn such cases, to give time for a satisfactory settlement to emerge, but when it did not, as often happened, the discontented seamen were given the choice of returning to work or imprisonment. Not all their masters were above reproach; Caernarfon, Aberystwyth and Newport magistrates warned them time and again that discharge notes had to be given and arrears of wages paid.[53]

Insubordinate apprentices, and other working men and women, were treated in a similar manner to these sailors. Domestic servants had an especially hard time. The very youngest were beaten and older ones were accused of 'ill behaviour', 'wasting her master's property' and other such misdemeanours. It was clear, from the court case of Margaret Jones of Cardigan in 1846, that some of the feeblest servants were deprived of wages for months and even years.[54] The annual hire of servants, both male and female, was generally made without any papers being signed, but the verbal contract was binding. Those servants who lived and worked at the farms soon discovered how little freedom they had; in the first two decades of the century they were fined, or more usually imprisoned for as much as a month, for being absent for a few hours, for being out at night, and for refusing to obey a command. Many, disillusioned by the low wages and attracted by the prospects in town and industry, 'deserted their service' in the mid-century and risked the one to three months imprisonment that awaited them if caught. Those servants who fled before the busy harvest time, for higher wages in the English countryside and in the mines of south Wales, were often ordered back to the farms, to work off their debt. Later in the century, when the balance of power between employers and workers in rural Wales was more equal, the latter took their masters to court in considerable numbers for wages unpaid, poor food and promises unfulfilled.[55]

The first industrialists were reluctant to waste time and money, and they had other controls like the discharge note, but there were economic conditions when it made sense for them to enforce work practices and contracts of employment through the courts. Workmen were charged with absenting themselves from work, ruining goods and machines, entering into combinations and leaving without the required month's notice. In 1799 the Dowlais company considered using both the combination and conspiracy laws to break one strike. The leaders were confined in the bridewell at Cowbridge, and this note, from John Davies to Thomas Guest, conveys the effects of gaol upon the protesters:

> I ham sorry that I abused your Honour in taking so much upon me to spaek for others. I hope you will get me out of this whole of a place so soon as your Honer shall think fitt as I shall be starved a live for my money is all spent...[56]

In Wales in the second half of the nineteenth century there were, on average, over 600 prosecutions annually in relation to servants, apprentices and masters. The Master and Servant Act of 1844, an extension of another one 21 years before, proved to be of immense 'disciplinary convenience', especially for employers who received preferential treatment under it. Daphne Simon, in her chapter on the Act, describes how in one case, at Wrexham in 1864, the mayor, without a pretence at impartiality, spoke grimly about the French revolution and the 'disunited states of America' and then sent a young workman to gaol for a month.[57] Many prosecutions under the Act were brought by the employers to stop a haemorrhage of good workmen and to prevent and end strikes. The typical fine, or one month's gaol sentence, for leaving a company without notice was sometimes rescinded if the defendant agreed to return to work. Some of the court proceedings, like those involving the redoubtable W.P. Roberts at Tredegar in 1864, made the national news, but most were very ordinary affairs. One is struck, reading the correspondence of the employers, by the care with which they used the judiciary and the police during the industrial troubles of the mid and late nineteenth century. The Dowlais Company letters illustrate, for example, how the Guests in the strike of 1853 consulted Henry Austin Bruce, magistrate, and superintendent Wrenn, at every stage of the conflict. Even then, the authorities occasionally got it wrong, as when they inflicted excessive punishment on the men at Pontymister in 1893, and provoked a public outcry.

Rather more interesting perhaps was the readiness of the same workmen to take employers and agents to court over contract and wage disputes. In hard times this was not unexpected. In the spring of 1842 the Petty Sessions at Bedwellty, Pontypool and Abergavenny were full of workmen successfully lodging claims for unpaid wages.[58] Even in the prosperous years, however, working people needed the courts, or just the threat of taking out summonses. In the Merthyr police district alone, between 1846 and 1864, an average of almost a hundred prosecutions a year were brought for non-payment of wages, with crowds celebrating the most spectacular victories. When John H. G. Owen of Pontypool, the 'people's attorney', told Henry Austin Bruce in these years that there was one law for the rich and one for the poor, he was being strictly accurate though not perhaps totally fair.

Certain years figure prominently in the court statistics; in 1873, for example, when there were good wages, strong trade unionism and industrial action on the south Wales coalfield, 1,487 offences relating to servants, apprentices and masters, were heard in the Petty Sessions. Well over a half of these cases were from Glamorgan. Two years later the Employers and Workmen's Act was passed, as part of an attempt to improve industrial relations, and more use seems to have been made of it in Wales, especially in the coal industry, than elsewhere in Britain.[59] Five or six hundred persons per year were charged under this legislation, many for breaches of contract, and a much smaller number for intimidation. Before the end of the century labour law was considerably extended, and more proceedings were brought against employers. Between two and three hundred of them found themselves in court every year during the 1890s for ignoring the terms of trade, factory, mine, shop, and other Acts for the protection of labour.

Those who could or would not work received less protection. The effort, symbolized by the Poor Law Amendment Act of 1834, to control expenditure on the poor and to enforce conditions for its receipt, would have been impossible without the expanding police force and police courts. Each year several hundred people were charged with crimes in connection with the poor-law. Before the settlement laws were changed, families were penalized for ignoring orders of removal or moving without a certificate. When this ceased to be a problem, paupers appeared in court on other charges, such as improper conduct towards relieving officers and refractory behaviour within the workhouse. In the former case, people were charged with defrauding overseers, threatening them, breaking into their homes, and destroying their property and that of other officials. One such rebel was Robert Jones, a pauper who burst into the Amlwch vestry room in 1868, shouted 'I can't live on 3*s.* a week', and grabbed the coins from the guardians' bowl.

When lodged in the workhouses the same paupers often refused to perform a work test and to obey the other demands of the masters and mistresses. The latter were given the authority to punish the rebellious, mainly by withholding food, though a few workhouses insisted on separate confinement for the worst offenders. Yet, as Daniel Kemp, master of the Wrexham workhouse, well knew, any such action had serious consequences.[60] The most determined of the inmates fled the buildings, wearing their parish clothes, whilst those inside took out their anger on property. Windows and furniture were smashed, partitions broken down, bedding ripped to pieces, and dormitories set on fire. Pauper Anne Evans of Aberaeron caused such disruption that, after six periods in Cardigan gaol, she was finally granted her request in 1849 to leave the workhouse. Her *alter ego*, Mary Wright, three years later received a two-month goal sentence for breaking windows in Haverfordwest workhouse, and another twelve for threatening to burn it down.[61]

The scapegoat for so much of this trouble was the poor vagrant, staying temporarily with the other workhouse inmates. The beggar and vagrant had been a special target of the forces of law and order for centuries. At the beginning of the nineteenth these people were still treated harshly, being put in stocks, beaten, sent to houses of correction and returned to their home parishes. It was said in these early years that magistrates, mainly for reasons of cost, were reluctant to send too many vagrants to gaol. During 1817, when south Wales was infested with them, some were simply escorted, in the 'Manchester manner', two or three miles outside town boundaries.[62] No more than about 200 of them were annually committed in the early 1820s to the prisons of Wales.

The Vagrancy Act of 1824 was partly responsible for a change in practice; it gave the authorities new preventive and discretionary powers, and laid down grades of punishment. The Act proved to be one of the most flexible and criminal-making statutes in our history. Apart from the offences of begging, being an incorrigible rogue and a disorderly prostitute, having no visible means of subsistence, frequenting enclosed premises, and sleeping rough, the vagrant could also be charged on suspicion of having committed, or being about to commit, an offence. The authorities used this Act to remove drunken and lewd women from the streets, and to clear undesirables from the vicinity of farms, mansions and factories. Charlotte Havard, who spent much of the late 1820s and early 1830s in Haverford-west gaol, was a classic victim of the Act, but there were many others who suffered the customary one month's imprisonment. Such were the numbers arrested that vagrancy crimes accounted for a large share of the rise in summary convictions before 1854. By 1848, when 877 vagrants were imprisoned, they represented well over a third of the total in Table 5.

Many more of these people appeared in court than ever entered gaol. Acquittals were extremely common, a tribute to the flimsy nature of the evidence against them. Imprisonment was the norm for those found guilty of vagrancy crimes, though a fortunate few were dismissed with a caution on promising to leave the district.[63] The Victorians, in their efforts to control pauperism, sought to separate the voluntary from the involuntary vagrant, and to separate them both from the legitimate street traders, the hawkers and pedlars. The poorest of the hawkers were little better than tramps, and were often charged, like them, with begging. By the early 1880s well over a thousand persons a year were proceeded against for this crime alone. It was committed by professional charlatans like Thomas Findlay, who feigned illness in order to obtain brandy and food, and 'Barmouth George' Hughes, who had a store of begging letters, by aggressive street musicians, and genuinely destitute individuals.[64] At Corwen and other small-town and rural Petty Sessions, where the offences of begging and sleeping in the open air constituted a third or more of the legal business, there was a suspicion in the 1880s that a recent change from prison sentences to fines and cautions had only increased the number of vagrancy crimes.

Graph 21 of these offences during the second half of the century reveals similarities with that of offences against property and with that of family crimes. This is hardly coincidental; the number of proceedings under the

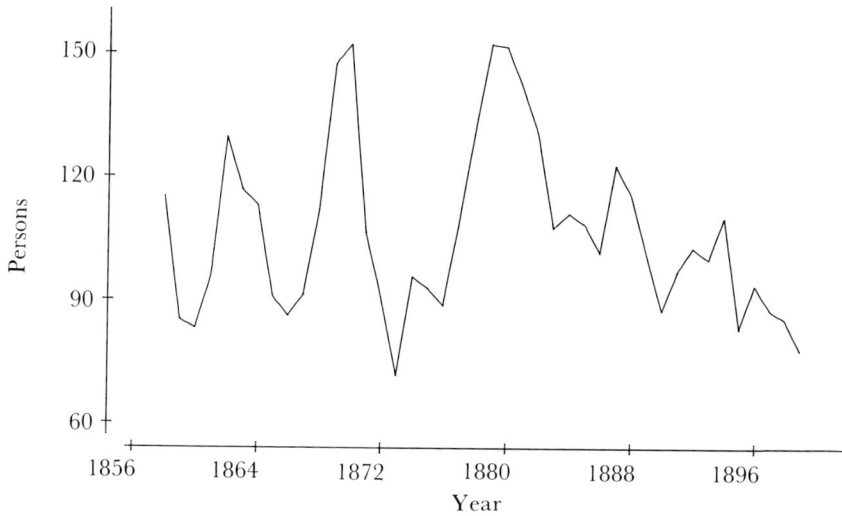

Basic rate: per 100,000 of population

Graph 21. Persons proceeded against for offences under the Vagrancy Act, 1858–1899.

Vagrancy Act frequently increased when times were hard and when those in authority were worried by the burden on the rates. The years 1869–70, when counties adopted new methods to deal with the problem, and 1879–80, stand out, and ought to be compared with other periods, like the post-war depression, the early 1830s and 1846–8, about which we have fewer details.[65] In the winter of 1848, at a magistrates' meeting in Carmarthen, William Morris expressed his concern at the number of hungry Irish vagrants wandering about the streets all night, and wondered if the strict regulations of the Poor Law Board was not forcing them into crime. In the case of Mary Ann Walters, an old and destitute Cardiff woman, there was little doubt about the matter. She applied at the police station in January 1880 for an order to be admitted to the workhouse as a tramp. As it was after 9 p.m., her request was too late, and at 1 o'clock on that cold night she smashed a window at the home of the chief constable and soon found shelter of a sort.[66]

The coming of the professional police made a significant difference to the statistics of vagrancy crime. In the mid-Victorian years they were appointed assistant poor-law officers with special responsibility for vagrants. Police diaries show that in parts of south-west Wales much of their time was devoted to registering, searching and arresting these outsiders. In Caernarfonshire, Montgomeryshire and Merioneth it was a similar story, but in their anxiety to move these people on, the problem was passed around the

Principality. Offences tended to rise in towns during the winter months, when the vagrants clung to the coke ovens and annoyed the middle-class residents, and to increase in the countryside during the summer, when they looked for odd jobs and slept against the hay ricks. Denial of help, encouraged by the new anti-mendicity societies, only turned more vagrants to crime, both in the workhouse and outside. Gaol for these people had its merits, especially in the coldest season. In the last years of the century, when deterrent wards and cells were built for persistent tramps, there was some gratification over the falling level of recorded vagrancy offences, but in 1894, and even more so ten years later, the graph soared again.

With the limited exceptions of vagrancy and family crimes, the statistics of all the offences discussed in this chapter did not closely follow the path of those described in chapters 3 and 4. This was neither surprising nor alarming. Reformers, who hoped for the diminution, even elimination, of crimes against persons and property, anticipated an initial growth in the incidence of victimless offences as governments imposed more sophisticated forms of order and civilized behaviour. The mid-Victorian period witnessed just such a growth. Some of the legislation used by the authorities had been on the statute book for a long time, whilst other Acts were comparatively new, but all were given impetus by enthusiastic pressure groups, dedicated central and local government officers, energetic watch committees, and, on occasions, public support. The police, too, played an important role in this area, something which historians have largely ignored. The men in blue, who were health, trade and vagrancy inspectors, as well as much else besides, reported many of the misdemeanours described in this chapter, and prosecuted a considerable number of the offenders. The police journals of policemen at Leeswood in Flintshire and Sketty in Swansea in 1868–70 show just how busy they were giving cautions, serving summonses, and executing warrants for arrears of maintenance, highway offences, non-payment of rates, public-health nuisances, and the like. Chief constables worried about the effect of such duties on the efficiency and popularity of their men when they returned to 'regular police work'.[67]

The Acts outlawing cruelty to animals and controlling behaviour on the highway provide two of the best examples of the way in which law was revitalized, partly with police assistance, in the later nineteenth century. The important Act protecting animals was passed in 1835, but was used fitfully thereafter. In 1858 there were only 101 prosecutions under it in Wales, though the newspaper accounts of that time prove that sports such as bull-running, dog- and cock-fighting, and badger-baiting had not been eliminated, and that domestic animals were tortured with sad, monotonous regularity. With the help of the police, and some members of the public, the inspectors of the RSPCA managed to breathe life into an old campaign. During the last forty years of the century, proceedings over cruelty to animals increased by more than seven times. Many of the cases were of neglect, especially of refusing to feed farm animals properly. Inspector Hampshire, of the Caernarfon and Anglesey branch of the RSPCA, also kept a close watch on the transportation and slaughter of these beasts. In one instance he prosecuted a butcher who needed an axe, a sledgehammer and a knife to kill a bull with an obvious zest for life.[68] Other people appeared in court for brutally disposing of unwanted cats and dogs, for cruelly marking cows and sheep, and for beating horses and donkeys. Inevitably perhaps, given their prominence in the streets, cab and cart-men were always a target for the police and RSPCA inspectors; most were convicted of using horses whose shoulders were raw and covered in sores.

Policing the highway illustrated, perhaps better than anything else, important developments in socio-legal history. Highway and turnpike Acts were not new; at the time of Rebecca hundreds of people were cautioned and fined for riding recklessly and without reins, for obstructing the highway with a cart, for not having a name on their vehicles, and for not paying tolls. It was all rather more serious than it seemed, for road deaths, especially of the very young, were already an unfortunate fact of country and urban life. The coming of the bicycle, and then motorized transport, only added to the problems. The Denbighshire chief constable admitted in 1894 that the police had been obliged to end their customary practice of being lenient towards farmers who allowed cattle to stray into the road.[69]

In 1858 just over a 1,000 people were prosecuted under the Highway Act, and soon the police diaries contained the following typical entry: 'left station and proceeded on patrol ... on look out for tramps and highway offenders'. In the towns the police, under pressure from the watch committees, did their best to keep the centres free of unwanted traffic and obstructions to road and pavement.[70] Amongst those who appeared in court were carters of manure, fair and circus families, boys playing football and bandy in the streets, 'young fellows...standing round street corners', noisy street vendors and musicians, carpet-beating housewives and other 'public nuisances'. 'Refusing to move on when requested', a frequent response to police intervention, indicates the feeling of these people as they lost another round in the modern battle for space. By the end of the century 3,000 persons were annually prosecuted under the Highway Act. In the seaside towns, where many of the offences occurred, the police pursued reckless and drunken drivers, careless cabbies, and, after 1895, cyclists without lights. This was just a small sign of things to come. Two generations later the driver would replace the drunkard as the most common visitor to the local police court.

The implications of this growth of victimless offences were discussed as much in the nineteenth century as they have been in recent times. Conservatives warned of the dangers of extending the arm of the state too far, and of the deterioration which it might cause in the attitude of the public towards authority and the police. William Meyrick, a Merthyr solicitor during the second quarter of the century, believed that, in the interests of liberty, criminal behaviour should stay narrowly defined. In his opinion drunkenness, for example, was an impropriety not an offence. For such traditionalists, widening the range of legislation had four damaging consequences: it put excessive power into the hands of the central government, undermined the majesty of the law, interfered with personal, family and class relationships, and brought too many respectable people into court. They doubted, too, whether directives from bureaucrats in central government, and the efforts of men like superintendent Lynn of Neath and Willett of Cardiff, could ultimately change deep-rooted human behaviour. 'Petty legislation is certain', said the *North Wales Chronicle* in 1868, to prove unequal to the task...'[71]

Others, who comprised the majority of respectable opinion, took a somewhat different view; for them 'a police-man state' was perfectly acceptable, so long as those who were watched and penalized were the 'residuum', the bottom third of society. Magistrates, confronted by a drunken solicitor or a wealthy tradesman, expressed sadness that such people should have been caught by laws intended for others, and much disapproval descended upon those professional policemen who failed to be cautious and selective in their choice of victims. For many respectable observers, the statistics of certain victimless crimes during the mid-Victorian years were an indication of the scale of the battle which had to be fought with the 'idle, the pauperised, the rebellious and the immoral', and the subsequent slow-down registered on Graph 3 was also to be welcomed. It was proof, which Charles Booth reinforced in his mammoth surveys, that society at the end of the century was becoming more civilized and the lowest social groups less dangerous. 'At last,' said F. W. Maitland in 1885, when reviewing the figures of cases dealt with under summary jurisdiction, they were 'turning towards the rising sun'.[72]

A few zealots managed to rise above class interest; these, the ideological children of Edwin Chadwick, demanded the greatest possible intervention of the state at every level of society, and in all aspects of human affairs, believing that it offered the best long-term prospect for a disciplined and civilized existence. They argued that breaches of the licensing, health, revenue and education laws, reckless driving and the like, should be treated as seriously, or almost as seriously, as theft and assault, and that no one of whatever class should be allowed to escape punishment for their foolish actions and, increasingly, inactions. A handful of the letters received by the police committees and county councils indicates that there was limited support for this totalitarian view, and it is one which has remained with us. It represented a very different approach to crime from that inherited in 1800, but, as we shall see, the term 'criminal' was not easily redefined.

6

The Criminals

The use of words is important in the study of delinquency. As we have seen, a rather wider collection of social types appeared before the courts than might have been expected from the results of some historical studies. Yet the butcher selling bad meat, or the farmer who had allowed his cattle to stray on the highway, was rarely called a 'criminal' even though he had broken the criminal law. He was 'the guilty party' or 'the defendant'. The term 'criminal' was largely confined to those people who committed acts against people and property, and, in the courts at least, these were most often members of the working class. The legislators, the watch committees and the police forces concentrated their efforts on apprehending the poorest of criminals. The ratios given in chapter 2, of prosecuted criminals to population, need to be adjusted to this political fact, and it means that over a period of just a few years a considerable proportion of urban working men experienced at first hand the power of the law. In fact, by 1900 these males might have been more aware of the presence of the 'police-man state' than at any time before or since.

Studies of the sixteenth and seventeenth centuries have shown that, in a society where the gap between rich and poor was widening, authority came down increasingly heavily and selectively on the latter group. When the propertied people began their gradual 'retreat into respectability', the rest of society looked more and more deviant. Wherever you look in the records of early modern England, writes Jim Sharpe, 'crime seems to have been committed by the poor as a whole'. There were, agrees Edward Thompson in his work on the eighteenth century, no special criminal sub-cultures. The problem of crime was part of the problem of the 'lower orders'. This association of crime with the poor can also be found in the early nineteenth century.[1] It seemed, said Edmund Hyde Hall, in his description of Caernarfonshire, that only the most vulnerable members of society were deserving of the legislators' attentions. The reforming vicar of Nefyn and the alarmist Dr Bowen of Carmarthen were activated by the belief that most, if not all, the 'lower orders' had the 'mark of Cain', and should be harried by poor-laws, vagrancy laws, and other discriminating statutes. Henry Mayhew, writing a few years later, said that if the fearful and the 'do-gooders' did not stop, there was a danger of the whole working class being turned into a proscribed criminal class.[2]

In truth, this association of crime with a complete class was never absolute. There were many people, especially in the rural counties, who were convinced that the 'lower orders' were mostly decent and law-abiding citizens, and even in the towns of the mid-century observers found signs of social improvement, much as Francis Place had done in London in 1825. Henry Austin Bruce and the Revd John Griffith of Aberdare identified crime with that part of the working class known as 'the residuum', the poorest and least civilized section of society. Mary Carpenter, writing about this time, gave the name of the 'criminal and dangerous classes' to those convicts, prostitutes, habitual drunkards, beggars, idlers and in-disciplined adults and children who comprised this bottom stratum. Mary Carpenter claimed that they presented a serious threat to society, espe-cially if they became attached to the political malcontents, but with relent-less effort, and government money, the dangers could be averted. 'If the criminal class of the lower part of the population' were placed in different circumstances, she told a select committee in 1852 'they would become different'.[3] By the late nineteenth century there was some optimism about the effects of policing, punishment and reform on this 'residuum', but we are told that a residue of inadequate 'habitual criminals' remained, together with a smaller and more successful group of 'professional criminals', a new and dangerous type of businessman. These were the last 'stain on our civilisation'.

Psychological theory as it developed in that century, as well as self-interest and ignorance, combined to produce images of the criminal as a special category of persons. The habitual criminals were often portrayed as deviants or outsiders, with a different mentality and culture from the rest of society. Dr Bevan Lewis, the distinguished Wakefield psychiatrist, said in the 1890s that they were 'simply a degenerate offspring of a very degenerate stock' and he, like the the deputy-superintendent of the Glamorgan Lunatic Asylum, saw a connection between mental illness and crime. Others, of a Lombrosian persuasion, detected physical as well as mental differences between 'regular criminals' and the rest of society, the result of 'hereditary influences' and a poor urban environment.[4]

The information supplied by police, court and prison officers on the physical attributes, background, education and parentage of offenders reinforced this image of a distinct criminal class. The idea that there was an alien race, located in criminal areas, was fostered by the police lists of 'known thieves and depredators', 'suspected persons', 'prostitutes' and 'vagrants and tramps' at large in the community, and by the returns from each police division of the number of brothels and 'houses of bad character' which such people frequented. Each year after 1857, as the annual chief constables' reports were presented to the police committees, the local newspapers warned their readers of the dangers that lurked in the dark corners of their particular town.

The gaol records provided details of the age, sex, literacy and previous convictions of offenders, and, after 1856, of their occupation and nationality. Even physical details were sometimes included; thus we know that the male inmates of Carmarthen gaol in the 1850s and 1860s measured on average 5 feet 4 inches and the female 5 feet.[5] Unfortunately, all prison statistics are by nature selective, in at least three ways. Firstly, they relate very largely to one class; for centuries 'jail sentences have been imposed far more freely on working-class offenders than on businessmen and shopkeepers who broke the law'.[6] Secondly, they do not give a complete picture even of working people who committed crimes. Magistrates often decided that only the most obvious members of the 'criminal class', by virtue of their depravity or recidivism, needed to be isolated from respectable society. Most of the working class who were convicted at the lower courts escaped with a fine and a warning. Thirdly, in each generation some crimes and some criminals were over-represented in the gaol records, as authorities changed their priorities. During the Napoleonic Wars the prisons were crowded with single mothers and disobedient workmen, whilst at other times prostitutes and vagrants were the main inmates. Prison statistics, to be of value, need to be set alongside other evidence on offenders.

That provided by court officers for the Home Office is perhaps the most interesting and valuable of all. These returns of people who appeared before the higher courts after 1834, and the lower courts after 1857, give details of their age, sex, literacy, and their actual or suspected criminal past. Some of this, as we shall see, reinforces the police and prison evidence, but much of it does not. Although many 'known thieves' and other criminal types came before the courts, a large number, especially at the Petty Sessions, were 'of previous good character' and of 'character unknown'. As John Coke Fowler, Glamorgan magistrate, pointed out, such a profile caused one to wonder if these criminals were not a perfect microcosm of society. In fact, they were not, partly for reasons already mentioned, a fully representative sample of the population, and the differences in the sexual ratio, age-structure, and social make-up form the starting point of our enquiry.

It seems, from all the above evidence, that the sexual ratio of offenders did change slightly both through time and across different communities. In the twelve months after October 1822, some eighty-two per cent of the people charged with minor and serious crimes in the Haverfordwest gaol register were males. This sexual breakdown, confirmed by the transportation registers of the time, sets the pattern for the rest of the century, and can be compared with the findings of a study of the Black Country in

Table 11.
Age and sex of persons committed to prison 1860–1892

Year	Under 12 years		12–16		16–21		21–30		30–40	
	m.	f.	m.	f.	m.	f.	m.	f.	m.	f.
1860	20	9	122	49	503	312	1056	480	581	199
1876	31	5	134	38	653	293	1520	588	1150	428
1892	35	0	87	20	554	151	1501	487	1193	445

Year	40–50		50–60		60 +		Age not known		Total	
	m.	f.	m.	f.	m.	f.	m.	f.	m.	f.
1860	313	102	132	44	72	19	11	4	2810	1218
1876	651	339	323	110	170	35	13	5	4645	1841
1892	700	281	324	130	231	48	6	0	4631	1562

Source: PP, 1861, LX, 1877, LXXXVI, and 1893–4, C111.

Victorian England.[7] In the 1830s, when there were slightly fewer men than women in the Welsh population, eighty-one per cent of the persons before the Assize and Quarter Sessions were male. The proportion fell in the middle years of the century, but by the 1890s over four-fifths of those arrested and summoned, and proceeded against at Petty Sessions, were male. At the same time about three quarters of gaol inmates were male, and the proportion was rising (Table 11).

Overwhelmingly, then, one has the impression from the records that crime in Wales was predominantly, and perhaps increasingly, a male activity. This was true of England, but possibly less so. Men were, as we have seen, responsible for the majority of crimes of violence and sexual attacks, most cases of burglary and breaking and entering, almost all white-collar crimes, and some kinds of larceny. They were also more likely than women to appear at the lower courts for game-law and vagrancy offences, malicious damage, cruelty to animals, and for breaches of the highway Acts and of other important national and local legislation described in the last chapter. Sometimes this was simply because men were the heads of households.

Women were charged with a narrower range of offences. In the mid-century, when female criminality was adjudged to be at its height, typical offences committed by women were larcenies, especially shop-lifting, thefts of clothes, food and coal, and stealing from employers and the person, together with some assaults, drunkenness and disorderly conduct, and vagrancy offences, and, of course, virtually all crimes associated with babies and prostitution. Although the last occupation was not an offence, many women in the main seaports were apprehended because of it, on charges of being a 'lewd woman', displaying 'indecency' and seeming 'idle and disorderly'. As we shall see later, these female criminals were often arrested several times for the same crime. Charlotte Havard, who was in Haverfordwest gaol twenty times between 1828 and 1834, Mary Ann Williams of Newport, in Monmouthshire, who appeared on her sixteenth charge of being disorderly in March 1880, and others like them, helped to ensure that female recidivism was proportionately more common than male.

In the samples used for this book, it seems that single women were associated with crimes like larceny from the person, concealing births and infanticide, but for most offences single and married women were arrested in fairly even proportions. Thus at Newport, Monmouthshire, between 1 September 1885 and 31 August 1886, forty-nine married women were charged with drunkenness and disorderly conduct, together with thirteen widows, thirty-seven prostitutes, and ten spinsters, out of a total of 436 men and women.[8] However, given the marital status of all females in the population of fifteen years and over, it seems that single women were almost twice as likely to be apprehended for a crime as married women. Was this an indication of different mentalities and opportunities, or did, as historians have suggested, the young and the single face greater hardships and receive less help from the poor-law guardians than the married and the widowed? The authorities were certainly aware of the results of imprisoning mothers; their youngest children had to be placed in care or accommodated in the gaols.

Graph 4 of females taken before the Assizes and Quarter Sessions closely follows that of the males, but the rise to the mid-century peak, and the fall, was sharper and more consistent than that of the male rate. The breakdown of male and female offenders imprisoned for lesser offences in Table 5 underpins this; in 1836 there were 121 women so gaoled, and over the next eighteen years the number rose steeply to 550. The rate of increase fluctuated less than that of the males, and was significantly faster. The results can be seen in the proportions of male and female offenders in the mid-century. By 1854 a quarter of the people fined or imprisoned after summary convictions were women. In the higher courts, too, between 1853 and 1855 the proportion of female defendants reached just under a third. This was unprecedented, and helps to explain why Welsh chaplains and ministers denounced 'female depravity' at this time in such strident tones.

The regional differences in recorded female criminality were more marked than those of the male. In the second quarter of the century the increase in the rate of women tried for indictable crime, and imprisoned for lesser offences, was much greater in Glamorgan and Monmouthshire than in the rural counties of Anglesey, Cardiganshire and Radnorshire. Seventy per cent or more of all the females in the mid-1850s tried at the Assizes and Quarter Sessions, proceeded against at the Petty Sessions, and gaoled for minor offences, were from Glamorgan and Monmouthshire, where only a third of Wales's females resided. Jelinger Symons, who was one of the education commissioners of 1847, spotted this discrepancy. He said that in iron districts such as the south Wales coalfield

> ...the lawless vices and rude habits of the men are communicated to the women. In murderous offences by females, no other district (not excepting London) affords so many instances. Even in offences against property committed with violence, the women there more largely participate than elsewhere. This is in some degree owing to the masculine pursuits in the works and the pits, which degrade them to the habits and brutalities of men.[9]

In the Merthyr police area between 1846 and 1866 the female proportion of persons committed to the Assize and Quarter Sessions reached 40 per cent.

These figures are a little misleading. As so many female crimes were of larceny, women were likely to appear more prominently at Assizes and Quarter Sessions than at Petty Sessions. Over the same period in Merthyr, only 17 per cent of the total number of persons apprehended and summoned for all offences were females, that is, an annual rate of about one in every 120 of the female population. This is less than was sometimes claimed, and it remained at that level for only a short time. Later in the century the amount of recorded criminality amongst the women of the mining communities fell so sharply that an appearance before magistrates was regarded 'as a badge of shame'. By 1892 only 8 per cent of apprehensions for reported indictable offences in the two most industrial counties, and only 12 per cent of summary proceedings there, involved females.

However, the position in their largest towns was very different; in Cardiff, Swansea and Newport, proportions of females apprehended for indictable crime and proceeded against summarily in 1892 were 24 and 30 per cent of the totals. It seems that female crime was comparatively high in these towns throughout the nineteenth century.[10] In the years 1857–61, when detailed records began, 40 per cent of the persons apprehended for serious offences in these three towns were female. At Swansea the proportion even rose to 50 per cent, and, in addition, women comprised almost a third of the town's defendants at the Petty Sessions.

The contrast between this and recorded female criminality in counties such as Anglesey, Cardiganshire and Radnorshire was stark. In 1861 whilst one female in 335 of the three above towns was apprehended for an indictable crime, and one in thirty-five proceeded against summarily, in the three rural counties the figures were one in 5,691 and one in 561. The chief constable of Cardiganshire reported six years later that only one in ten of the people apprehended by his force was female.[11] No one seemed absolutely certain why there should have been such differences. It was said that urban women were both more independent and somehow more vulnerable than those in the countryside. As Angela John reminds us, and their stealing of coal, food and clothes probably confirms, they bore the brunt of periodic unemployment and indebtedness. Contemporaries claimed that urban females desired more than their country friends to 'have the good things in life', and had better opportunities to get them illegally. They were also subjected to close scrutiny. In mid-nineteenth century Cardiff, Newport and Swansea women were policed with an intensity which has rarely been equalled in modern times.

Despite this, it is hard to believe that the above statistics were a complete guide to female criminality.[12] By their nature, typical female crimes like removing vegetables and milk from the fields and shop-lifting in the towns were not easy to detect. It was assumed that people were more reluctant to report women, particularly older women, than men for offences, and that the police were more ready to caution and dismiss them. A glance at the police diaries suggests that there was something in the notion, but the treatment was not that different. In some towns as many young girls as boys were seized by the police, but this was not fully reflected in the court records. At least a third of the females apprehended for indictable offences in the mid-Victorian years were not proceeded against. For some reason, males were less fortunate in this respect, though by the end of the century the gap between them had closed. When, however, females actually appeared on trial at the Assizes and Quarter Sessions, they were not treated more generously than males.[13] A sample of 519 males and 340 females from the Merthyr police district who were tried at the Assizes and Quarter Sessions between 1846 and 1866 gives acquittal rates of 20 per cent for the men and 17 per cent for the women, and the sentences, for property crimes, were similar for both sexes.

Perhaps it is significant that the police, in their annual returns of 'known thieves and depredators' and 'suspected persons' at large in the community, always gave a higher ratio of females to males than one might have expected from the court records. As we can see in Table 15, of 12,909 such people listed in 1860, 1876, and 1892, about a third were female, and in addition, it was estimated that they comprised about the same proportion of receivers of stolen goods. A few of the latter were notorious, like Harriet Thomas, a lodging-house keeper of Carmarthen, and Glamorgan's Mary Noble, a keeper of a 'bawdy house', who was sentenced to be transported for fourteen years in 1833. Such women, and the prostitutes who supplied them with goods and money, were regarded as the antithesis of the virtuous female and mother, and thus a special threat to society.

In the last third of the nineteenth century the statistical and literary records pointed in the same direction; outside one or two of the largest towns, the problem of female criminality was small and decreasing. Even the rate of females proceeded against at Petty Sessions reached its peak in 1882 and not 1899 as did that of the males. A common view was that in the criminal, as in the religious, temperance and other spheres of life, Welsh women were showing their menfolk the respectable way. No doubt the shift owed something to the wider social changes, summed up in the phrase 'the retreat into the home', especially in industrial Wales, and to the improved economic conditions and better policing. 'In all countries where social habits and customs constrain women to lead retiring and secluded lives', said William Morrison in 1891, 'the number of female criminals descends to a minimum.'[14] Moral reformers rather approved of the contraction of female job opportunites after the 1870s, but attributed much of the change in recorded criminality to their own campaigns to eradicate female ignorance, alcoholism and prostitution. 'When the female of the lower classes shall have been more universally educated', said the Reverend E. G. Williams at Swansea in 1867, 'crime will become less frequent among them'. Perhaps, too, the Welsh ideal, propounded by 'Ieuan Gwynedd', of a highly moral family life, with the stern religious mother at its heart, had a continuing influence. Women at the end of the century would go to great lengths to appear honest and respectable.[15]

There was, as the century progressed, a growing interest in the ages of both female and male criminals.[16] For many people it was a shock to discover just how young these people were. In 1834, when the details were first given in the parliamentary papers, 29 per cent of the people committed for trial or bailed to appear at the Assizes and Quarter Sessions were twenty-one years of age and under, and 35 per cent were between twenty-two and thirty. The first percentage dropped in difficult times, a trend which is initially surprising, but which has been confirmed by research elsewhere in Britain. Ten years later the proportions were not very different, but the new age classifications revealed the large number of offenders – about a quarter – who were in their early twenties. When people were aged twenty to twenty-four years they were indicted for more than twice as many offences as might have been anticipated from the age distribution of the population; they also received the most severe sentences and filled the convict ships to Australia.[17] Perhaps, as historians of the eighteenth century claim, this period of one's life brought a unique combination of independence, vulnerability and temptation.[18] It also brought undue police attention; the highest rate of male acquittals in nineteenth-century Wales was in this age range. As people grew older, so the differential between the age of criminals and the age of the population gradually closed until, when people were in their thirties and forties, the proportions were about equal. These age statistics varied a little from district to district; in the most industrialized counties, the men and women appearing at the Assizes and Quarter Sessions were, as contemporaries feared, slightly younger than the national average. Of the offenders at the Petty Sessions we have fewer details, but in the 1830s and 1890s they were rather older than the people in the higher courts.

Such evidence tells us little about the age when people first committed criminal acts. In fact, it actually conveys the wrong impression, that a life of crime began rather late. The prison records reinforce this conclusion. Thus in 1837 only 21 boys and 4 girls under fourteen years of age were sent to gaol in Wales, for all types of crime. Of course, more and possibly younger children were fined, whipped and cautioned, and hundreds of other delinquents must have escaped the best efforts of constables and victims. To discover when these youngsters turned to crime, we have to rely on the literary sources. According to diaries, letters and newspapers, many children of twelve years age in the nineteenth century were already established criminals, and the boys amongst them committed their first offences a couple of years before the girls.

The records of the reformatory schools reveal something of their early criminal careers. Amongst the boys at the Monmouthshire institution near Pontypool in 1859–60 were Charles Peake, an eight-year-old of Abergavenny, with no previous convictions, and three Newport boys, George Aplin, John Roberts and John Carney, ten-, eleven- and twelve-year olds, who had been in custody a total of six times.[19] They can be compared with the Merthyr boys, Griffith Rees aged seven years, who took a watch, and Jonathan Davies, aged eight years, and David Thomas, aged nine years, both of whom stole coal. All three in 1848–9 received a whipping, whilst their friend Mary Davies, aged eight years, who removed clothes, was imprisoned for three days. One of the youngest to appear in court was James Williams, a six-year-old Pontypridd boy, who was charged in 1875 with stealing coal. The main aim of the authorities was to prevent such children from going down 'the criminal path'. The fear was that Williams would follow the example of a young illiterate male labourer of Cardiff, who in 1876, at the age of thirteen years, was given two months hard labour for stealing boots, and appeared at the Petty Sessions, Quarter Sessions and Assizes in the next six years for similar offences.

The recidivism of people in their late teens convinced contemporaries that this was the most criminal age for males and females, though it was also the time, of course, when they had a high profile and confronted the police on their street patrols. So far as women were concerned, many of them, like thieves Mary Ann Cooney of Merthyr, Jane Benson of Swansea, and Catherine Brian of Cardiff, entered the official records in their early teens.[20] The chaplain of Swansea gaol said that when girls of thirteen and fourteen years of age committed petty larcenies 'it often appears to be their first step to ruin, resulting in the majority of instances in them supplying the town with prostitutes'.[21] A glance at the age structure of known female offenders suggests that the chaplain was only partly correct; on reaching eighteen or nineteen years of age many young women gave up criminal activity completely. Others returned to it five years later or in their late twenties. There was also one distinctive group of older female criminals, represented perfectly by a Cardiff housewife who committed her first offence at forty-seven years of age, and then three others by the time that she was fifty. Males, on the other hand, had a less disturbed age-pattern to their criminal activity, with a sharp rise to a peak of offences committed between the ages of eighteen and twenty-three years, and a long decline thereafter. 'There was', we are told, 'an endlessly repeated migration from a condition of more or less criminal fecklessness in youth to a condition of greater or less respectability in maturity'.[22]

Each age group, in both sexes, was identified with certain types of offences. The very young were apprehended for illegally taking food, clothing and fuel, and for vagrancy offences and trespass, the men of about eighteen to twenty-four years of age for assaults, malicious damage and attacks on the police, and those a little older for poaching and house-break-ins. Males in their thirties and forties were accused of family and white-collar crimes. Women of about twenty years of age in the largest towns were often convicted of stealing from the person, whilst the same people ten or twenty years later were more attracted to shop-lifting. The elderly were accused of a range of offences, including the collection of free fuel, refusing to pay rates and rents, and receiving stolen goods. People of all ages were charged with vagrancy offences, and all but teenagers were likely to appear in court for being drunk. On very rare occasions, whole families entered the dock together; thus in September 1843 Ann Moss, a 45-year-old laundry woman from Yorkshire, and her three children Rosamund, John and Eliza, aged between three and a half and fourteen years, were convicted of vagrancy at Haverfordwest, and imprisoned.

Cases studies of people such as John Wylde, who became an 'Emperor' of Merthyr's 'China', show that they graduated from petty to serious offences, but this, the pattern which reformers so denounced, was less common than assumed. With many, if not most recidivists, one can detect by the age of twenty the nature of their future career. Those who had been apprehended for violence at this age, for breaking and entering, or for poaching, tended to follow that particular branch of criminal activity.

There are innumerable examples. Hugh Roberts of Penycae near Rhiwabon was a prodigious poacher of the late nineteenth century, whilst Charles Tomkins, bus-driver of Aberdyfi, and John Owen, the mad cyclist of Tywyn, were unrelenting in their opposition to highway regulations. Drunks and prostitutes also returned to court time and again on the same charge, and received the same punishment. Jane Griffiths, a Caernarfon prostitute, faced seventy-six charges associated with her profession between June 1877 and June 1896, and was sentenced on most occasions to one to three months gaol. John Stone, a Bangor tailor, and Thomas Rowlands, a pedlar from Conwy, were less of a nuisance, but were still convicted seventy times in twenty years for drunkenness and disorderly conduct. Isaac Hughes, a labourer of Llansantffraid in Merioneth, spent all his adult life being 'riotous', and died in 1875, his last crime, like his first, being an assault on a policeman.[23] Whole families specialized in certain offences; in the mid-century the Johns of Amroth were expert burglars and the Jones fraternity of 14 Friars Field, Newport, begged and scavenged.

After the mid-century there were changes in the age-structure of criminals, but they are difficult to follow. Complications include the tendency to move juvenile crime cases from the higher to the local courts, and the increasing reluctance in the last decades to send the very young to prison. When all allowances are made, however, it seems that the average age of offenders rose even faster than might have been expected from the ageing of the population. The average age of people charged with an offence by the Tywyn police in the 1870s and 1880s was thirty-four years, about six years older than the figure of forty years before. Only 9 per cent were under twenty years of age, 34 per cent were in their twenties, 21 per cent in their thirties, 22 per cent in their forties and 14 per cent were even older.

By the 1890s over half of the people awaiting trial in Wales for indictable offences, and over two-thirds of those proceeded against at Petty Sessions were over thirty years of age. As a comparison, the proportions of inmates in Welsh gaols aged thirty years and over rose from 36 per cent in 1860 to 54 per cent by 1892, with the increase being especially marked in the case of women (Table 11). According to some historians, this indicated that 'proportionately more offenders later in the century came from a hardened and perhaps an experienced criminal class than was the case in earlier decades–...'[24] Less young and new blood was replenishing the stream of criminal life. In fact, the proportions of prisoners under twenty-one years in Wales fell in the years 1860–92 from 25 to 14 per cent, which, as we shall see later, gave limited support to the claim made in 1891 by a Caernarfonshire judge that the greatest decrease in crime had been amongst the young.[25]

The problem of juvenile delinquency received more attention than perhaps it warranted in the nineteenth century. The social literature of the years following the Napoleonic Wars was full of comment on the size and treatment of this problem. One historian, who has examined the judicial and prison statistics of that era, concludes that there was 'some justification' for the fear of increasing juvenile crime, but the anxiety also grew out of living in a changing world.[26] Although there were many young offenders in the countryside, juvenile delinquency was associated with urban and industrial communities, whose streets were full of children and young people. These places provided, it was said, job opportunities, temptations, and independence for the young without an appropriate amount of parental and religious discipline. They also experienced hardship, in the form of overcrowding, the death and desertion of parents, poverty and unemployment. 'The city streets, for some of the nation's rapidly increasing number of children, [were] their principal means of survival'.[27]

The presence, precosity, and behaviour of street children shocked the more refined contemporaries. When the Reverend St George Armstrong Williams settled in Pwllheli in 1841 he found 'no order or decency; nothing like civilisation among them'. 'They would create an uproar, and throw stones in the streets at the passers-by, breaking the church windows when a marriage service was being solemnized, till it became necessary to call out the constables to restrain them with their whips.' Five years later there was 'a visible improvement'.[28] There was agreement, amongst employers, tradesmen and council leaders, as well as amongst clergymen, that forms of disorderly behaviour by children and teenagers, tolerated perhaps in the villages, had no place in towns like Caernarfon, Wrexham, and Merthyr. Energetic games, playing pitch and toss, throwing stones, and breaking branches for street fights were just some of the activities outlawed first on Sundays, and then on other days of the week as well. In the mid-century, when the problem seemed at its worst, people even wondered about the connections between juvenile delinquency and the rash of popular disturbances. Reformers like Lord Ashley and Mary Carpenter argued that an effective response to the problems of youth offered the best long-term solution to both crime and revolutionary protest.[29]

It is impossible to estimate the extent of juvenile delinquency. Policemen, journalists and reformers were prone to exaggeration. In their lists of 'known thieves and depredators' and 'suspected persons' at large in the community, the police of Glamorgan and Monmouthshire reckoned that well over a quarter of the former, and precisely a quarter of the latter, were under sixteen years of age (Table 15). The legal and prison records have to be regarded with care, as many child offenders under seven, and a few between seven and fourteen years, were released from custody for being 'without understanding' of their actions. However, the records, such as they are, suggest that juvenile delinquency was less of a problem than contemporaries feared. At Michaelmas 1834 only nine youngsters under seventeen years of age were in the Welsh gaols, and no more than 10 per cent of people committed to trial and imprisoned after summary convictions in the early Victorian years, were of this age group.

The peak in these statistics of juvenile crime was reached in the mid-century. The numbers imprisoned rose sharply in years such as 1844, 1848 and 1851. New legislation like the Juvenile Offenders (Larceny) Act of 1847 encouraged people to pursue actions against children in the lower courts. By 1857, 231 males and 115 females under seventeen years of age, convicted at these courts were committed to prison, almost three-quarters in Glamorgan and Monmouthshire, and an unspecified number were fined and discharged. Subsequently, the number of juveniles sent to prison declined, though the figures for young males held up well from the late 1860s to the early 1880s. By 1899 only 48 males under seventeen years of age and 9 females were committed to Welsh gaols, and 27 males and 5 females to reformatories.[30] The improved legal statistics of the 1890s also indicated that the rate of juvenile convictions for indictable crime was falling, and probably for misdemeanours as well. 'The (inevitable) conclusion was drawn that crime amongst the young was declining faster than crime amongst the population at large'.[31]

All the records leave no doubt that juvenile delinquency was more common in the heavily urbanized and industrialized counties than in the rural. After the Juvenile Offenders Act was passed in 1847, four-fifths of the under-sixteen year olds charged under the Act came from Glamorgan and Monmouthshire, and about half of these appeared in the Cardiff, Swansea and Newport courts. During the late 1870s, when the figures were high, especially of boys, the annual number of child thieves taken before the magistrates of these three towns was 170. They took coal and metals, food and drink, clothes, boots and shoes, cigars and tobacco, and money, and were sentenced to a few days or weeks imprisonment, whippings, and perhaps a transfer to a reformatory school. It was estimated that for every one of these convicted juveniles there were about two or three that escaped the police's attention. This formed the basis for the statement at the Glamorgan Quarter Sessions in 1856 that 150 youngsters in Merthyr earned their living by 'dishonest practices', 200 in Cardiff, and 110 in Swansea.[32] Many of these lived rough, by the furnaces, around the docks and even in the sewers, and they were said to have been in league with pawnbrokers, metal dealers and other receivers of stolen goods. In one case, in 1879, Llewellyn Price of Cardiff was accused of keeping young girls in his house, without the knowledge of their parents, and instructing them in the art of pickpocketing.[33]

Some of these youngsters joined gangs, which committed break-ins and other serious crimes, and one or two of their number, such as Richard

Matthias in Merthyr, later became notorious adult offenders. Punishment for these could be heavy. One fourteen-year-old of Merthyr, with a long troublesome history, was sentenced to ten years transportation in 1850 for stealing one and a half loaves of bread. No one had much sympathy for him. The chief interest of reformers was in the other, more redeemable, juveniles: the tramping orphans, the unemployed sand-girls and the homeless market-boys, who wandered aimlessly about until the police apprehended them for a vagrancy offence or another petty misdemeanour. Amongst them were Hugh Evans, Hugh Owens, and John Thomas, three boys under sixteen years of age from Caernarfon, who begged by day, and slept at the lime-kilns at night. In January 1860 they were brought before the magistrates on a vagrancy charge, given fourteen days imprisonment and sent to a reformatory for two years.[34]

In the 1850s, when concern about these delinquent children was at its height, Henry Austin Bruce declared that their upbringing, by parents and the parishes, was a 'scandal'.[35] He identified a number of types at risk, namely orphans, neglected children and truants, as well as people like Hannah Davies, a fifteen-year-old Swansea girl, whose mother, brothers and sisters were convicted criminals.[36] The chaplain of Swansea goal stated in the 1860s that most of the juveniles whom he saw were orphans and the neglected offspring of the 'very lowest' social class, though there was a very small group of rebellious children from 'better' homes. The records of the Glamorgan and Monmouthshire reformatories reveal that the juvenile delinquents in their care were from 'very poor' and 'poor' families. A handful had 'respectable' parents like engine fitters and marble polishers, but most were the sons of labourers, hobblers, basket makers, rag-and-bone men, charwomen and the unemployed.

About half of the juvenile delinquents in these reformatories had parents described as 'good', 'honest' and of 'unknown' character, and the rest had 'indifferent', 'middling', 'dissipated', 'drunken', 'neglectful' and 'criminal' mothers and fathers, or none at all. Richard Baldwin, fourteen years of age, William Seward, thirteen years, and Daniel Smith, fifteen years, were orphans who had journeyed alone from the English counties to beg and steal in south Wales. The first entry in the Monmouthshire reformatory stands for another prominent group. It was of Michael Collins, a ten-year-old of King's Parade, Newport, who was convicted of stealing coal. His father was a dock worker, who had been in prison for the same offence. The authorities, in their wisdom, allowed Michael six month's reprieve from his five years at Pontypool, on condition that he joined a ship bound for the Mediterranean.[37]

Henry Austin Bruce and the chaplains of Swansea and Cardiff gaols demanded more education for the children of the 'destitute and depraved' poor. Together with John Coke Fowler and like-minded friends, they

Table 12.
Birthplace of prisoners, 1860–1892

Year	Total		England		Wales		Scotland	
	m.	f.	m.	f.	m.	f.	m.	f.
1860	2810	1218	930	359	1151	581	61	5
1876	4645	1841	1528	538	2162	928	71	15
1892	4631	1562	1831	451	2148	917	65	6

Year	Ireland		Colonies & East Indies		Foreign countries		Not ascertained	
	m.	f.	m.	f.	m.	f.	m.	f.
1860	484	248	37	0	119	3	28	22
1876	697	339	46	3	105	6	36	12
1892	453	176	27	3	81	5	26	4

Source: PP. 1861, LX, 1877, LXXXVI, and 1893–4, CIII.

supported social and religious initiatives designed to prevent and eradicate juvenile delinquency, as we shall see in the next chapter. A generation later, when much of this had been provided, and firm action had been taken against receivers, there was relief at the changing age-profile of apprehended criminals. Yet it was not all plain sailing: in 1880 the chief constable of Swansea bemoaned the number of children under twelve years of age sleeping in the streets and the sudden increase in juvenile larceny; in 1891 there was incomprehension when educated boys were caught shop-lifting in Carmarthen and Caernarfon; and before the century was out, the outcry over London's 'hooligans' and street 'arabs' found an echo in Wales's largest towns.

Although we know a little of the age and sex of nineteenth-century criminals, it is probable that the most interesting questions about their background will remain unanswered. Prison governors were obliged to fill in annual returns of the nationality, occupation, literacy and criminal career of the men and women in their charge, but their information was suspect and, of course, it covered only a minority of offenders. Table 12 indicates that almost half the prison inmates were of Welsh origin, more than 30 per cent were English and less than 20 per cent were Irish. In 1860 three-quarters of all the English prisoners in Wales were split evenly between the Monmouthshire and Glamorgan gaols, and six out of every ten of the Irish prisoners were in Glamorgan. In Anglesey, Cardiganshire, and Radnorshire, by contrast, only 36 per cent of the prison population at this time had been born in England or Ireland, and in a few county goals the proportion was nearer a quarter. Even so, the prominence of these outsiders in the statistics was greater than their share in the population as a whole, a fact which strengthened Henry Richard's claim that the worst crimes in the Principality were executed by outsiders.

In all, but especially the more isolated, parts of the country, magistrates and chief constables found it convenient to blame sharp upswings in the crime figures on travellers, vagrants, seamen, navvies and other non-residents. 'Strangers' were said to have made up two-thirds of the inmates of Rhuthun gaol in the 1830s. Henry Leach, chairman of the Pembrokeshire Quarter Sessions, said in April 1848 that 'by far the greatest number of those convicted of the highest class of crimes tried here, have not been natives of the county', but 'trampers', and many of the lesser offences were attributed to the marines and sailors along that county's coastline.[38] At a Quarter Sessions in Cardiganshire, devoted to the problem of tramps, it was estimated that of the 760 prisoners in the county between 1858 and 1867, 358 had been of this type.[39] In truth, trampers or vagrants in the nineteenth century committed comparatively few serious crimes; they were arrested in large numbers in places such as Aberaeron, Haverfordwest and Holywell, but generally for petty offences, chiefly begging and other breaches of the Vagrancy Act.

Migrant road and railway workers inspired greater fear. As they pushed westwards across north and south Wales, they were accused of trailing crime in their wake. 'The introduction of a Railway', said Captain Napier in 1845, 'invariably leaves in its train, a scum, demanding constant vigilance and increasing activity on the part of the police'. Welsh navvies had a better reputation than most, but in Bangor and Caernarfon they, too, were blamed for riot and crime. At Caernarfon in 1847 the goaler reported that the people engaged on the Chester to Holyhead railway committed many of the larcenies in the district.[40] Extra policemen, as well as company officials, were appointed to keep an eye on them, something repeated during the damn-building many years later in mid-Wales. However, it was easy to become obsessed with the thieving habits of these mobile workers; much of their spare time was spent in drinking and fighting each other. When, at Bala in 1881, a major construction project came to an end, the authorities were reluctant to reduce police cover as 'the greatest transgressors [in property crimes such as poaching] were natives not navvies'.[41]

In Glamorgan, where Henry Thomas was at pains to deny the existence of a native and permanent 'criminal class', strangers were again blamed for the majority of serious crimes. Both Irish men and women had a particularly bad reputation in mid-century Glamorgan, as they had in Holyhead, Caernarfon, Bangor and other towns along the Welsh coast. At

Brynsiencyn on Anglesey 'the characteristic surnames Sweeney, Riley, McNally and Kelly recur intermittently' and explosively in the story of its crime.[42] The Irish were arrested on theft, and more commonly on vagrancy, assault and drink charges. Mary Sullivan, who always seemed to appear in court with a babe in her arms, promised repeatedly to give up begging, but nothing, not even a short enforced return to her native land, could stop her annoying the authorities of Cardiff and Swansea during the 1850s and 1860s.[43] In these towns, where such people gathered in the slum districts, their criminality was a testimony to their poverty, and possibly a reflection of cultural differences and a ghetto-mentality, but there were other equally important reasons why all outsiders figured large in the gaol statistics. They were an identifiable target, and courts imprisoned them more readily than the indigenous population.

When one looks at the police and court books, especially for counties in mid and west Wales, it is apparent that local people were more heavily involved in criminal activity than was sometimes apparent from the prison files and the biased comments of chairmen of Quarter Sessions.[44] Sixty per cent or more of the recorded crimes were committed by natives of these counties, and most of these lived close to the scene of their crime. Even in Caernarfon, which was said to have been cosmopolitan in its criminals, registers of charges in the 1880s show that eight out of ten persons were natives of north Wales, most of these lived within a six-mile radius, and half of them were inhabitants of the town. By comparison, Criccieth deserved its reputation for having law-abiding citizens; fewer than a third of those on its charge sheets in the late nineteenth century were from the immediate vicinity. Much of its drunkenness and disorderly conduct was imported by sailors and hawkers from Liverpool, Manchester, Ireland and Caernarfon.[45]

Of all the information on offenders, that on the occupations and literacy of prisoners has to be regarded with the greatest caution. Convicted criminals in the nineteenth, as in the eighteenth, century were overwhelmingly working class, and the gaol records indicate that they were drawn increasingly from the ranks of Edward Carpenter's 'fringe labour', the very poorest and least educated sections of society. By the 1890s more than two-thirds of male prisoners were identified as labourers, who were often single or married with just a few children, and a similar proportion of the females were collectively returned as needlewomen, charwomen, domestic servants and without employment (Table 13). About 35 per cent of male and 45 per cent of female prisoners in the late nineteenth century could neither read nor write, and an even larger proportion could do so only imperfectly.[46] There were some oustanding exceptions, especially amongst the men. 'We have had', wrote the chaplain of Swansea gaol in 1867, 'a high proportion of fairly educated male prisoners...', but the average literacy ratings were well below those for the population generally. This

Table 13
Occupations of prisoners, 1860–1892

Year	Total		No occupation		Domestic servants		Labourers charwomen needlewomen		Factory workers		Mechanics & skilled workers	
	m.	f.	m.	f.	m.	f.	m.	f.	m.	f.	m.	f.
1860	2810	1218	115	697	37	161	1514	322	14	3	600	7
1876	4645	1841	119	525	16	119	2807	483	8	13	939	11
1892	4631	1562	85	531	16	72	3365	520	11	2	631	0

Year	Foremen		Shopmen shopwomen clerks		Shopkeepers & dealers		Professional employments		Sailors mariners soldiers	Prostitutes	Not known	
	m.	f.	m.	f.	m.	f.	m.	f.	m.	f.	m.	f.
1860	9	1	14	0	76	18	4	0	420	–	7	9
1876	11	0	31	3	149	92	11	1	540	589	14	5
1892	2	0	85	1	106	105	6	4	318	326	6	1

Source: PP. 1861, LX, 1877, LXXXVI and 1893–4, CIII.

was one reason why Henry Austin Bruce and others spoke of criminals as 'the dregs of society', an element from the uncivilized substratum.

As the forces of law and order were largely directed against these people, it was no surprise that the gaols were full of them. It is interesting, however, to compare the information on prisoners with other evidence on the occupations of criminals. Various court and police lists, and the transportation registers, confirm that most of the people apprehended were of the working class, but they give a wider range of job details than in Table 13. In two samples of 345 males and females proceeded against for indictable offences in the Merthyr police district in the mid-century, and of 541 people charged with less serious crimes in Tywyn, Barmouth and Corwen thirty years later, 32 and 28 per cent respectively were called labourers. Another 28 per cent of the first sample were colliers, miners, puddlers and other skilled workers of the ironworks and collieries, and the same proportion of the second sample were tramps and vagrants. The occupations of the women in these samples were rarely given; of those that were, most were domestic servants, charwomen and prostitutes, and just over half were single women.[47]

Another sample, of 272 people charged at Caernarfon in 1880, gives a figure of 48 females, 25 of whom were prostitutes and 16 wives. Of the 224 males, 61 were labourers, at least 32 worked at the quarries, 27 were tramps, vagrants, hawkers and pedlars and 18 were seamen. In addition, over twenty other professions were represented, including 7 masons, 7 potters, 3 agents and one gentleman.[48] There were, in all these lists, rather more unemployed males, and just a few more employers, dealers, shopkeepers, agents and professional people than might have been expected from the prison records. The extension of summary jurisdiction, and a greater willingness to punish breaches of public-health, highway and similar legislation, brought farmers, tradesmen and other middle-ranking people before the magistrates. Even so, it needs to be emphasized that such people rarely appeared at the Assizes and Quarter Sessions. As we saw in the study of white-collar and commercial crimes, it was a long time before the middle-class were pursued for serious offences with the same vigour as those below them, and even then the accused tended to be clerks and lesser mortals.

The records, with all their limitations and bias, indicate that each occupation had its own criminal profile: farm servants were apprehended for poaching, sex, work and family crimes, female servants for theft, concealing births, and infanticide, boatmen for stealing, unemployed labourers for drunken and disorderly behaviour and break-ins, and clerks and agents for embezzlement and fraud. Of those above them in the social scale we know very little; occasionally gentlemen were charged with financial irregularities, employer crimes, and sexual offences, but it was a rare event. Great efforts were made to keep respectable families out of court, and, above all, out of prison. When a banker appeared at the Montgomeryshire Assizes in 1842 on a charge of forgery, and when respectable ladies had to explain their shop-lifting, the courts were crowded with gawping spectators. Certainly, these persons were not regarded as being members of the 'criminal class'.

It must be apparent, from the evidence in the rest of this book, that the tables on the criminal careers of offenders cannot be completely relied upon. In the early nineteenth century the information is particularly suspect. Expert observers at Dolgellau and Montgomery said that re-committals were few, and according to the Welsh gaol statistics of 1834 only one in thirteen of admissions had been in prison before.[49] If this were remotely accurate, it means that prison was not only a new experience for more and more people, but also one which they did not wish to repeat. Soon, however, the records tell a different story. In the mid-century the reports of prison chaplains were full of the difficulties of reforming prisoners, and of complaints about the effects of both drink and incarceration on men, and especially women. 'Habitual drunkards', were, it was generally agreed, 'the most hopeless class' and 'fallen women' the 'most discouraging'. As many as a quarter of gaol inmates in the 1850s and 1860s returned to haunt their erstwhile religious teachers. In October 1877 the governor of Cardiff gaol said that in the previous twelve months he had received 2,211 into his establishment and of these 935 had former convictions. Table 14 confirms that an increasing proportion of those committed to prison in the second half of the century had previous convictions.[50] By 1892 four out of ten male prisoners had them and as many as six or seven out of ten females. Moreover, a third of the women in gaol had at least six previous convictions each.

This information strengthened the widely held opinion that crime in the late nineteenth century was becoming ever more the activity of skilful professionals and unreformable petty offenders. Whether this development posed a growing threat to society, or alternatively was a sign of a well-policed and law-abiding community, no one seemed very sure. Certainly, the habitual criminal was at the very heart of discussions over penal policy in this period, and considerable efforts were made to identify, register, and deal with these personal 'centres of corruption'. Politicians, no less than the press and the public, became hypnotized by the prison statistics of recidivism, and tended to ignore the evidence of those offenders who were punished in other ways. If one compares the judicial with the prison statistics a very different picture emerges. Of the 806 males and 144 females proceeded against on indictment in 1892, only 38 per cent and 50 per cent respectively were labelled suspected or known criminals, whilst of the

Table 14
Number of persons committed to prison, with the number of their previous convictions, 1860–1892

Year	Total commitments	Once	2 times	3 times	4 times	5 times
1860	4596	549	238	112	77	44
1876	6891	1024	503	318	208	139
1892	6656	1006	491	306	207	166

Year	6–7 times	8–10 times	Above 10 times	Total	Others
1860	49	41	78	1188	
1876	165	142	283	2782	20
1892	244	172	590	3182	26

Source: PP. 1861, LX, 1877, LXXXVI, and 1893–4, CIII.

39,888 males and 7,393 females proceeded against summarily the comparable percentages were only 16 and 29. In view of the types of crime then being dealt with at the Petty Sessions, the last figures were hardly unexpected.

The existence of recidivism was the result of several factors, including police attitudes and sentencing policy. When serious offences were reported, the police had their suspicions of likely offenders. One such was John Jones of Tregaron, apprehended, indicted and then released on a charge of arson in 1847. He was a bankrupt farmer, who had already been to the Petty Sessions about thirty times before, and had spent three periods in gaol. Other police suspects were Owen Jones of Holyhead, who faced eighteen charges between 1879 and 1906, for drunkenness, stealing, and hawking without a licence, and Joseph Abraham, his counterpart in south Wales, who had eighteen convictions between 1881 and 1908 in various towns, almost all for thefts of clothing, as well as twenty-three for drunkenness and assaults. Once people were convicted of their first offence, however early or late in life, there was a good chance that they would reappear quickly on the charge sheets. So it was that Catherine Roberts, coal stealer of Penrhyndeudraeth, came before the Easter Quarter Sessions of 1892 on her tenth charge, in a short space of time, a record matched by 'Burglar Bill', 'Bob the Goose' and their criminal friends at the Cardiff docks. These were constantly under surveillance. Besides being convicted of burglary and stealing, Bill was also found guilty of desertion from the army, trespass, and gaming, whilst Bob, whose hobby was collecting fowls, had a record of using obscene language, threatening behaviour, assaulting his wife, and stealing metal and tools.[51] Some of the prostitutes who worked close to them had several times as many convictions. Mary Ann Smith of Canton, 'the pest of the place', was gaoled on twenty-six occasions before being escorted to the Magdalen House of Mercy in Bristol.[52]

Each year the Welsh police had to return to the Home Office the number of known thieves and depredators, receivers of stolen goods, prostitutes, vagrants, tramps, and suspected persons at large in their district. Almost two-thirds of them were located in Glamorgan and Monmouthshire. Handwritten lists, which have survived from the Overton and Holywell divisions of Flintshire for 1877–81, show that once again most of the persons named by the police were middle-aged labourers, both employed and unemployed, females like Ann McManus of St Asaph, who earned money from sex and thieving, and a few respectable people, such as William Boddington, the Rhyl watchmaker, who were secretly identified as receivers and suspected poachers.[53] As Table 15 shows, in 1860 there were 8,537 of these people in Wales, just over half of whom were males, and 1,561 of the total were under sixteen years of age. It was claimed that they used 1,872 brothels, pubs and other houses of 'bad character'. Holywell had six of these in 1880, in Penyball Street; St Asaph three, in Irish Square, and Rhyl two, in New Road.

These police records ought to be compared with those compiled by the clerks of the courts. They classified the people proceeded against on indictment and summarily. As can be seen from Tables 16 and 17, they used slightly different headings from the police authorities. In 1860 it appears that 792 offenders from five different 'depraved' groups came before the Assizes and Quarter Sessions, and 6,072 before the Petty Sessions. By 1892 the number of vagrants and habitual drunkards proceeded against at the lower courts had more than doubled, but significantly the number of known thieves, prostitutes and suspicious persons alongside them had changed little. During the same thirty-two years the number of known thieves who were tried at the Assizes and Quarter Sessions fell by over a half, as had, according to the police, the number of their colleagues still at large in the lodging-houses, brothels and beerhouses of Wales.

This statistical reduction of the criminal world into people and places of 'bad character' tells us a good deal about the compilers of these tables. Nineteenth-century society, unlike its predecessor, felt the need to locate delinquency in certain people and certain areas.[54] Dr Tobias, who has written most about this, believes that the 'concept [of a separate race of criminals]...is a tenable one', offering 'an acceptable explanation' for much of the town-based recidivism and the illegal activities of migratory groups.[55] With the help of the writings of H.-A. Frégier, the notion proved

Table 15
Depredators, offenders, and suspected persons at large, 1860–1892

Year	Known thieves & depredators				Receivers of stolen goods				Prostitutes		Suspected persons				Vagrants and tramps				Total				Houses of bad character
	−16yrs		16+		−16yrs		16+		−16yrs	16+	−16yrs		16+		−16yrs		16+		−16yrs		16+		
	m.	f.	m.	f.	m.	f.	m.	f.	f.	f.	m.	f.	m.	f.	m.	f.	m.	f.	m.	f.	m.	f.	
1860	313	373	1349	895	0	0	230	93	99	1516	240	137	1213	465	204	195	820	395	757	804	3612	3364	1872
1876	166	61	556	370	1	0	90	62	—	—	296	168	1586	843	—	—	—	—	463	229	2232	1275	300
1892	242	77	728	310	4	0	68	47	—	—	417	113	1420	571	—	—	—	—	663	190	2216	928	281

Source: PP. 1861, LX, 1877, LXXXVI, and 1893–4, CIII.

Table 16
Class of persons proceeded against on indictment, 1860–1892

Year	Known thieves		Prostitutes	Vagrants, tramps, etc		Suspicious characters		Habitual drunkards		Previous good character		Character unknown		Total	
	m.	f.	f.	m.	f.	m.	f.	m.	f.	m.	f.	m.	f.	m.	f.
1860	173	106	97	51	8	251	84	19	3	224	60	210	46	928	404
1876	159	36	41	33	7	123	27	40	10	367	116	186	32	908	269
1892	91	18	31	20	1	167	19	26	3	385	63	117	9	806	144

Source: PP. 1861, LX, 1877, LXXXVI, and 1893–4, CIII.

Table 17
Class of persons proceeded against summarily, 1860–1892

Year	Known thieves		Prostitutes	Vagrants, tramps, etc		Suspicious characters		Habitual drunkards		Previous good character		Character unknown		Total	
	m.	f.	f.	m.	f.	m.	f.	m.	f.	m.	f.	m.	f.	m.	f.
1860	426	162	787	607	119	1991	373	1406	201	7546	1058	4697	792	16673	3492
1876	318	108	640	911	130	1785	376	3242	635	18555	2865	4150	1128	28961	5882
1892	379	132	696	1717	223	1996	537	2354	554	28453	4551	4989	700	39888	7393

Source: PP. 1861, LX, 1877, LXXXVI, and 1893–4, CIII.

extremely popular in our period. Some social investigators, including the public-health pioneer Edwin Chadwick, compared crime to a disease that initially affected only special people and districts, but which could, depending on the resistance, be transmitted or expelled. In the early Victorian era there was a strong feeling that the number of criminally diseased people was growing, and that this infected class might undermine a society already threatened by economic fluctuations, uncontrolled urbanization and seditious ideas.

Such a view was shared by Edmund Head, the assistant poor-law commissioner. He believed that the south Wales coalfield, for instance, was in danger of becoming a criminal area. By 1839 it was, he said, little better than 'a penal settlement', where large numbers of working people 'were lost to the law'. It was a community which seemed to stimulate and attract illegality. Amongst those who arrived there about this time were William Jones, the Tregaron tinker, who deserted from the army and found sanctuary at Merthyr, and Thomas Evans of Penboyr, another well-known thief, who disappeared in Dowlais. 'Without any police worth speaking of to watch newcomers of suspicious appearance, or control the resident bad characters', wrote Head in November 1839, 'the whole mass of Welsh, Irish, runaway criminals and vagrants has fermented together until this outbreak has demonstrated of what materials it consists.'[56] 'There is ground for fear...', said another writer, 'lest England herself become a penal settlement'.[57] In fact, the defeat of the Newport rebellion of 1839, and of the other public-order challenges in the mid-century, enabled people to adjust their fears. During the mid-Victorian years they talked less about the dangers from the fermenting masses, and rather more about the nature, organization and psychology of a smaller body, a more precise 'criminal class'. *The Times* in September 1859 defined it as the 100,000, or more, people who actually lived by crime.[58]

The question which so intrigued contemporaries was whether this group or class actually comprised a separate social unit.[59] There were a few families in the villages and small market towns of Wales, like those of Sarah Evans of Llandysul and William Williams (Wil Tatws) and Edward Edwards (Ned y Ffidler) of Corwen, which seem to have committed criminal acts for generations, but they were not seen as part of a 'class', unless, that is, they were connected in some way with travelling gangs of thieves. The real criminal class lived, so it was believed, solely by dishonest means, and was 'in the community but [not] of it'. It was a hereditary body, close-knit, organized, mobile, and permanently at war with the rest of society. Henry Mayhew, who met and interviewed these people, claimed that 'the criminal tribes' were 'that portion of our society who have not yet conformed to civilised habits'.[60] They included the last remnants of old criminal associations, and many of the vagrants, prostitutes and habitual offenders who lived in, and between, the biggest towns of the nineteenth century.

In 1800 the medieval world of bandits and travelling fraternities of thieves and highway robbers had not completely disappeared.[61] During the Napoleonic Wars, there were reports of husbands and wives touring mid-Wales, looking for anything 'to fill their large pockets', and, working alongside them were large gangs, who specialized in particular crimes and had networks of receivers and purchasers. One set of horse stealers, for example, made a great deal of money trawling Pembrokeshire, Carmarthenshire and Glamorgan in 1810, but success, like the gangs themselves, seems to have been short-lived. There was general agreement that the coming of the professional police made life more difficult for them. Gangs of burglars, who covered the same counties in 1828, 1833–5 and 1855, were apprehended and punished.[62]

'Swell mobs' committed the occasional burglary, but their speciality was pickpocketing. These 'mobs', or loose collections of pickpockets, gamblers, thieves and counterfeiters, were the most obvious manifestations of a separate criminal class, though their peripheral members seem to have moved in and out of crime with great alacrity. According to the Royal Commission on the Constabulary Force in 1839 'the migration of thieves into Wales takes place from March up to May; the time of the fairs'. Large gangs of young and adult men from London, Bristol and the Midlands visited Welsh towns at regular intervals throughout the first half of the century. They were closely watched by the parish and police constables, and severely punished. The most famous of the 'swell mobs' was that of 'Cockney Bill', who was accused of invading south Wales in 1833 with 115 'travellers' or 'thieves'. Some of these, such as John Lewis ('Hatch'), John Strawberry ('Jack Straw'), and Frederick Johnson, were convicted of breaking into shops and warehouses, and pickpocketing at fairs. Like 'Bill' himself, who was cleared of stabbing a Caerphilly constable but found guilty of stealing, these three men were sentenced to transportation at the autumn Assizes of 1834. Subsequently, there were other, smaller, 'mobs', like that of Francis Parker, Thomas Parker, John Gee and the Bath pickpockets caught in Newport market in 1842, but after the 1850s there were fewer references to them, in marked contrast to the vagrants.[63]

The latter were, during the first two-thirds of the century, chiefly English and Irish males in their twenties, ex-labourers, seamen, miners and craftsmen, who moved in groups along well-defined routes. In the last decades, at least according to a Rhuthun census of 1895, there were more of the Welsh poor amongst these travellers, and fewer women. Although no one knew the precise numbers, there were many more vagrants than the 1,614 estimated by the police in 1860. They were, said the master of Wrexham workhouse in 1866, 'outcast from society, knowing no home, counting all men their enemies, and thus educating themselves for the most flagrant crimes, and [they] are ready, on a day's notice, without remorse, to concentrate themselves for mischief in any part of the country.' They were denounced for having their own culture, slang and communications network. As in early modern times, it appears that the number of professional rogues amongst these vagrants was exaggerated; many of them were simply poor people seeking temporary employment and an abode. Gradually, but very gradually, 'crude stereotypes' of these nuisances 'began to give way to more subtle differentiations'.

Perhaps a fifth of them had criminal records, and some, like John Stanmore (alias Stafford), the tatooed and much-travelled Irishman, and his colleague, 25-year-old Henry Smith, had very bad ones indeed. The latter, when sentenced to eight years penal servitude at the Rhuthun Assize in March 1866, had ten previous convictions, and had spent over five years in gaol, for larceny and vagrancy. When times were very hard, vagrants openly flouted their criminality by breaking windows, stealing goods, and waiting for the police to arrest them. As the present writer has shown elsewhere, they committed as many as a quarter of the known indictable crimes in a few of the isolated rural communities. They broke into houses, stole goods and set fire to property, and even confessed to offences which they had not committed.

In the early 1830s, the late 1840s and the late 1860s they were blamed, more than anyone else, for the sharp increases in the Welsh criminal statistics. A glance at Tables 16 and 17 shows that, in the mid-Victorian years at least, they were actually prosecuted for remarkably few offences against property and the person, but this was not the impression given by police and magistrates. A Denbighshire police clerk in 1866 said that 'most of the crimes committed in this county have been done by vagrants', a view shared by the chairmen of the Radnorshire, Cardiganshire, Montgomeryshire, and Merioneth Quarter Sessions.[64] They were, agreed the chief constable of Anglesey in 1857 'a great burden to the community, especially the farmers, and were the chief instruments of crime and robbery'.[65] By the end of the century such views were heard rather more in the counties with a substantial industrial population.

The first instinctive response to the arrival of vagrants was to move them on. Notices were put up at the gates of north Wales towns in the post-war depression warning tramps not to enter, and those who broke through the cordon were escorted by the poor-law officers and constables to their home parishes. During the years of the Irish famine, when they were associated with crime and disease in equal measure, Cardiff and Holyhead returned them to their native land. In Pembrokeshire, where probably more vagrants were arrested than anywhere else in the 1840s, the authorities spent hundreds of pounds passing them to Galway, Cork, Wiltshire,

Middlesex, Kent, Durham, Lancashire and further afield. They soon reappeared, and such was the exasperation that several contemporaries wanted to dump them all on an island in the Bristol Channel, one of a number of half-baked schemes which preceeded the agricultural labour colonies of the early twentieth century.

The new police forces were created partly to deal with the problem of vagrants, and much time was devoted to searching, cautioning and arresting them. It became the practice, in some districts, to 'search every tramp' within a few days of an unsolved property crime. When the first policemen made their life unbearable in Haverfordwest, Welshpool, and Monmouth the vagrants camped outside the town boundaries or moved into the villages. Their capacity to evade the forces of law and order convinced Edwin Chadwick that crime could only be extinguished by a national police force. In time the improvements in communications and transport, and police registers of tramps, hawkers and pedlars, enabled the constabularies to deal more effectively with the mobile criminal, but the modern age also brought benefits for the latter. At Barmouth and Swansea plain-clothed policemen waited at the railway stations in the 1890s for those about to prey on holiday-makers.

The connections between the mobile and the settled criminals were of considerable interest to the social investigators of the nineteeenth century. Thomas Plint, Henry Mayhew and other writers of the mid-Victorian era found that the criminal class had established strong roots in the largest towns of Britain, and in particular in certain districts or 'criminal areas'. Research has shown that there were areas of Cardiff, Swansea, Newport and Merthyr where travellers of all kinds, as well as other 'low characters and habitual offenders', existed in close proximity.[66] Thieves, prostitutes, their protectors, receivers and tramps congregated in 'low' lodging-houses, drinking places, and other houses of 'ill-repute'. The three seaports alone had 570 such houses in 1860; 243 of these were brothels, 107 were beershops, 86 were lodging-houses, and 74 were the homes of known receivers. PC James James of Merthyr recounts in his diary how, in plain clothes, he entered the house of Rachel Griffiths, Riverside, on 6 October 1860 and found it, as he expected, 'full of thieves and prostitutes drinking'.[67] Although the number of such places was reduced later in the century, when legislation like the Habitual Criminals and Prevention of Crimes Acts of 1869 and 1871 punished the 'harbouring' of thieves, the value of 'flash houses' to the police was obvious. So long as they existed the authorities had a good idea of who the criminals were, where they were, and with whom they associated.

At the centre of these urban networks were the 'women of the pave'. According to the Welsh police and court records there were more than 1,600 of these in 1860, and they represented over a fifth of the females prosecuted in that year. How many of these were really prostitutes is not easy to determine. Compilers of records used the term loosely. Thus, for instance, not all the average of 380 females annually prosecuted under the Vagrancy Act for being disorderly prostitutes were actually that. One thing, however, is clear; although there were pockets of prostitutes in Holyhead, Caernarfon, Carmarthen, and Haverfordwest, the main body, of almost a thousand in 1860, lived in the four towns mentioned in the last paragraph. Most of these were young females in their late teens and early twenties, with Irish, Welsh and English surnames – in that order – and about a third of them were recent arrivals in the district.

The development of prostitution, and its related crimes, is especially well documented in Merthyr and Cardiff. One elderly gentleman described how, to accommodate them, the more respectable inhabitants of Ponty-storehouse in Merthyr were pushed and bought out in the second quarter of the century.[68] These prostitutes were the first residents of the dreaded underworld of 'China', a place which bears comparison with the rookeries of pre-industrial English cities. Although the occupation of prostitutes like 'Big Jane' Thomas, and 'Buffalo' Margaret Evans was not illegal, stealing from the person and many of their other activities were. Alongside these ladies in 'China' were young 'bullies' such as Thomas Davies ('Tom Tit'), and brothel keepers and receivers like Tom Robbins ('the Navvy'). These in turn were the leaders of gangs, which planned robberies and supported one another in and out of trouble. What concerned the authorities was not just the physical threat of 'China', but the danger of anti-social attitudes and the fear of 'moral contagion'. The criminal hierarchy, with its 'Emperor' and 'Empress', and the swaggering behaviour of its inhabitants in court, was a deliberate affront to respectable society. In the late 1840s the Merthyr magistrates and police launched a direct assault on what had become virtually a 'no-go area'. Scores of prominent criminals from 'the Celestial Empire' were arrested, and, when convicted, were sent to a new life in Australia.[69]

The same kind of confrontation took place in Cardiff twenty years later. At that time the middle and lower classes were still living uncomfortably close. One commentator in 1860 wrote that 'it is a melancholy fact that...the respectable portion of the inhabitants [of Bute Town], whether of the working classes, tradesmen, brokers, or merchants, appear to be elbowed and thrust out of that part of the parish, one by one, by the inroads of brothels...'[70] The police estimated in this decade that there were well over 500 prostitutes in the town, about half of whom were Irish. It was claimed in 1860 that the parish of St Mary, with its 2–300 brothels and disorderly houses, produced 'a third of the whole of the crime of the county'. During the 1860s the notorious Caroline Davies, together with about 40 per cent of the other Cardiff prostitutes, were annually proceeded against at the higher and lower courts, for about a quarter of the city's reported female crime, and there was a growing interest in James Wall, Thomas Williams and the other shadowy Welsh, English and Italian brothel owners who took much of the profits from sex and crime.[71] The Cardiff Improvement Act of 1871 made it easier for the authorities to proceed against these 'managers' of crime. Campaigns against Bute Street vice, drunkenness and violence were launched in these years, but, as at Merthyr, hopes of a complete victory were dashed when the problems re-emerged in districts to the north-east. One chief superintendent, Major Bond, who left under a cloud, wondered whether the results were worth the effort expended.

If the conflict between the authorities and the prostitutes always lacked a certain conviction, that with the 'habitual criminals' was conducted in deadly earnest. In the last quarter of the century, as fears of a large and expanding criminal class declined, interest was focused on this smaller group of people who were such a burden on the police, the courts and prison governors. Analysts divided them into three groups, the 'feeble-minded offenders' and the 'habitual drunkards', whose reappearance in gaol, usually for short periods, was a sign of their confused state, and the 'professional criminals', who made a business of crime. According to Table 17, about two or three thousand, mainly male, habitual drunkards were proceeded against for lesser crimes each year. They included David Davies ('Dai Bach'), the labourer of Llandrillo in Merioneth, and that remarkable prostitute, Ellen Sweeney of Swansea, who notched up her 255th conviction in 1895. Her prison chaplain said that he saw little hope of rescuing these drunkards, and the Inebriates Act of 1898, and later reforming legislation, proved unworkable.

The professional criminal was regarded more seriously. There had always been people who lived by crime, and writers such as Charles Dickens and Henry Mayhew described in absorbing detail their craft skills.[72] William Jones of Monmouthshire, the burglar who was eventually transported in 1817, and Thomas Thomas of Llanfynydd, the sheep-stealer and highway robber, were classic exponents of their trade. At his hanging in 1845 the 24-year old Thomas entertained the Brecon crowd with the tale of his misdoings, and finished, as expected, with a warning for them to do otherwise. Until the mid-century the death penalty and transportation were the typical punishments for these 'habitual offenders', but in later decades changes had to be made. The last of the Merthyr 'emperors' and 'empresses', for example, had to be accommodated within the prison system, and returned sooner or later to the society from whence they came.

This unpleasant fact, together with the prison statistics of recidivism, created the fear that the state was threatened by a small but growing band of highly skilled professional criminals. In Wales during the later nineteenth century they included John Ford, who worked in London, Leeds and Hull before bringing his thieving talents to Anglesey and Caernarfon, William Williams of Amlwch, who established a small trade in stealing and re-selling tools, William Graham, a native of Birmingham, who travelled across Wales and the north-west of England, stealing from the person, and John Jones and Frederick Reidell, who followed a similar route, but were specialist house-breakers.[73] These professionals were accused of ruthlessly exploiting the opportunities for crime in the modern urban world, and the most skilful of them were able to circumvent each new method of protecting commercial and domestic property.

When lucrative burglaries and violent robberies hit the headlines in the 1860s, and on subsequent occasions, newspaper reporters claimed that these people were immune from police influence and the forces which were curbing other criminal behaviour. Yet estimates of the numbers of such people, outside the towns and industrial districts of Glamorgan, were always fairly small. Table 15 shows that there were 2,930 known thieves at large in the community in 1860, but this number was reduced by more than a half thirty-two years later and their chances of escaping capture had decreased. In 1896, when asked to give the number of thieves, receivers and others, outside prison, who were 'habitually engaged in crime', the Welsh police returned only 117, ninety-seven of whom were male.

Some contemporaries wanted to give these characters indeterminate or life sentences to prevent them from contaminating others. Under the Penal Servitude, Habitual Offenders and Prevention of Crimes Acts of the second half of the century, which are examined in the next chapter, these criminals were subjected to exceptionally tough punishment, and to unprecedented police supervision after they were released from the special prisons built for them. Charles Williams, alias Owen Pritchard, is a good example of one caught by this system. He was imprisoned in Cardigan, Stafford and Rhuthun gaols, before being committed in Carmarthenshire on 3 November 1865 for burglary and stealing money. He managed, not for the first time, to break out of his cell, but was re-captured and sentenced to fifteen years penal servitude at Pentonville. In a felon's register of over 1,400 people, we are told that he stands out as the 'incorrigible criminal who made his living, such as it was, from crime', but after 1865 this career was not revived.[74] In this respect he could be contrasted with other gaoled convicts like James Price of Holywell, and William Phoenix of Bangor, who returned, after penal servitude, to their old professions.

Each year in the last three decades the police kept an official eye on about 100–150 people who were either released convicts on licence or persons needing supervision under the Habitual Criminals Act of 1869 and the Prevention of Crimes Act of 1871. Such people were required to report regularly to the police, and could be detained on the least suspicion, a policy extended by the infamous Prevention of Crime Act of 1908. Their numbers proved to be smaller than expected, and declining. Under examination, these professional criminals were rather disappointing anti-heroes; 'they were only a little more systematic in [their] depredation than the opportunistic larcenist'.[75] Several of the Welsh examples were so harrassed by the probationary procedures that they fled to America and Australia, an act of disobedience which their guardians half welcomed. In Cardiff, where there was a 'remarkable' dimunition of crime in the 1890s, the chief constable attributed the change to the impact of his detective force on such offenders. 'This [force] has been kept up ever since [1893]', he said in 1900, 'and the number of habitual criminals at large within the borough has gradually diminished, and this class is now practically extinct.'[76] By that year there were only eighty-four such people requiring police supervision in Wales, one in Anglesey, Cardiganshire and Radnorshire, twenty-eight in Glamorgan and Monmouthshire, and forty-two in Cardiff, Swansea and Newport.

As the literature of the end of the century vividly demonstates, the interest in murderers, violent robbers, burglars and talented professional rogues never waned, but the general fear of, and obsession with, a criminal class and criminal areas undoubtedly subsided. The political confidence of late-Victorian Britain, the fall in the rate of recorded attacks on people and property, greater surveillance of habitual offenders, and social action in slum areas, all helped in this regard. In the 1870s and 1880s there was an acknowledgement that few people lived well by crime, and that many of those who did appear regularly in court were just inadequates and unfortunates, no match for the policemen who reeled them in. 'There is no reason to suppose', said Sir James Mathew at the Glamorgan Assizes in the summer of 1886, 'that we have amongst us a class of persons professionally dishonest'. Henry Austin Bruce was also optimistic; he claimed that, besides the few 'hardened criminals' locked up in the bleak convict gaols, only a small minority of people in the county and borough prisons could be said to 'belong to the criminal class'.[77]

Such statements are welcomed by historians.[78] Although the notion of a criminal class was, in many ways, an important one, historians increasingly believe that the prominence given to it by contemporaries has distorted the real picture of nineteenth-century crime. There was not one united criminal class, but a mass of people moving in and out of crime. The search for the 'criminal type' had been largely a delusion; it made sense only if one isolated the few and ignored the many. If one gives due weight to *all* the people defined as criminal by the courts, three main groups of offenders can be identified, none of which were entirely self-contained. These were the habitual criminals, divided into the 'utterly weak' and the 'deliberately wicked', the part-time criminals, who committed an illegal act when the opportunity presented itself or when necessity called, and the persons who appeared perhaps once on minor technical charges at the Petty Sessions and were never likely to join the others in gaol.

The last two groups were, of course, much more numerous than the first, for after all, most reported offences were petty affairs, carried out by people who were in employment and had no criminal record. It is instructive to follow the police enquiries in Merioneth and Flintshire through the records, and to see how often the time spent following leads about 'strangers', 'tramps' and 'convicts' proved wasteful. The guilty parties turned out to be neighbours and employees instead, people not on the police files. By 1892 as many as 48 per cent of males and 44 per cent of females proceeded against in Assizes and Quarter Sessions, and 71 per cent of males and 62 per cent of females at Petty Sessions were returned as being of 'previous good character' (Tables 16 and 17). This was twice the proportions of 1860, and the increases were especially marked in Cardiff, Swansea and Newport. The value of these figures can be questioned, but the appearance of so many 'good characters' in the dock was a testimony to the extraordinary efforts of the legislature, the courts and the police.

7

Police, Punishment and Reform

The nineteenth century witnessed probably the most important changes ever in the policing and punishment of criminals. During the previous century Britain had the reputation of being a comparatively free society, where the law was supreme and above class interest, where liberty was preferred to the efficiency of a 'French police', and where many assaults, disorders and other misdemeanours went unpunished, or were left to popular rather than state justice.[1] Serious offences in 1700 were punishable by death, transportation and the ignominy of beatings, branding and the pillory, and in this retribution, as in the policing and prosecution of criminals, the ordinary people were expected to play a part. By 1800 there were well over 200, mainly property, crimes for which one could be hanged in public. The purpose and effect of this eighteenth-century 'bloody code' has been much discussed by historians, but all are agreed that it was best suited to a world of decentralized rural communities, where there was neither the ambition nor the machinery to pursue the majority of criminals.[2] As we saw in chapter 1, people had their own ways of dealing with these, outside the official channels; arbitration, reparation, informal punishments, and community shaming were as much a part of eighteenth-century life as the 'order' of the parish constable, the magistrate and the court.

By 1800 and more especially in the years after the Napoleonic Wars, things began to change. The state, growing in power and bureaucracy, the social missionaries with their coercive and reforming mentality, and other people simply worried by the scale of crime, sedition and violent protest, all turned their back on the ways of the past.[3] On the south Wales coalfield, an extreme but relevant example, employers, magistrates and clergymen claimed that they were helpless before a rising tide of crime, intimidation and disorder. As the *Merthyr Guardian* put it in 1834, 'from Dowlais to Abergavenny,...THERE IS NO LAW'.[4] In these new communities old forms of control broke down; circumstances demanded a more effective system of policing, prosecution and punishment, one which we can recognize as distinctly 'modern'.

The criminal administration was remodelled in the first decades of the nineteenth century, and Robert Peel has taken most of the credit for this. Law was codified, the death penalty removed for most crimes, and greater emphasis placed on the merits of detection and a range of suitable punishments. In Wales capital punishment had been used more sparingly than in England, so that this aspect of legal reform had less of an impact here.[5] Other signs of change were more obvious. At the turn of the century there were the first examples of professional policing in the Principality, summary jurisdiction grew in popularity, and the building and improvements of prisons heralded another important shift in attitudes. By the mid-Victorian years all these developments had proceeded with astonishing speed, and the modern methods of deterring, apprehending, punishing and reforming offenders had been established. Whilst this was progressing, the question often asked was this: if Wales were as free of crime as its defenders claimed, were such developments really necessary?

The answer to this question depended largely on the class and community within which one lived, but not entirely so. There were conservatives in all classes, and the old ways of doing things had some 'passionate defenders'. The attraction of the eighteenth-century legal system was that, for all its inadequacies, and sometimes because of them, it allowed for a good deal of tolerance, discretion and local initiative, and the private prosecutions and trial by jury seemed to set it above political and class interests. By contrast, the changes in law, and in the machinery of law and order, in the nineteenth century were identified more closely with the central government, and with new forms of wealth, interfering and efficient administrators, and courts without juries. This was resented, as we have seen, by reactionary gentlemen like Henry Thomas in Glamorgan, as much as by William Miles, a Chartist of the same county. Whatever their reservations, however, large numbers of people of all classes came to use, and admire aspects of, the reformed criminal law and the agencies of government.[6] The greatest strength of the modern police forces, and of the legal and penal institutions associated with them, has been our inability to conceive of alternatives.

Policing in pre-industrial Wales had been a matter for, in principle, the whole community. In a real sense the victim of crime was his or her own 'policeman'. It was common practice for the victim to set out in search of the offender, making use of publicans, tradesmen and other contacts along the way. In the more sparsely populated regions it was easy to spot strangers and stolen property, and many were brought to justice in this manner. When the criminal was hard to find, people turned to the local wise man to discover his or her identity. In the report on education in Wales of 1847 there is an account of a subscription 'lately made by his fellow-workmen in order to enable a carpenter to travel fifty miles from Monmouthshire to Lampeter, to consult a wise man how to recover some tools he had lost'.[7] If they had the means, victims also publicized the crime by handbill and newspaper advertisement.[8]

It is impossible to estimate the success rate of these *ad hoc* measures, but acting as one's own policeman had its difficulties. One type of problem can be seen in the case of the murder in 1812 of Mary Jones, described in chapter 3. When the family discovered her body, they grabbed the suspect Thomas Edwards, tied him to a horse, and set off on a long journey to find a magistrate. During the night Edwards escaped. A hue and cry was set up, and once again he was caught, and eventually committed to Dolgellau gaol. As in this instance, the offended party could call upon the help of the people of the village, though it was not uncommon for the latter to switch their support to the wrong side! Criminals were rescued from the clutches of their victims, as well as from constables and gaolors.

The formal system of eighteenth-century policing consisted of the parish constables, the high or chief constables of the hundred, and the county magistrates. The first of these were appointed annually, usually from farmers and tradesmen in the parishes and from small shopkeepers and artisans in the townships, and their duties included making presentments of offences, serving summonses and executing warrants. They were re-munerated by fees, allowances and rewards. It was not an easy job, for they suffered from 'the strains of their mediating position between their com-munities and the law'. A 'studied negligence' explains part of their failure to apprehend and prosecute people.[9] The 'efficiency', in the modern sense, of the parish-constable system depended on many things, not least the speed with which information was received, the nature of the crime, and the availability of lock-ups and magistrates. Fear, sympathy, self-interest and plain indifference could reduce them to inactivity, but when there was a firm promise of financial rewards for an easy arrest, things worked well. Parish constables were, after all, responsible to a degree for the rising figures of apprehensions and committals in the early nineteenth century. In fact, in parts of rural Wales, and some of the smallest townships, they continued to operate alongside their professional replacements well into the nineteenth century.[10]

This familiar machinery of law and order was at its weakest in com-munities undergoing rapid industrialization and urbanization, and in particular when such places were racked by public disorder and riot. On the south Wales coalfield there were only a few paid and unpaid constables in the early years of the century, and even fewer places to detain suspicious individuals. In 1830, when the leader of striking ironworkers was incar-cerated in the Pontypool lock-up, he was soon released by his followers, a fact which encouraged the ratepayers of Trevethin industrial parish to establish an effective and highly paid professional force. John Roberts, the superintendent of this force, and his colleague William Homan, appointed by Samuel Homfray at Tredegar, achieved some notable arrests, and became bitter enemies of the Chartists. Their offices were threatened by crowds during the rising of November 1839.

It is not easy to obtain a balanced view of the quality and impact of policing in the early nineteenth century. Some urban leaders, including those at Montgomery and Conwy in the 1830s, stated that the borough police were perfectly sufficient in normal times, but the mayor of Caernarfon, comparing the old with the new in 1861, summed up the opposing view: 'the old borough police...was about as disgraceful a farce as can easily be conceived. The appointments resting in the hands of so many persons were not always well bestowed, and owing to the paucity of men, the town was often quite unwatched at night'.[11] In the largest towns the first preventive policing, of paid night and day watchmen, was introduced about the turn of the century, but numbers were small, and they needed, on fair days and holidays, the assistance of specials. Tradesmen in Haverfordwest and Newport also took the precaution at such times of boarding up their shops.

'This small body [4 or 5] of active persons is wholly inadequate to the necessities of the place, and is not even sufficient to execute the orders of the magistrates', ran one report from Newport, Monmouthshire, in 1835. 'Considering the increase of the town and the character of the population employed upon the river, this subject is one of growing importance, and demands immediate attention.'[12] Even the acquisition in that decade of Moses Scard and his Bristol colleagues by the Newport corporation did not please everyone. They were criticized for being unable, and sometimes afraid, to arrest burglars, vagrants and the crowds of drunken inhabitants at weekends. At Beaumaris and Monmouth the 'principal inhabitants' formed 'a voluntary police' to give their paid officers support, whilst in Mold and Newtown, in the face of marching gangs of strikers and election fever, magistrates swore in hundreds of special constables and called for the military.[13]

The disturbances of the Reform crisis of 1830–2, and government circulars, forced the urban authorities to review their policing arrangements. Merthyr, Carmarthen, Haverfordwest and several other towns appointed experienced head constables, sometimes from the Metropolitan area, to organize their bands of part-time officers, a development which had long been recommended. Under the terms of the Municipal Corporations Act of 1835, which complemented the Lighting and Watching Act of two years before, such places were obliged to establish a watch committee and a constabulary force. The number of salaried officers at Aberystwyth, Welshpool and four other Welsh boroughs can be seen in Table 6. In 1838 they had twenty policemen, and thirteen years later twenty-three had been added. These borough forces were obviously small, and were assisted by parish constables and by the watchmen of private associations for the defence of property. Tenby in 1836 had only two paid policemen, Carmarthen had five, and Swansea seven. By 1851 the number in the last town had tripled, to one for every 1,498 of the population, and there was also the presence of the docks police.[14]

Outside the major towns, police development was uneven. Much was done on a temporary basis, as when magistrates and employers on the south Wales coalfield created a mountain police of armed out-pensioners in 1834 to combat the Scotch Cattle terrorists, and a considerable number of company policemen kept watch on the new railways, canals, mines and quarries. Another expedient was to obtain temporary help from police forces outside Wales, usually from the large Metropolitan body. This happened in the mid-Wales factory towns during the riots and strikes of the 1830s. The central government, however, was becoming wary of sending too many policemen and troops into Wales. The events of 1839, when hundreds crossed the border to contain the Chartist threat, acted as a warning and a catalyst. After that date, the reply of the Home Office, seen especially during the Rebecca riots of 1839–44, was that London was prepared to sanction police and military assistance in an emergency so long as the local forces of law and order agreed to reform themselves.[15]

The Rural Police Act of 1839 laid down conditions for the establishment of county police forces, and an Act of 1842, also permissive, gave counties the opportunity of reorganizing rather than replacing the framework of parish constables. In Wales, in contrast to many other parts of Britain, the authorities were quick to take advantage of these Acts. Decisions were precipitated by the fear of disorder and sedition, and by concern over the crime statistics and the perceived threat of Irish immigrants and vagrants. Montgomeryshire and Denbighshire in 1840, Glamorgan in 1841, Carmarthenshire in 1843 and Cardiganshire a year later, established police forces, of 18–57 men each. In these counties, the opponents of change, including a minority of prominent landowners and industrialists, lost the argument but then concentrated on reducing the number of policemen and their salaries. Meanwhile, Anglesey, Caernarfonshire, Flintshire, Radnorshire, Pembrokeshire and Monmouthshire, which were less innovative, added a layer of paid superintending constables to the existing system of parish constables. It was an experiment much praised. Altogether, it meant that well before the compulsory County and Borough Police Act of 1856 the basis for professional forces had been laid in Wales. This probably explains the muted opposition to the Act; there were fears in the Principality that the legislation would reduce local sovereignty and the control of magistrates, as well as substantially increase the rates, but the Welsh MPs registered little protest.[16]

NO POLICE!!

WELL DONE ABERYSTWYTH BOYS!

Your Month's Trial is past; and right nobly have you acquitted yourselves! Your behaviour has been admirable; your conduct deserves the utmost praise. The quiet, peaceable, and orderly state of the Town, is the greatest credit to you. It has been emphatically the MOST peaceable and happy Month enjoyed by the Town of Aberystwyth for Years! Even the Trees on the North Parade, so lately the objects of silly revenge, have not been touched. This is as it ought to be. Whoever destroys or injures them, is an Enemy to the Town, and an Abettor of the detested Police System! The fact of a Row of beautiful Trees growing there, cannot injure or annoy one single individual; nor could their removal benefit any one. There let them remain. Does not your voice already echo, Yes, there they shall remain!

Your conduct hitherto is a guarantee for the future; for to no one single act of disorder can even the finger of envy point! This has raised your character immeasurably; and proved, beyond the possibility of contradiction, that the Inhabitants of Aberystwyth do not require the surveillance of a couple of Bludgeon-men to keep them from becoming Pickpockets and Thieves. The question at the beginning of the Month was,

Police or No Police?

That problem has been solved; the question is answered. The Watch Committee appealed to the Town. The Inhabitants have responded—they have supplied the answer; and that answer is,

NO POLICE!!

The state of the Town for the last Month has proved to the satisfaction of the most timid and incredulous, that they were not required. As far as Aberystwyth is concerned, the Cutlasses and Truncheons of hired Spies may henceforth be consigned to oblivion in the Commissioners' Yard, along with rusty old Iron, rotten Timber, and broken Pipes, as perfectly useless Lumber, and Relics of bygone days.

PERSEVERE IN YOUR PRAISEWORTHY CONDUCT!

THE

£200

WILL BE SAVED,

And the Victory won!

April 6th, 1850.

E. WILLIAMS & SON, PRINTERS, ABERYSTWYTH.

Opposition to the new police at Aberystwyth, 1850

The Act, which ultimately meant the replacement of parish with uni-
formed and salaried police constables throughout Britain, was of overwhelming importance. The government required all counties and large
towns to establish professional police forces, with stations, cells and houses,
all paid for out of the rates, with aid from the Exchequer. For a while, small
towns like Pwllheli and Tenby refused to join the county constabularies,
but independence was a difficult and expensive business, and by the end
of the century only the boroughs of Cardiff, Swansea, Neath, Newport and
Carmarthen had separate forces. In the counties the new police forces were
placed under the control of chief constables, who were often ex-military
men of high social status, and these in turn were answerable to police
committees of JPs, appointed at Quarter Sessions. The influence of these
committees varied greatly. Some of them, in contrast to the typical urban
watch committee, were virtually ignored by their chief constables, but late
in the century, when dissenters, radicals and nationalists joined the committees, there were some explosive conflicts, culminating in the dismissal of
the Cardiganshire police chief in 1890.[17] The Home Office regarded with
great suspicion this and other attempts to interfere with the independence
of chief constables, for they were important figures in transmitting the
values and standards of central government.

The rate of dismissals and resignations of the first professional policemen
was high in certain counties and boroughs, as young and fit recruits from
the countryside proved to be more ambitious for good wages, and more
insolent, incompetent and drunken than expected. The minutes of the
Cardiff Watch Committee show that men were disciplined for 'not com-
municating' with each other, for being in 'idle conversation' with the
public, for receiving money 'in suspicious circumstances', for being found
in brothels, and, above all, for being drunk and absent without leave.[18] In
the Glamorgan and Monmouthshire county forces thirty-four men
resigned in 1859 and twenty-two were dismissed. Although superannua-
tion schemes were introduced, the weekly salary at this time for constables
was only 20s. a week in south Wales, and 17s. in the north, well below that
obtained by miners and navvies. Thirty years later the weekly income had
risen by only 7s.[19] Local police committees trod a careful line between the
expense of extra policing and the cost of crime. The Home Office had
limited control over this and other aspects of the police forces, though the
grant-in-aid of a quarter and then a half of police costs, and the annual
reports of inspectors, ensured that the voice of central government was
increasingly heard. At the end of the century there was pressure from the
top for greater liason between constabularies, and talk of mergers.[20]

The number of policemen appointed under the Act can be seen on
Graph 22. When related to population, the rate did not reach average
English county and borough levels. 'The nature of the country [north

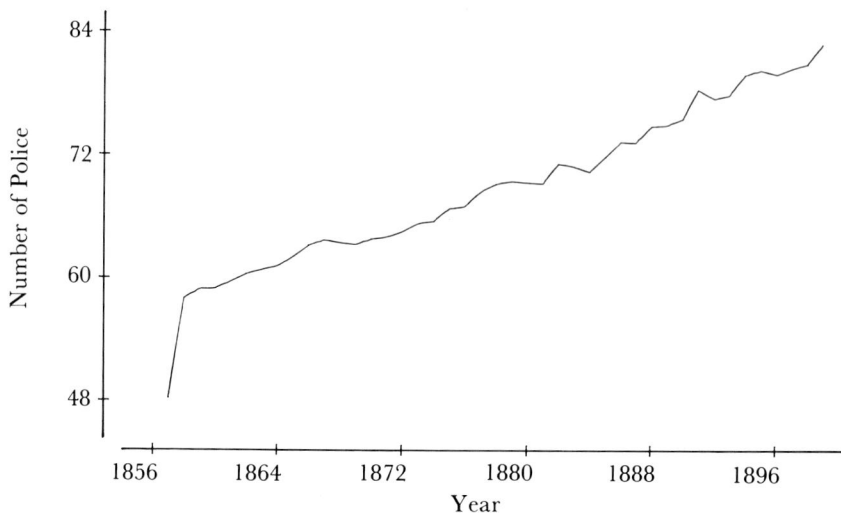

Basic rate: per 100,000 of population

Graph 22. Police numbers, 1857–1899.

Wales]', said the first inspector of constabulary in 1857,' does not require the same amount of force as in the English counties'.[21] Nevertheless, there was, under pressure from these inspectors, a consistent increase in manpower. The number of Welsh policemen in 1857 was 596, or one for every 2,073 of the population, whilst in 1899 there were 1,622 officers, one for every 1,209. In Great Britain the comparative rate in the 1890s was one per 720. The variations within Wales are just as striking. Whilst Cardiff, Swansea and Newport, with a total of 434 men, had a combined rate of one per 728 at the end of the century, lower than that of most large English towns, the rural counties of Anglesey, Radnorshire and Cardiganshire had only one per 1,535. It is difficult to compare their work-loads, but in the three seaports there was one officer for every thirty reported crimes in 1891, whereas in the three counties it was one per twenty.

These 'Bobbies' were regarded, first and foremost, as the servants of the local authorities and the ratepayers.[22] Police committees took much interest in the character and priorities of their forces; central police stations and cells were often in, or close to, guild and county halls, and leading citizens were inclined to treat constables as personal bodyguards. At Cardiff and Monmouth the watch committees simply 'instructed the superintendent to take action' over boys annoying residents, women soliciting, and publicans ignoring licensing regulations. Much in the spirit of the old constables of the parish or township, the new men were required to perform all manner of activities on behalf of their paymasters. They were appointed inspectors of weights and measures, and had to check on common lodging-houses, hygiene regulations and animal diseases. In many areas, too, they became assistant relieving officers, doubled as firemen, impounders, and dog-retrievers, and registered the users of petroleum and gunpowder. In Carmarthenshire, for a while in the 1860s, they even took nominal charge of the men employed by the fishery boards, and the Summary Jurisdiction Act of 1879 also confirmed that they were obliged to assist bailiffs in their unpleasant tasks.[23]

There were differing opinions about the value of this police work. 'I am myself most anxious that the Police should stand well with the Rate Payers', wrote the chief constable of Flintshire in June 1858, '& that their services should be made generally available if not at the expense of the faithful discharge of their more important duties'.[24] Some contemporaries argued that this work, described more fully in chapter 5, actually helped policemen to deal with crime; in this way, for example, they came into regular contact with vagrants and other doubtful characters, but towards the end of the century the Home Office grew more insistent that officers should, where possible, serve only one master and confine their attention to preventing, reporting and detecting crime.

Police instructions always emphasized the task of prevention, but there were, at the start, few men, large areas to patrol, and, on occasions, an unhelpful public. The first inspectors claimed that it would take time to create 'efficient' forces and to establish the communications needed within and across counties.[25] Once this had been done, and the new policemen had gained experience, their impact on crime could be properly assessed. In the event, such assessments varied widely. In Anglesey, Cardiganshire and Radnorshire, where there were only eighty-eight policemen in 1899, or one for 10,464 acres, people said that 'efficient supervision' was impossible; hundreds never saw the forces of law and order. Henry Richard, the Cardiganshire minister and politician, insisted that the policeman of the villages and towns of rural Wales was a lonely and under-worked figure, little more than the personal servant of the gentry, a charge taken up by the elected police committees after the local government reforms of 1888.[26]

For others, the men in blue were the most successful of Victorian missionaries, both in the towns and in the countryside. They were praised for encouraging the reporting of offences and for increasing the rate of apprehensions. Their very presence was said to have a beneficial impact on the incidence and nature of crime itself. In Anglesey, which had one of the smallest forces, the inspector reported in 1859–62 that it had become increasingly successful in preventing delinquency, and in the town of Denbigh, John Robinson, the head of police from 1844 to 1848, produced figures to show that in his time, and under his influence, felonies, vagrancy offences, assaults and drunken and disorderly behaviour had decreased dramatically.[27]

Llewelyn Turner, the mayor of Caernarfon, stated the case for the new police in this way:

> I know some men who lived for years by thieving, and sometimes by highway robbery, who have now [1861] resorted to honest modes of living, the risks of their former pursuits having become too great...
>
> To my certain knowledge, numbers of robberies were [once] committed of which no information was given to the [old] police; the present system of proper registration of officers is fast doing away with this anomalous state of things, and persons are now afraid to compromise felonies as they formerly did.
>
> On the score of expense, I feel satisfied that the gain is very great; property is much more secure, and the detection of offences more certain.[28]

On reflection, one can see the dangers of attributing too much to the police. The events of the second half of the twentieth century have removed some of the Turner's certainties about policing and crime. The statistics of the time offer few clues. Those of indictable, chiefly property, offences rose in counties such as Denbighshire as soon as county police forces were introduced, but not in Montgomeryshire. In Glamorgan and Carmarthenshire, although the rate of summary convictions moved sharply upwards about the time that their forces were established, the police were not, as Captain Napier admitted, initially responsible for bringing more property or serious crimes to court. The county police undoubtedly had an effect on the way in which crime was reported, but it is difficult to see exactly what it was. In the largest towns of the Principality the comments of contemporaries indicate that the biggest rise and fall in serious crime probably took place before professional policemen were appointed in large numbers. Even later, well into the second half of the century, the incidence of reported property offences does not seem to have been closely related, positively or negatively, to the changing size of the police establishment in Wales (Graphs 15 and 22).

Chief constables, naturally enough, argued for a connection. In Anglesey the chief claimed that serious crime, especially sheep stealing, had become 'rare' within a few years, due to police control of vagrancy and their 'unremitting vigilance...during night duty'.[29] An examination of some of the police diaries supports this favourable impression. The keenest constables had an agricultural labourer's eye for changes in the landscape.[30] They kept watch where property was vulnerable, such as along hedgerows and railway lines, called regularly at the homes of informers, and travelled many miles after known and suspected thieves. The diaries of constables Evans of Pennal, Merioneth, and his namesake of Deri, near

Bargoed, reveal that they knew, and did, a great deal more about property crime than the official statistics indicated. On their patrols they took into custody people who had poultry, animals, watches and other goods which might have been stolen, and apprehended others who just looked suspicious and then searched them and their homes for proof of their criminality. Not all were charged, though many were cautioned.

Critics of the police, and short-tempered newspaper editors, who hardly knew of this preventive and detective work, wondered aloud if these men had any impact at all on the level of major property crimes. In a county such as Radnorshire, which had 275,000 acres and 25,000 people in the second half of the century, 10–18 constables struggled to control the poaching gangs, and there were other country districts where wood and milk thefts continued much as before. Even in the towns, not every one shared Llewelyn Turner's belief in the efficiency of the new policing regimes. Watch committees passed votes of censure on the performance of their forces, declaring, often correctly, that the incidence of break-ins and burglaries seemed immune from changes in police methods. Angry chief constables replied with demands for more experienced officers, better salaries, and responsible property owners. Their annual reports were full of suppressed rage at the number of windows and doors found unlocked and goods left unwatched in the street. Whatever people's criticisms, chief constables knew that no one, in the great centres of commerce and population, was prepared to risk removing police patrols altogether.

In general, the impression remains that initially the police were most effective in preventing those property offences like street robberies and pickpocketing which had once flourished in unprotected places. When superintendant Wrenn of Merthyr and his officers physically fought their way into 'no-go' areas like 'China', they confronted established and open forms of criminal behaviour, and, so we are told, had a devastating effect upon them.[31] Scores of prominent 'bullies', members of 'swell mobs', female pickpockets and receivers were brought to court and transported. Much care was taken over the location of police stations and patrols in these 'dangerous' areas. Middle-class requests, and tradesmen's petitions, about such matters were carefully discussed in the watch committees. As for the poorer inhabitants, a few undoubtedly welcomed the permanent police presence and the thirty-minute patrols which promised greater security for property.

Of the effect of the police on other forms of delinquency, contemporaries were less grudging in their praise. The evidence from Denbighshire and Glamorgan, though not from all the Welsh counties, indicates that the introduction of the police forces was immediately accompanied by a rise in prosecutions for assault.[32] The first priority of these law enforcers was to

take charge of the streets. Much of a policeman's day was spent in preventing and suppressing disorder. There were patrols, visits to public houses,
and conflicts with noisy beggars, aggressive husbands, and revellers. A
constable at Leeswood in Flintshire during the 1860s cautioned virtually
everyone who showed the slightest sign of causing a disturbance.

Police chiefs argued that the 'unceasing exertion' of their men had a
long-term impact on the decline in violence in the later nineteenth century.
They were thinking mainly of policing the streets at nights and weekends,
when the forces battled with disorderly men and women reeling from the
public houses, but they also had in mind the suppression of the vengeful
crowd, fair-day celebrations, football and fireworks. Although there were
many reasons for the emergence of peaceful forms of community politics
and recreations, the new police proved to be an important arm of the
reformers. The chief constable of Cardiganshire, in the last report of the
nineteenth century, concluded in this way: 'since the police force was
established the carrying of effigies [*ceffylau pren*] has disappeared, the selling
of beer without a licence is a thing of the past... [and] affrays and other
unseemly conduct of young people attending fairs has been entirely eradi-
cated from the county'.[33]

Imposing police order was perhaps a more brutal business than we
imagine. Sergeants Toohill at Holyhead and Gill at Barry in the late
nineteenth century were no-nonsense policemen, willing to settle 'all
disputes with fists and staff'. One night in January 1860 another police
sergeant was called to the Strand in Swansea, where Margaret Thomas, a
young prostitute, was challenging twenty people to a fight. She fell to the
ground as sergeant Neale and a fellow officer approached, and they
dragged her several hundred yards to the police station. 'I felt my heart
beat for her', said an onlooker, 'knowing that I was a woman myself. She
was all over mud. Inside the station she was dropped down like a piece of
filth. It made me cry all the way home. I thought the poor woman's back
was broken'.[34] Late in the century, when the steelworks opened at East
Moors, Cardiff, the chief constable insisted that a permanent police
presence there, preferably of hefty recruits, would have a 'wonderfully
civilising effect' on a certain portion of the population; and Llangollen and
Llandudno, swamped at the time by rowdy day-trippers, also pleaded for
more officers 'able to keep the peace'.

Police intervention sometimes turned drunken hooliganism into worse,
but, on the whole, they were more effective than the old parish constables
in controlling public violence and popular disturbances. The latter success
is, perhaps, more apparent to historians than it was to contemporaries.
There were times when the police were seen as agents of those with power
and wealth, censored for causing industrial, agrarian and political
violence, and obliged, even at the end of the century, to call for additional

constabulary and military help. Minister William Thomas of Whitland, speaking at the Carmarthenshire Standing Joint Committee in January 1890, blamed much of the tithe troubles in his county on the numbers, character and arrogance of the police.[35] Yet in the south Wales strikes of the 1850s, at some of the later election contests, and even during the Tithe riots, the police were publicly thanked for adopting a low profile, preventing 'the disorder which usually prevails on such occasions'. Was it achieved, one wonders, by an element of restraint on both sides?

Historical debates have begun about the relationship between the police and the public, and over the reporting of crimes to the police and their efficiency in solving them. It is possible that, at the very start, the new policemen received limited support and information from ordinary people. That is the impression given in a few of the police diaries. How much this was due to the origins and attitudes of the new constables is hard to estimate. In urban and industrial south Wales a considerable proportion of the first policemen were from across the border, especially from the south west of England, and there were a number of Irish and Scotsmen as well. The problems were exacerbated, in some areas, when the recruits were non-Welsh speakers.[36] Bilingual policemen were preferred, and even required, in many districts, but it was not always possible to obtain them. The chief constable of Anglesey, who demanded better pay for his men, said in 1860 that 'a Welshman, of good character, speaking the two languages can readily obtain very lucrative employment' in Liverpool, Manchester and other towns with a strong Welsh connection.[37] Monoglot Welsh-speakers had advantages, but these were not of the kind which appealed to police bureaucrats. 'On my inspection', wrote William Cartwright of Caernarfonshire in 1857, 'I found some constables who could not understand the English language, which I considered an insuperable objection to their retaining their appointment'.[38] Within a generation, the same argument, against English-speaking monoglots, was being used to exclude applicants for the post of chief constable.

As we saw in chapter 3, the early days of professional policing were not easy. The first recruits soon realized, and their successors accepted, that their first requirement was to police the streets and the poorest members of society. Although this brought them approbation from their rate-paying masters, it did not always please those with whom they came into everyday contact. When, for instance, people were arrested for drunken and violent behaviour, the first paid constables had to run the gauntlet of angry mobs, the nearest Wales came, perhaps, to genuinely anti-police riots.[39] Although attacks on the constabulary declined later in the century, the poor appreciated, more than anyone, the selectivity and harshness of nineteenth-century policing. 'Reports being treated with contempt' ran an entry in the diary of police constable John Davies of Maesteg for 1867.[40] Resentment was perhaps a better word, and in the records of Margaret Thomas, the bedraggled Swansea prostitute, Thomas Williams, the defiant Pontypridd teenager of the 1890s, and other street characters arrested for 'beating and kicking a constable', it echoes down the corridors of time.

And yet the working-class victims of crime also saw the advantages of handing to the police the task of discovering and prosecuting offenders. Each year, in Wales as in other parts of Britain, they brought thousands of incidents to the attention of the men in blue. Within a couple of years of the establishment of the county constabulary, the chief constable of Anglesey explained the improvement in his detection rate to more information being given more quickly to his policemen, whilst, at the same time, his counterpart in Monmouthshire attributed the increase in reported petty thefts to the 'greater inclination being now shown by the public to apply for the services of the Constabulary...'[41]

The diaries of John Davies of the Bridgend police division, James Row of Pontypridd and Thomas Roberts of Aberdyfi in the 1860s and 1870s illustrate how much information came their way, and how policemen were used, not only by gentlemen, shopkeepers and publicans, but also by working men and women to sort out their problems and prosecute their enemies. These three policemen were brought stories of husband-and-wife quarrels, murderous street fights, attempted suicides, goods snatched, gardens raided, obstructions on railway lines, suspicious strangers, stray animals and lost dogs. Mrs Edwards of Aberdyfi even reported her husband drunk to Thomas Roberts, and wanted to know where he had been.[42] There were, it must be said, other people who consistently refused to contact and help the police. In the village of Bangor-on-Dee, 'such a wretched place', they seem to have been in the majority, and of every class.[43] However, one must not exaggerate the point; whatever people's ideological objections to the new policing, they soon regarded the constables as 'user friendly'.

The emergence of a growing acceptance of professional policing is well documented. In 1844 Colonel Yale in Denbighshire, speaking for many of his friends, complained of the police running after 'every little petty offence', thereby putting the county to expense and enriching the legal profession, but fifteen years later the inspector of the north Wales police district said that the 'popularity of the force increases year by year with its efficiency,....'[44] In Carmarthenshire Lord Cawdor echoed these sentiments: 'there was dissatisfaction with it once – at its introduction – but now [1857] if they were told that the police were to leave, the whole of Carmarthenshire would rise up in arms against their going.'[45] After a short while the doubters amongst the landowners and industrialists became converted to the value of professional policemen. So, it seems, did the lower middle class, who suffered more than most from petty crime.

The police's own records suggest that, in spite of the slow development of the detective force in Wales, their clear-up rate of indictable crimes encouraged people to trust them. It rose rapidly, from just over a half in the late 1850s to a high plateau of more than three-quarters for much of the 1860s and 1870s. The figures are a little deceiving; as can be seen from the police diaries and letters, not all the reported crimes were entered on the official returns. From the 1870s until 1893, when the calculations changed, the apprehension rate fell back towards 50 per cent. There were significant differences in the rate between areas and crimes. In Anglesey, Cardiganshire and Radnorshire the combined detection rate was over 50 per cent better than that of Cardiff, Swansea and Newport, where the police had to deal with many more reported offences. In these towns crimes such as burglary and simple larceny proved especially hard to solve. 'What robbery of any importance has been perpetrated, of which the rioters have been detected by the Swansea police during the past ten years?', asked *The Cambrian* newspaper in December 1857. 'We recollect none.'[46]

The detection rates, well above those of the late twentieth century, were not a perfect index of efficiency, but many people were convinced that the police achieved outstanding results in the mid-Victorian era, and ascribed this to the advantages which they enjoyed over the criminal. Constables were given wide powers to caution and arrest people whom they suspected of having committed, or being about to commit, a crime. Sometimes, as we have seen, they raided lodging-house after lodging-house, taking in anyone who might have committed a crime, and stopped hundreds of people on the street for 'felonious intent' and 'being without visible means of subsistence'. Welsh chief constables pressed hard for the Poaching Prevention and Prevention of Crimes Acts of 1862 and 1871. This legislation gave them the right to apprehend various groups of suspected and convicted offenders, who in turn had to prove their innocence. Such police sweeps were not popular with the victims, nor with many of those who witnessed them. People gathered round at the moment of arrest, and followed the parties to the station, all the while cursing the police. Mistakes were made. As many as 40 per cent of the people summoned and apprehended by the Welsh police were never convicted of a crime. In 1860, a constable stopped two men carrying a bag of apples between Brynmawr and Beaufort. They told him that they had got the fruit in Merthyr Tydfil, and when he tried to take them into custody, one of them pulled a gun on him. After protests on their behalf, the two men were acquitted at the Breconshire Assizes.[47]

The misuse of police power was, like excessive police violence, impossible to estimate. They were accused, especially by poachers, vagrants and prostitutes, of making false charges and of accepting bribes for keeping silent. The fact that respected characters like inspector Ellis of Holyhead and superintendent Lynn of Neath left their forces under a cloud is a reminder of the temptations facing all officers. The watch-committee minutes for Swansea and Cardiff reveal that some men took 'hush-money' from prostitutes, pawnbrokers and runaway seamen, and other constables perjured themselves in court. The abuse of police authority was probably greater than we will ever know, as the newspapers implied when discussing Cardiff cases in 1860, but as the years passed the forces learnt how to close ranks.[48] Even judges and magistrates, who suspected 'a fixed case', found it hard to undermine police evidence and solidarity, although juries occasionally came to their rescue.

One historian has used the term 'no contest' to describe the battle between the few professional criminals, with their primitive organizations and techniques, and the new professional policemen.[49] The latter were given enhanced powers of supervision over serious offenders by the Penal Servitude Acts of 1853–64, the Habitual Criminals Act of 1869 and the Prevention of Crimes Act of 1871. Scores of Welsh prisoners were annually let out on licence, and these had to report regularly to the police, and notify changes of address.[50] They could be taken into custody at any time, and obliged to give proof of their good behaviour. Such measures were, said Henry Austin Bruce, against natural justice, but he believed that they had proved their worth.

The police of the late nineteenth century also had the novel benefits of fast transport, photography, detailed record keeping, and telegraphic communications. Within hours of robberies at Holywell in the 1890s the police at Rhyl, Denbigh, Rhuthun, Mold, Rhos, and Wrexham had descriptions of the goods stolen and the likely offenders. Some astonished Welsh convicts were picked up as they arrived in London, or disembarked in America, whilst lesser fry, who fell more easily into the net, hardly had the confidence to deny the charges. Altogether, one can see why criminals talked gloomily of 'the big eye' of authority, and why others so praised the police for restraining known, and deterring potential, offenders.

These important developments in policing were matched by those in punishment. When people were arrested for indictable offences in the nineteenth century they had different prospects from those of their grandfathers and grandmothers. About seven out of ten of the males and six out of ten of the females apprehended were eventually committed for trial or bailed to appear either at the Great Sessions/Assizes, held twice a year, or at the Quarter Sessions. As we saw in chapter 1, only a small number of people came before the first court; great efforts were made to save the time and costs of Assize cases. Judges, when presented with the white gloves at a maiden Assize, praised the honest character of the Welsh people, but

The winter Assizes at Haverfordwest, 1898

added a note of thanks to the hard-working justices at Quarter Sessions. Apart from cases of murder, manslaughter and a few other felonies, these magistrates could deal with virtually every serious offence. They also heard a decreasing number of appeals against the lower-court verdicts in bastardy, settlement, licensing, rating, highway and game law cases.[51] Although things changed as the century progressed, the main factors which decided whether cases came before these higher courts, or were determined summarily, were the nature of the crime, the plea, the age of the accused, and his or her criminal record.

The disadvantages of the Assizes and Quarter Sessions were the long gaps between meetings, the inconvenience of travel for witnesses and the high costs, though in Wales, prior to the abolition of the Great Sessions, it seems that legal redress at this level was both cheaper and easier than that in England.[52] The great benefit of an appearance before these higher courts was trial by jury. The jury system was one of the foundations of an Englishman's rights and liberties; it gave some legitimacy and independence to the law. In truth, the discretion which juries displayed was probably exaggerated, though it had a symbolic importance, especially in Wales.[53] Grand juries threw out about 13 per cent of the bills that were presented to them, whilst the petty juries at Assizes and Quarter Sessions acquitted rather more than the authorities would have liked. Although this did not compare with the Irish situation, it was 'worse' than that in England.[54] Whereas a quarter of the defendants at the Welsh Petty Sessions were acquitted, or discharged because of missing prosecuters and for other technical reasons, in the higher courts the figure was about a third. The latter was below the eighteenth-century rate, but slightly higher than its English equivalent.

For those charged with offences against the person, except for murderers, the expectation of acquittal was higher still, in marked contrast, as we shall see, to the situation at the lower courts. With property crime the reverse was true. More than eight out of ten offenders from the Merthyr Tydfil police district who were charged with property crimes were convicted at the Assizes and Quarter Sessions in the mid-century. The Glamorgan juries liked to convict robbers and burglars, but were more generous towards women over twenty-five years of age who stole fuel and money from the person, and towards males under twenty-five years who took food and goods at work. According to Susan Ellis the chance of escaping scot free was also improved if a defendant 'was able to have himself professionally represented rather than attempt to conduct his own defence'.[55] If he were before a Carmarthenshire court, the most tolerant in the land, his prospects were even brighter. All in all, one can see why many people preferred trial by jury, to the annoyance of magistrates and judges.

As the legal correspondence over the Rebecca riots and Newport rising illustrates, the government always gave careful consideration to the location of the trials of Welshmen charged with treason, sedition and riot. Some of the keenest private prosecutors also wanted their cases heard outside the Principality, either in the superior courts in London, or in Chester, Shrewsbury and Hereford. In 1886–7, for instance, the cases of a man accused of killing a gamekeeper in a brawl at Dinas Mawddwy, and of tithe rioters of the same county, were transferred to Chester. Other matters could be left confidently to the Welsh juries. Dr Lewis Lloyd cites the case of Ann Lewis, who was charged in 1833 at the Merioneth Quarter Sessions with stealing clothes from her employer. It took only 'a few minutes' for the court to decide on her guilt, and Lewis and her two female receivers were sentenced to transportation.[56] The example illustrates how, in contrast to civil cases, criminal proceedings at this level were over very quickly, and how most offenders against property had neither legal representation nor expectation of mercy. Towards the end of the century, when prosecutions were better presented, and punishment less severe, conviction rates of those brought for trial in Wales rose nearer to 70 per cent at the higher courts and 80 per cent at the lower, and magistrates and the police expressed themselves more satisfied.

No one seemed to know exactly why the Welsh acquittal rates were a little higher than those in England. Critics of the Great Sessions, prior to its demise in 1830, put some of the blame for this on the 'Welsh judges [who] are men of inferior ability', but most of their anger was reserved for the 'numerous and unscrupulous' attornies, the 'lying witnesses' and the wilful juries.[57] Mr Serjeant Heywood, addressing the Carmarthenshire grand jury in 1812, talked of the prevalence of perjury, and the 'ignorance of the common people at the solemn nature of an oath'. It was a prominent theme over the years, mentioned at the time of the report of 1847 on Welsh education, and resurrected by the Bishop of St Asaph in 1889. The people were, it was said, 'so combined and lie so confoundedly' that the system of justice was gravely undermined. Yet proceedings for perjury were rare in nineteenth-century Wales; rather than tell untruths in court, one senses that men and women preferred not 'to give the evidence of which they are possessed'.[58]

Welsh jurymen, grand and common, although selected with care, were said to have been rather independent, as well as generous in the treatment of their countrymen. Grand juries were composed of gentlemen, yeomen and the upper middle class. Service was valued for its social side, and the chance to make the first, important, decisions on the fate of defendants of a lower rank. The judicial statistics indicate that their decisions did not vary much from good to bad years, though in Anglesey, Cardiganshire and Radnorshire the grand juries threw out a much smaller percentage of bills than their colleagues in Glamorgan and Monmouthshire or Wales as a whole. In a legal system which permitted a considerable amount of discretion, the prosecution and defence were careful to keep on the right side of the grand jury, but the attention did not always compensate for the frustrations of the task. There were times when those on the jury lists found, at the last minute, that they were not needed. It was especially galling in Glamorgan, where Sessions were held alternately at either end of a wide county. In the harvest period, the gentry and yeomen were prepared to pay the fine of £1–2 for non-attendance. Sometimes, to fill the grand jury, the sheriff had to corral gentlemen who just happened to be in the vicinity when the court was in sitting. It was a responsibility which had to be taken seriously, for the wrong decision on a bill of indictment might bring anonymous letters, maiming and arson. If the rich had the power, the poor set some of its limits.[59]

The grand jury was given legal advice on the bills before them, but it was only of the superficial kind. It is obvious, from their work, that they were concerned about the wisdom, and cost, of proceeding with malicious and doubtful cases, and were perhaps 'unduly affected' by the character of the prisoners. In Wales, or at least parts of it, people were known to each other, and the weeks of the Great Sessions and Assizes were a time of consultation and bargaining. One writer claimed, for example, that when respectable people were charged with indecent assault, 'every man of the Grand Jury is seen before [the trial] comes on.'[60] 'No true bills' were indeed returned frequently for crimes such as rape and infanticide, whereas the opposite was true for offences such as murder and burglary. Robert Oliver Jones, chairman of the Glamorgan Quarter Sessions, told a legal commission in 1872 that 'uncertain finding of bills' was an important administrative matter for his colleagues, and suggested that grand juries should be retained only for Assizes.[61] Their importance declined in the late nineteenth century, and they were abolished in 1933.

The petty juries came in for even more criticism. The British freehold and income qualification for being common jurors had to be reduced in Wales, and this was frequently cited as the reason for their 'poorer quality'.[62] In 1836 some 16,000 men were qualified and liable for jury service, and their social composition has some similarities with the tables of victims and prosecutors in chapter 1. The many farmers, tradesmen and artisans on the lists could expect to be called about once every five or ten years, and there were reservists in the Assize and Quarter Session towns who made a casual, 1s. per day, living out of being available. In Wales, rather more than elsewhere, counsel challenged people on the proferred jury lists, and later accused those who were appointed of being unreliable and of arbitrarily going against judges' directions. The *Quarterly Review* in 1844 berated them for their 'shameless disregard of the evidence'.[63] One view was that the Welsh legal system had not fully emerged from the eighteenth century, when juries played a more interventionist and independent role, and counteracted the severity of the penal code by reducing charges, deliberately undervaluing stolen property, and bringing in conditional verdicts. Mr Serjeant Heywood, appearing before a Select Committee of the House of Commons in 1820, stated that the number of 'wrong verdicts' in the Principality had been exaggerated, but attributed them to the isolation of the Welsh and their backward mentality.[64]

Others, like William Williams, the Coventry MP, and Edward Lloyd Hall, the Newcastle Emlyn attorney, claimed that the petty juries either did not understand the proceedings in English, or were swayed by the sight of one of their own people struggling to cope without interpreters and legal advisers. In the counties of north-west Wales, early in the century, the judge's charge to the jury had to be translated into English, and official and unofficial interpreters were constantly used in their higher courts. Augustus Brackenbury, the Lincolnshire gentleman who was driven from Cardiganshire in the 1820s, told a London court that a judge at the Great Sessions had refused to allow an interpreter to translate the statements of his English witnesses. As a result, so he claimed, the Cardiganshire jury did not understand a word, and the man charged with destroying his home was acquitted.[65]

Although they had a right to give evidence in their own language, defendants were sometimes denied this by magistrates and judges anxious to speed up the course of justice. Thus Thomas Jones, who appeared at the Glamorgan Quarter Sessions in 1850 to appeal against a conviction for industrial violence, was unable to plead his case for lack of money and the English language until solicitor John Owen offered to pay someone who could assist him.[66] Even then, said Revd Henry Griffiths of Brecon, taking up a point made by Benjamin Malkin thirty years earlier, the process of working through two languages, especially when a life was at stake, was 'painful in the extreme'.[67]

There was undoubtedly resistance, even by those who had some English, to take the oath and give evidence in the official language of the courts. Contemporaries, commenting on a case in 1829, spoke of the 'determined doggedness with which the lower class of inhabitants of the Principality refuse to be questioned in any other than the ancient tongue of their country.'[68] For some the answer to this problem was simple; judges in criminal, as in civil courts, must be Welsh-speaking, a point made repeatedly by Lloyd George, Tom Ellis and David Thomas, MPs, in the last years of the century. It was, after all, a linguistic concession granted in other areas of official life. Osborne Morgan, addressing the House of Commons in 1872 on the subject, claimed that, until judges were Welsh-speaking, defendants were being deprived of a natural right.[69] Henry Austin Bruce had some sympathy with this view, but William Williams and the legal establishment thought otherwise. Judge Baron Gurney, at the Carmarthenshire Assizes in March 1834, said that the proceedings had convinced him of the need for every Welsh child to be taught English.[70] In his eyes, and those of Edward Lloyd Hall, the linguistic divide accounted for the exceptional tolerance of Carmarthenshire juries when set against those of Anglicized Monmouthshire. The Cymreigyddion Society rose to the bait, and the editor of the local paper warned that although Gurney's plan would speed up justice a change in the language would also bring an English level of crime!

From the anger of prosecutors, and the laughter in the gallery, it was apparent that juries, as they had done for centuries, decided guilt on other than strictly legal merits. So far as one can tell from the statistics, the verdicts were not affected by the economic conditions of the time; the acquittal rate did not rise, or fall, markedly in years such as 1839 and 1842. Juries were concerned, however, in many instances with justice rather than order and punishment, and with their own particular interests. The quick and guilty verdicts on sheep stealers and arsonists, and the acquittals of Brackenbury's enemies, of angry and distressed servants, and of women who had allowed their children to die, were all rather more understandable than at first appeared.[71] As Serjeant Heywood pointed out, jurymen in Wales often lived in small and close communities, and knew intimate details of a case and of the defendant before the court sat. They were also deeply suspicious of malicious prosecutors, professional thief-takers and paid informers. Musing upon some of the 'doubtful' jury decisions, Heywood said that they had, on reflection, been made for a 'very good reason'.[72] At a much later date the charitable *Cornhill Magazine* wondered if the situation owed something to the cautious nature of the Celts, who did not wish to offend their neighbours.[73]

Judges were astonished not only by some of the acquittals, but also by the frequent recommendations to mercy. Such pleas can be related to the age, respectability, and circumstances of the guilty person, and perhaps to less tangible motives. When the jury asked for mercy in 1840 for the killers of Shadrach Lewis, 'on the grounds of previous good character', the judge realized just how unpopular the man had been. Judges were so shocked by some of the foremen's declarations that they asked juries to reconsider their verdicts, usually without the desired result. In Radnorshire in 1834, when a jury returned an unexpected acquittal, it emerged that, as they were divided on the man's guilt, the twelve men had drawn lots to reach a verdict. They were each fined £5. Judge Taylor Coleridge, speaking at Brecon in 1837, wished that the prejudicial or 'partial feeling' of jurymen could itself be punished.[74] One suspects that, like several of the great

Table 18

Persons apprehended and summoned in the Merthyr police district, 1855–1858, and the outcome of the charges brought against them

Offence	Number apprehended and summoned	Conviction (%)	Discharge & acquittal (%)
Larceny	945	55	45
Larceny by juveniles	111	66	34
Wilful damage to property	413	74	26
Common assault	2145	80	20
Assault on the police	333	90	10
Drunk	1480	90	10
Disorderly prostitutes	53	91	9
Vagrancy	141	52	48
Bastardy	326	89	11
Deserting the family	120	83	17
Non-payment of wages	136	77	23
Non-payment of rates	526	99	1

Source: MGRO, Q/E 1/9F, Chief constable's reports, 1855–8. In addition there were 398 males and females who were dealt with at the Assizes and Quarter Sessions in these four years.

landowners, he believed that the law was best left in the hands of gentlemen.

Significantly, much of the preoccupation with the faults or otherwise of the jury system occurred in the earlier part of the century. In later years, as we saw in chapter 2, the overwhelming majority of defendants were convicted or acquitted by magistrates sitting in Petty Sessions. 'From being the epitome of the English criminal law in the eighteenth century, the jury trial became the little-used symbol of it in the nineteenth'.[75] In the lower courts, where only a small minority of defendants had solicitors and interpreters, the conviction rate was, on average, over 75 per cent. Table 18 is a breakdown of the types of offenders who were charged in the Merthyr Tydfil police district in the mid-century. Not all of these were convicted or acquitted by the magistrates; some were discharged, for various technical reasons, and others entered into last-minute compromises which rendered legal proceedings unnecessary.

Many of the charges which were then decided upon by the Bench, including those of not paying rates and of being drunk, could hardly be disputed, and people accused of family offences had little chance of acquittal. More interesting is the trend, which runs counter to that of the higher courts, of a high rate of convictions for assault, and a moderate one for larceny. Ironically, it was sometimes in the very categories where acquittals were common that the magistrates were attacked for being too ready to convict. There were loud complaints from tramps and poachers, for instance, that justices of the peace were happy to accept the unsupported evidence of informers, watchmen and police officers. In a few cases magistrates' decisions were overturned on appeal, and prisoners released. More commonly the convicted men and women, as they were being dragged to the cells, cursed the Bench for their class-ridden and vindictive decisions.

Claims of partiality were often made, with magistrates condemned for 'leaning...towards the course of the rich and powerful' and for mixing politics with justice, thereby losing respect for the Bench.[76] As we saw in chapter 1, the social composition of justices of the peace made such accusations almost inevitable, but it is revealing that several popular movements of the time, including the Rebecca riots, contained the demand for stipendiary or independent justices. Josiah John Guest, who consulted privately with magistrates before, and during, a prosecution, said in 1841 that no one could pretend that justice in Merthyr was even-handed. It was customary for magistrates with a personal interest in a case to withdraw from the Bench, but a few, especially in proceedings over truck, turnpikes and the game laws, refused to hide their opinions. A policeman who stopped the publican of the Bowling Green Inn, Overton, in 1867 under the Poaching Prevention Act, admitted that 'we shall have uphill work but being a poaching case the Justices are of course with us.'[77] As the century came to a close, so, in the rural counties, the criticisms of the Bench came from opposing directions.[78] Whilst the old-style country magistrates were denounced for being too severe on poachers and too lenient on publicans, the new ones were accused of being the reverse, and of being too accommodating to prominent chapel-goers on assault, theft, highway and public-health charges.

The other complaint was the lack of uniformity in punishment, particularly at Petty Sessions. The Howard Association noted that in Anglesey, as well and in other counties, magistrates gave very different sentences for the same minor offences. Unless one had a permanent chairman of Petty Sessions, with legal training, who attended regularly and communicated with colleagues elsewhere, it was difficult to impose one standard. In some districts even the attendance of sufficient magistrates was not guaranteed; sittings were postponed, and everyone became over-dependent on the industry, knowledge and integrity of magistrates' clerks. Petty Sessional divisions were changed, and more justices appointed, but it was recognized as early as 1835 that the towns of Wales needed better administration.[79] In the largest of them the pressure of business, the difficulty of obtaining suitable candidates for the Bench, and concern over the growing power of the police, both as prosecutors and witnesses, led to the appointment of stipendiary magistrates.[80] Whatever their faults, these were at least more consistent in their sentencing. In 1872, when two were appointed at Pontypridd and Swansea, following the earlier ones at Merthyr (1843) and Cardiff (1858), Wales had a quarter of the professional magistrates outside London.[81] John Coke Fowler at Swansea and Robert Oliver Jones at Cardiff, on salaries of £600 p.a., won praise for being outstanding legal administrators and for increasing respect for the law, but in the eyes of the public they were perhaps too closely identified with town-hall bureaucrats and police inspectors.

The punishment of those found guilty of crimes at the higher and lower courts can be seen in Tables 19 and 20. In the missing period, prior to 1834, the main developments were the increasing commutation of death sentences, except for the offence of murder, the ending of shaming punishments like public whippings and the pillory, the continued rise in the popularity of transportation, and the emergence of imprisonment as the dominant form of punishment. At the beginning of the century, when 'the Bloody Code' was still in being, up to 20 per cent of those committed for trial at the higher Welsh courts were sentenced to the death penalty, chiefly for murder, burglary, housebreaking, robbery, forgery, and the stealing of farm animals. A number of them tried to cheat the hangman by committing suicide and by escaping from their gaolors.[82] Fear of death also affected the juries, and encouraged them to recommend mercy whenever possible. Only a tenth of those convicted of a capital offence during the first two decades of the nineteenth century were actually executed, a proportion generally regarded as the lowest in Britain.[83] This was not necessarily a sign of failure. 'The old sytem seems to have worked tolerably enough', writes one historian of early modern society, who believes that it was heavily and rightly balanced in favour of the accused.[84] When John Wyatt, the attorney-general of the north Wales circuit, addressed a parliamentary enquiry in 1829, he praised the civilized conduct of the Welsh and their Great Sessions, and claimed that only four people had been hanged in Anglesey, Caernarfonshire and Merioneth in the previous forty years. In Monmouthshire, the bloodiest county, during the years 1800–30 the figure was twenty-six, almost half the Welsh total.[85]

When, where and why the death sentence was respited are questions which have recently occupied the minds of social and legal historians. The reasons actually given at the time for reprieves were the 'aggravated'

Table 19.
Committals for trial or bailed: result of proceedings, 1834–1892

Year	Total offenders	Acquitted & discharged	Death sentence	Transportation	Penal servitude	Gaol over 6 months	Gaol under 6 months	Whipping, fined & discharged on sureties	To Refm. schools	Insane	Commutation & pardon
1834	575	200	13	85	–	60	187	29	–	1	13
1844	1075	397	0	86	–	98	460	30	–	4	–
1860	845	315	1	–	85	88	304	42	8	2	–
1876	831	275	2	–	56	195	289	4	8	2	–
1892	677	196	1	–	24	112	308	33	0	3	–

Source: PP, 1835, XLV, 1845, XXXIX, 1861, LX, 1877, LXXXVI, and 1893–4, C111.

Table 20.
Offences determined summarily: result of proceedings, 1860–1892

Year	Discharged	Convicted	Gaol: Above 6 months	Above 1 month	Above 14 days	14 days & under	To Refm. & Ind. schools	Fined	Whipped	To find sureties & recogns.	Delivered to army & navy	Other punishments
1860	6908	13257	10	628	863	1111	23	8404	26	653	113	1426
1876	8682	26161	2	850	1348	2645	39	17978	63	1002	83	2151
1892	9151	38130	3	519	871	1942	141	29659	219	807	112	3857

Source: PP, 1861, LX, 1877, LXXXVI and 1893–4, CIII.

nature of the crime, the age, sex and character of the convicted persons, and their criminal records.[86] When a gang of burglars was captured, for instance, it was usual for only the leader to be executed. Pleas on behalf of these prisoners, 'almost [a matter] of course' in Wales, were made by friends, employers, gaolors, clergymen, chairmen of the Quarter Sessions, and the gentry. The main impressions, gained from reading the government correspondence, is that petitions from men 'of consequence and weight in the County' had more influence than the rest, and that little known young adults in the urban and industrial districts had the least hope of saving their skins.[87] There were times, however, when it was felt that, whatever the circumstances, a death was necessary. The *Hereford Journal*, commenting on the hanging of a lad in 1816 for setting fire to a farm building, said that it was 'a sacrifice requisite for the welfare of society and the preservation of property'.[88] The numbers attending the public hangings were invariably large. In April 1817, for example, 10,000 arrived at Carmarthen to see the end of the part-time minister who had administered poison to his pregnant girlfriend. Sometimes, as we saw in chapter 3, the large crowds vented their anger on the condemned persons, especially if they were wife-killers, but the authorities could never be certain of the response. In 1801 a man going to his hanging was rescued in Brecon, and there were protests on behalf of the dying elsewhere.[89]

Doubts about the efficacy of the death penalty grew quickly in the years after the Napoleonic Wars. Robert Peel and other reformers of the criminal code argued that the limited risk of being caught and hanged for property offences should be replaced by the certainty of apprehension and a punishment appropriate to the crime. During the 1820s and 1830s the option of the death sentence was removed for most crimes, including burglary, the stealing of farm animals and arson. Between 1834 and 1837, when the last crime ceased to be a capital offence, forty-five death sentences were recorded in the courts of Wales, and all but one were commuted. Over the next seventeen years about the same number of people (forty-six) were sentenced to death, almost all for murder, and ten of these were executed. For the rest of the century executions were, as we have seen, rare in the Principality; after the Act of 1868, which banned public hangings, the death sentence was carried out on average no more than once a year. In spite of this, a small band of MPs and several Welsh ministers of religion felt compelled to campaign, on principle, for the abolition of capital punishment.

Transportation, which had been used extensively since the early eighteenth century, was the main alternative to the death penalty, though a number of females and children received the lesser punishment of 1–3 years imprisonment instead. During the whole history of transportation to Australia between 1787 and 1868, only 2,200 of the 160,000 convicts were from

Wales.[90] In the early 1830s, when the popularity of this form of punishment was at its height, over a quarter of the men and women convicted at Assizes and Quarter Sessions in Wales, as in England, were sent abroad, mostly for the duration of seven years. Even in the late 1840s and early 1850s almost a hundred people a year on average were sentenced to join them. One of these was William Williams, a Bangor boy, who was convicted of larcenies in 1848. Like Williams, transportees were usually people with previous convictions for indictable, mainly property, offences. Single people predominated, as did labourers in their late teens and early twenties, and there were particular criminals whom the authorities were determined to remove. They included persistent juvenile thieves, leaders of 'swell mobs', the professional criminals and receivers of the towns, and the prostitutes who stole from the person. Classic victims, if that is the right term, were Margaret Presdee and Morgan James of Caernarfon in the 1840s, small-time criminals who specialized in stealing purses. Females accounted for about a seventh of the people transported from Wales. Professor Deirdre Beddoe tells us that 283 women were sent between 1787 and 1852, less than 2 per cent of the United Kingdom total. Almost half were from Glamorgan and Monmouthshire, and almost two-thirds of them had criminal records.[91] It seems that female domestic servants, who were seen as colonial marriage fodder, were occasionally punished more severely than male offenders who comitted similar crimes, but in general, as the figures show, transportation was not greatly favoured by magistrates in Wales.

For those who believed in the existence of a criminal class the attraction of this type of punishment was obvious; although it was costly, it was the most effective and permanent solution. Up to a fifth of the convicts, who left via London, Portsmouth and Plymouth, for Van Diemen's Land and New South Wales, died on the crossing, and most of the others never returned. 'Convict life in New South Wales is the most dreary and miserable than can be imagined,...' ran one newspaper letter in 1843, when the government was desperately trying to reinforce the deterrent effect of transportation. It was, ironically, a punishment which, after that date, increasingly met with the criminals' approval. When transportation fell into disuse a decade later, there were still vagrants in Wales who begged to be sent across the world to begin a new life. Unfortunately, neither the penal reformers in Britain nor the colonists themselves wished to accommodate them. After a series of enquiries into possible alternatives, transportation came to an end quite suddenly in the mid-1850s.

Thereafter, instead of a journey overseas, serious offenders faced long periods in prison. This was a new development, part of the triumph of the prison system which has been the most significant trend in modern penal history. The interest in the prison system, which greatly revived after the late eighteenth century, and the huge commitment of state resources to its reform, have been the subject of much debate. It has been suggested that behind this outwardly humanitarian attempt to 'institutionalize a social problem', with its stories and statistics of success, was a formidable battle by a determined state to control deviants and 'a hidden agenda' to make them 'detestable' to society at large.[92]

In the eighteenth century there were common gaols and houses of correction at Beaumaris, Bangor, Dolgellau, Aberystwyth and other centres of population, but they were not large long-stay penitentiaries. The houses of correction, if they were ever truly intended as reformatories, had long ceased to deserve their name. Only a few hundred people were imprisoned in these Welsh gaols during the 1770s, when John Howard found them in a terrible state. They were financed and run by all manner of urban and private agencies. They had few individual cells, unrestricted association of all types of offenders, and part-time gaolors. At Welshpool, where a handful of prisoners were locked up in a dark and primitive shelter.in the centre of the town, they spent their time conversing, through a small grating, with passers-by. At Monmouth, when Charles Homfray, adjutant of the militia was gaoled for assault, he was allowed the company of friends and 'such wine, spirits, beer and provisions as may be necessary for his own consumption.'

Sixty years after John Howard's visit to that particular county prison, Wales had sixteen gaols, together with four smaller prisons which sometimes held only debtors. As we have seen, they were, for Edmund Hyde Hall, part of the 'war on immorality' which revived in Britain after the 1780s. Two thousand people, chiefly males over seventeen years of age, were sent to these prisons in the twelve months ending March 1834. Considerable efforts were made in the years after the Napoleonic Wars to turn these places into healthier but intimidating penal institutions, set apart from the community. With the encouragement of Robert Peel's gaol legislation of the 1820s, the liberties and association once enjoyed by inmates, male and female, were curtailed, and the treadwheels and other forms of hard labour were introduced. Even so, the condition of some of the north Wales institutions, like those at Wrexham and Bala, was so bad that magistrates were reluctant to commit people to them, and escapes were common.[93] The exceptions were Beaumaris and Montgomery; the former, opened in 1830, was regarded by the new prison inspectors as one of the best in Britain. Presteigne's gaol was about the worst; in 1814 a woman forger was rescued from the death cell by her family, and eleven years later there was a mass break out.[94]

In the early and mid-Victorian years most of these institutions, including the gaols at Rhuthun, Cardiff and Swansea, were rebuilt and extended, borough and county gaols were consolidated, and a new one opened at Mold. The central government, which had first insisted on uniformity and

Montgomery gaol in the nineteenth century

annual inspections, chose this period to take over responsibility for the running of prisons. The Prison Act of 1865 laid down minimum building, hygiene and educational standards, forcing Beaumaris, Brecon, Carmarthen and Presteigne gaols to enlarge and up-grade their accommodation. In 1876, one year before the establishment of the Prison Commission, 6,486 men and women were committed to the Welsh gaols. Two-thirds of these entered the county prisons at Cardiff, Swansea and Usk. During the remaining years of the century the number of inmates fell or kept steady, and half the local prisons closed. Beaumaris, Presteigne, and Montgomery were amongst them. In 1892, when overcrowding was a problem, the number of committals was slightly down on that of sixteen years before (Table 11).

The debate on the purpose of imprisonment was rather swept aside by the sheer popularity of this form of punishment. There were a number of experiments, at Flint, Rhuthun, Montgomery and elsewhere, with silent and separate prison regimes during daylight hours, and there was, too, the general introduction of short periods of solitary confinement. At the Usk House of Correction in the mid-century the governor was even able, because of unusually fortunate circumstances, to keep prisoners 'strictly separate by day and by night.'[95] Prison chaplains, surgeons and teachers were appointed to take care of the bodies, minds and souls of inmates, and hundreds were persuaded to take communion and sign the teetotal pledge. 'The majority of prisoners appear to appreciate [these] efforts', said one chaplain in 1869, but nothing brought lasting delight to evangelists or utilitarians.[96] At Brecon gaol, where remand prisoners were kept separate from the rest, and where the silent system prevailed during the daytime, the chaplain and the visiting magistrates stated in 1847 that a stay in their institution made people only more determined 'for the commission of fresh crimes almost as soon as they have gained their liberty'.[97]

In fact, the typical gaol sentence was so short as to make all reform programmes, of whatever value, practically unworkable. It is important to realize that long-term imprisonment was rare in our period, especially in Wales. Penal servitude, which replaced transportation, and consisted of separate confinement and hard labour, was given in exceptional circumstances, as when Lydia Williams of Fishguard poisoned her husband in 1863.[98] It was usually for periods of 3–7 years, and spent in purpose-built convict prisons like Chatham and Portland, all of them outside Wales. When the ticket-of-leave system was introduced for these people in 1853, it was given a mixed reception by the public, who had read stories about dangerous criminals being free to walk their streets. In the early 1860s, as concern mounted over violent robberies, burglaries and arson attacks, judges and magistrates sentenced on average just over a hundred men a year in Wales to the convict prisons. One of these was William Rees, a Cardiff boatman, with a string of previous convictions, who stole 5 lb of pork from Emma Nixon in 1860.[99] The Penal Servitude Act of 1864, which set the pattern for the next thirty years, lengthened the sentences, and ensured that in future Rees and his colleagues faced an even more rigorous regime. In 1874 the Howard Association complained about the seven-year sentence passed at the Anglesey Assizes on a man, with two minor convictions, who had taken a hen.[100]

There was, in some quarters, 'legitimate satisfaction' with the deterrent effect of such severe punishment, a feeling which has returned in almost cyclical fashion in modern times. But Sir John Byles, addressing the

Denbighshire Assizes in 1865, doubted the wisdom of long-term incarceration. He wondered, as did Henry Austin Bruce, whether its real purpose was to placate public, or more especially middle-class, opinion, a question which has been asked of most penal reforms of the nineteenth century. After the fears of the 1860s the number of people punished by penal servitude declined to a very low level indeed. In 1876, fifty-six persons only were given that sentence. During the same year 195 people at the Assizes and Quarter Sessions received gaol sentences of from six months to two years, for aggravated offences against the person and property, 147 received 3–6 months, and 142 less than that. Over the last two decades the proportion of convicted criminals in the last group increased considerably. Many of them were first offenders, people of 'good character', very young males, and females caught stealing other than from the person and from employers. This sentencing at the higher courts was, perhaps, less harsh than we have imagined, though many people, guilty and innocent, also spent months just waiting for trial.

At the Petty Sessions, four-fifths of those sentenced to terms of imprisonment in the second half of the century stayed there for a month or less. Most of these had been convicted of minor larcenies, common assault, breaches of the vagrancy and game laws, and family, work, drink and prostitution offences. The precise length of the sentence depended on the idiosyncrasies of magistrates, the past record and current behaviour of the defendants in court, the sex and age of the offender, and the nature of the crime. Women were sometimes treated better than men in minor property cases, but when they threw aside the perceived female role, by not caring for their children and behaving in an indecent and disorderly fashion, punishment could be heavy. The worst age to be sentenced was in one's early twenties; the very young and very old had some kind of excuse or sympathy. Amongst the unluckiest individuals were poachers and industrial militants, who were convicted on multiple charges, and stayed longer behind bars than the rest, whilst the most fortunate prisoners were those who had beaten their wives, girl-friends, work-mates and neighbours, and returned to the fray after a few weeks. A number of people, mainly those guilty of non-property crimes, were also granted remission, being 'forgiven part of his [or her] time' by committing magistrates.

In gaol all of them experienced 'rigid discipline tempered with much kindness and sympathy', or so the governors and chaplains would have us believe.[101] Prisoners were kept occupied by breaking stones, making bags and mats, picking oakum and cleaning the kitchens, and a few institutions offered tailoring, dressmaking and gardening. Only the very youngest received any educational training outside the Bible classes. The Revd E. G. Williams at Swansea paid special attention to the worst and oldest inmates, so that, although they had failed in life, there was the possibility of 'a hopeful death'. The annual reports of governors, chaplains and inspectors of gaols make gloomy reading. Hard labour of the 'first class' kind meant, after the second quarter of the century, exercising on the treadwheel and/or crank mill, for up to ten hours a day, and the range of punishments for idleness, disobedience and unruly behaviour in prison was extended. Hundreds each year were flogged, put in irons, placed in dark cells, subjected to solitary confinement and deprived of food for prison offences, a reminder that the nineteenth-century state took its revenge on the criminal in a more hidden and disturbing manner than its predecessors.[102]

In 1835 the number punished for prison offences was 169; by 1894 it had risen to 518 males and 99 females. Women and children escaped some of the worst aspects of prison regimes after the mid-century, but it was a hard, brutal and lonely existence for all. There were a handful of angry protests by the families of prisoners subjected to corrective punishments, but in general one is struck by the isolation, of every sort, endured by those sentenced to gaol in the nineteenth century. Thomas Haweek, removed from his wife and seven children in 1868 for taking clothes on a train, was only one of a number of depressed inmates who made repeated attempts at suicide. Others, too, emerged from prisons psychologically marked, and demarcated from the rest of the working class.[103]

There was, said Henry Austin Bruce, no more than a faint hope that anyone would be changed by the prison experience; some vagrants even appeared to relish it, and bread and water diets were introduced to deter them. 'These persons [tramps or vagrants] are turned out even in a worse condition than when they were brought in', said the Swansea prison chaplain in 1867, 'for they bear the stigma of having been in gaol'. He wanted them to be returned to 'normal' society via a system of public works. In his opinion the alcoholics and prostitutes whom he met in gaol had also lost 'self-respect...they look upon themselves as outcasts from society, rejected, despised, and irrecoverable'.[104] A quick return to prison was guaranteed. Recommittal rates are unreliable, but the evidence of Table 14 suggests that, on past experience, about 40 per cent of the prisoners in 1876 would be returning. John Heaton, the chairman of the Denbighshire Quarter Sessions, said in 1848 that where inmates had been positively influenced by the 'reformatory discipline' of the gaol and the 'instruction of the chaplain', they should be given a leaving certicate to that effect, a letter to their local clergyman and help with finding employment.[105] Goal visitors, religious associations, and county prisoners' aid societies carried out some of this work. Most of them published optimistic annual reports, but added words of caution. The Glamorgan Society, which provided gaol leavers with small sums of money and jobs as servants and pedlars, declared in its tenth report that many of those emerging from Cardiff prison 'belong to a class almost impossible to reclaim.'[106]

This reality and, even more, the large number of people passing through the courts and the financial costs of imprisonment, encouraged magistrates to seek other methods of punishment. Some had been tried for generations. In the early nineteenth century branding was outlawed, but offenders were still placed in the stocks and whipped through the streets. Male vagrants, juveniles and the disorderly suffered most. In August 1812, for example, three boys who robbed the orchard of Henry Eaton, collector of customs at Llanelli, were publicly whipped through the town, and one of the constables was officially reprimanded for allowing the demonstration to proceed too quickly.[107] His task had been an unenviable one, for spectators were in the mood to turn upon those responsible for this punishment. Sometimes whipping in public was imposed in addition to a gaol sentence, though increasingly, and permanently after 1862, it was done within the walls of the House of Correction. The public punishment of placing people in the stocks was also on the decline; when a Cardiganshire man, convicted of being drunk and disorderly, underwent the experience for six hours in August 1856, the local newspaper felt bound to record it.[108]

This sentence was inflicted because the man was not in a position to pay a fine. Fines had already become the most convenient alternative to imprisonment, especially useful for first-time offenders, women and youths. Early in the century fines were the norm for breaches of excise and highway regulations, and for common assault, trespass and profane swearing. The point has often been made since, but rarely at the time, that people were treated much more leniently for attacks on people than for offences against property. By 1860, as we can see on Table 20, well over half the people convicted at Petty Sessions were fined, and thirty years later the proportion had risen to three-quarters. Typical fines ranged from 2s. 6d. for throwing stones and 5s. for being drunk and disorderly, to £1 for an assault and £2 for poaching. Like many other aspects of legal administration, the system of fining worked to the disadvantage of the poor, for it was not related to the ability to pay. Only after the Summary Jurisdiction Act of 1879 were people allowed to pay by instalments, and even then it was difficult. In the 1890s about half of the inmates of gaols were there because they could not pay fines.

Whipping, often in addition to imprisonment, regained some popularity at the time of the garotting panic of the early 1860s, and again very late in the century when people were worried by the behaviour of young hooligans. Reformers had an ambivalent attitude towards corporal punishment. A juvenile offenders committee, which met at Usk on 3 January 1881, recommended reformatory schools for all young delinquents, but only after a short gaol sentence and whipping, with 12 strokes for boys over twelve years of age or 18 strokes if they had been violent.[109] In the previous year, when fifty-six juveniles were prosecuted for larceny in Swansea, half of them were whipped, and the rest fined, imprisoned and sent to reformatories. In 1892 the total Welsh figure of whippings as a result of proceedings at Petty sessions was 219. The birch was often inflicted on children who stole drinks, sweets, cigarettes, fruit, eggs and ice-creams. Nine-year olds Thomas Maldoon and Andrew O'Neill of Treherbert were birched in 1875 for helping themselves to beer and soda water, but in other instances the courts dismissed the culprits if their parents promised to administer corporal punishment instead.

Probation, in form if not name, had always been a part of the legal system. At the start of our period large numbers of people were put under recognizances to be of good behaviour; many were wife-beaters and other violent and disorderly characters. As we can see in Table 20, about 5 per cent of those convicted at Petty Sessions in 1860 were asked to find sureties and enter into recognizances. This method of dealing with petty offenders was recognized in the Criminal Law Consolidation Acts of 1861 and the Summary Jurisdiction Act of 1879. After furious lobbying from Henry Vincent, who was concerned by the presence of so many first offenders in prisons, the Probation of First Offenders' Act was passed in 1887. It was, said Merioneth magistrates, 'a very useful Act', but it was little used, and cannot be really compared with the Probation Act of 1907. Courts, wishing to give offenders the benefit of the doubt, proceeded much as before. They were placed under recognizances to come up for judgement when called upon, and the Salvation Army and other voluntary agencies gave commitments to help them. In some cases, promises were exacted over signing teetotal pledges and getting medical help, and dozens were allowed to escape gaol each year by joining the army and navy.

The ultimate prospect of reforming offenders increasingly exercised the minds of nineteenth-century evangelicals, whether secular or religious. The vagrant and the drunkard were given some of their attention. Refuges were established for the former in Swansea and Cardiff, and societies were created to suppress both begging and drunkenness and to give aid to those who showed signs of remorse about their past conduct. Dr Lambert has written about some of this, and the religious drive behind it, but of all the evangelicals' targets, the most favoured ones were the prostitute and the juvenile delinquent. Moral missionaries like the Revd John Griffith preached about the evils of prostitution, and ministers visited their homes and places of work. With the opening of the penitentiary for 'fallen women' at Llandaf in the 1862, magistrates were able to send wayward prostitutes there, instead of confining them in gaols or dispatching them to the sixty-three refuges in England and Scotland. When they entered prison, the chaplain at Cardiff pursued them relentlessly, looking for any changes in character, and begging them to accept a place with a good family. The chaplain at Swansea took a more cynical view. So long as society 'tolerates it [the evil of prostitution] in its most aggravated forms', he saw little prospect of reformation. The raucous support for the Contagious Diseases Acts in his town underlined his point. 'Our only chance', he concluded in 1877, 'is with the young.'[110]

Others agreed, and by the mid-century the notion of institutionalizing and destroying juvenile delinquency had gained much ground. The new reformatories and industrial schools were intended to be 'moral hospitals', where abandoned, neglected and criminal children received the missing dose of religious education, discipline and training. Wales was a little slow in establishing such institutions, though the reformatory at Hendref Ganol, Neath, was certified by the government in 1858, and that at Little Mill, near Pontypool, a few months later. Initially there were problems with both places, because of inadequate resources and the 'extreme idleness', misconduct and endemic thieving of the new arrivals, but in time conditions improved. On average two dozen boys aged 12–16 years were sent each year to these schools, usually for stealing, and this figure represented half of the Welsh inmates. The children were, as we have seen, mostly from poor homes, and many of them had no previous convictions. A typical case was William Breen, a fifteen-year-old of Cardiff, who stole a bullock's head worth 10*d.* and was sentenced in 1865 to fourteen days gaol and two years at the reformatory. Under the Reformatory Schools Act of the following year all these children had to serve a preliminary period of imprisonment, but in 1893 this was made optional and later abolished. They stayed several years in the reformatories, doing gardening and farming, but were sometimes released early on promises of good behaviour. In north Wales opportunities for reform were fewer; until the opening of the Catholic reformatory at Mold in 1899, the magistrates had to send juvenile candidates out of Wales, or to the industrial school at Bangor.[111]

Ragged and industrial schools supplemented the work of the reformatories. 'There is a vast number of children who never attended any school, who have never been convicted of any crime,' claimed Henry Austin Bruce at a public meeting in Cardiff in April 1860, 'but who are felt to be the source from whence the criminal classes are recruited.'[112] Ragged schools and children's homes for such 'neglected' youngsters were established at Cardiff, Swansea and other large towns during the 1850s and 1860s. They offered them religious education, lessons in obedience and independence, and an introduction to the world of work. In addition, Bruce and his friends identified another class of rebellious children, beyond the control of their parents, who sometimes lived rough, in the company of thieves and beggars, and enjoyed a life of 'wild liberty'. These needed the discipline and training of industrial schools. Money was collected in Cardiff for this purpose, and a frigate, the *Havannah*, was chosen in 1861 as the home of the school. At first some eighty boys were taught there, either as boarders or day scholars, and about a quarter of that number, mostly in the age range 8–14 years, arrived each year. They learnt nautical skills, and worked in Cardiff market as porters and shoe-blacks. Some were sent, under warrant, to the ship by magistrates, and, under the Industrial Schools Act of 1866, parents were obliged to contribute towards their expenses. In 1877 another ship, the *Clio*, was certified for similar use at Bangor, and over £7,000 was spent on the refitting. This had room for more than twice the number of boys, and most of them were eventually sent to sea.

Before the century came to its close the provision for neglected, rebellious and criminal children had become quite extensive. Apart from the institutions mentioned above, there were Board truant schools at Bonymaen, Swansea (certified in 1882), Quakers' Yard, Merthyr Tydfil (1893), and Barry (1899), the Girls Home at Mumbles in Swansea (1885), which was run by the Church of England Waifs and Strays Society, and a small auxiliary Home for Boys in Cardiff (1899).[113] In addition, magistrates still sent children to schools at Bristol and other English towns for rehabilitation. How effective all these were at civilizing and training youngsters cannot be ascertained. Many of the inmates of reformatories and industrial schools were found employment, in the armed forces, at sea, and in service, a good number were simply 'returned to friends', and a few were sent abroad. From the doubtful statistics compiled of the careers of those leaving the Welsh establishments, it seems that over two-thirds of them kept away from a life of crime.[114] In spite of the reports at the end of the century of staff brutality, and of juveniles absconding from detention and disappearing when on probation, hopes remained high that these educational institutions offered the best chance of breaking the 'hereditary cycle' of delinquent behaviour in modern Britain.

This view was only part of a wider optimism about the policing and punishment of offenders. Many people, including Henry Austin Bruce, had no doubt that justice in the late nineteenth century was altogether more certain and effective than it had been at the beginning. The judge at the Anglesey Assizes in 1895 insisted that the diminution of crime owed much to a more merciful administration of the criminal law, and the better care of offenders whilst in gaol and on leaving it.[115] Such adjectives and opinions belonged, of course, to a particular moment in time; a generation earlier or later and his statement would have brought murmers of dissent from his audience. Opinions on the intention and effect of punishment constantly change. At the very moment when the judge in Anglesey was penning his address, William Morrison, the assistant chaplain at Wandsworth, asked the explosive question; 'Are our Prisons a Failure?'[116] In the early years of the twentieth century the enthusiasm for incarceration, both long-term for serious offenders, and short-term for the idle, the awkward, the drunk and the disorderly, quickly disappeared. Each generation since 1900 has looked for new ideas, re-discovered old arguments, and questioned endlessly whether the reforms and institutions of the nineteenth century actually work. Perhaps, in one sense, it does not matter too much. The most careful historical assessment of changes in punishment and the crime rates has shown that the former have no discernible effect on the latter.[117]

Epilogue

This short survey of nineteenth-century Wales has given some support to the thesis that countries and regions have their own distinctive criminal patterns and traditions. Henry Richard was correct in his opinion that Wales was a land where both the nature of delinquency and its treatment was somewhat different from that of England and Scotland, and certainly of Ireland. The scale of crime and disorder did not begin to match that of other Celtic or Latin countries. In a European context, Wales had, as the education commissioners of 1847 noted, about the best record of all.[1] It was not a land of 'great crimes', or horrific violence, but of common assaults, petty thieving and many misdemeanours. According to the court records, this continued to be true into the twentieth century; in 1951, and to a lesser extent in 1971, fewer Welshmen than Englishmen came before the higher courts, but more were proceeded against for non-indictable crimes at the lower ones.

Those who sought to define 'Welshness' in the mid-nineteenth century, insisted that in this area of human behaviour, the difference between them and their Irish cousins across the sea could hardly have been greater. 'No landowner, proprietor of works, nor any other member of the upper class in the Principality, has cause to fear the dagger of the assassin, the fire of the incendiary, or the rude assaults of an infuriated mob', said Thomas Rees, the Swansea minister in 1867. Even compared with the people of England, he continued, his countrymen were twice as good 'in their morals, so far as criminal statistics prove the point,...'[2] As we have seen, Rees and his friends offered thanks for this to their dissenting religion, which had moulded the civil and social character of their countrymen. The Welsh had developed a great respect for the life and property of others. 'I attribute this paucity of punishable offences in Wales', stated one observer, 'partly to the extreme shrewdness and caution of the people, but much more to a natural benevolence and warmth of heart, which powerfully deters them from acts of malice and all deliberate injury to others'.[3]

To place the comments of Richard and Rees in context, we must remember that they were ignoring the many cases at the lower courts, and the various non-legal ways in which Welsh society dealt with delinquency. The Petty Sessions were busy in the Principality; in 1899, when one per thirty-six of the population attended them, the rate reached one of the highest points in modern times. In the towns, where the rate was higher still, the inhabitants developed a close and ambivalent relationship with the police and court officers. At the same time, there were other communities where policing was minimal, the reporting of crimes 'leaves much to be desired', and disputes were settled much as in pre-industrial society. Offenders in these places were disciplined through their relationships, their work and their chapels, and, for certain misdemeanours, there was the humilation of the *ceffyl pren* and its various offshoots. It is possible that such unofficial sanctions and justice, which diminished sharply in the mid-Victorian years, accounted for some, though by no means all, of the differences between recorded crime in Wales and that in the outside world.

The evidence of this book also demonstrates that Henry Richard was right about the disparities between rural, urban and industrial districts. In rural Wales there was perhaps less concern about crime and it was dealt with rather differently, but even so, most of the records indicate that all types of offences, violent as well as property, were less common there. Those who, like George Rice Trevor, argued that the people of the villages were 'brutal and immoral' were not supported by the statistics. We are told by Alan Macfarlane that these places had been comparatively law-abiding and peaceful for centuries, and had used official methods to sort out conflicts.[4] It is just feasible that the popular image of the eighteenth century, with its drunken squires and riotous villagers, has caused us to exaggerate the violence of ordinary people in pre-industrial Wales. Lawrence Stone believes that serious attacks on the person were in decline by 1800, due to 'a cultural softening of manners, greater sensitivity to cruelty and violence, and to the social rise of a middle-class culture and a more market-orientated society'.[5] There was an increase in recorded assaults for a while in rural Wales during the first half of the nineteenth century, but it was less striking than in the industrial districts and reached its peak by the mid-1830s. The contrast between rural Wales, and rural Ireland, Sicily and France at that moment in time is very marked; vendetta, feuding, warring and violence were much less common in this country.

Grievous bodily harm and sexual attacks were more common in industrial and urban than in rural Wales, but the rate of both was not as high as might have been expected from popular history and historical novels. Another student, of the Black Country, has seized upon this. 'There is' he writes, 'much evidence that it [industrial society] was a rough society, but little to show that people feared for their lives, or felt themselves unable to use the roads at night'.[6] If they were female they would have been less relaxed about this than David Philips, but his point is a good one. What is missing perhaps is an awareness of the scale of all this; as we have seen, when compared with Wales in the 1930s Victorian society was much more violent. In the seaports the statistics reveal that working-class adults had reason to be concerned for their safety. Weekends carried a danger, as they still do, and there were parts of Cardiff, Swansea and Newport where the police always anticipated violence. Offences against the person remained high in these places until the 1870s. In the 1880s and 1890s, too, when a ripple of anxiety over muggings and rape broke the complacency about the declining rate of violent offences, it was the large towns which attracted attention.

All the communities which we have been discussing had a similar balance between violent, property and victimless offences. There was not in Wales the contrast between a rural crime pattern, with a high proportion of personal conflicts, and an urban one, where property offences predominated, as has been described by Eugene Weber and other scholars. Both categories were evenly reported, though many more property crimes were dealt with at the higher courts. As other historians have pointed out, the pattern of serious crime had not altered much since the fourteenth century, in spite of major economic and legislative changes.[7] The turning-point in this respect was the Second World War. Since then, violence against the person, sexual offences, and burglary and break-ins have increased at a much faster pace than the rest of indictable crime. In Cardiff, Swansea and Newport, where the recent increase in burglaries and serious assaults has been greatest, newspapers have written in the 1980s and 1990s about 'fearful homeowners', 'terrified females', 'juvenile hooliganism', and 'weekends of crime, drunkenness and violence'. Some of this is an exaggeration, part of the 'fixed vocabulary of complaint [which] rumbles on through British history almost without interruption', but it sets the fears of the 1850s and 1890s in some perspective, and revives memories of Henry Richard's strictures on the morals of the Anglicized urban population when compared with those of the inhabitants of the 'gwlad y fenig wen'.[8]

The Welsh, of whatever kind, have never been as 'innocent' or as 'loyal' as Henry Richard and Thomas Rees claimed. This book has shown that they were writing at a convenient moment in history; the indictable crime rate was declining by the 1860s, and rural, as well as some urban districts, were regaining a reputation for being law-abiding and peaceful. Significantly, neither writer made too much of the events of the preceding half century. The rise in the rate of recorded crime in Wales during that time was truly remarkable, faster even than the increase in the rate of indictable offences between 1945 and 1985. The tables produced in this book show that the rise encompassed minor as well as serious offences, and affected rural as well as industrial communities, natives as well as newcomers, women as well as men, and the young as well as the old. It continued until 1854, just a few years later than the English 'crime boom'.

Like the 'crime booms' of the early seventeenth century and that of very recent times, the criminal statistics in the early nineteenth century probably reflected both a genuine increase in delinquent behaviour and less tolerance of it. It is surely too much to argue that all the statistical increase, especially of property crimes, was due to changes in prosecution policy, though one can see why Dr Gatrell puts the case.[9] There *was* at that time a new awareness of the dangers posed by the rapidly expanding population, and by the existence of poverty, vagrancy and crime after the Napoleonic Wars. Efforts were made to outlaw the practices of the 'marginal people', and to control everything which reduced the income of the wealthy and the importance and discipline of wage labour. The disorderly and the riotous were also confronted by improved police arrangements.

How much these changes in prosecution and policing contributed to the crime figures we cannot tell, though one suspects it was a large amount. The impression, however, from much of the literature of the time, is that people were also committing more offences. Why exactly this happened remains a mystery; as in the 'crime wave' after the Second World War, people offered very different reasons for it. The general, and yet short-term, nature of the rise, made simple economic and socio-economic explanations about the impact of capitalism and urbanization rather doubtful. John Wade said in 1833 that 'crimes have increased among men because property and transactions connected with property have increased', but, like other speculations about the effects of anomie, alienation, relative and actual deprivation, and affluence, it was difficult to match the fluctuating statistics to the theory.[10] Critics of modernization were unnerved by the subsequent decline in criminal indices, and turned elsewhere for signs of moral decay.

Whilst some analysts struggled to make sense of the growth and contraction in the crime figures, others cast doubt on the real danger and seriousness of criminal behaviour. Some cynics, precursors of present-day radicals, suggested that the problem of crime in modern society had been deliberately exaggerated, to permit the state to extend its powers and influence. It is difficult, as Benjamin Disraeli stated in his opposition to the early police legislation, to obtain an objective measurement of the threat posed by crime. The statistics take us only so far. In 1858 the combined rate of known indictable and summary offences was one per forty-eight of the population, slightly worse than that in 1931 but several times better than that of 1971. As we have seen, criminal violence continued at a comparatively high level until the 1870s, but it was rarely of an extreme nature, and property offences, too, were usually of a minor kind.

Nor was there much evidence of an extensive and well-organized body of criminals. There were gangs, receivers and flash-houses, and considerable planning behind the many 'acquisitive offences', but there was no large criminal class.[11] In the nineteenth, as in the twentieth century, most offenders were rather pathetic recidivists and ordinary people without a criminal record. Crime in Britain has never been the glamorous and rewarding profession portrayed in films and novels. Thomas Plint, one of the best-informed of observers, said that stealing was 'as poor and ill-paid a business as one could enter into'.[12] Throughout this book, it has been the ordinariness of crime and criminals that stands out.

The cost of these crimes was low by recent standards. Court cases involving the embezzlement of hundreds of pounds, and lucrative raids on jewellery shops and the houses of the rich were rare. Crime in 1851 was chiefly a collection of petty thefts worth only a few pence or shillings. Some victims preferred to ignore the losses, and pressure had to be applied by governments and reformers to convince them of the need to prosecute. One can estimate, from various sources, that the value of reported indictable offences against property in the 1850s was in the region of £15–25,000 p. a., about the same as the expenditure on the police in Glamorgan and Monmouthshire, or on all the Welsh prisons.[13] As a comparison, in the area covered by the South Wales Constabulary, the value of property stolen in 84,002 offences during 1982 was estimated at well over £15,000,000. Some of the modern embezzlers, drug dealers and car thieves make a much better living than the smugglers, robbers, burglars and other 'high earners' of the nineteenth century.

In the light of these comparisons, students of twentieth-century policing and crime might be a little surprised that the people of the early and mid nineteenth century were so obsessed with the problem of crime. Of the interest, and alarm, there is no doubt. Edwin Chadwick saw delinquency as a threat to the workings of the capitalist economy, and Lord Ashley believed that the rising figures, especially of juvenile crime, were the beginnings of a social revolution. Friedrich Engels, in a famous passage from his book of 1844, praised criminals for having the 'courage and passion ...enough to resist society, to reply with declared war upon the bourgeoisie.'[14] There are historians, too, who see much of the delinquency in this book as 'social crime', a form of primitive rebellion, which had considerable support from the oppressed classes. Howard Zehr and Ted Gurr tell us that 'sharp increases in indicators of crimes of theft and violence usually coincide with episodes of strife.'[15] This book gives examples where crime was a form of displaced rebellion, but a large amount of the delinquency which we have described does not fall into this category. It was a serious threat to no one, and had no connections with the wider world of protest. Many human actions contain an element of rebellion, but in a typical theft or assault it was a small and, probably, unconscious one.

What gave crime such a high profile in the early and mid nineteenth century was not so much the scale and nature of the offences as the prevailing anxieties about change, dislocation and rebellion. This, says Geoffrey Pearson, in his book on respectable fears, has always been the way of things.[16] Modern writers, looking backwards, have been impressed by the orderly nature of the economic revolutions of the period, and by the restraint and limitations of the popular protests. At the time, however, the governors were not quite as detached in their judgements. The Merthyr and Rebecca riots, and the Chartist risings in mid and south Wales, undermined the old clichés about Welsh passivity. The remarks on 'the peaceful character' of the Welsh, by travellers of 1800, were replaced by fears that some districts, rural, urban and industrial, were 'beyond the law'. For those who wished to receive it, the *ceffyl pren* in the west and the Scotch Cattle in the south-east provided proof that there was now a sinister and permanent threat confronting the authorities. Comparisons with the arson campaign and the miners strikes of the 1970s and 1980s have been suggested, but the context of, and reactions to, these troubles were different. For a while in the mid-nineteenth century ministers saw exceptional dangers on this side of Offa's Dyke, though never, it must be said, on the scale of the Irish rebellions of 1798 and 1848.[17]

The immediate response to these perceived threats, namely the stationing of soldiers and the establishment of professional policing, was impressive, and the longer-term developments in education and language policy were equally momentous. In Wales, where there was less resistance to the centralizing policies of the British government than in Ireland, much was achieved in a short time, or so contemporaries believed. Well before the publication of Richard's *Letters and Essays on Wales* (1866), the level of serious offences and popular disturbances had begun to fall, and subsequently the rates of most types of crime and disorder turned in the right direction. Agrarian outrages hardly reappeared after Rebecca, and industrial troubles became more spasmodic and less dangerous. According to Ted Gurr, since the 1850s, with the possible exception of the years before the First World War, public order 'has rarely been more than a secondary concern for most of the élite or the public at large.'[18] During the last decades of the century, even the increase in the rate of victimless offences slowed down, to be followed by an actual decline early in the twentieth century. In the context of unprecedented urban and industrial growth, and the great shifts of population, the improvement in social behaviour seemed remarkable. For many people, it had been an essential ingredient in the economic miracles of the period.

In the history of modern crime since the mid-eighteenth century there has been nothing to compare with this 'triumph over crime'. It was much wider than a Welsh phenomenon; places as far apart as Stockholm and New South Wales shared in the low figures. But the British had the greatest sense of pride; the fall in the statistics was broadcast to the farflung corners of the empire, and compared favourably with the records of the French, Germans and Russians. This, perhaps the most satisfying of the Victorian achievements, continued, with some fluctuations, into the first years of the twentieth century. The rate of serious crime rose only slowly until the Second World War, and that of minor offences remained low. In 1931 one indictable crime was reported for every 255 of the population, and one person in sixty-five was prosecuted for a non-indictable offence. Then, as if part of a great cyclical plan, the war brought a change, and the mood of confidence vanished. Since the mid-1950s the increase in recorded crime had been extraordinary, and some of the anxieties of the early Victorian years, about the pace of economic and social change, the nature and violence of city life, and the evils of juvenile delinquency, have returned.[19] In 1971, when the collection and recording of statistics had improved, one indictable offence was reported to the police for every thirty of the population, and one person in twenty-eight was prosecuted for non-indictable crimes. It now seems, as it did to the judge in 1855, that soaring crime figures and ever-growing numbers of policemen are the mark of a modern society. If Henry Austin Bruce's optimism runs through much of this volume, it is worth recalling his footnote that human nature does not change very much and that there is, in the modern industrial world, the potential for almost unlimited crime. The Italian Philippo Poletti and Emile Durkheim, writing about the same time, caused a furore by asking whether a high crime rate was not an inevitable, and perhaps welcome, price to pay for rapid social progress.

One of the most difficult questions, frequently asked at conferences on the history of crime and policing in Britain, is how the people of the second half of the nineteenth century were able to halt the upward spiral of crime in modern society. The explanations given by contemporaries were inextricably bound up with discussions over the emergence of political stability and social respectability. Although contemporaries praised the changes in policing and punishment, they devoted most of their attention to the economic climate, social philanthropy, and educational and religious endeavour. Modern writers understand this emphasis; increased policing, so we are told, can only reduce criminal behaviour 'when it reinforces improving socio-economic conditions'.[20] The report on Welsh education of 1847, which was concerned with delinquency as much as schooling, had predicted that with the English language, and a good education, the people will 'in all probability assume a high rank among civilized communities.' Control was thus to be of an internal as well as external character. No doubt some of the population, wishing to live in an orderly society, hardly needed persuading. 'Coercion', two legal historians insist, 'is almost always accompanied, and sometimes replaced, by consent.'[21]

It was widely believed in 1900 that a judicious mixture of external controls and self-discipline had produced the desired result. People seemed more unwilling to commit and tolerate crime. In the early twentieth century there was, says Terence Morris, 'a greater degree of consensus about the canons of social propriety as they related to behaviour...to have been before a criminal court charged with dishonesty, however trivial, was regarded as socially disgraceful'.[22] The reduction in the number of women appearing before the courts was particularly marked, and this was attributed to a growth of respectability and the 'retreat into the home'. The rate of female crime has remained low, relative to male, in twentieth-century Wales, as fewer women have been prosecuted for street and prostitute offences and as males have been convicted in great numbers for breaches of traffic regulations. In 1971 fewer than ten per cent of those at the courts were female. Of juvenile crime, the evidence is more contradictory, but at the turn of the century the figures also suggested a decline, though one reversed since the Second World War.

According to some writers, the rejection of crime in the later nineteenth century permeated large sections of the working class. We must remember, however, that most people, even in 1800, never wanted to be associated with crime. Of the period 1660–1800, one writer has said that 'the court records suggest that most men given the opportunity to work and support themselves would do so, and...when employment was available and prices were moderate property crime was likely to be at a low level.'[23] Although popular support existed for some illegal protests, and sympathy, too, for actions inspired by poverty, it is a mistake to exaggerate the acceptance of crime. The appeal of the Owenite analysis of the roots of delinquency probably narrowed after the 1840s. In an age of money wages and growing prosperity, the working class, who experienced much of the property crime and most of the violence, became, one suspects, more dismissive of the ex-prisoners in their midst. Labour leaders in the Mabon mould were keen to condemn any form of illegal action, and the media did its best to turn people against recidivists. Those just above the working class in the social scale, people like petty clerks, shopkeepers and publicans, gave these criminals even less sympathy. Henry Austin Bruce declared in 1875 that when people felt that they had a stake in progress, they accused Liberal Home Secretaries of having a secret pact with burglars.

The attitudes of people towards the legal, penal and policing systems were, and have remained, complex and pluralist. Alan Macfarlane claims that one of the differences between Britain and other countries was the early development of the common law and the respect which it engendered. Writing of society in the seventeenth century, he finds 'no indication of a popular opposition to national laws or to the activities of Justices or other law-enforcement officers.'[24] Law was the 'ideological cement' of modern society. One is struck, from the beginning of the nineteenth century, by the respect for the rule of law. With the exception of the game and fishing laws, and some of the regulatory Acts described in chapter 5, people held the law in high regard. There were times when men and women abused both the law and those who enforced it, but they saw its virtues and used it. Even Rebecca, with her preference for 'Welsh law' in certain areas of life, was content for her followers to seek redress for most complaints through the Queen's courts.

Respect for the law, however, was not the same thing as a belief in impartial justice. Although everyone in 1900 was offered accessible, cheap and efficient justice, not everyone was treated equally. The most vulnerable members of society, who crowd the pages of this book, experienced the realities of power, or as Marx put it, 'the dominant will'. They knew at first hand how legislation and policing worked in practice, and saw for themselves the bias of the courts in favour of those with money and legal representation. At this distance in time, things appear in sharper focus; if nineteenth-century crime was composed of thousands of petty offences rather than of great commercial scandals and middle-class larceny, and if the very poor were imprisoned in exceptional numbers, it was in part because the state decided that these things should be so. It would be wrong, nevertheless, to drift into the extreme labelling position, and insist that everything was determined solely by a small ruling élite. Governments, to be effective, needed public support in this area, and the law had always served other than simply the narrow interests of a privileged few. People in 1800 used the law partly because they believed it belonged to them.

During the nineteenth century important changes took place in the character and control of justice and policing. The 'high level of popular participation' in legal processes and law enforcement, which was a feature of early modern Wales, was much reduced in our period. By the mid-nineteenth century informal, local, religious and seigneurial justice had given way to crown jurisdiction. The courts of Great and Quarter Sessions, and especially Petty Sessions, dominated the field. At first the prosecutions in these courts were largely private ones, as in the past, but later in the century much of the legal work was taken over by the police, officials and attorneys, and this continued until the radical overhaul of the prosecution service in 1985. The people also withdrew from law enforcement, first in the towns and industrial districts, and then, after 1856, across the whole country. Although there were links between the old parish constables and the new, professional policing marked a revolution in attitudes and politics. Policing and prosecuting were more efficient in 1900 than they had been a hundred years before, but the consequences of the changes, in terms of power, control and individual rights, are still the subject of heated debate.

One of the rights which was discussed within legal circles in the nineteenth century was that of language. Since the Act of Union English had been the official language of the courts, and it was used exclusively by judges, magistrates, and counsel in our period. Despite protests, Welsh was heard less in the courts as the century worn on. If Welsh was the 'language of morality', English was very much the language of authority. Governments were willing to make language concessions in other fields of life, even in the civil courts and in the police and prison services, but not in the criminal courts. The abolition of the Great Sessions, one of the last Welsh institutions, was symbolic; legal, administrative and cultural sovereignty passed to London in the nineteenth century. Ironically, magistrates' courts after the Second World War became an arena for the battles over language policy, with a number of justices expressing sympathy, as few did in the nineteenth century, for the rights of Welsh speakers. The Welsh Language Act of 1967 at last gave Welsh the same official status as English.

One of the most interesting changes described in this book was the triumph of 'magisterial justice', at the expense of trial by jury. In 1899 only one case in eighty-five went before the higher courts. The grand and petty juries had once been regarded as a central and glorious feature of the British legal system, the point at which the community had a final and decisive say in the whole apparatus of administration. As we have seen, Welsh juries had a reputation for being generous in their verdicts. After the the merging of judicatures in 1830, and pressures from above, the rate of acquittals did fall a little, but even in 1899 only 67 per cent of those sent for trial were actually convicted. There was a feeling, in some quarters, that here was a counterweight to insensitive English justice and judges. During the twentieth century the use made of these higher courts fluctuated. After the Second World War the numbers attending Assizes and Quarter Sessions increased. By 1971 about one in fifty-five legal cases was conducted before a jury, but the chance of acquittal had fallen significantly since 1900.

The great majority of offenders in the nineteenth century were taken before the Petty Sessions, where the acquittal rate was low. It was quick and cheap justice, but it was, in one very obvious sense, 'class justice'. The defendants, and the prosecutors for that matter, were often poor, but their fate was always decided by men of a different social class. Apart from a handful of stipendiary magistrates, with a legal background, most of the justices on the bench were unpaid volunteers whose main qualifications for the task were property and status. They were, even at the end of the century, chosen overwhelmingly from the upper ranks of county and urban society. In spite of the useful legal services which they provided, and the independence from Whitehall which they sometimes displayed, they were regarded, perhaps increasingly, as the 'right hand of the police and the propertied classes'. Nor did things change much in the early twentieth century; appointments to the Bench were made on political and social grounds, and proper training for the role was not introduced until the 1960s. The appointment of John Frost, the Chartist draper, is a reminder that there have been some representatives of 'the people' on the commission of the peace, but until quite recent times they have been few and far between.

By contrast the police forces, in the nineteenth and for some of the twentieth century, have been heavily stocked by members of the working class. The typical recruit in 1850 was an unmarried agricultural labourer of just over twenty years of age. Miners, craftsmen and others were also appointed but they lacked certain virtues. As the early figures of dismissals and resignations indicate, these men were set basic standards of behaviour and discipline. Initially they were regarded very much as the servants of the ratepayers, but in time the Home Office, which increasingly paid the piper, called the tune. The photographs of the forces, the wage-complaints of the 1890s, and the beginnings of formal training, reveal that these men were being welded into a proud and self-supporting nationwide profession.[25] They were not uncritical of legislation, or unaware of the selective nature of their work, but they were committed to upholding the law in the manner dictated by their betters. This brought some clashes with the working class, especially over the policing of strikes and the fight for quiet streets, a confrontation which was exacerbated during the years 1910–26.[26] The history of the modern police has been one of extending legal powers and a decline in local accountability, well illustrated during the miners' strike of the 1984–5.

We should, of course, not allow recent events to cloud our judgement of the relationship between police and people in the past. Outside the major towns, the physical presence of the nineteenth-century police was very different from the situation today. Even in 1899 there were only 1,622 policemen in Wales, or one for every 1,209 of the population, a much lower ratio than the British average of that period, and only about a half of that in 1971. Initially, there was some resistance to the permanent presence of men who were very different, in style and responsibility, from the old parish constables. Yet they soon became an indispensible force, the first contact for people with a grievance, and security for those who feared attacks and robberies. It is often stated in present-day society that the police, like the prisons, have little impact on crime, but this was not the view of the people of the second half of the nineteenth century, nor of the criminals. Few citizens in 1900 doubted the 'moral influence' of the men in blue and their ability to prevent and contain unwelcome behaviour.

Some writers have drawn a line through the middle of the working class, and claimed that those above it were favourably inclined towards the police, and those below were hostile, but there was a range of views in all social ranks. There was, in many families, and even individuals, a 'moral pluralism' about the response to the new policemen. If, as we are often told, the 'overwhelming majority of ordinary people' held the police in 'high regard' from the 1880s until the mid-1950s, it was a critical regard. One can perhaps make too much of the violence towards the police, in the mid-nineteeth, as in the late twentieth, century, but one cannot ignore completely the angry voice of working men and women. There were degrees of frustration that the policemen were beyond their reach, and a suspicion of the growing police powers and, ultimately, of the real purpose of modern policing. 'Why do you not go after proper criminals?' was a recurring and revealing protest.

This leads us to perhaps the most interesting development discussed in this volume, which was the growth of a policed society, in the widest sense. The chapters have been about power and control, as well as about the defence of property and the person. It is easy to forget, especially in Liberal Wales, that the 'age of reform' was a period when thousands of people were pursued through the courts for breaches of minor regulations, and when state intervention, police surveillance, and harsh penal experiments were unceasing. Sir Robert Anderson, ex-head of the Criminal Investigation Department, writing on 'Our Absurd System of Punishing Crime' in 1901, said that the emergence of the 'police-man state' had been infinitely more important and successful than the changes in the penal system.[27] He believed that the prisons, as they existed, were unsuitable for the inebriated, the feeble-minded, the vagrant, the prostitute, the juvenile and the other people who so concerned the penal reformers at the turn of the century. Prisons were ineffective and actually spread the disease which they were supposed to cure. They should be, said Anderson, remodelled with only 'the aristocracy of crime' in mind. The inadequate recidivists should be put in asylums, whilst the mass of other offenders could be dealt with outside penal institutions.

It was Anderson's belief, shared by Charles Booth and the Gladstone committee on prisons in 1895, that the numbers of this last group of offenders would be reduced in time by other agencies. Anderson argued that the modern state could be seen as a huge house of correction, with the capacity, through its laws, civil service and police, to make men and women more moral. He expressed 'wonder and admiration' in 1901 at the orderly, law-abiding and even deferential nature of the population in general, and attributed it, not to greater severity or leniency in the courts and prisons, but to the broad sweep of social legislation and reforms 'which have improved the condition and raised the tone of the humbler classes of the community,...' These included the education and public-health measures, and the Welsh Sunday Closing Act of 1881, a rare legal acknowledgement of a separate Welsh identity and a tribute to its desire for respectability.

The process, which Anderson and others recommended, has been examined in some detail in previous chapters. The law was being used in 1900, in a way only half foreseen a hundred years before, to regulate a wide range of human activites. Historians are perhaps inclined to forget that the policy affected all classes, and was resisted by stubborn men and women at every level of society, but it remains true that the main target was the poor. It is not just the half-hourly police patrols which elderly people of working-class Cardiff and Swansea recall from the beginning of our century, but also the visits of the school-attendance officers, public-health officials, inspectors and priests, as well as the licensing and trading restrictions, the bans on gambling and street football, and the cautions for breaches of medical, animal and housing regulations. It was a battle for urban peace, space and health, remembered with both rancour and humour. Interviews with these aged residents reveal that they sometimes welcomed such intrusion, or social policing, for the effect which it had on their relationships. Awkward neighbours, aggressive and spendthrift husbands, and rebellious and noisy street children were shown the error of their ways.

The extension of summary jurisdiction, and the growing interest in victimless offences in the second half of the nineteenth century turned a large number of the public into criminals. This development continued into the twentieth century, and was given greater impetus after the 1950s by the laws controlling the ownership, licensing and use of motor transport. At the present time a member of every Welsh family can expect to appear in court at least once during his or her lifetime. The results of this are still a matter of controversy. What is certain is that since the late 1960s, as the confidence of the professionals has been undermined by alarming rates of offences against people and property, there has been a growing conviction that the same Welsh families should be drawn back more positively into the battle against crime. There is even a belated awareness that the manner in which the communities of 1800 dealt with delinquency, not least their emphasis on self-policing, arbitration, and reparation for victims, has some relevance to our situation today, as much perhaps as the police and prison reforms of the nineteenth century. History occasionally teaches us the value of that which we have left behind.

Notes

Preface

1. PP, 1847, XXVII, Report of the Commissioners on the State of Education in Wales, Caernarfon, Appendix A, p. 42.
2. A point superbly elaborated in D. Hay, 'Property, Authority and the Criminal Law', in D. Hay et al. (eds), *Albion's Fatal Tree* (London, 1975).
3. See, for instance, R. Fine et al. (eds), *Capitalism and the Rule of Law* (London, 1979). For a general approach to the definitions, ideologies, and other aspects of crime, see L. Radzinowicz and J. King, *The Growth of Crime* (London, 1977).
4. Terence Morris has said recently that 'of all the social statistics, those relating to crime are probably the most inaccurate'. *Crime and Criminal Justice since 1945* (Oxford, 1989), p. 4. Yet it would be foolish to ignore them altogether. See the comment by Lawrence Stone, 'The History of Violence in England: Some Observations', *Past and Present*, CVIII, 1985, p. 218, and see the beginning of chapter 2 in this book. For two useful surveys of modern crime statistics, and popular conceptions of the extent of crime, see M. Hough and P. Mayhew, *The British Crime Survey* (London, 1983), and R. Kinsey, J. Lea and J. Young, *Losing the Fight against Crime* (Oxford, 1986).
5. There are, of course, problems with using the literary evidence as well. For a good account of the nature, and deficiencies, of all records used by historians of crime, see J. A. Sharpe, *Crime in Early Modern England, 1550–1750* (Harlow, 1984), chapters 2 and 3.
6. One development which I have necessarily omitted from this study is the growth of civil law, and the use made of the county courts. Breaches of contract and several other offences were switched from the criminal to the civil courts. There is much need for research in this area of nineteenth-century social history.

Chapter 1

1. *Cambrian News*, 8 April 1871.
2. PP, 1837, XXXII, Report of the Inspectors of Prisons, North Wales, p. 64.
3. H. Richard, *Letters and Essays on Wales* (London, 1866, ed. of 1884), pp. 52–70.
4. CJ, 17 Dec. 1830. For praise of the quiet Welsh by judges, for the association of the English language with sedition, and for the contribution of Welsh squires, being resident, to the light calendars, see ibid., 2 Aug. 1833, 28 March 1834, and 5 Aug. 1836.
5. PRO, HO 40/51. Letter of 6 July 1839. PP 1847, XXVII, Report on Education, Breconshire, Cardiganshire and Radnorshire, p. 57.
6. See, for instance, the reply in the *Cambrian News* to the *Standard*'s attack. Edition of 9 April 1870. For 'Adfyfyr', see T. J. Hughes, *Landlordism in Wales* (Cardiff, 1887), pp. 35–8 and 51. Dr David Howell kindly gave me a copy of this last source.
7. These, and other comments in this paragraph, are taken from many sources, such

as MM, 15 Aug. 1829, and the reports on several dozen Welsh boroughs in PP, 1835, XXIII, First Report of the Commissioners on Municipal Corporations, and PP, 1837–8, XXXV, Report on Certain Boroughs, by T. J. Hogg. See, too, PP, 1862, XLV, Reports of the Inspectors of Constabulary, North Wales, p. 11.

8. PRO, HO 73/55. Report of 14 November 1839.
9. S. H. Jones-Parry, 'Crime in Wales', *Red Dragon*, III, 1883, p. 524. The quotation is copied as written, but the double negative is surely an error.
10. CJ, 29 Oct. 1830 and 12 Jan. 1866.
11. MRO, Constabulary Records, Z/H/12/1. The list of 1885 is reprinted in K. Birch, 'The Merioneth Police, 1856–1950', MA thesis, Aberystwyth, 1980, p. 313.
12. E. R. Baker, 'The History of the Glamorgan Constabulary(1)', pp. 8–9, from a collection of Mr Baker's notes, articles and papers kept in the Police Museum, Bridgend. I am grateful to Jeremy Glenn, curator, for sending me a copy of this paper, and for his assistance in finding other sources.
13. CMG, 1 Jan. 1859.
14. V. A. C. Gatrell, 'Crime, authority and the police-man state', in F. M. L. Thompson (ed.), *The Cambridge Social History of Britain 1750–1950*, vol. 3 (Cambridge, 1990), p. 248. This work is a most stimulating introduction to the study of nineteenth-century crime. In subsequent references, only the title of the chapter will be footnoted.
15. G. H. Jenkins, *The Foundation of Modern Wales, 1642–1780* (Oxford, 1987), pp. 334–8.
16. Michel Foucault has been one of the most influential writers on the state and deviancy. See especially his *Discipline and Punish*, translated by A. Sheridan (New York, 1978).
17. See, for instance, D. Parry-Jones, *My Own Folk* (Llandysul, 1972), pp. 117–123.
18. MRO, Constabulary Records. Z/H/12/1.
19. Cardiff Central Library. The First Report of the Cardiff Associate Institute for Improving and Enforcing the Laws for the Protection of Women, 1860, p. 10. Neil Evans kindly sent me a copy of this pamphlet.
20. MRO, Constabulary Records. Z/H/14. Towyn Occurrence Book, 1885. Z/H/4. Barmouth Occurrence Book, 1886.
21. F.P.C. (anon.), 'The Celt of Wales and the Celt of Ireland', *The Cornhill Magazine*, XXXVI, 1877, p. 674. David Howell pointed me in the direction of this source.
22. Another historian, who has written a splendid book on this subject, has noted the difference in attitude between small and large companies. D. Philips, *Crime and Authority in Victorian England* (London, 1977), p. 189.
23. MGRO, Quarter Session Records. Q/E 1/9 F. Chief Constable's Report of 28 June 1842. Compare CMG, 16 July 1842.
24. See the comments on the case of cutting timber in *The Welshman*, 12 Dec. 1845.
25. A. Macfarlane, *The Justice and the Mare's Tale* (Oxford, 1981), p. 195.
26. CJ, 4 Jan. and 12 April 1867. GRO, Constabulary Records. Q/CR. Chief Constable's Report of 1865. For just a couple of settlements, which made the court cases redundant, see TC, 13 Jan. 1860, and CDH, 3 and 10 May 1895.
27. SWPM, Police Note-books. D/D CON 176.
28. W. H. Howse, *Radnorshire* (Hereford, 1949), p. 82.
29. NWC, 14 Jan. 1860.
30. CLRO, Constabulary Records. FP/3/5.
31. TC, 24 March 1810.
32. J. Davis, 'A Poor Man's System of Justice: the London Police Courts in the Second Half of the Nineteenth Century', *The Historical Journal*, XXVII, 2, 1984, p. 310.
33. TC, 24 March 1893.

34. CJ, 20 June 1862.

35. For a little on this, see D. J. V. Jones, *Rebecca's Children* (Oxford, 1989), p. 160.

36. CJ, 28 July 1848.

37. H T. Evans, *The Gorse Glen (Cwm Eithin)* (Liverpool, ed. of 1948), p. 74.

38. NLW, Great Sessions Records, Gaol Files, Radnorshire 1819, Wales 4/534/8. For some examples of forced entry and expulsion, see ibid., Radnorshire 1800, Wales 4/532/3, Radnorshire 1820, Wales 4/536/2, and Breconshire 1816, Wales 4/394/3.

39. CJ, 27 July 1849. Compare the destruction of a house and furniture on the lower slopes of Pencarreg Mountain, and the burning of a home of a shepherd, by about fifteen men with blackened faces, on the Breconshire–Cardiganshire border. Ibid., 22 March 1850, and 18 Sept. 1868.

40. D. Parry-Jones, *Welsh Country Upbringing* (London, 1948), p. 98, and idem, *My Own Folk* (Llandysul, 1972), p. 117.

41. On the cases mentioned in the paragraph, see NWC, 6 May 1830, NLW, Great Sessions Records, Gaol Files, Montgomeryshire 1823, Wales 4/201/8, and CJ, 4 April 1851.

42. CJ, 14 April 1854.

43. CJ, 7 March 1856 and 17 Oct. 1862. See also ibid., 4 and 18 Oct. 1861.

44. The essential background on this is the excellent article by R. A. N. Jones, 'Popular Culture, Policing, and the Disappearance of the Ceffyl Pren in Cardigan, c. 1837–1850', *Ceredigion*, 1988–9, pp. 19–39. Perhaps she has slightly pre-dated the decline of the practice.

45. CMG, 13 June 1845 and 24 July 1847.

46. *The Welshman*, 25 April 1845.

47. CDH, 29 March and 12 April 1895.

48. J. A. Sharpe, op. cit., p. 21. For a good summary of the findings regarding the earlier use of the courts, which seems to decline after the early seventeenth century, see ibid., pp. 41–72.

49. L. Stone, 'The History of Violence in England: Some Observations. A Rejoinder', *Past and Present*, CVIII, 1985, p. 220.

50. PP, 1828, XX, Return of the Number of Causes instituted in the Ecclesiastical Courts, 1824–6, pp. 2, 3, 7, and 12.

51. Most of the material on the urban courts is taken from P.P. 1835, XXIII, First Report of the Commissioners on Municipal Corporations, and P.P. 1837–8, XXXV, Report on Certain Boroughs, by T. J. Hogg.

52. PP, 1888, LXXXII, Return of the Number of County Court Plaints, p. 14.

53. PP, 1817, V, 1820, II, 1821, IV, and 1829, IX. Of these reports on the administration of justice in Wales, the last is the most substantial and important.

54. PP, 1829, IX, First Report into the Practice and Proceedings of the Common Law, Appendix E, Query 29. Lord Cawdor claimed much of the credit for the merger of judicatures. There is a huge amount of material, in this report, and elsewhere, on the debate over the Great Sessions. All the Welsh newspapers gave the issue much attention.

55. PP, 1837–8, XXXV, Report on Certain Boroughs, by T. J. Hogg. Report on Conwy, p. 17.

56. The situation changed somewhat later in the century. In 1890 Cardiff obtained a separate court of Quarter Sessions. For just a little on the requests to have, and to move, Quarter Sessions, in Glamorgan and Cardiganshire, see TC, 22 Nov. 1817, and CJ, 3 Jan. and 21 Feb. 1868.

57. See the case presented in the letter from Robert ap Hugh Williams in CDH, 26 April 1895.

58. PP, 1862, XLV, Reports of the Inspectors of Constabulary, Cardiganshire and Carmarthenshire, pp. 125–6. The problems of finding more than one magistrate,

so that a Petty Sessions could be held, was a common problem in west Wales. See CJ, 10 June 1853, and 24 March 1854.
59. CJ, 17 Feb. 1832.
60. PP, 1837–8, XXXV, Report on Certain Boroughs, by T. J. Hogg, p. 78. At Bala, as this report records, there had been a formal protest over the appointment to the Bench of a Methodist grocer. Ibid., p. 5.
61. PP, 1886, LIII, Return of Justices of the Peace in Boroughs and Cities of England and Wales. Of 267 magistrates for the seventeen Welsh boroughs, there were, for example, thirty-one physicians and surgeons, twenty-seven tradesmen, thirty merchants, twenty-seven esquires, thirty-nine gentlemen, and twenty-eight, mainly upper-class, people were given no occupation. For the stipendiaries, at Merthyr, Cardiff, Pontypridd and Swansea, see PP, 1873, LIV, Return of Stipendiary Magistrates.
62. See the impact of the Act on courts in Monmouthshire. MM, 9 Jan. 1880.
63. D. J. V. Jones, *Before Rebecca* (London, 1973), p. 164.
64. PP, 1826–7, VI, Report on the Causes of the Increase in Criminal Commitments and Convictions, p. 5.
65. CDH, 19 Feb. 1848.
66. V. A. C. Gatrell and T. B. Hadden, 'Criminal Statistics and their Interpretation', in E. A. Wrigley (ed.), *Nineteenth-Century Society* (Cambridge, 1972), p. 356.
67. E. H. Hall, *A Description of Caernarvonshire* (Caernarfon, 1809–11, ed. of 1952), pp. 313–4.
68. Lord Aberdare (H. A. Bruce), *Letters and Addresses* (London, 1917), p. 265. Unless otherwise stated, subsequent references to Lord Aberdare's comments in 1875 are taken from his lecture of that date, reprinted in this volume. In the text I have, to simplify things, not used Bruce's title.
69. See, for example, the battle between two females, prosecutor and defendant, described in NWC, 21 Jan. 1860.
70. PP, 1862, XLV, Reports of Inspectors of Constabulary, North Wales, p. 11.
71. In Monmouthshire this happened, but more research is needed on other Welsh and English counties. See D. Philips, op. cit., pp. 125 and 130. For some useful information on this, see D. Hay and F. Snyder (eds), *Policing and Prosecution in Britain, 1750–1850* (Oxford, 1989), pp. 3–54. Also vital is D. Hay, 'Controlling the English Prosecutor', *Osgoode Hall Law Journal*, XXI, 1983, pp. 165–86. For background to all this section, consult the impressive J. M. Beattie, *Crime and the Courts of England, 1660–1800* (Oxford, 1986), chapter 2. See, also, R. B. Shoemaker, *Prosecution and Punishment: Petty Crime and the Law in London and Rural Middlesex, 1660–1725* (Cambridge, 1991).
72. J. Davis, op. cit., p. 318.
73. See, for instance, MGRO, P/S D (Calendars 1862 and 1868), GRO, CRB 0002, CRO, XJ/1377, and MRO, ZH 4/20.
74. SWPM, Police Note-books. D/D CON 174.
75. This comment, taken from a General Order Book, 1857–1880, of the Pembrokeshire Constabulary, was sent to me by Mr R. W. Jones, who had obtained the book. Much of his excellent collection of police material has been deposited in the Dyfed (Pembrokeshire) Record Office, Haverfordwest.
76. CRO, Constabulary Records. XJ/462. Letter of 19 Dec. 1859.
77. See the section on the police in chapter 7 of this book.
78. PP, 1874, XXIV, Fourth Report of the Judicature Commissioners, p. xv.
79. For this, and later information, on costs, see PP, 1836, XVII, 1854, LIV, 1861, LX, 1874, XXIV, 1877, LXXXVI, and 1893–4, CIII, Reports and Returns on County Rates and Criminal Prosecutions.
80. 'Crime in Wales', *Red Dragon*, III, 1883, p. 526.

81. PP, 1872, XX, Second Report of the Judicature Commissioners, p. 165.
82. S. C. Ellis, 'Observations of Anglesey Life through the Quarter Sessions Rolls, 1860–69', *Transactions of the Anglesey Antiquarian Society and Field Club*, 75, 1986, p. 122. This is an invaluable article.
83. CJ, 17 March 1837. Only nine years before the chief justice of the Great Sessions welcomed the financial help then being made available to prosecutors, and the assistance which they could thereby obtain from attornies. Ibid., 26 Sept. 1828.
84. For a little on this, see the Reports of the Select Committee on the Administration of Justice in Wales. PP, 1820, II, p. 40, and 1821, IV, p. 6.
85. PP, 1872, XX, Second Report of the Judicature Commissioners, p. 165.
86. P. King, 'Decision-Makers and Decision-Making in the English Criminal Law, 1750–1800', *Historical Journal*, XXVII, 1, 1984, p. 29.
87. For a comparison, see D. Philips, op. cit., pp. 125–9.
88. ARO, Quarter Session Records. Uncatalogued box of recognizances, 1838–79.
89. A small working party is currently calendaring the Quarter and Petty Session material of this period, in the Mid Glamorgan Record Office at Cardiff. Similar projects have been launched, on the criminal information in newspapers, in the Carmarthen and Swansea libraries. Soon, we should have a much clearer picture of the prosecutors, the crimes, and the criminals.
90. J. H. Langbein, '*Albion's* Fatal Flaws', *Past and Present*, XCVIII, 1983, p. 105. See Dr. Beattie's comments on the use of the courts, the criminal law and shared values. Op. cit., p. 197.
91. U. Henriques, 'The Jews and Crime in South Wales before World War I', *Morgannwg*, XXIX, 1985, p. 70.
92. CLRO, Constabulary Records. FP/3/4A. Reports of robberies, Holywell Division.
93. The Bangor and Abergavenny Associations are good examples. See, for instance, NWC, 4 March 1830, and MM, 12 March 1842.
94. See, for instance, the work of the society to control salmon fishing in the Teifi, the appointment of water-guards, and the bonuses for convictions, in CJ, 10, 17 and 24 Dec. 1852.
95. I. Waters, 'The Salmon Fisheries at Chepstow in the Nineteenth Century', *Gwent Local History*, 42, 1977, p. 26.
96. CJ, 10 Jan. 1890.
97. See, for instance, CDH, 24 July 1891 and 21 July 1893, and CJ, 10 July 1891.
98. CRO, Constabulary Records. XJ/2. Police Committee Minutes, March and April 1893.
99. CDH, 17 Feb. 1893.
100. V. A. C. Gatrell, 'Crime, authority and the police-man state', p. 255.
101. Edition of 15 Sept. 1875. This quotation was found by Audrey Philpin, and I thank her for the reference.
102. See, for instance, the demand of Dr. Howell Rees that county councils should have more administrative control of police forces. CJ, 30 May 1890.
103. For more on all this, see chapter 5 of this book.

Chapter 2

1. PP, 1897, C, Criminal Statistics, p. 35. Cited in L. Radzinowicz and R. Hood, *A History of English Criminal Law*, vol. 5 (London, 1986), p. 111. I have used this book a good deal as a source for this chapter.
2. PP, 1861, LII, Reports of the Inspectors of Constabulary, North Wales, p. 11.
3. The Committee's report is conveniently abstracted by J.J. Tobias, *Nineteenth-Century Crime* (Newton Abbott, 1972), pp. 90–6.

4. G. Pearson, *Hooligan. A History of Respectable Fears* (London, 1983), p. 219.
5. V. A. C. Gatrell and T. B. Hadden, 'Nineteenth century criminal statistics and their interpretation', in E. A. Wrigley (ed), *Nineteenth Century Society* (Cambridge, 1972). Both writers do, however, stress the problems of changes in compilation, as in 1893. Compare the views on statistics of J. J. Tobias, *Crime and Industrial Society in the Nineteenth Century* (London, 1967), pp. 256–67, and D. Philips, op. cit., pp. 16–24.
6. For comparisons, at this point and throughout the book, see the general survey of T. R. Gurr, *Rogues, Rebels and Reformers* (London, 1974).
7. Lord Aberdare, op. cit., p. 222.
8. CDH, 12 April 1895.
9. See, for instance, MRO, Quarter Session Calendars, 1810–20. Z/QS.
10. CLRO, Quarter Session Minute Books. QS/MB/6–8.
11. DRO, Haverfordwest Prison Registers, 1813–44. PQ/AG/1–7. The Rhuthun figures can be found in PP, 1837, XXXII, Reports of the Inspectors of Prisons, North Wales, p. 60.
12. This breakdown, largely taken from the Haverfordwest and Dogellau gaol registers, can be compared with the summary of information from other parts of Britain in J. Innes, 'Prisons of the Poor: English Bridewells, 1555–1800', in F. Snyder and D. Hay (eds), *Labour, Law and Crime* (London, 1987), p. 99. The Dolgellau register is in MRO, Prison Records. Z/QA/G/14.
13. TC, 11 April 1851, and D. J. V. Jones, *Rebecca's Children* (Oxford, 1989), p. 156. The Merthyr information is in MGRO, Quarter Session Records. Q/E 1/9F. Chief Constable's Reports, 1842–51.
14. Unfortunately, the nature and the survival of the evidence is such that one cannot make, at least consistently, a more detailed comparison between rural, industrial and urban areas. See the section on Sources and Data at the end of the book for further details. Where regional comparisons are made, for the period after 1857, between rural, industrial and urban areas, the population figures for Cardiff, Swansea and Newport have been deducted from the county totals for Glamorgan and Monmouthshire. Some of the problems with regional analysis are outlined in V. A. C. Gatrell and T. B. Hadden, op. cit., p. 358.
15. MGRO, Quarter Session Records. Q/E 1/9F. Chief Constable's Reports and Quarterly Returns, 1851. I have used the divisions, and sub-divisions, which he gives, and have tried, with the aid of the 1851 census, to give the best estimate of the crime rate for each.
16. CRO, Constabulary Records. XJ/2. Minutes of the Police Committee, 21 Jan. 1897.
17. For just some of this, see W. Bingley, *North Wales*, II (London, 1804), p. 264, and T. Roscoe, *Wanderings and Excursions in South Wales* (London, 1854), p. 45. An excellent background to this, and all aspects of eighteenth-century crime, is the chapter on crime in T. M. Humphreys, 'Rural Society in Montgomeryshire in the Eighteenth Century', Ph. D. thesis, University of Wales, Swansea, 1982.
18. PP, 1847, XXVII, Report on Education, Brecon, Cardigan and Radnor, Appendix, p. 120.
19. PP, 1842, XVII, Report on the Employment of Children in Mines, Appendix, Part II, South Wales, p. 506.
20. B. H. Malkin, *The Scenery, Antiquities and Biography of South Wales*, II (London, 1807), p. 28.
21. PP, 1893–4, XXXVI, Report of the Royal Commission on the Agricultural Labourer, Wales, pp. 65 and 105. I am grateful to Dr D. W. Howell for the Lleufer Thomas reference.

22. PP, 1896, XXXIV, Report of the Royal Commission on Land in Wales and Monmouthshire, p. 641.
23. PP, 1847, XXVII, Report on Education, Monmouthshire, p. 290, and Brecon, Cardigan and Radnor, p. 63.
24. TC, 27 July 1855. For the contrasting delight at the changing situation in Cardiganshire and Pembrokeshire by 1848, see CJ, 17 March 1848.
25. PP, 1846, XXIV, Report of the Royal Commission on the State of the Mining Districts, Monmouthshire and Breconshire, p. 32.
26. PP, 1842, XVII, Report on the Employment of Children, South Wales, Appendix, Part II, p. 498. Summary of cases disposed of, 1839–41 (Table B).
27. A great deal has been written on the urban–rural differences. For three examples, see T. Plint, *Crime in England. Its Relation, Character and Extent as developed from 1801 to 1848* (London, 1851), H. Zehr, *Crime and the Development of Modern Society* (London, 1976), and D. Cohen and E. Johnson, 'French criminality: urban–rural differences in the nineteenth century', *Journal of Inter-disciplinary History*, XII, 1982.
28. For a study which helps to undermine this myth, see D. J. V. Jones, *Crime, Protest, Community and Police in Nineteenth-Century Britain* (London, 1982), chapters 5 and 6.
29. H. Richard, op. cit., p. 68.
30. See, for instance, CDH, 4 Jan. 1889.
31. See George Rudé's criticisms of such divisions. *Criminal and Victim* (Oxford, 1985), pp. 78–9. Both John Beattie and David Philips decided not to examine the offences in the third category. Both books cited above.
32. MGRO, Quarter Session Records. Q/E 1/9 F. Chief Constable's Reports and Quarterly Returns, 1850.
33. H. Zehr, op. cit., p. 83.
34. A. Macfarlane, op. cit., p. 199.
35. L. Radzinowicz and R. Hood, op. cit., p. 119.
36. MRO, Constabulary Records. Z/H/14, Z/H/4, and Z/H/7. Alan Bainbridge kindly provided me with this sample.
37. Lord Aberdare, op. cit., p. 241.
38. V. A. C. Gatrell, 'Crime, authority and the policeman-state', p. 250.
39. PP, 1840, XXIV, Reports of the Assistant Commissioners on the Handloom Weavers, Part IV, Report of W. A. Miles, pp. 563–4.
40. E. H. Hall, op. cit., pp. 313–14.
41. *The Welshman*, 7 April 1848.
42. PP, 1836, XXXV, Reports of Inspectors of Prisons for the Home District, pp. 83–4. Cited in S. Margarey, 'Juvenile Delinquency in Early Nineteenth-Century England', *Labour History*, XXXIV, 1978, p. 18.
43. PP, 1847, XXVII, Report on Education, Caernarfon, Appendix A, p. 42, and Monmouthshire, p. 295.
44. CMG, 20 Feb. 1841. Compare the Pembrokeshire opposition to Henry Leach over the extent of crime, and need for more policing, in 1839. CJ, 5 July 1839.
45. TC, 5 March 1842.
46. Lord Aberdare, op. cit., pp. 241–2.
47. C. Emsley, *Crime and Society in England, 1750–1900* (Harlow, 1987), p. 246.
48. TC, 8 March 1850.
49. The reports on Merthyr, including a break-down of its recorded crime, are in the *Morning Chronicle*, 4 March–29 April 1850.
50. NWC, 14 Jan. 1860.
51. V. A. C. Gatrell, 'The Decline of Theft and Violence in Victorian and Edwardian England, 1834–1914', in V. A. C. Gatrell, B. Lenman, and G. Parker (eds), *Crime*

and the Law (London, 1980), p. 240. Subsequent references will contain just the chapter title.

52. L. O. Pike, *A History of Crime in England* (London, 1876), pp. 480–1. Cited in L. Radzinowicz and R. Hood, op. cit., p. 115.
53. CDH, 4 July 1885.
54. See, for example, PP, 1882, XXXII, Report of the Commissioners on Criminal Lunacy, Appendices 6, 7, 13 and 14. For background, see J. Saunders, 'Magistrates and Madmen: Segregating the Criminally Insane in Late-nineteenth-century Warwickshire', in V. Bailey (ed.), *Policing and Punishment in Nineteenth-Century Britain* (London, 1981).
55. R. S. Stewart, 'The Relationship of Wages, Lunacy, and Crime in South Wales', *Journal of Medical Science*, 1904. Reprint in the Central Library, Cardiff.
56. TC, 18 October 1861.
57. Ibid., 7 April 1871.
58. There are innumerable references to the evils of heavy drinking and beerhouses, and their association with crime. The comment about the clergymen and magistrates is taken from PP, 1847, XXVII, Report on Education, Breconshire, Cardiganshire and Radnorshire, p. 57.
59. CMG, 3 July 1858.
60. PP, 1839, XIX, Royal Commission on the Constabulary Force in England and Wales, p. 181.
61. See the debate in CMG, 5 Jan. 1850.
62. The present writer has touched on this before in *Crime, Protest, Police and Community in Nineteenth-Century Britain* (London, 1982), chapter 7. The quotation is from V. A. C. Gatrell, 'Crime, authority and the policeman-state', p. 305.
63. Cited in the valuable article by A. E. Davies, 'Wages, Prices, and Social Improvement in Cardiganshire, 1750–1850', *Ceredigion*, X, 1, 1984, p. 44.
64. PP, 1878, XLII, Report of the Inspector of Reformatory and Industrial Schools, p. 3.
65. CJ, 30 March 1838.
66. CDH, 28 March 1863.
67. CMG, 21 July 1860.
68. MGRO, Prison Chaplain's Reports. QG/Cardiff, 1869–77.
69. The comment, by H. A. Bruce, is set in context by W. R. Lambert, *Drink and Sobriety in Wales, c. 1820–1895* (Cardiff, 1983), pp. 25 and 44.
70. MM, 16 April 1880.
71. The most recent debate over the relationship between crime and living standards in the nineteenth century was begun by V. A. C. Gatrell and T. B. Hadden, op. cit., 368–71. Amongst their main findings was the beginning of an 'imprecision in the correlations' between property crimes and depression in the 1880s.
72. PP, 1826–7, VI, Report on the Cause of the Increase in Criminal Commitments and Convictions, p. 4.
73. The point has been made, though largely discounted, that the high figures could have been the result of more people, especially the working class, being prepared to prosecute at such times. C. Emsley, op. cit., p. 34.
74. CJ, 9 Sept. 1853.
75. PP, 1847, XXVII, Report on Education, Carmarthen, Glamorgan and Pembroke, p. 489. As the years passed, the police seemed to expect only limited increases in crime at such times. See, for instance, GRO, Constabulary Records. Q/CONS R. Chief Constable's Report, March 1861.
76. This analysis is based on the information in the Chief Constable's Reports and Quarterly Returns, 1842–66, in MGRO. Q/E 1/9 F.
77. For the sources of the sample of 723 crimes, see footnote 36. For just one example

of the seasonal pattern of commitments to gaol, at Wrexham, see PP, 1837, XXXII, Reports of the Inspectors of Prison, North Wales, p. 61.
78. SC, March 1890.
79. Lord Aberdare, op. cit., pp. 266 and 272. To set the contemporary debate in sociological, geographical and historical context, see C. Emsley, op. cit., pp. 78–97.
80. W. Kay, *Report on the Sanitary Condition of Merthyr Tydfil* (Merthyr Tydfil, 1854), p. 71.
81. CMG, 4 July 1845. Compare the editions of 5 Jan. 1850, and 7 Jan. and 25 Feb. 1854.
82. TC, 15 March 1872.
83. PP, 1842, XVII, Report on the Employment of Children, Appendix, Part II, p. 506.
84. This reference is given in the valuable thesis by J. O. Jones, 'The History of the Caernarvonshire Police Force, 1856–1900', MA thesis, University of Wales, Bangor, 1956, p. 84.
85. GRO, Monmouthshire Reformatory Records. Q/MR 0009. Register of Boys, 1859–86.
86. TC, 8 March 1850. Griffith's views were very different from those of speakers at the Merthyr meeting of 1847. CMG, 20 March 1847.
87. TC, 6 April 1860.
88. *The Welshman*, 13 July 1860.
89. PP, 1895, LVI, Report from the Departmental Committee on Prisons, p. 12. Cited in L. Radzinowicz and R. Hood, op. cit., p. 86.
90. F.P.C., op. cit., p. 678. For Dr. V. A. C. Gatrell, the key development in this later period was the change in the nature of economic depressions when they came. Unemployment and high prices did not, as in the first half of the century, hit the working class simultaneously. 'The Decline of Theft and Violence in Victorian and Edwardian England, 1834–1914', pp. 310–12.
91. This paragraph is based on the reports of the two important commissions on Welsh agricultural labourers and Welsh agriculture. PP, 1893–4, XXXVI, and PP, 1896, XXXIV.
92. Cited in R. Powys, 'From Alienation to Accommodation: Merthyr Tydfil's Industrial Relations, 1842–70', MA thesis, University of Wales, Swansea, 1988, p. 68.
93. NWC, 14 Jan. 1860. The effects were important, we are told, in the decline of violence. V. A. C. Gatrell, 'The Decline of Theft and Violence in Victorian and Edwardian England, 1834–1914', p. 300.
94. A. H. Williams (ed.), *Public Health in Victorian Wales*, II (Cardiff, 1983), pp. 1023–4.
95. Royal Institution, Swansea. Box 87/9.
96. See, for example, CDH, 4 July 1885.
97. British Library, Add. MSS, 44/199. Gladstone's Papers, vol. 114, pp. 146–7. Cited in L. Radzinowicz and R. Hood, op. cit., p. 116.

Chapter 3

1. For the differing views on this, see L. Stone, 'Interpersonal Violence in English Society, 1300–1980', *Past and Present*, CI, 1983, and J. A. Sharpe, 'The History of Violence in England: Some Observations', ibid, 108, 1985. Compare J. S. Cockburn, 'Patterns of Violence in English Society: Homicide in Kent, 1560–1985', ibid., CXXX, 1991.

2. W. C. Taylor, 'The Moral Economy of large Towns', *Bentley's Miscellany*, VI, 1839, p. 481.
3. Cited in the excellent study by L. Lloyd, *Australians from Wales* (Caernarfon, 1988), p. 32.
4. PP, 1837–8, XXXV, Report on Certain Boroughs, by T. J. Hogg, pp. 37 and 89.
5. For background to all of this, see the chapter on crime in T. M. Humphreys, op. cit.
6. J. M. Beattie, op. cit., p. 132–9.
7. L. O. Pike, op. cit., pp. 480–1. Cited in L. Radzinowicz and R. Hood, op. cit., p. 115.
8. J. M. Beattie, op. cit., p. 136.
9. H. Zehr, op. cit., p. 127.
10. MGRO, Chaplains Reports. QG/Swansea, 1866–77. Report for 1874.
11. Quotation and source cited in V. A. C. Gatrell, 'The Decline of Theft and Violence in Victorian and Edwardian England, 1834–1914', p. 291.
12. French historians are at the front of this comparative work, but see the doubts expressed by A. Macfarlane, op. cit., pp. 188–9, and C. Emsley, op. cit., p. 83.
13. H. A. Bruce is interesting on all aspects of crime and violence in the town. *Merthyr in 1852* (Cardiff, 1852), pp. 7–9.
14. PP, 1847, XXVII, Report on Education, Brecon, Cardigan and Radnor, Appendix, p. 89.
15. GRO, Constabulary Records. C/PB – 1. Bedwellty Court Register, 1892–3.
16. PP, 1847, XXVII, Report on Education, Monmouthshire, p. 294.
17. The reports on Merthyr are in the *Morning Chronicle*, 4 March–29 April 1850.
18. *Chester Chronicle*, 25 Sept. 1812, cited in E. V. Jones, 'A Merioneth Murder of 1812', *Journal of the Merioneth Historical Record Society*, VI, 1969, p. 65.
19. PP, 1839, XIX, Report of the Commissioners on the Constabulary Force, p. 37.
20. CJ, 12 Sept. 1851, and J. F. Jones, 'The Kidwelly Borough Police Force', *The Carmarthen Antiquary*, IV, 3, 1963, p. 156.
21. Harry killed and buried his wife, and Griffith, after marrying another bigamously, returned to seek his revenge. Both cases excited much interest, and popular anger. TC, 19 April and 23 Aug. 1817, and the NWC, 2 and 16 Sept. 1830.
22. See also the exceptional case of accusations of infidelity by both husband and wife, which resulted in three deaths, at Llanwenog. CJ, 4 May 1849.
23. For the opposite situation, where a crowd became sympathetic to the person about to be executed, see K. Birch, op. cit., p. 87.
24. For a little detail on these cases, see TC, 26 April and 17 May 1817, and MM, 26 Sept. 1829.
25. Elizabeth Gibbs of Laugharne, who was acquitted in another poisoning case, was driven from the area. CJ, 4 April 1851.
26. E. V. Jones, op. cit. This particular crime, and the chase after Davies, had a wide press coverage. See SC, 18 Sept. 1812.
27. The government, worried by such deaths, launched several inquiries into the deaths of people killed in poaching affrays. See, for example, PP, 1844, XXXIX, Return of Inquests, since 1833, on the Bodies of Gamekeepers.
28. The story of Shadrach Lewis has been well told by Gwylon Phillips, *Llofruddiaeth Shadrach Lewis* (Llandysul, 1986). For Thomas, see the CMG, 23 Feb. 1850.
29. W. W. Hunt, *To Guard My People* (Swansea, 1957), p. 61.
30. L. Rose, *Massacre of the Innocents* (London, 1986), pp. 58–9.
31. NWC, 31 March 1860.
32. See, for example, the comments on the Act of 1834 in CJ, 15 May 1835, and 30 March 1838.

33. The three were very exceptional cases. Ibid., 17 March 1848, 11 Oct. 1850 and 30 April, 7 May and 16 July 1847.
34. Ibid., 15 July 1864. Audrey Philpin, who is studying female criminality in Pembrokeshire, has much information on Mary Prout. For more information on female criminals, see chapter 6 of this book.
35. See, for instance, PP, 1846, XXXIV, A Return of all Murders committed between 1842 and 1846.
36. The first important study of the garotting panic of the 1860s was by Jennifer Davis, 'The London Garotting Panic of 1862', in V. A. C. Gatrell, B. Lenman and G. Parker (eds), *Crime and the Law* (London, 1980).
37. *Western Mail*, 18 August 1898. Compare G. Pearson, op. cit., p. 74.
38. *The Silurian*, 6 March 1852.
39. For one example, see CJ, 21 March 1851.
40. TC, 19 April 1817.
41. What follows can be compared with the important work of Anna Clark, *Women's Silence, Men's Voice; Sexual Assault in England 1770–1845* (London, 1987).
42. TC, 6 April 1860, and similar attacks 'on the hills' reported in the edition of 23 March 1860, and in MM, 13 Feb. 1880.
43. TC, 30 Aug. 1817.
44. CJ, 5 Aug. 1831.
45. See, for example, ibid., 14 March 1851, and NWC, 17 March 1860.
46. MM, 29 Aug. and 12 Sept. 1829.
47. In the years 1886–99, the average annual number of court cases of sexual attacks was twice that of the previous fourteen years.
48. PP, 1847, XXVII, Report on Education, Denbighshire, Appendix A, p. 75.
49. O. Anderson, *Suicide in Victorian and Edwardian England* (Oxford, 1987), pp. 99–101.
50. See, for example, NWC, 6 May 1830.
51. 'Few violent encounters gave rise to a court case in the eighteenth century'. J. M. Beattie, op. cit., p. 124.
52. NWC, 10 March 1860. The usual punishment for ill-treating servants was a small fine.
53. On the eighteenth-century situation, see J. M. Beattie, op. cit., p. 74. For the nineteenth century, see N. Tomes, 'A "Torrent of Abuse"', *Journal of Social History*, XI, 1978. The trend is confirmed in G. K. Behlmer, *Child Abuse and Moral Reform in England, 1870–1908* (Stanford, California, 1982), pp. 15 and 237. This book also provides the context for the next paragraphs on violence against children.
54. CJ, 29 April 1864.
55. Compare the case of J. Candy in TC, 30 March 1860. For some comparative work on family violence, see M. May, 'Violence in the Family: an Historical Perspective', in J.P. Martin (ed.) *Violence and the Family* (London, 1979). Since the writing of this book, Carolyn A. Conley has produced an interesting study of women, children and justice in Victorian Kent. *The Unwritten Law: Criminal Justice in Victorian Kent* (Oxford, 1991).
56. For a couple of these cases, see CJ, 9 Aug. 1833, and TC, 24 March 1893. The John Roberts reference is in PP, 1842, XVII, Report on the Employment of Children, Appendix, II, South Wales, p. 595.
57. Behlmer, op. cit., pp. 9–15.
58. CDH, 11 Jan. 1895
59. MM, 6 Feb. 1880.
60. CJ, 2 June 1854. Compare the female fight over trespassing cattle in ibid., 30 Sept. 1853.

61. CDH, 11 Jan. 1889.
62. Percy FitzGerald was the writer. His comments are recorded by J. Davis, 'A Poor Man's System of Justice', *The Historical Journal*, XXVII, 2, 1984, p. 316.
63. CDH, 24 May 1895. See, too, ibid., 14 June 1895.
64. NLW, Great Sessions Records, Gaol Files, Carmarthenshire 1807, Wales 4/756/2.
65. TC, 27 Jan. 1810.
66. CDH, 10 May 1895.
67. SWPM, Police Notebooks. D/D CON 172/1. Just this one, of his notebooks has survived, for 1867, though his work can be traced in the newspapers.
68. CJ, 14 April 1854.
69. The story is told in D. J. V. Jones, 'The Second Rebecca Riots', *Llafur*, II, 1976.
70. See, for instance, NLW, Great Sessions Records, Gaol Files, Denbighshire 1815, Wales 4/70/4, and Montgomeryshire 1817, Wales 4/200/8. See the treatment of constables who tried to levy a distress, described in the report of the Petty Sessions at Carmarthen. CJ, 6 April 1832.
71. SWPM, Police Notebooks. D/D CON 174, and 178.
72. See the interpretation of early police history in R. D. Storch, 'The Plague of Blue Locusts. Police Reform and Popular Resistance in Northern England, 1840–57', *International Review of Social History*, XX, 1975, and idem., 'The Policeman as Domestic Missionary: Urban Discipline and Popular Culture in Northern England, 1850–80', *Journal of Social History*, IX, 1976. It is possible, as has been suggested, that the changing nature of modern policing has prevented many assaults, at least until very recent times when they have returned to patrolling on foot.
73. CJ, 25 July 1845, and *The Welshman*, 14 March 1845. Note the resentment of the police, for the way they executed the licensing laws at Lampeter. Ibid., 2 Jan. 1852.
74. He was lucky to escape with a fine. CDH, 10 May 1895.
75. Many of the names and records of these people, in this, and the next three chapters, have been taken from the registers of previous convictions, and the reports on prisoners, which are to be found in most record offices. For these, see CRO, XJ/1821, and 1443.
76. In the late 1850s the Glamorgan and Monmouthshire chief constables said that only in 'extreme' cases were people taken up. See, for example, GRO, Constabulary Records. Q/CON R. Report of Chief Constable, Oct. 1858. W. R. Lambert provides the background. op. cit., p. 46.
77. CMG, 25 Feb. 1860.
78. See, too, the comments of Sir Fitzroy Kelly. CJ, 19 March 1869.
79. Ibid., 16 Jan. 1891.
80. PP, 1847, XXVII, Report on Education, Brecon, Cardigan and Radnor, Appendix, p. 96.
81. J. Ingram, 'Notes on Some Old Bangor Inns', *Transactions of the Caernarvonshire Historical Society*, x, 1949, p. 52.
82. Note the comments on Caernarfon's Ellen Roberts, and the sympathy for her husband, in the NWC, 18 Feb. 1860.
83. PP, 1847, XXVII, Report on Education, Monmouthshire, Appendix, p. 300.
84. At the Caernarfon Petty Sessions in the spring of 1860 the first gaol sentence was given in a case of drunkenness without the option of a fine. NWC, 14 April 1860.
85. Cited in W. H. Jones, 'A Strike at Talargoch Lead-Mine one hundred Years ago', *Transactions of the Flintshire Historical Society*, XVI, 1956, p.23.
86. Quoted in R. M. Jones, *The North Wales Quarrymen* (Cardiff, 1981), p. 45.
87. CLRO, Constabulary Records. PS/3/9. Overton Division Letterbook, 1865–76.
88. MGRO, Borough Records. B/C 18. Watch Committee Minutes, 1860–78.

Compare PP, 1847, XXVII, Report on Education, Caernarfonshire, Appendix A, p. 32.

89. See, for instance, the clashes at Beddgelert between farm servants and quarrymen. CDH, 17 May 1895.

90. For the Cardigan episode, see CJ, 7 Jan. 1859. For background to the paragraph, see D. J. V. Jones, *Rebecca's Children* (Oxford, 1989), pp. 78 and 179.

91. CJ, 19 Jan. 1838, and T. M. Owen, *Welsh Folk Customs* (Cardiff, ed. of 1974), p. 47. Some of the disturbances which did occur during the 1850s were caused by attempts to revive old habits, by residents and itinerant workmen. See CJ, 2 Jan. and 11 June 1852.

92. PP, 1843, XV, Second Report on the Employment of Children, North Wales, p. 158, CMG, 22 April 1845, and 18 April 1846.

93. CMG, 6 June 1857, and 14 April 1860. SWPM, Police Notebooks. D/D CON 176.

94. Nine were stabbed in the Carmarthenshire troubles. CJ, 4 July and 12 Dec. 1851.

95. PRO, HO 40/19. Letter from W. Forman, 7 March 1826.

96. For just some of the background, on the Irish story alone, see P. O'Leary, 'Anti-Irish Riots in Wales', *Llafur*, V, 1991, J. V. Hickey, 'The Origin and Growth of the Irish Community in Cardiff', MA thesis, University of Wales, Cardiff, 1959, pp. 174–6, J. Parry, 'The Tredegar Anti-Irish Riots of 1882', *Llafur*, III, 1983, and MM, 2 Jan. 1880. The beginnings of later anti-Jewish and anti-Black feelings are explored in several articles. See U. Henriques, 'The Jewish Community in Cardiff, 1813–1914', *Welsh History Review*, XIV, 1988, and N. Evans, 'The South Wales Riots of 1919', *Llafur*, III, 1980.

97. N. Gibbard, 'The Tumble Strike, 1893', *The Carmarthenshire Antiquary*, XX, 1984.

98. D. C. Davies, 'The Present Condition of the Welsh Nation', *Red Dragon*, IV, 1883, p. 444.

99. For this paragraph, see D. J. V. Jones, *Before Rebecca* (London, 1973), chapters 1 and 2, and D. W. Howell, *Land and People in Nineteenth-Century Wales* (London, 1977), chapters 6 and 9. The quotation by Lewis is in PP, 1844, V, Report of the Select Committee on Commons Enclosure, Evidence, p. 100, qu. 1238.

100. D. Williams, *The Rebecca Riots* (Cardiff, 1855), chapters 7–10, and D. J. V. Jones, *Rebecca's Children* (Oxford, 1989), chapters 5 and 6.

101. There are many good accounts of the acrimonious discussions in the police committees in the *Carmarthen Journal* and the *Caernarvon and Denbigh Herald* during the period of the Tithe riots. For the context here, see D. C. Richter, 'The Welsh Police, the Home Office, and the Welsh Tithe War of 1886–91', *Welsh History Review*, XII, 1984.

102. PP, 1840, XXIV, Reports of the Assistant Commissioners on Handloom Weavers, Report of W. A. Miles on Mid-Wales, p. 564, and CJ, 25 April and 15 Aug. 1856.

103. For more on this, see D. J. V. Jones, *Before Rebecca* (London, 1973), chapters 3 and 4.

104. R. Powys, op. cit, p. 12, and I. G. Jones, 'The Merthyr of Henry Richard', in G. Williams (ed.), *Merthyr Politics: the Making of a Working-Class Tradition* (Cardiff, 1966), pp. 43–44.

105. There is so much on all of this. For just one occupation, see P. J. Leng, *The Welsh Dockers* (Ormskirk, 1981), and T. J. McCarry, 'Labour and Society in Swansea, 1887–1918', Ph. D. thesis, University of Wales, Swansea, 1986. The important work of Emlyn Rogers has been edited by R. Roberts. See especially his chapter X, 'Trade Unionism in the Coal Mining Industry of North Wales to 1914', *Denbighshire Historical Transactions*, XX, 1971.

106. G. A. Williams, *The Merthyr Rising* (London, 1978).

107. The two most recent, and diverging, interpretations are I. Wilks, *South Wales and*

the Rising of 1839 (London, 1984) and D. J. V. Jones, *The Last Rising* (Oxford, 1985).
108. D. J. V. Jones, *The Last Rising* (Oxford, 1985), pp. 221–222.
109. A total of 122 people were charged in connection with rioting at four polling stations in Monmouthshire in 1868. GRO, Constabulary Records. Q/CON R. Chief Constable's Report, Jan. 1869.
110. D. C. Richter, *Riotous Victorians* (Ohio, 1981).
111. H. Zehr, op. cit., pp. 89–90, and T. R. Gurr, op. cit., 168.
112. J. Saville, *1848. The British State and the Chartist Movement* (Cambridge, 1987), p. 223.
113. Cited in the perceptive article by G. W. Williams, 'The Disenchantment with the World: Innovation, Crisis and Change in Cardiganshire, *c.* 1880–1910', *Ceredigion*, IX, 4, 1983, p. 314.
114. J. M. Beattie, op. cit., p. 138.
115. See, for example, C. Emsley, op. cit., p. 246. There are also some interesting speculations, in this direction, in N. Evans, 'Philanthropy in Cardiff, 1850–1914', MA thesis, University of Wales, Swansea, 1973, chapter 1.
116. It was a time of depression. CDH, 22 March 1895.
117. *Western Mail*, 16 Aug. 1898.
118. A. Marshall, *Future of the Working Classes* (Cambridge, 1873), quoted in R. McKibben, 'Working-class gambling in Britain, 1880–1939', *Past and Present*, 82, 1979, p. 173.
119. Vivian's comment is in J. H. Morris and L. J. Williams, *The South Wales Coal Industry, 1841–75* (Cardiff, 1958), p. 284.

Chapter 4

1. J. A. Sharpe, op. cit., p. 150.
2. See D. Hay, 'The Criminal Prosecution in England and its Historians', *Modern Law Review*, XLVII, 1, 1984, pp. 25–8.
3. Compare M. Ignatieff, 'State, Civil Society and Total Institution: a Critique of Recent Histories of Punishment', in D. Sugarman (ed.), *Legality, Ideology and the State* (London, 1983), pp. 197–9.
4. For a couple of slander and suicide cases, over theft accusations, see, for example, CJ, 6 July 1860, and 19 Feb. 1864.
5. See the useful chapter on crime in T. M. Humphreys, op. cit.
6. J. M. Beattie, op. cit., chapter 5.
7. D. Parry-Jones, *My Own Folk* (Llandysul, 1972), p. 79.
8. PP, 1893–4, XXXVI, Report on the Agricultural Labourer, p. 33.
9. CLRO, Quarter Session Records. QS/MB/6–8.
10. MRO, Constabulary Records. Z/H/4/5–9, Z/H/7/7–10, Z/H/14/2–5. Again I thank Alan Bainbridge for his help with these. The sample is of 176 offences.
11. The sample, of 420 property crimes, is taken from an analysis of crime in Merthyr, 1846–66, based on the police records and the reports of Quarter Session and Assize cases, and from an analysis of crime in Cardiff, 1862–82, based on the Petty Session, Quarter Session, and Assize cases. The sources used are in the MGRO, Quarter Session Records, Petty Session Records, and Constabulary Records, 1846–82, and, for the gaps, the reports in the *Cardiff and Merthyr Guardian* for the period.
12. PP, 1907, XLVII, Criminal Statistics, p. 12. Cited in L. Radzinowicz and R. Hood, op. cit., p. 117.
13. CRO, Constabulary Records. XJ/27.
14. PP, 1839, XIX, Report of the Commissioners on the Constabulary, p. 63.

15. S. C. Ellis, pp. 134–5, and for a few other examples, in just one year, TC, 1 Feb., 29 March, 4 Oct. and 29 Nov. 1817.

16. TC, 9 June and 25 Aug. 1810. Compare ibid., 16 Aug. 1817, and SC, 7 Aug. 1812.

17. TC, 24 May and 23 Aug. 1817. D. Beddoe, *Welsh Convict Women* (Barry, 1979), pp. 65, 160, and 163.

18. TC, 13 and 20 Dec. 1817. See D. J. V. Jones, 'Life and Death in Eighteenth-Century Wales: a Note', *The Welsh History Review*, X, 4, 1981, 542.

19. The point has often been made that the law was slow to act against abuses in the commercial world. C. Emsley, op. cit., pp. 6–7.

20. See R. Sindall, 'Middle-Class Crime in Nineteenth-Century England', *Criminal Justice History*, IV, 1983, pp. 23–40, and the interesting study by C. Goring, *The English Convict: a Statistical Study* (Montclair, 1913).

21. CDH, 14 July 1893, and J. O. Jones, op. cit., p. 169.

22. Caleb Phillips, a man of 'good character', received a year longer for a similar offence, and was 'staggered' by his treatment. MM, 13 Feb. 1880.

23. Ibid., 16 April 1880.

24. For some examples of all this, see TC, 13 Oct. 1810 and 20 April 1860, and CJ, 27 April 1849.

25. D. Beddoe, op. cit., pp. 54–5.

26. *Cambrian News*, 3 July 1885.

27. Dr. V. A. C. Gatrell points out that even the latter group of crimes was 'contained' in the second half of the century. 'The Decline of Theft and Violence in Victorian and Edwardian England', p. 333.

28. On this, and the changing nature of highway robbery, burglary and other property crime, through the period, see M. McIntosh, 'Changes in the Organisation of Thieving', in S. Cohen (ed.), *Images of Deviance* (London, 1971), pp. 98–133.

29. TC, 17 and 24 March, and 29 Sept. 1810, and SC, 13 March 1812.

30. On the interference with commercial and post office deliveries, see, for example, TC, 20 Jan. 1810, and 13 April 1860.

31. For examples, see CJ, 22 Feb. 1828, and 13 Feb., 13 March, and 10 April 1835. On an execution of a burglar, as a warning to others, see TC, 21 April 1810. For the female burglars, see D. Beddoe, 'Carmarthenshire Women and Criminal Transportation to Australia, 1787–1852', *The Carmarthenshire Antiquary*, XIII, 1977, p. 69.

32. See the complaints about gangs of tramps and burglaries in the Teifi valley. CJ, 3 May 1850.

33. MM, 28 Nov. 1829.

34. The quotation is from J. Grant, *Sketches in London* (London, 1838), p. 397. Cited in J. J. Tobias, *Nineteenth-Century Crime* (Newton Abbot, 1972), p. 118.

35. TC, 19 April 1817.

36. NWC, 21 Jan. 1830, and CJ, 23 and 30 March and 4 May 1855.

37. TC, 18 Dec. 1857, and CDH, 24 July 1891.

38. There were a few exceptions. Under the Summary Jurisdiction Act of 1879, for example, a small number of receivers were prosecuted at the lower courts.

39. MRO, Constabulary Records. Z/H/14. Towyn Occurence Book, report of 17 April 1885.

40. MM, 2 Jan. 1880.

41. See typical cases of stealing sheets and such like from hedges and walls. NWC, 10 March 1860.

42. TC, 29 Sept. 1810, and 3 May 1817.

43. See the Chepstow example in ibid., 1 Nov. 1817.

44. SC, 14 Feb. and 22 May 1812.

45. Much has been written recently about perks, fiddles and customs. See, for example, G. Mars, *Cheats at Work* (London, 1983), and B. Bushaway, *By Rite: Custom, Ceremony and Community in England, 1700–1880* (London, 1982). For an earlier period, see P. Linebaugh, *The London Hanged: Crime and Civil Society in the Eighteenth Century* (London, 1991).
46. CJ, 10 April 1840, and CDH, 26 April 1895.
47. For some English background on this section, see J. Rule, 'Social crime in the rural south in the eighteenth and early nineteenth centuries', *Southern History*, 1, 1979, pp. 135–53.
48. See, for instance, the crime and comment in CJ, 16 Jan. 1818.
49. TC, 26 April 1817, and MM, 2 and 16 Jan. 1880.
50. For some of the cases, and comment, see CJ, 23 July 1830, 26 Jan. 1844, 20 Feb. 1863, and 28 Feb. 1868.
51. Some of this long story can be followed in the Carmarthenshire Record Office, Carmarthen. Quarter Session Order and Minute Books, 1831–49.
52. *Aberdare Times*, 5 Feb. 1876. This reference was kindly sent by Huw Williams. On the interesting connections between the nature of crime pursued, and the occupations of magistrates, in industrial communities, see D. Philips, op. cit., pp. 48–9, and 180–195.
53. MM, 20 Feb. and 30 April 1880.
54. For a little more on this coal stealing, at Merthyr, see D. J. V. Jones, *Crime, Protest, Community and Police in Nineteenth-century Britain* (London, 1982), pp. 98–99.
55. For background to, and examples of, street thefts by women and youths, see ibid., pp. 97–8, and 107–8.
56. TC, 2 Aug. 1817.
57. MM, 2 Jan. 1880. For a little on juvenile and female pickpocketing at Newport and Cardiff, see ibid., 6 Feb. 1880, and CMG, 21 and 28 Jan. 1860.
58. CMG, 24 March 1860.
59. See the debate on juveniles and thieving, in ibid., 10 April 1852.
60. SC, 4 July 1862, and NWC, 21 Jan. and 31 March 1860.
61. D. Beddoe, 'Carmarthenshire's Convict Women in Nineteenth-Century Van Diemen's Land', *The Carmarthenshire Antiquary*, XV, 1979, p. 69.
62. PP, 1896, XXXIV, Report on Land in Wales, pp. 507–10. Reference cited by D. W. Howell, op. cit., p. 77.
63. PP, 1819, VIII, Report from the Select Committee on Criminal Laws, Appendix 21. The appendices to the report have details of death sentences and executions for the Carmarthen, Montgomery, and south-east Wales circuits, and for Monmouthshire. Compare, for the period after 1805, the returns in the PRO, HO 27.
64. For this, and other stealing cases, in the eighteenth and very early nineteenth centuries, see D.J. V. Jones, 'Life and Death in Eighteenth-Century Wales: a Note', *Welsh History Review*, X, 1981, p. 540.
65. MM, 23 Oct. 1829.
66. See, for example, CJ, 22 Dec. 1848, 4 Oct. 1850, and 11 Jan. 1856.
67. *Cambrian News*, 20 Oct. 1882.
68. H. Hopkins, *The Long Affray* (London, 1985), p. 5. For a general background on poaching at this time, see D. J. V. Jones, 'The Poacher: a Study in Victorian Crime and Protest', *Historical Journal*, XXII, 1979, pp. 825–60.
69. Cited by S. C. Ellis, op. cit., p. 132.
70. PRO, HO 45/6812. Letter from T. Mostyn, 31 Dec. 1859.
71. CRO, Constabulary Records. XJ/1443 and 1821. Registers of Previous Convictions, and Character.

72. For the miners, and gangs, see, for example, CJ, 27 Nov. and 11 Dec. 1835, 29 Oct. 1847 and 26 Aug. 1853.
73. For just one reference to this, see ibid., 20 Feb. 1857.
74. Ibid., 21 Jan. 1853, and TC, 29 June 1860.
75. PP, 1846, XXXIV, Returns of numbers of people convicted under the Game Laws. Of the figures given in Table 5 in this book, about fifty persons each year were imprisoned in the years 1836–54 for breaches of the Game Laws, after being convicted at the lower courts.
76. For a start on this, see D. J. V. Jones, *Rebecca's Children* (Oxford, 1989), p. 374, and idem., 'The Second Rebecca Riots: a Study of Poaching on the Upper Wye', *Llafur*, II, 1976, pp. 32–56. See the classic statements of the importance of 'custom' and 'rights' in CJ, 26 April 1867.
77. MRO, Constabulary Records. Z/H/2/1. Journal of J. Hughes.
78. For just some of this paragraph, see CJ, 9 July 1830, and 21 April 1865, and NLW., Great Sessions Records, Gaol Files, Caernarfonshire 1805, Wales 4/278/4, Flintshire 1816, Wales 4/1086/6.
79. CJ, 17 Oct. 1851, and *Cambrian News*, 12 Feb. 1870. For context, and contrasts, see J. E. Archer, *By a Flash and a Scare* (Oxford, 1990).
80. Of the figures given in Table 5, 364 were imprisoned under the Malicious Trespass Act in the years 1842–4, more than double the yearly average at this time. For the popularity of malicious activities at the earlier period, see D. J. V. Jones, *Before Rebecca* (London, 1973), pp. 58.
81. CJ, 19 April 1850.
82. For some background to this, and the story of arson by vagrants, see D. J. V. Jones, '"A Dead Loss to the Community": the Criminal Vagrant in Mid-Nineteenth Century Wales', *Welsh History Review*, VIII, 1977.
83. TC, 14 and 28 April 1810.
84. See, for example, CJ, 27 April 1855, 28 Jan., 4 and 11 Feb. 1859, and 1 July 1864.
85. Ibid., 10 Aug. 1838.
86. MM, 5 March 1842, and CJ, 14 Feb. 1833. See the awful problems faced by the police at Pembroke Dock. Ibid., 10 July 1868.
87. CJ, 11 June 1847.
88. CRO, Constabulary Records. XJ/28.
89. CLRO, Constabulary Records. FP/3/4A.
90. V. A. C. Gatrell, 'Crime, authority and the police-state', pp. 249–50. Deirdre Beddoe, writing of the females transported, also notes 'the pettiness of their crimes'. *Welsh Convict Women* (Barry, 1979), p. 40. Of course, to some extent, this reflected a decision by society to concentrate on petty rather than great property crimes. See the Epilogue of this book.
91. The two historians are J. Rule, op. cit., p. 138, and G. Rudé, op. cit., p. 79.
92. MGRO, Quarter Session Records. Q/E 1/9 F. Chief Constable's Report of 31 Dec. 1841.
93. Many pawnbrokers, whom Henry Thomas and others blamed for much crime, were Jews. For the Jews and crime, see U. Henriques, 'The Jews and Crime in South Wales before World War I', *Morgannwg*, XXIX, 1985, pp. 59–73.

Chapter 5

1. PP, 1895, CVIII. Cited by J. J. Tobias, *Nineteenth-Century Crime* (Newton Abbot, 1972), pp. 90–6.
2. See the note on the omission in V. A. C. Gatrell, 'Crime, Authority and the Police-man State', pp. 244–5. Historians of earlier times, who note the broad

nature of 'the pre-industrial definition of crime', have looked in some detail at the subject. See especially R. B. Shoemaker, op. cit., p. 5.

3. A. C. Hall, *Crime in its Relations to Social Progress* (New York, 1902, 1910 ed.), pp. 377, and 406.

4. K. Wrightson and D. Levine, *Poverty and Piety in an English Village; Terling, 1525–1700* (London, 1979), p. 177.

5. See, for example, the comment of G. K. Behlmer on the 'sacrilege' of the state interfering in the home. Op. cit., p. 9.

6. PP, 1828, XX, A Return of the Informations and Convictions for Breaches of the Malt Laws, 1806–7.

7. NLW, Great Sessions Records, Gaol Files, Pembrokeshire 1805, Wales 4/829/3, and G. Smith, *Smuggling in the Bristol Channel, 1700–1850* (Newbury, 1989), pp. 147–8.

8. See the comment on the impact of the coastguard on smuggling, in CJ, 3 April 1835. The quotation is from PP, 1859(2), XIV, Report of the Commissioners of Customs, p. 7.

9. CMG, 20 July 1850.

10. See the sympathetic response of the magistrates to one such case, involving a ship's broker. TC, 28 Feb. 1873.

11. CJ, 10 and 24 Dec. 1847.

12. MGRO, Quarter Session Records. Q/E 1/9 F. Chief Constable's Reports, and Quarterly Returns, 1855–8. A recent Act had made it easier to proceed against persons who had not paid their poor and highway rates. CJ, 13 July 1849.

13. See the many non-payments of a special sanitary rate, and distress warrants, referred to in CDH, 12 April 1895. The Tweeney case is reported in TC, 27 Jan. and 17 Feb. 1893. He claimed that he could not be rated as the shop was owned by the family.

14. TC, 27 Jan. and 9 March 1860.

15. For one example of the numbers annually granted and endorsed, see PP, 1872, XXX, Reports from the Inspectors of Constabulary, for North Wales, South Wales and Monmouthshire.

16. MGRO, Borough Records. B/C 18. Watch Committee Minute Book, 1860–78. Entry for 1878.

17. CDH, 28 June 1895.

18. MM, 12 March 1880.

19. See the market toll case reported in TC, 24 Feb. 1860. One of the complaints of poor-law reformers like Edwin Chadwick was that the rural parishes of early nineteenth-century Wales had been too generous to defaulters, and did not put enough pressure on collectors and overseers of the poor. Concessions were still made to non-payers of poor-rates in the mid-century, but their cases were more carefully considered. For examples from north Wales, see CDH, 22 and 29 Jan. 1848.

20. NWC, 11 Feb. 1860.

21. CMG, 14 Jan. 1860. Compare Newport examples in MM, 20 Feb. 1880.

22. For part of this story, see TC, 6 April 1860.

23. For his case, and others like him, see D. J. V. Jones, '"A Deal Loss to the Community": the Criminal Vagrant in Mid-Nineteenth Century Wales', *Welsh History Review*, VIII, 1977.

24. TC, 2 March 1860.

25. CJ, 9 Jan 1846.

26. See the complaint, of a 'leaning of the magistrates toward the course of the rich and powerful', cited in chapter 7 of this book.

27. DRO, Haverfordwest Prison Register. PQ/AG/4.

28. PP, 1844, XIX, Tenth Report of the Poor Law Commissioners, Administration of the Poor Law in South Wales, pp. 21–2.
29. Brigstocke's comment is in PP, 1836, XXIX(1), Second Report of the Poor Law Commissioners, Carmarthen Union, p. 369. For an interesting case in Brigstocke's area of refusing to maintain a child, and consequent 'dropping', see CJ, 25 June 1847.
30. MRO, Constabulary Records. PS/42/1. Petty Sessions Register for Tywyn, 1866–1905.
31. TC, 20 Jan. 1860.
32. MRO, Constabulary Records. PS/32/1. Petty Sessions Register for Corwen, 1858–77. See, too, the classic case of desertion, and not sending wages back, reported in CJ, 26 Feb. 1847.
33. TC, 25 Jan. 1884.
34. PP, 1889, XLII, Thirty-Second Report of the Inspector of Reformatory and Industrial Schools, Appendix II(C).
35. For a few of the pollution incidents, see TC, 8 Sept. 1810, and CJ, 15 Dec. 1848 and 31 Jan. 1890. See, too, A. H. Williams, op. cit., III, pp. 1301–17.
36. CLRO, Constabulary Records. PS/3/9. Overton Division Letter-book, 1865–76.
37. TC, 9 March, 11 May and 8 June 1860.
38. MM, 27 Feb., 5 March, 12 and 19 March 1880.
39. NWC, 17 June 1830.
40. For these references, see ibid., 7 Jan. and 5 May 1860, and TC, 24 Feb. 1860. Frequently people were only cautioned for using unjust weights, but many were convicted. See the numbers punished at the Chepstow and Pontypool courts in July 1853, and May 1856. GR0, Quarter Session Records. LSCR 0001. List of Summary Convictions, 1848–70.
41. CDH, 21 July 1893.
42. The battle to keep refreshment houses, mainly fish and chip shops, closed after 11 p.m. produced some hilarious moments. See ibid., 12 and 26 April 1895.
43. Ibid., 12 April 1895.
44. SWPM, Police Note-books. D/D CON 182.
45. The *Western Mail* played a central role in the debate over the licensing laws, and was especially critical of the Sunday Closing Act.
46. CDH, 29 March 1895.
47. Op. cit., p. 227. On the rise of the shebeens after the attacks on the drinking clubs, see the *Western Mail*, 11 August 1898.
48. CMG, 25 Feb. 1860.
49. MM, 2, 9 and 16 Jan. 1880.
50. For background, see O. O. G. MacDonagh, 'Coal Mines Regulation: the First Decade, 1842–52', in R. Robson (ed.), *Ideas and Institutions of Victorian Britain* (London, 1967).
51. PP, 1842, IX, Report of the Select Committee on the Payment of Wages, p. 76. For some cases, of breaches of child employment legislation and of mines' regulations, see CJ, 17 May 1867, TC, 13 Jan. 1860, and MM, 27 Feb. 1880.
52. PP, 1852, XXI, Report of the Commission on the Operation of the Truck Act in the Mining Districts, p. 5.
53. For just a few cases, see TC, 3 and 24 Feb. 1860 and MM, 12 March and 30 April 1880.
54. See, for example, TC, 11 Oct. 1817, and CJ, 20 March 1846 and 12 Nov. 1847.
55. For some of this, see CJ, 3 Aug. 1849, 11 March 1853, and 4 April 1890.
56. M. Elsas (ed.), *Iron in the Making: Dowlais Iron Company Letters, 1782–1860* (Cardiff, 1960), p. 36.

57. D. Simon, 'Master and Servant', in J. Saville (ed.), *Democracy and the Labour Movement* (London, 1954), pp. 170–1.

58. MM, 19 and 26 Feb. and 5 March 1842.

59. For background to this section, see J. H. Morris and L. J. Williams, op. cit., chapter 10, L. J. Williams, 'Miners and the Law of Contracts, 1875–1914', *Llafur*, IV, 1985, and R. Challinor, *A Radical Lawyer in Victorian England* (London, 1990).

60. CDH, 1 April 1848. See, too, NWC, 18 Feb. 1860, and *Cambrian News*, 19 March 1870.

61. CJ, 9 March 1849, and 10 Dec. 1852.

62. TC, 1 March 1817.

63. See Captain Freeman's comment on this, at the Cardiganshire Quarter Sessions. CJ, 7 Jan. 1853.

64. Findlay's theatrical performances are reported in MM, 20 Feb. 1880, and 'Barmouth George's' career is in MRO, Constabulary Records. PS 32/1.

65. There was, for example, much anxiety in Bangor about the problem during the early 1830s. NWC, 7 Jan. 1830.

66. For Morris and Walters, see CJ, 8 Dec. 1848, and MM, 16 Jan. 1880.

67. ARO, Quarter Session Records. Uncatalogued box of Reports of Chief Constable, 1857–1910. Report of summer of 1890.

68. CDH, 5 April 1895. For a few of the other types of cruelty cases mentioned in the text, see ibid., 1 and 8 March 1895, and MM, 5 March 1880.

69. CDH, 20 July 1894.

70. See, for instance, the Cardiff material in MGRO, Borough Records. B/C 18. Watch Comittee Minutes, 1860–78.

71. NWC, 6 Feb, 1868. The newspaper was thinking mainly of the idleness of vagrants. Cited in the useful booklet, M. Aris, J. Latham, and J. Pott, *Crime and Punishment – A Welsh Perspective. Nineteenth Century Crime and Protest* (Caernarfon, 1987), p. 70.

72. F. W. Maitland, *Justice and Peace* (London, 1885), p. 129. Cited in L. Radzinowicz and R. Hood, op. cit., p. 119.

Chapter 6

1. J. A. Sharpe, op. cit., pp. 95–103, and E. P. Thompson, 'Eighteenth-century Crime, Popular Movements, and Social Control', *Bulletin of the Society for the Study of Labour History*, XXV, 1972, p. 10, and idem, *Whigs and Hunters: the Origins of the Black Act* (London, 1975), p. 194.

2. 'It is almost impossible for a poor man to escape gaol'. H. Mayhew, *The Criminal Prisons of London* (London, 1861), p. 341, cited by M. Ignatieff, *A Just Measure of Pain. The Penitentiary in the Industrial Revolution, 1750–1850* (London, 1978), p. 186.

3. PP, 1852, VII, Report of the Select Committee on Juvenile Offenders, pp. 97–102. Quotation from the abstract, reprinted in J. J. Tobias, *Nineteenth Century Crime* (Newton Abbott, 1972), p. 47.

4. For some background to these views, see L. Radzinowicz and R. Hood, op. cit., 84–90, and V. A. C. Gatrell, 'Crime, authority and the police-man state', p. 253.

5. John Owen, 'Crime in Victorian Carmarthenshire: the Evidence of the Felon's Register', *The Carmarthenshire Antiquary*, XXIII, 1987, p. 70.

6. E. Smithies, *The Black Economy in England since 1914* (Dublin, 1984), p. 132.

7. D. Philips, op. cit., pp. 147–50. Peter King tells us that twelve per cent of those accused of property crimes on the Home Circuit, 1782–87, were female. Op. cit., p. 35.

8. W. R. Lambert, op. cit., p. 49.

9. J. C. Symons, *Tactics for the Times*, 1849 (ed. by M. J. Wiener, New York, 1984), p. 47. Reference given in D. Beddoe, *Welsh Convict Women* (Barry, 1979), p. 25.

10. For a comparison, see J. M. Beattie, 'The criminality of women in eighteenth-century England', *Journal of Social History*, VIII, 1975, pp. 80–116.

11. Ratios varied. At a later quarter, the Cardiganshire ratio was 1:6.5. CJ, 4 Jan. and 12 April 1867.

12. A number of people are now working on the history of female criminality in modern Britain, including Audrey Philpin in Pembrokeshire. The results of their researches are eagerly awaited. In the meantime, there is a valuable comparative study by Judith A. Allen, *Sex and Secrets. Crimes Involving Australian Women since 1880* (Oxford, 1990). Since writing this chapter, Lucia Zedner has given us *Women, Crime, and Custody in Victorian England* (Oxford, 1991).

13. John Beattie finds that, at the preliminary discussion of bills of indictment, grand juries were more generous to women in the eighteenth century. *Crime and Courts in England, 1660–1800* (Oxford, 1986), p. 404.

14. Cited in D. Philips, op. cit., p. 150.

15. For the quotation, see MGRO, Prison Chaplain Records. QG/Swansea, 1866–77. Report of 1867. For an interesting study, see E. Roberts, *A Woman's Place: An Oral History of Working-Class Women, 1890–1940* (Oxford, 1984).

16. One useful comparison, which dicusses possible inaccuracies, is P. King, op. cit., pp. 35–42.

17. L. L. Robson, *The Convict Settlers of Australia* (Melbourne, 1965), p. 182.

18. J. M. Beattie, *Crime and Courts in England, 1660–1800* (Oxford, 1986), p. 247.

19. GRO, Reformatory Records. Q/MR 0009. Register of Boys, 1859–86.

20. For these, and the other Glamorgan cases in the previous paragraph, see MGRO, Quarter Sessions Records. QS/JC 1/12, 36, 41, 87, and 10/102. Juvenile Convictions.

21. MGRO, Prison Chaplain Records. QG/Swansea. 1866–77. Report of 1871.

22. V. A. C. Gatrell, 'Crime, Authority, and the Police-man State', p. 304.

23. MRO, Constabulary Records. Z/PS/32. Petty Sessions Register for Corwen. Isaac Hughes's criminal record covered 1 Nov. 1858–25 Sept. 1874. He died on 18 Sept. 1875. For the other people mentioned in this paragraph, see, for instance, CRO, Constabulary Records. XJ/1443 and 1821, and MRO, Constabulary Records, PS 32/1, and 42/1.

24. V. A. C. Gatrell and T. B. Hadden, op. cit., p. 385.

25. CDH, 3 July 1891.

26. S. Magarey, op. cit., pp. 16–17.

27. Ibid., p. 14.

28. PP, 1847, XXVII, Report on Education, Caernarfon, Appendix A, p. 28.

29. For just a little background to all this, see J. Manton, *Mary Carpenter and the Children of the Streets* (London, 1976), and J. R. Gillis, *Youth and History. Tradition and Change in European Age Relations, 1770–Present* (London, 1974).

30. PP, 1863, XXIV, Report of the Inspector of Reformatory and Industrial Schools, Appendix VII, and PP, 1902, XLVII, Report of the Inspector of Reformatory and Industrial Schools, Appendices IX(A) and IX(B).

31. L. Radzinowicz and S. Hood, op. cit., p. 120.

32. M. Moggridge reckoned that there were 720 juvenile delinquents in the largest towns of Glamorgan who lived by illegal means. CMG, 18 Oct. 1856.

33. MM, 2 Jan. 1880.

34. NWC, 28 Jan. 1860.

35. See, for instance, the important meeting to discuss juveniles, and Bruce's comments, in CMG, 21 April 1860.

36. TC, 20 April 1860.

37. GRO, Reformatory Records. Q/MR 0009. Register of Boys, 1859–86.
38. PP, 1837, XXXII, Report of the Inspectors of Prisons, North Wales, p. 60. *The Welshman*, 7 April 1848, and PP, 1862, XLV, Reports of the Inspectors of Constabulary, South Wales, p. 130.
39. CJ, 8 Jan. 1869. Compare the complaints in ibid., 10 April 1868.
40. MGRO, Quarter Session records. Q/E 1/9 F. Chief Constable's report of 1845. PP, 1847–8, LII, Reports of the Inspectors of Prisons, North Wales, p. 35. Compare CJ, 29 July 1853.
41. *Cambrian News*, 7 Jan. 1881.
42. S. C. Ellis, op. cit., p. 145.
43. For one reference to her, see TC, 11 May 1860.
44. For a start on this kind of analysis, see D. J. V. Jones, *Rebecca's Children* (Oxford, 1989), p. 164.
45. CRO, Constabulary Records. XJ/1377, and 1399. Registers of Charges, Caernarfon and Criccieth.
46. For comparisons on literacy, see V. A. C. Gatrell and T. B. Hadden, op. cit., pp. 379–380, and for comparisons on occupations and literacy, see D. Philips, op. cit., pp. 154–61 and 164–8. Peter King tells us that at the Essex Quarter Sessions 1748–1800, 73.5 per cent of the accused were called labourers. Op. cit., p. 30.
47. Evidence kindly provided by Alan Bainbridge, based on years 1846–66 for Merthyr, and 1875–87 for those charged at Barmouth, Tywyn and Corwen.
48. CRO, Constabulary Records. XJ/1377. Register of Charges, Caernarfon. First 272 people whose occupations were given.
49. PP, 1837, XXXII, Report of Inspectors of Prisons, North Wales, pp. 62 and 68.
50. MGRO, Governors' Reports. QG/Cardiff. Report for 1877. The quotations in the paragraph are taken from chaplains reports, of Cardiff and Swansea gaols, in the same record office.
51. Information on the dock offenders from the Prisoners' Description Book, 1905–22, deposited in 1975 at the British Transport Office, West Bute Street, Cardiff.
52. MGRO, Chaplains' Reports. QG/Cardiff, 1869–77. Report for 1874. She could not, however, be compared to the nationally famous Ellen Sweeney who was convicted on her 255th charge in 1893, for being drunk and disorderly. TC, 24 Feb. 1893.
53. CLRO, Constabulary Records. FP/3/5, and PS/3/11. The recording of such information changed. See the note on Table 15 in Sources and Data.
54. J. M. Beattie, *Crime and Courts in England, 1660–1800* (Oxford, 1986), p. 629.
55. J. J. Tobias, *Crime and Industrial Society in the Nineteenth Century* (London, 1967), p. 62.
56. PRO, HO 73/55. Report of 14 Nov. 1839. For Jones and Evans, CJ, 21 March 1828, and 26 Nov. 1841.
57. *The Economist*, 1847, vol. 5, p. 835. Cited in L. Radzinowicz and R. Hood, op. cit., p. 74.
58. *The Times*, 10 Sept. 1859.
59. There are two important modern theses on the 'criminal class', by S. J. Stevenson, 'The "criminal class" in the mid-Victorian city', D. Phil., Oxford, 1983, and J. Davis, 'Law breaking and law enforcement: the creation of a criminal class in mid-Victorian London', Ph. D., Boston College, 1984. For comments on these, and other references, see C. Emsley, op. cit., chapter 6.
60. See the section in H. Mayhew and J. Binny, op. cit., p. 381–6.
61. On the changes from simple to craft and project thieving, see M. McIntosh, 'Changes in the Organisation of Thieving', in S. Cohen (ed), *Images of Deviance* (London, 1971), and see, too, M. McIntosh, *The Organisation of Crime* (London, 1975).

62. See, for example, TC, 11 Aug. 1810 and 7 June 1817, and CJ, 23 March 1855.

63. For some of this, see CJ, 20 March and 10 July 1835, and 25 Feb. 1853 and MM, 5 Feb. 1842.

64. All this information, of the last two paragraphs, is given in more detail in D. J. V. Jones, '"A Dead Loss to the Community". The Criminal Vagrant in Nineteenth-Century Wales', *The Welsh History Review*, VIII, 1977. The commissions and parliamentary papers on vagrancy in Wales are very useful. PP, 1847–8, LIII, 1850, XXVII, 1866, XXXV, and 1906, CIII.

65. ARO, Quarter Sessions Records. Uncatalogued box of Chief Constable's Reports, 1857–1910. Report for 1857.

66. It is difficult to say much, of real value and detail, about the geography of crime in the nineteenth-century city. R. N. Davidson, *Crime and Environment* (London, 1981) is a starting point for those who are interested in this approach. There are obvious limitations. The historian does not have the kind of data available to modern social geographers. For one primitive attempt, which adds an historical dimension to the work of Professor David Herbert at Swansea, see D. J. V. Jones, '"Where did it all go wrong?" Crime in Swansea, 1938–68', *Welsh History Review*, XV, 2, 1990.

67. SWPM, Police Note-books. D/D CON 174.

68. NLW, MS 4943 B. Diary of a Scripture Reader.

69. For more on all this, see D. J. V. Jones, *Crime, Protest, Community and Police in Nineteenth-Century Britain* (London, 1982), chapter 4.

70. First Report of the Cardiff Associate Institute for Improving and Enforcing the Laws for the Protection of Women (Cardiff, 1860), p. 19. See, too, the concern in Swansea when prostitution began to expand to new areas. TC, 22 June 1860.

71. See the family reminiscences about Jack Matthews, beerhouse and brothel keeper, in the area at this time, see E. O'Neill, 'The Notorious Jack Matthews' (typescript of 1985), deposited in the Central Library, Cardiff.

72. Their findings, and those of others, have been brought together in J. J. Tobias, *Crime and Industrial Society in the Nineteenth Century* (London, 1967), chapter 4.

73. Some of these can be found in CRO, Constabulary Records. XJ/1443.

74. J. Owen, op. cit., pp. 69–70.

75. V. A. C. Gatrell, 'Crime, authority and the police-man state', p. 307.

76. PP, 1901, LXXXIX, Reports of Inspectors of Constabulary, Cardiff, p. 77.

77. TC, 6 Aug. 1886, and Lord Aberdare, op. cit., p. 248.

78. Like D. Philips, op. cit., p. 287.

Chapter 7

1. A good starting point, comparing France and Britain, is C. Emsley, *Policing in its Context, 1750–1870* (London, 1983).

2. The number of Acts, especially of recent origin, used for that purpose, has been exaggerated. An excellent beginning to such discussions is J. M. Beattie, *Crime and the Courts in England, 1660–1800* (Oxford, 1986), chapter 8.

3. For one survey of the literature on this, see M. Ignatieff, 'State, Civil Society and Total Institution: a Critique of Recent Social Histories of Punishment', in D. Sugarman (ed.), *Legality, Ideology and the State* (London, 1983).

4. CMG, 14 June 1834.

5. For background, see D. J. V. Jones, 'Life and Death in Eighteenth-Century Wales: a Note', *The Welsh History Review*, X, 4, 1981.

6. In addition to Ignatieff, cited in footnote 3, see P. King, 'Decision-Makers and Decision-Making in the English Criminal Law, 1750–1800', *Historical Journal*,

XXVII, 1, 1984, pp. 53–55, and J. Langbein, '*Albion's* Fatal Flaws', *Past and Present*, XCVIII, 1983, p. 105.

7. PP, 1847, XXVII, Report on Education, Brecon, Cardigan and Radnor, p. 64.
8. The details are set out in D. Hay and F. Snyder, op. cit., chapters 1 and 2. Of course, it was not just the victims, or constables, who set out after suspected offenders.
9. K. Wrightson, 'Two Concepts of Order', in J. Brewer and J. Styles (eds), *An Ungovernable People* (London, 1980), p. 31.
10. James O. Jones is perhaps too critical of the parish constables, but his account of policing early in the century is impressive. See op. cit., chapters 1 and 2. Compare the excellent study by C. Emsley, *The English Police: A Political and Social History* (London, 1991).
11. PP, 1862, XLV, Report of the Inspectors of Constabulary, North Wales, p. 11. The material for the mid-1830s is gleaned from two sources. PP, 1835, XXIII, First Report of the Commissioners on Municipal Corporations, and PP, 1837–8, XXXV, Report on Certain Boroughs, by T. J. Hogg.
12. PP, 1835, XXIII, First Report of the Commissioners on Municipal Corporations, Appendix, Part I, p. 345.
13. Ibid., Part IV, p. 2587, and MM, 13 June and 15 Aug. 1829.
14. PP, 1854, LIII, Return of the Police and Prisoners in the Cities and Boroughs, pp. 38–40, and 63–68.
15. There are many interpretations of the police changes, of the role of central government in the transformation, and of the nature of the opposition to the developments. The most comprehensive study is by S. Palmer, *Police and Protest in England and Ireland, 1780–1850* (Cambridge, 1988). Also useful are the part-historical surveys of M. Brogden, *The Police: Autonomy and Consent* (London, 1982), and P. Cohen, 'Policing the Working-Class City', in R. Fine et al. (eds), *Capitalism and the Rule of Law* (London, 1979).
16. For police developments mentioned in this paragraph, see PP, 1846, XXXIV, Return of Parishes or Districts adopting the Acts of 1839 and 1842. Breconshire later adopted the second scheme of superintending constables. There was some opposition to the Act of 1856, as being unnessary in Wales. See, for example, CJ, 9 Jan. 1857.
17. For just a taste of the Cardiganshire saga, see CJ, 17 Jan. 21 Feb. and 11 April 1890. There was also conflict over who controls the police in Carmarthenshire. Ibid., 16 Aug. 1889 and 30 May 1890.
18. MGRO, Borough Records. B/C 18. Watch Committee Minute Books, 1860–78.
19. This, and some of the other, general material on policing is taken from the annual reports of Inspectors of Constabulary. For a sample of some of the best of these, see PP. 1857–8, XLVII, 1859(1), XXII, 1860, LVII, 1861, LII, 1862, XLV, 1882, XXXIII, and 1892(1), XLI. They contain details of numbers, pay, duties, efficiency, and occasionally an interesting piece of analysis and comment.
20. The full story is recounted in the many county studies of the police. See, for example, W. C. Maddox, *A History of the Radnorshire Police Force* (Llandrindod Wells, 1959), R. W. Jones, *The History of the Pembrokeshire Police* (Haverfordwest, 1957), J. O. Jones, *The History of the Caernarvonshire Constabulary* (Caernarfon, 1963), H. Owen, *The History of the Anglesey Constabulary* (Llangefni, 1952), and G. Lerry, 'The Policemen of Denbighshire', *Transactions of the Denbighshire Historical Society*, II, 1953.
21. PP, 1857–8, XLVII, Reports of the Inspectors of Constabulary, North Wales, p. 9.
22. For some interesting early police rules and advice, covering points in this, and the next, paragraph, see the booklets in the Royal Institution, Swansea. Box 87.

There is also comparable material in the South Wales Police Museum, Bridgend. D/D CON 38/1–3. Instructions Books, 1856–72.

23. CJ, 12 April 1867. The relationship of the police with bailiffs and keepers was a perennial problem, and source of radical discontent. The importance of the Act of 1879 is underlined in C. Steedman, *Policing the Victorian Community* (London, 1984), p. 159.

24. CLRO, Constabulary Records. FP/2/1. Letter-book, 1857–8.

25. See, for example, PP, 1861, LII, Reports of the Inspectors of Constabulary, North Wales, p. 6. It is worth noting that once the police were established in a place, there was a reluctance, even on the part of critics, to see them depart. See, for example, the comments of Saunders in CJ, 18 Oct. 1850. Note, too, the petitions for police to be stationed at places like Llangeler and Penboyr. Ibid., 5 Jan. 1849.

26. H. Richard, op. cit., p. 73.

27. ARO, Quarter Session Records. Uncatalogued box of Chief Constable's Reports, 1857–1910, and CDH, 5 Feb. 1848.

28. PP, 1862, XLV, Report of the Inspectors of Constabulary, North Wales, p. 11.

29. ARO, Quarter Session Records. Uncatalogued box of Chief Constable's Reports, 1857–1910. Report of 1858.

30. C. Steedman, op. cit., p. 158.

31. There is an interesting discussion on this aspect of policing by V. A. C. Gatrell, 'The Decline of Theft and Violence in Victorian and Edwardian England', pp. 275–78.

32. This is the expected pattern. R. Lane, 'Urbanization and Criminal Violence in the Nineteenth Century; Massachusetts as a Test Case', in H. D. Graham and T. R. Gurr (eds), *The History of Violence in America* (London, 1969), pp. 468–84.

33. Cited by G. W. Williams, op. cit., p. 314.

34. TC, 13 and 20 Jan. 1860. Compare C. Emsley, '"The Thump of Wood on a Swede Turnip": Police Violence in Nineteenth-Century England', *Criminal Justice History*, VI, 1985.

35. CJ, 10 Jan. 1890.

36. As at Tregaron. Ibid., 10 Oct. 1851.

37. ARO, Quarter Sessions Records. Uncatalogued box of Chief Constable's Reports, 1857–1910. Report of 1860.

38. PP, 1857–8, XLVII, Reports of the Inspectors of Constabulary, North Wales, p. 23. The difficulty of getting bilingual constables was mentioned in Montgomeryshire a few years later. PP, 1872, XXX, Report from the Inspectors of Constabulary, North Wales, p. 79.

39. For just one example, of a crowd at Solva annoyed by the police taking suspected pickpockets to a lock-up, see CJ, 2 and 9 Jan. 1846. In the same county Henry Leach, magistrate, was delighted by the extra powers given to arrest on suspicion. Ibid., 23 Oct. 1846.

40. SWPM, Police Note-books. D/D CON 172/1.

41. GRO, Constabulary Records. Q/CON R. Chief Constable's Reports, 1857–70. Report of 1859.

42. MRO, Constabulary Records. ZH/1/2. Notebook of T. Roberts, vol. 2. The books of James Row and John Davies are in the South Wales Police Museum.

43. For some of this, see CLRO, Constabulary Records. PS/3/9. Overton Division Letter-book, 1865–76.

44. G. Lerry, op. cit., p. 110, and PP, 1860, LVII, North Wales, p. 10.

45. CJ, 9 Jan. 1857.

46. TC, 18 Dec. 1857.

47. Ibid., 6 April 1860.

48. On police corruption, extortion, and perjury, see, for instance, CMG, 3 and 31 March, and 7 April 1860, and TC, 20 and 27 Jan. and 3 Feb. 1860.
49. V. A. C. Gatrell, 'The Decline of Theft and Violence in Victorian and Edwardian England', pp. 263–4. Compare D. J. V. Jones, 'The new police, crime and people in England and Wales, 1829–88', *Transactions of the Royal Historical Society*, XXXIII, 1983, pp. 162–3.
50. Details on all of this can be found in the reports of the Inspectors of Constabulary. See, for example, PP, 1882, XXXIII, North and South Wales, and Monmouthshire. See, too, P. W. J. Bartrip, 'Public Opinion and Law Enforcement: the Ticket-of-Leave Scares in Mid-Victorian Britain', in V. Bailey (ed.), op. cit.
51. PP, 1872, XX, Second Report of the Judicature Commission, p. 164.
52. For this, and the background to these paragraphs, see PP, 1817, V, 1820, II, and 1821, IV. Reports of the Select Committee on the Administration of Justice in Wales. See also PP, 1829, IX, First Report into the Practice and Proceedings of the Common Law.
53. For some background, and debate on this, see the work of King, op. cit., and of Langbein, op. cit. The seminal piece on decisions and pardons in eighteenth century courts is by D. Hay, 'Property, Authority and the Criminal Law', in D. Hay et al. (eds), *Albion's Fatal Tree* (London, 1975).
54. On Ireland's rate, see S. Palmer, op. cit., p. 371.
55. S.C. Ellis, op. cit., pp. 130–2. D. Philips estimated that 25 per cent of indictable cases were defended in 1843. Op. cit., p. 104.
56. L. Lloyd, op. cit., pp. 36–7.
57. See the complaints in PP, 1820, II, Report of the Select Committee on the Administration of Justice, and in PP, 1829, IX, First Report into the Practice and Proceedings of the Common Law, Appendix E, Evidence of H. Evans and others seeking a change from the old system of Great Sessions.
58. For the quotations, see SC, 21 Aug. 1812, the National Library of Scotland, MS. 2843. Letter from Col. Hankey, 11 Nov. 1844, and PP, 1847, XXVII, Report on Education, Caernarfon, Appendix, p. 41.
59. For a little on these grand jury problems, see NWC, 7 April 1860, and PP, 1821, IV, Report of the Select Committee on the Administration of Justice in Wales, p. 27. But there was praise, too. CDH, 25 March 1848.
60. *Carmarthen Weekly Reporter*, 25 July 1902, cited in R. Davies, 'In a Broken Dream', *Llafur*, III, 1983, p. 29.
61. PP, 1872, XX, Second Report of the Judicature Commission, pp. 164–5.
62. PP, 1867, IX. Report of the Select Committee on Special and Common Juries, p. 12, and PP, 1820, II. Report of the Select Committee on the Administration of Justice in Wales, p. 13.
63. *Quarterly Review*, LXXIV, 1844, p. 138.
64. PP, 1820, II, Report of the Select Committee on the Administration of Justice in Wales, p. 13.
65. CJ, 10 Nov. 1826. The *North Wales Chronicle*, which was against the disappearance of the Great Sessions, reminded its readers of the translation work done in this court, for juries, defendants and witnesses, and wondered if, under the new system of Assizes, the judges would be so patient. Edition of 28 Jan. 1830. Charles Morgan, clerk of the peace in Carmarthenshire, also pointed to similar problems. See PP, 1829, IX, First Report into the Practice and Proceedings of the Common Law, Appendix E, Evidence of Morgan.
66. TC, 12 April 1850.
67. PP, 1847, XXVII, Report on Education, Brecon, Cardigan and Radnor, Appendix, p. 114.
68. MM, 29 Aug. 1829.

69. Hansard, Third Series, 1872, CCCIX, cols 1648–73. I thank Dr D. W. Howell for helping me to locate this reference. Compare ibid., Fourth Series, 1892, 1, cols 827–63.

70. CJ, 28 March and 18 April 1834.

71. For just a few of the 'surprising' acquittals, see TC, 7 April 1810, and CJ, 10 April 1840 and 13 July 1855.

72. PP, 1820, II, Report from the Select Committee on the Administration of Justice in Wales, p. 13.

73. F. P. C., 'The Celt of Wales and the Celt of Ireland', *The Cornhill Magazine*, XXXVI, 1877, p. 674.

74. CJ, 31 March and 7 April 1837.

75. D. Hay, 'The Criminal Prosecution in England', *Modern Law Review*, XLVII, 1984, p. 4.

76. Quotation used in J. H. Morris and L. J. Williams, op. cit., p. 269. But Lord Aberdare, in the House of Lords, defended the record of magistrates. See C. Emsley, *Crime and Society in England, 1750–1900* (Harlow, 1987), op. cit., p. 161. For interesting detail of urban magistrates, politics and sentencing, see PP, 1837–8, XXXV, Report on Certain Boroughs, by T. J. Hogg. North Wales Boroughs.

77. CLRO, Constabulary Records. PS/3/9. Overton Division Letter-book, 1865–76. Letter of 14 July 1867.

78. See, for example, NWC, 25 Feb. 1860. At Narberth Petty Sessions there was a complaint as late as December 1863 that the chairman, James Child, was sitting on his own, game-law, case. He had to withdraw. CJ, 1 Jan. 1864.

79. See, for instance, PP, 1837–8, XXXV, Report on Certain Boroughs, by T. J. Hogg. North Wales Boroughs, pp. 48, 78 and 101.

80. Note the concern over police powers at the courts in TC, 13 Jan. 1860.

81. PP, 1873, LIV, Return of Stipendiary Magistrates in England and Wales.

82. See, for example, TC, 17 May 1817, and MM, 1 Aug. 1829.

83. For some background, and statistics, on this, see PP, 1819, VIII, Report of the Select Committee on Criminal Laws as relate to Capital Punishment, Appendices 11, 22, and 23. Compare D. J. V. Jones, 'Life and Death in Eighteenth-Century Wales: a Note', *Welsh History Review*, X, 1981.

84. J. A. Sharpe, op. cit., p. 174.

85. PP, 1829, IX, First Report into the Practice and Proceedings of the Common Law, Appendix E, Evidence of John Wyatt. On the Monmouthshire statistics, see the annual lists, after 1805, of county convicts in PRO, HO 27. See, too, PP, 1819, VIII, Report of the Select Committee on Criminal Laws as relate to Capital Punishment, Appendix 11, and PP, 1846, XXXIV, Returns relating to Executions in the Twenty-One Years preceding 1834. The returns do not always tally.

86. Peter King has looked at all this in detail, and notes the great importance of the age factor. Op. cit., p. 39.

87. The two short quotations are from PRO, HO 47/11. Letter from G. Hardinge, 28 Jan. 1790. Note that petitions on behalf of convicts came even after capital punishment was removed for a crime. See, for example, CJ, 8 April 1864.

88. W. H. Howse, op. cit., p. 59.

89. See, for instance, TC, 26 April 1817, NWC, 16 Sept. 1830, and NLW, Great Sessions Records, Goal Files, Breconshire 1801, Wales 4/390/10.

90. L. LLoyd, op. cit., p. 17.

91. D. Beddoe, *Welsh Convict Women* (Barry, 1979), chapter 2. Compare the UK table, of female arrivals, in A. G. L. Shaw, *Convicts and Colonies* (London, 1966), pp. 363–8. Two other books used for background were L. L. Robson, *The Convict Settlers of Australia* (Melbourne, 1965), and C. Bateson, *The Convict Ships 1787–1868* (Glasgow, 1959). The parliamentary papers on transportation are disappointing

for Welsh historians. See, for example, the returns in PP, 1819, VII, 1837, XIX, 1837–8, XXII, 1851, XLVI, and 1856, XVII. The vital transportation registers, with details on each person sent, are in the PRO, HO 11.

92. A useful introduction to the development of prisons in early modern times is J. Innes, op. cit. One Welsh story is chronicled by H. J. Owen, 'The Common Gaols of Merioneth during the Eighteenth and Nineteenth Centuries', *Journal of the Merioneth Historical and Record Society*, III, 1, 1957. The starting-point, for all recent debates on the purpose of these prisons, is M. Foucault, op. cit.

93. Useful for these paragraphs are PP, 1834, IV, Report on the State of the Goals in England and Wales, pp. 417–9, and PP, 1837, XXXII, Reports of the Inspectors of Prisons – the Welsh Gaols. For an early estimate of the benefits of the treadwheel in some Welsh gaols, see PP, 1825, XXIII, Return of Inquiries regarding the Treadwheel, p. 23.

94. Useful articles on gaols in the nineteenth century are by W. K. Parker, 'John Howard and Radnor County Gaol', and 'Radnor County Gaol: the Last Decade, 1868–78', both in *Radnorshire Society Transactions*, LII, 1982, and J. W. H. Greaves, 'A Study of Prison Administration in the Nineteenth Century', *Presenting Monmouthshire*, 40, 1975.

95. PP, 1847–8, LII, Reports of the Inspectors of Prisons, p. 155. I have also used the annual reports of these inspectors as background for the paragraphs. The best of these include the reports to be found in PP, 1837, XXXII, 1847–8, LII, 1871, XXIX, and 1895, LVI. See, too, M. Ignatieff, *A Just Measure of Pain: the Penitentiary in the Industrial Revolution, 1750–1850* (London, 1978), and U. Henriques, 'The Rise and Decline of the Separate System of Prison Discipline', *Past and Present*, LIV, 1972.

96. MGRO, Chaplains' Reports. QG/Cardiff. Reports of 1869–77.

97. PP, 1847–8, LII, Reports of the Inspectors of Prisons, South Wales, p. 23.

98. Lydia Williams had penal servitude for life. CJ, 10 July 1863. Compare H. Tomlinson, 'Penal Servitude 1846–65: a System in Evolution', in V. Bailey, op. cit.

99. For Rees, see TC, 6 Jan. 1860. A useful survey of penal servitude can be found in PP, 1878–9, XXXVII, Report on the Working of the Penal Servitude Acts.

100. L. Radzinowicz and R. Hood, op. cit., p. 744.

101. MGRO, Chaplains' Reports. QG/Cardiff, 1869–77. Report of 1874.

102. In the year 1870, for example, 210 offenders in Caernarfon gaol were punished by loss of food, whilst at Cardiff 120 males and 115 females were placed in dark cells. PP, 1871, XXIX, Report of Prison Inspectors, Southern District, Wales, pp. 40 and 89.

103. M. Ignatieff looks at the contributions made by the authorities, and the working class itself, to such a demarcation. 'State, Civil Society and Total Institution: a Critique of Recent Social Histories of Punishment', in D. Sugarman (ed.), *Legality, Ideology and the State* (London, 1983), pp. 197–8.

104. These comments, and Haweek's case, are in MGRO, Chaplains' Reports. QG/Swansea, 1866–77.

105. CDH, 25 March 1848.

106. The report was otherwise optimistic. TC, 6 Jan. 1871. Compare ibid., 6 April 1860.

107. Ibid., 16 Aug. 1817. Compare the whipping of a person through Llanbadarn. SC, 7 Feb. 1812.

108. CJ, 22 Aug. 1856. The pillory was used in Carmarthenshire in 1802. NLW, Great Sessions Records, Gaol Files, Carmarthen 1802, Wales 4/753/4.

109. GRO, Quarter Sessions Records. Q/JOAC. 0002. Report of Juvenile Offenders Committee, 1881–2.

110. MGRO, Chaplains' Reports. QG/Swansea, 1866–77. Reports of 1869 and 1877.

111. One can follow the establishment and intake of reformatory and industrial schools, and reports on each one, in the annual reports of the inspector appointed to oversee them. Those used for these paragraphs can be found in PP, 1863, XXIV, 1870, XXXVI, 1878, XLII, 1889, XLII, and PP, 1899, XLIV. The detailed appendices to these reports provide the figures used in the text. See also PP, 1857, XXX, General Report of J. Symons on Parochial Schools, and GRO, Reformatory Records. Q/MR 0009. Register of Boys, 1859–1914.

112. CMG, 21 April 1860. For reports on ragged schools in Cardiff and Swansea, see, for example, ibid., 12 May 1860, and TC, 20 April 1860.

113. There was room for about ninety boys per truant school, and for about twenty girls at Mumbles. PP, 1899, XLIV, Report of the Inspector of Reformatory and Industrial Schools, Appendices 1(C) and II(B).

114. Mary Carpenter and others conducted a vigorous campaign over the success rates. There were claims that the worst youngsters were kept out of the corrective schools, and that the evidence on the criminal careers of ex-inmates was suspect. The success rate given is usually well over the two-third minimum. See, for example, the reports of the inspector in PP, 1870, XXXVI, Appendix VI(1a), 1889, XLII, Appendix II(A), and 1899, XLIV, Appendix III(D).

115. CDH, 14 June 1895.

116. L. Radzinowicz and R. Hood, op. cit., 575.

117. V. A. C. Gatrell, 'Crime, Authority and the Police-man State', p. 333, and V. A. C. Gatrell and T. B. Hadden, op. cit., p. 352.

Epilogue

1. For a European context, see T. R. Gurr, op. cit., H. Zehr, op. cit., L. A. Knafla (ed.), *Crime and Criminal Justice in Europe and Canada* (Ontario, 1981), A. Blok, *The Mafia of a Sicilian Village 1860–1960* (Oxford, 1974), and A. D. Lodhi and C. Tilly, 'Urbanization, Crime and Collective Violence in Nineteenth-century France', *American Journal of Sociology*, 79, 1973.

2. T. Rees, *Miscellaneous Papers on Subjects Relating to Wales* (London, 1867). pp. 15–17.

3. PP, 1847, XXVII, Report on Education, Brecon, Cardigan and Radnor, p. 62.

4. A. Macfarlane, op. cit., pp. 196–7.

5. L. Stone, 'The History of Violence in England: Some Observations. A Rejoinder', *Past and Present*, 108, 1985, p. 219.

6. D. Philips, op. cit., p. 284.

7. J. A. Sharpe., op. cit., p. 171.

8. The quotation is from G. Pearson, op. cit., p. 230.

9. V. A. C. Gatrell, 'Crime, authority and the police-man state', p. 250.

10. For a summary of contemporary explanations, including Wade's, see D. J. V. Jones, *Crime, Protest, Police and Community in Nineteenth-Century Britain* (London, 1982), chapter 1,, and for a modern model of the causation and progress of disorder, see T. R. Gurr, op. cit., chapter 6.

11. Comparisons on the criminal class can be found in D. Philips, op. cit., p. 287, and G. Rudé, op. cit., p. 126.

12. T. Plint, *Crime in England* (London, 1851), p. 145. Cited in L. Radzinowicz and R. Hood, op. cit., p. 82.

13. Police and prison finances based on PP, 1859 (1), XXVI, Police and Criminal Statistics for 1858.

14. For this, and the fascinating and changing views of Engels and Marx on crime, see L. Radzinowicz and R. Hood, op. cit., pp. 40–8. Compare G. Rudé's

comments about crime and the class war. Op. cit., pp. 118–9. See, too, C. Emsley's scepticism. *Crime and Society in England, 1750–1900* (Harlow, 1987), p. 124.

15. Quotation from T. R. Gurr, op. cit., p. 90. H. Zehr, op. cit., pp. 26 and 142. D. Philips finds the links between crime and protest not proven. Op. cit., p. 287.

16. G. Pearson, op. cit., p. 243.

17. David Philips, in his study of industrial people in the Midlands during the most disturbed period, argues that society was not about to break down. In general he believes that the British deserved their reputation for being peaceful, orderly and law-abiding people. Op. cit., pp. 284–5. My own impression, after working on the Newport rising and the Rebecca riots, is that conditions were, for a short time in the second quarter of the nineteenth century, rather more dangerous than that. At other times in the century, one is inclined to agree with his judgement.

18. T. R. Gurr, op. cit., p. 96.

19. The British story is set out in, for instance, F. H. McClintock and N. H. Avison, *Crime in England and Wales* (London, 1968), and for a local Welsh story, see D. J. V. Jones, '"Where did it all go wrong?" Crime in Swansea, 1938–68', *The Welsh History Review*, XV, 2, 1990, and idem, 'Crime, Order and the Police', in R. A. Griffiths (ed.), *The City of Swansea: Challenges and Change* (Stroud, 1990).

20. T. R. Gurr, op. cit., p. 134.

21. F. Snyder and D. Hay, op. cit., p. 23.

22. T. Morris, op. cit., p. 27.

23. J. M. Beattie, *Crime and the Courts in England, 1660–1800* (Oxford, 1986), p. 264.

24. A. Macfarlane, op. cit., p. 196.

25. C. Steedman, op. cit., p. 159.

26. The story of this is told in J. Morgan, *Conflict and Order. The Police and Labour Disputes in England and Wales, 1900–1939* (Oxford, 1987).

27. *The Nineteenth Century*, XLIX, 1901.

Sources and Data

Records

A wide range of sources, judicial and otherwise, has been used for the writing of this book. The footnotes give an indication of the main records consulted. The sheer scale of the legal records, being the largest collection of documents in most record offices, prevents one assembling a comprehensive bibliography. The Great Sessions papers are in the National Library at Aberystwyth, and the surviving Assize records are at the Public Record Office, Chancery Lane, London. The voluminous rolls, books, and letters of the Quarter Sessions are either at the National Library or, more commonly, at the local record offices, and the registers and papers of Petty Sessions are likewise scattered about the country. In London, in the Public Record Office at Kew, are to be found annual returns from these courts, together with records of transportation and punishment, letters from and to magistrates, documents on popular disturbances, and legal decisions on cases, pleas and pardons.

Much of this information was compiled annually, and transformed into the Parliamentary Papers. There is a huge number of these of interest to historians of crime. The annual statements of delinquency are divided into three main groups; judicial statistics, which start, backdated, in 1805 and are improved after 1834 and 1857, prison returns, which can be traced back to 1814, and police information, which begins in 1857. The last is perhaps the most used, and contains lists of reported indictable crimes. These annual tables were changed somewhat after 1893. There is, in addition, a large number of enquiries by royal commissions and select committees on policing, offences, disturbances, the judiciary, magistrates, juries, transportation, reformatories, and much more. There are also reports by inspectors, on policing, prisons and schooling, as well as occasional papers demanded by parliament, details of which are in the footnotes.

The newspapers are a valuable source, though they need to be handled with care. The main collections of Welsh papers are in the National Library, and the gaps can be filled by those at the British Newspaper Library at Colindale, London. There are also small collections of newspapers at most record offices and large libraries in Wales. The main ones used for this book are identified in the Preface, and in the footnotes. The historian, working alone, is obliged to sample, but a number of research projects are underway which promise a complete computer analysis of references to crimes in selected Welsh papers. Several local historians have already used these newspapers extensively for articles on crime, policing and punishment, and I have noted their main contributions in the footnotes. So far, within Wales, few books have been compiled on this subject, though there are some valuable studies of the history of crime in other countries since the eighteenth century. I have acknowledged the information and ideas gleaned from these in the text and notes.

The police records are worthy of more attention than academic historians have so far shown in them. The Police History Society has been a turning-point in terms of awareness, and police museums, large and small, are being established. That at Bridgend, of the South Wales Constabulary, owed its existence to the inestimable Mr Baker, and there is a smaller collection of historical documents at the Gwent Constabulary Headquarters at Cwmbrân. Many other papers have sadly been destroyed, most during the merging of the forces in the late 1960s, but there are some interesting police books, diaries and letters in most record offices. I have been through a selection of these, the ones which seemed most valuable and less repetitive than the rest. The same was true of the prison records, which are again formidable in scale. Only the registers of prisoners, and reports by governors and chaplains were consulted, again in the record offices.

Graphs

All except one (No. 7) of the graphs are based on the judicial, police and prison statistics returned annually after 1810, in the Parliamentary Papers. These are now available on microcards at most university libraries, and at the National Library of Wales at Aberystwyth, but many of the reprints are of poor quality. The present writer transcribed the statistics from the volumes of Parliamentary Papers, 1810–1902, kept in the State Paper Room of the British Library, London. In the graphs and tables based on these statistics, the figures refer to the twelve-month period used by contemporary compilers, but 'Wales' has been expanded to include Monmouthshire.

The graphs give rates of crime, and police strength, related to the changing population. The population figures were taken from L. J. Williams (ed.), *Digest of Welsh Historical Statistics*, vol. 1 (Cardiff, 1985). Of all the graphs those comparing rural, industrial and urban districts were the most difficult to draw. Initially it was intended to make a more detailed comparison of rural, industrial and urban parishes, but the records would

not permit such a project. Graphs 5, 6, 10 and 16 are therefore a compromise, but they do illustrate important differences within the Welsh
crime rates. In the last three of these graphs, and where references are
made to them in the text, the population figures of Cardiff, Swansea and
Newport have been deducted from the county totals for Glamorgan and
Monmouthshire after 1857.

A particular problem was posed by the police districts of Cardiff,
Swansea, and Newport. The returns of cases dealt with at the Assizes and
Quarter Sessions in Glamorgan and Monmouthshire include offenders
from these towns, but the reports, after 1857, of indictable offences committed and of cases dealt with summarily, provide separate figures for these
towns. Unfortunately, the police districts of Cardiff, Swansea and Newport
are not clearly defined, nor were they always synonymous with the urban
districts. Of course, the boundaries of the latter changed considerably in
the century. As a result, Graphs 5, 6, 10 and 16, which contain the rate of
urban crime, are more approximate than the others. They have to be used
as a guide, for comparative purposes only.

The information for Graph 7 is taken from B. R. Mitchell and P. Deane
(eds), *Abstract of British Historical Statistics* (Cambridge, ed. of 1971),
pp. 343–5, P. H. Lindert and J. G. Williamson., 'English workers living
standards during the industrial revolution: a new look', *Economic History
Review*, XXXVI, 1983, pp. 11, and E. W. Evans, *The Miners of South Wales*
(Cardiff, 1961), pp. 242–3. The problems of using the above, not least for
the Welsh situation, are obvious, but the graph is again useful for comparative purposes.

In two of the graphs certain figures have been deliberately omitted.
Game law offences have been removed from Graph 15, and given their
own graph, and the prostitutes proceeded against under the Vagrancy Act
have been omitted from Graph 21. The reasons for these omissions are
discussed in the text. Both poachers and prostitutes were regarded as being
rather different from other offenders in these categories.

Tables

The source for each table is included with the information. However, a
number of them deserve special mention. Table 1 is admittedly from a
rather late date, but it provides more comprehensive material than
previous returns.

Table 2 is based on the Quarter Session Recognizances (QSR. 0161–68),
1843–44, in the Gwent Record Office, Cwmbrân. The records are fragile
and some of the occupations are missing. Where, in a few instances,
prosecutors and witnesses were listed together on the recognizances, I have
taken just the former. The categories need little explanation, except

perhaps the skilled manual workers, who comprised people such as smiths, carpenters, and shoemakers, and the unskilled manual workers who were labourers, colliers, sailors, farm servants, gardeners and the like. Some of the retailers, like the beer-sellers, were not far removed from the working class.

Table 3 is taken from the Quarter Session Depositions (QSD), 1818–42, conveniently calendared in the Gwent Record Office, Cwmbrân. Some of the depositions have disappeared, and not all the victims can be easily identified. As in Table 2, most of the cases are of larceny. The social categories are identical to those in Table 2.

Tables 4, 5 and 6 illustrate the difficulties of obtaining complete and continous information for the first half of the nineteenth century. The fluctuating number of returns in Table 4 represents both missing data and gaols closed and opened. One can fill the gaps, in these years, from other sources, but the nature of the information is slightly different. Table 6 is particularly unsatisfactory; we do not know how many of the prisoners were actually arrested in the towns named. There are also a few missing returns in this Table.

Tables 7, 8, 9 and 10 are samples to illustrate particular themes and points. The first, being of indictable crimes, refers mainly to property offences, and the monthly breakdown is dictated by the nature of the police returns in the Parliamentary Papers. Table 8 is a statement of the most serious offences against the person, though, from the text alone, it is clear that a considerable number of the common assaults also resulted in painful and permanent injury.

Tables 11–14 are based on the annual prison statistics, Table 15 on the annual police returns, and Tables 16, 17, 19 and 20 on the judicial statistics, all in the Parliamentary Papers. In Table 15 there are no returns for prostitutes and vagrants in 1876 and 1892, because a decision was made in the late 1860s to exclude these from the lists.

Table 18 is based on the Chief Constable's Reports and Quarterly Returns in the Quarter Sessions records (Q/E 1/9 F) in the Mid Glamorgan Record Office, at Cardiff. A number of the discharge and acquittal rates look very low, but the rates are returned as given.

Index